The Question of the Gift

The Question of the Gift is the first collection of new interdisciplinary essays on the gift. Bringing together scholars from a variety of fields, including anthropology, literary criticism, economics, philosophy and classics, it provides new paradigms and poses new questions concerning the theory and practice of gift exchange.

In a culture awash with the rhetoric of self-interest, understanding the gift is more important than ever. Thus this collection raises essential questions for social life:

- How do non-commercial exchanges form and solidify communities?
- How do humans and objects interact outside of consumerism?
- What are the relationships between gifts and commodities?
- To what degree are artworks gifts?
- Is a truly free gift possible, or even desirable?

In addressing these questions, contributors not only challenge the conventions of their fields, but also combine ideas and methods from both the social sciences and humanities to forge innovative ways of confronting this universal phenomenon.

Mark Osteen is Professor of English and Director of Film Studies at Loyola College, Baltimore. He is the author of *American Magic and Dread: Don DeLillo's Dialogue with Culture* (2000) and *The Economy of Ulysses: Making Both Ends Meet* (1995); the editor of the Viking Critical Edition of Don DeLillo's *White Noise* (1998) and co-editor, with Martha Woodmansee, of *The New Economic Criticism* (Routledge, 1999).

Routledge Studies in Anthropology

The Question of the Gift

Essays across disciplines

Edited by Mark Osteen

 Routledge
Taylor & Francis Group

LONDON AND NEW YORK

First published 2002
by Routledge
2 Park Square, Milton Park, Abingdon, Oxon OX14 4RN

Simultaneously published in the USA and Canada
by Routledge
711 Third Avenue, New York, NY 10017

Routledge is an imprint of the Taylor & Francis Group

Transferred to Digital Printing 2006

First issued in paperback 2014

© 2002 Selection and editorial material, Mark Osteen; individual chapters,
the contributors

Typeset in Baskerville by Taylor & Francis Ltd

British Library Cataloguing in Publication Data
A catalogue record for this book is available from the British Library

Library of Congress Cataloging in Publication Data
A catalog record for this book has been requested

ISBN 978-0-415-28277-2 hardcover
ISBN 978-0-415-86914-0 paperback

Contents

Notes on contributors

Jack Amariglio is a professor of economics at Merrimack College. He was the founding editor of the interdisciplinary journal *Rethinking Marxism*, and is the co-editor (with Stephen Cullenberg and David Ruccio) of *Postmodernism, Economics, and Knowledge* (Routledge, 2001), and the co-author (with David Ruccio) of *The Postmodern Moment in Economics* (Princeton University Press, forthcoming).

Antonio Callari teaches economics at Franklin and Marshall College and serves on the editorial board of *Rethinking Marxism*. He has edited *Marxism in the Postmodern Age* (Guilford, 1995; with S. Cullenberg and C. Biewener), and *Postmodern Materialism* (Wesleyan University Press, 1996; with D. Ruccio), and is now working on a book of essays, *How Economics Was Invented* (Ashgate, forthcoming).

Stephen Collis is an assistant professor of American literature at Simon Fraser University. He is currently working on a manuscript on poet Robert Duncan, *The Poetics of Derivation*, and has published his own poetry widely in Canada and the United States.

Andrew Cowell teaches French and Italian at the University of Colorado. He specializes in the Middle Ages, but also has a broader interest in economic theory and economic anthropology. His book *At Play in the Tavern: Signs, Coins and Bodies in the Middle Ages* was published by University of Michigan Press in 1999. Recent publications include articles in *Cultural Studies* and *Poetics Today*. His current book project is entitled *The Gift, Performance and Alterity: Reciprocity with the Past*.

Lee Anne Fennell is an assistant professor at the University of Texas Law School. Her teaching and research interests include property, distributive justice, local government law, and law and literature.

Anthony Fothergill teaches English literature at the University of Exeter, UK, having previously taught at Heidelberg University and Kenyon College. He has written extensively on Joseph Conrad, Virginia Woolf and other modernist writers, and on German critical theory, as well as publishing editions of Oscar Wilde's and Conrad's works. His current project is a book, *Joseph Conrad and Germany: The Politics of Cultural Reception*.

Charles H. Hinnant is Emeritus Professor of English at the University of Missouri-Columbia. He is the author of books on Thomas Hobbes, Samuel Johnson, Jonathan Swift and, most recently, Anne Finch. He is currently at work on a book-length study of the relevance of Marcel Mauss's *The Gift* to an understanding of the Bible.

James Laidlaw is a Fellow of King's College and a university lecturer in social anthropology at the University of Cambridge. His publications include *The Archetypal Actions of Ritual* (Clarendon Press, 1994; with Caroline Humphrey), *Riches and Renunciation* (Clarendon Press, 1995), and *The Essential Edmund Leach* (Yale University Press, 2000; with Stephen Hugh-Jones).

Eun Kyung Min is an assistant professor of English at Seoul National University in Korea. She studied philosophy at the Graduate Faculty, New School for Social Research, and completed her PhD in Comparative Literature at Princeton in 1998. She is currently working on the intersections of contemporary virtue ethics and eighteenth-century moral philosophy, and her next major research project is on the literary uses of China in eighteenth-century England and France.

Mark Osteen is Professor of English at Loyola College, Baltimore, and has published widely on film and on twentieth-century literature and economics. He is the author of *The Economy of* Ulysses: *Making Both Ends Meet* (Syracuse, 1995) and *American Magic and Dread: Don DeLillo's Dialogue with Culture* (University of Pennsylvania, 2000), as well as editor of the Viking Critical Library edition of DeLillo's *White Noise* (Penguin, 1998). His other publications include *The New Economic Criticism: Studies at the Intersection of Literature and Economics* (Routledge, 1999), co-edited with Martha Woodmansee.

Nicoletta Pireddu teaches Italian and Comparative Literature at Georgetown University. Her scholarly work revolves around European literary relations, with emphasis on Italian, English and French literature and culture from the nineteenth century to the present. She has published numerous articles in volumes and journals such as *Annali d'italianistica*, *Comparatistica*, *The Comparatist*, *Orbis Litterarum* and *études Anglaises*. She is the author of the book *Antropologi alla corte della bellezza. Decadenza ed economia simbolica nell'Europa fin-de-siècle* (Fiorini, 2001).

Jacqui Sadashige is an assistant professor of classical studies at the University of Pennsylvania where she also teaches comparative literature, film studies and ashtanga yoga. She is completing a book, *Roman Things: Staging the Material Object in the Plays of Plautus*.

Martha Kendal Woodruff is assistant professor of philosophy at Middlebury College. She received a PhD from Yale University, and studied at Universität-Freiburg with a research grant from DAAD (German Academic Exchange Service). Her main areas of interest include ancient Greek philosophy, post-Kantian German thought, and philosophy of art and literature. She has published pieces on Nietzsche, Heidegger and the Greeks, and she is currently working on a book entitled *The Pathos of Thought: Aristotle and Heidegger on Mood, Poetry, and Philosophy.*

Yunxiang Yan is an associate professor of anthropology at the University of California, Los Angeles. He is the author of *The Flow of Gifts: Reciprocity and Social Networks in a Chinese Village* (Cambridge University Press, 1996) and *Private Life under Socialism: Individuality and Family Change in a Chinese Village, 1949–1999* (in press). His current research interests include urban consumerism and the impact of transnational culture on Chinese society.

Acknowledgments

The axiom that all scholarly work is collaborative is especially true of *The Question of the Gift*. To fail to acknowledge those who have helped complete this collection would, indeed, violate its very spirit. Thus, I would like to thank a number of people who have acted as midwives to this volume.

The initial impetus for *The Question of the Gift* emerged from discussions at the Culture and Economics Conference at Exeter, UK, in July 1998, where I heard early versions of the chapters by Jacqui Sadashige, Anthony Fothergill and Antonio Callari. The conference co-sponsors – Regenia Gagnier, John Dupre, and Martha Woodmansee, the executive officer of the Society for Critical Exchange – thus deserve grateful acknowledgment. The Society for Critical Exchange also sponsored a panel on the gift at the following year's MLA convention, from which the idea for this collection, as well as its title, sprang.

Originally this was to be a co-edited volume. Although my collaborator, Max Thomas, elected to withdraw from the project, his advice in soliciting, selecting and editing papers at the early stages was indispensable. I would also like to thank Professors Jonathan Parry, Chris Gregory and Marilyn Strathern for recommending the work of James Laidlaw and Yunxiang Yan. Closer to home, my colleagues at the Loyola College English department have offered unflagging support, and the Loyola Faculty Development Committee saw fit to give me a summer research grant in 2000 that aided immensely.

As always, however, the greatest thanks are due to my wife, Leslie Gilden, for her faith, and to my son Cameron, for his existence. They are gifts for which no gratitude could be adequate.

Two of these essays were originally published elsewhere: Chapter 1, "A free gift makes no friends," by James Laidlaw, was previously published in the *Journal of the Royal Anthropological Society* 6.4 (December 2000). Chapter 6, "Adam Smith and the debt of gratitude," by Eun Kyung Min, was previously published in *Studies of English Languages & Cultures* 4 (1996): 47–75. I gratefully acknowledge both journals for granting permission to reprint.

Introduction

Questions of the gift

Mark Osteen

The nature of gifts and gift giving has intrigued thinkers since the beginning of Western civilization. We can see the outlines of modern ideas about generosity, gratitude and obligation forming in both the Old Testament and *The Odyssey*. More recently, thinkers as different as Adam Smith, Ralph Waldo Emerson, and Friedrich Nietzsche have explored the meanings of gifts. In the twentieth century, Marcel Mauss's landmark 1925 anthropological study-cum-historical romance *Essai sur le don* prompted scholars from a variety of disciplines to reopen the question of the gift. Yet despite Mauss's thesis that gifts are complex social practices governed by particular norms and obligations (Mauss 1990: 76), in recent years they have usually been either explained away as disguised self-interest or sentimentalized as a remnant of a golden age of pure generosity. This volume seeks to transcend these trite polarities by posing new questions and offering new paradigms regarding gifts and the discourses surrounding them. If, as Jacques T. Godbout argues, "the implicit and the unsaid reign supreme" in the realm of the gift (1998: 4–5), this collection aims to unseat that reign and hold those implicit norms up to the light of critical analysis.

The present volume represents innovative scholarly thinking about gifts in fields ranging from anthropology and sociology to literature, philosophy, ethics and economics. Each discipline asks a different set of questions, determined not only by the disparate areas of human behavior that each addresses, but also by the biases inherent in each field. Yet beneath this wide span of fields and interests a group of common questions will emerge: to what degree are human interactions motivated by self-interest? Is it possible to give without expectation of reward? When obligations are attached to gifts, what form do they take? Why, after all, do human beings give presents and to whom do we give them?

These questions seem to belong to the realms of anthropology, sociology and ethics. But the questions of the gift are also narrative matters: that is, they interpret the stories we tell about social interaction. Not only do we informally tell such stories to ourselves every day, but we also create more formal narratives about gifts in poems, novels, plays and letters. With the belief that we can acquire an adequate comprehension of gift behaviors only by scrutinizing these more formal linguistic constructs, this volume presents a group of literary interventions into questions of the gift. But these essays by no means stand apart from the anthropological or theoretical contributions; rather, they illustrate and enrich them, demonstrating how literary artists in societies as different as republican Rome and the twentieth-century USA have portrayed and analyzed gift relationships. Finally, the following essays, and particularly the final group of theoretical forays, offer not only new narratives – sociological, anthropological, literary, historical – but also new metanarratives about the gift. These stories about our stories will, we hope, inspire scholars in numerous disciplines to propose more nuanced and authentic ways of representing how and why human beings give presents. Such work is essential because, as Alan Schrift observes in his introduction to *The Logic of the Gift*, the question of the gift "addresses fundamental issues of intersubjective interaction" (1997: 18); explaining its motives and meanings is hence necessary to a fully ethical conception of social life.

Mauss's legacy

Definitions

Jacques Godbout and Alain Caillé state that "any exchange of goods or services with no guarantee of recompense in order to create, nourish, or create social bonds between people is a gift" (Godbout 1998: 20; cf. Caillé 2001: 37). Like many definitions of the gift, this one begs a key question: are gifts given freely, or do they involve some implicit expectation of reward? Godbout and Caillé stipulate that there is "no guarantee," but many theorists – Mauss himself, as well as more recent writers such as Jacques Derrida and Pierre Bourdieu – argue that all gifts arrive burdened with obligations, and hence that a truly free gift is impossible. It is clear from the outset, then, that any useful definition of gift practices must begin not merely by describing behavior but by analyzing motives. More specifically, according to Helmuth Berking, the gift may be divided into four related but discrete components: the gift object; the sequence of giving and taking; the actors' own understandings of their acts and motives; and the rules or principles governing their behavior (1999: 4). Each of these components invites concentrated inquiry. Berking goes on to define gift giving as a "ritual practice through which the current value of a relationship may be communicated and maintained" (1999: 5). Gifts, in other words, are concrete representations of social relations. What kind of relations? Certainly we do not give gifts to everyone whom we encounter, and most gift theorists recognize a distinction between the domains of market and gift. This distinction has been delineated in diverse ways, as we will see. What seems obvious, however, is that defining the gift is no easy task, because it immediately raises the question of whether any such thing exists.

The most influential and detailed definition of the gift is surely found in Mauss's *Essai*: as economist Philip Mirowski notes, "in economic anthropology, all roads to the gift lead back to Marcel Mauss" (2001: 438). Indeed, it would be difficult to find a text in the human sciences that has had more impact than Mauss's brief monograph. Yet his *Essai* was hardly without precedents: as a nephew of Emile Durkheim, Mauss was both Durkheim's intellectual heir and the scion of a distinguished tradition of French social thought. Mauss voices a set of ideas that challenges the definition of liberal society that dominates Anglo-American social thought even today, particularly the tenacious faith in autonomous, freely choosing individuals (Douglas 1990: x). Furthermore, if *The Gift* both heralded and catalyzed the rise of modern anthropology, it also manifested a trend toward comparativism and an attention to "primitive" cultural practices that was already well underway in Modernist art: T.S. Eliot's *The Waste Land* refers repeatedly to Jessie L. Weston's work on ritual and romance; post-impressionist painters were incorporating the techniques and forms of African and Melanesian art; Stravinsky's *Rite of Spring* had presumed the universality of ritual. Still, Mauss's work has become one of anthropology's sacred texts (Parry 1986: 455). Like any such foundational text, it has been subject to numerous, often contradictory interpretations. For *The Gift* is not just a synthesis of anthropological research; it is also a history of culture and a work of moral philosophy. Scholars with diverse disciplinary and political allegiances have emphasized different passages and drawn different conclusions from it, so that *The Gift* bears within it the seeds of virtually every important study of gift giving that has succeeded it.

Mauss boldly states his thesis right at the beginning: in many societies – not just "archaic" or "primitive" societies, although more clearly in them – "exchanges and contracts take the form of presents; [though] in theory these are voluntary, in reality they are given and reciprocated obligatorily" (1990: 3). Gift exchanges are "total social phenomena" in which "all kinds of institutions are given expression at one and the same time" (1990: 3). Thus the first question of *The Gift* remains the essential question of the gift: "What rule of legality or self-interest ... compels the gift that has been received to be obligatorily reciprocated? What power resides in the object given that causes its recipient to pay it back?" (1990: 3).[1] Within this question, however, is concealed an assumption: that the essence of the gift resides in the object given.

Basing his interpretation upon the words of a Maori sage named Ranaipiri, Mauss held that a spirit – named *hau* by the Maori – within the objects given causes them to be passed on. Claude Lévi-Strauss objected to this apparently uncritical acceptance of indigenous explanations, and further argued that the definition is merely circular (1997: 55). *Hau*, he countered, is nothing but an empty signifier that reveals the true nature of the gift to be a consequence of a surplus of signifiers without signifieds.[2] Raymond Firth criticized Mauss for confusing the *hau* of the gift with the *hau* of the giver (Yan 1996: 6): that is, it is not the object but the person giving it who frames the obligations and rewards required. Later, in his highly influential treatise *Stone Age Economics*, Marshall Sahlins equated *hau* with a general principle of increase. According to Sahlins, the secular meaning of *hau* is "profit" or "product of"; in religious terms, it may be translated as "fertility" (1972: 160, 167). More recently, Yunxiang Yan argues that the spirit *conveyed* by the gift, not the spirit *of* the gift, constitutes its social force (1996: 216–17; emphasis in original). This controversy may in fact be nothing more than a difference of emphasis, for clearly it is givers and receivers who imbue objects with the personality of the original giver and who therefore perceive some spirit within objects that preserves the imprint of the original owner. For my purposes, what is more significant is the assumption beneath the definition: that for "primitive" people, "everything speaks" (Mauss 1990: 44). Persons and things partake of each other. Thus Mauss emphasizes that things possess a personality because they continue to be identified with the giver or, in some cases, the recipient.[3] Hence, by "giving one is giving *oneself*, and if one gives *oneself* it is because one 'owes' *oneself* – one's person and one's goods – to others" (1990: 46; emphasis in original). The "persons" who live in these societies, in other words, represent themselves not as the self-interested individuals of neoclassical economics but as a nexus of social obligations.

Redefining reciprocity

Most famously, Mauss wrote that the "system of total prestations" in archaic societies involves members who seek prestige in three interlocking obligations: to give, to receive, and to reciprocate (1990: 39). These obligations are particularly coercive in societies such as the Kwakiutl of the Pacific Northwest who practice rituals of squandering and excessive giving called potlatch ceremonies. Here the aim is to crush a rival with obligations he cannot repay, to give so much that eventually reciprocation becomes impossible. Ironically, then, as Maurice Godelier has pointed out, the ultimate aim of the potlatch is to break the chain of reciprocity (1999: 58). Although Mauss dubbed the potlatch a "monstrous product" of the gift system (1990: 42), and although later ethnographic research has discovered that the forms studied by Mauss's sources were exaggerated distortions of earlier ceremonies, the potlatch has been analyzed more than any other "primitive" gift system other than the *kula* ring. Georges Bataille, in particular, expands the potlatch into a grand synecdoche for what he perceives to be a universal human desire for expenditure. We will return to Bataille and his influence on literary theory below. For Mauss, however, the important point about potlatch is that "to refuse to give, to fail to invite, just as to refuse to accept, is tantamount to declaring war" (1990: 13); the exchange of gifts supplants the exchange of blows because the former creates tangible and enforceable but non-violent modes of coercion. Make no mistake: these "gifts" are obligatory.

Although Mauss claims that the essence of the potlatch is the obligation to give (1990: 39), in every other respect the most important of the three obligations is the requirement to reciprocate. Thus we may rephrase Mauss's opening question as follows: what is the nature and reach of reciprocity? What sorts of payments surround gifts that distinguish them from other transactions? The principle of reciprocity has long been a crux in social theory. In 1960 Alvin Gouldner named the "norm of reciprocity" as the pivotal "starting" and "stabilizing" mechanism for social interaction (1996: 65). For Gouldner, reciprocity both initiates relationships, by encouraging those who have received attention to return it, and solidifies already established relationships, by ensuring that they involve relatively equal give and take. A few years later, Sahlins devised a spectrum of social relations based upon the mode of reciprocity most prevalent in each transaction. Hence, in the family, "generalized reciprocity" reigns. Here obligations remain implicit and may extend for a time or even indefinitely. "Negative reciprocity," characterized by suspicion and exploitation, dominates interactions among strangers. Somewhere between these poles lies "balanced reciprocity," where transactions tend toward equivalence (see Sahlins 1972: 193–9). The emotional connection among parties determines the nature of their transactions, so that "if friends make gifts, gifts make friends" (Sahlins 1972: 186). While this schema provides a useful model for categorizing social expectations, Sahlins himself warns that the term "reciprocity" can be so vague as to disguise all varieties of bad faith: "everywhere in the world," he cautions, "the indigenous category for exploitation is 'reciprocity'" (1972: 134).

Despite Sahlins's warning, the principle of reciprocity has until recently dominated anthropological discourse about the gift. Consequently, the gift has often been reduced to another form of equivalence that permits theorists to elide inequities of power and blur the myriad forms that exchanges can take. Anthropologists have tended to represent exchanges as dyadic transactions between self-interested persons and downplayed both communal norms and supernatural forms (Parry 1986: 455). As Parry observes, for theorists such as Sahlins and Peter Blau, "the gift is always an 'Indian gift' – that is, one 'for which an equivalent return is expected' – and the notion of a 'pure gift' is mere ideological obfuscation" masking the "supposedly *non*-ideological verity that nobody does anything for nothing" (1986: 455). In other words, ethnography tends to reduce exchange to an "'objective' core of an economic truth which seems to correspond more to the observer's picture of the world than to the practices" under study (Berking 1999: 40). Such economism, as we will see, is the land mine of gift theory. The problem may lie in the assumed definition of selfhood. Whereas Western thought represents exchanges as undertaken by autonomous individuals, in many other societies, as Mauss notes, it is not individuals but groups who carry on exchange, and the persons who exchange do so as representatives of ritualized positions or roles.

How, then, to forge a more useful definition of the obligation to reciprocate? Several social theorists have contested the principle as Mauss presents it. Stephen Gudeman, for example, would displace reciprocity from its central position. He argues that reciprocity "is an expression of community," but that communal allotment "does not come 'after' reciprocity"; rather, "moments of reciprocity or the gift are tokens of existent community" (2001: 467). The gift may extend the commons to outsiders but, Gudeman claims, "reciprocity is never contained within a community." Rather, the gift is a "probe into uncertainty" aimed at extending the borders of a community (2001: 467). What lies behind reciprocity, for Gudeman, is really status, or what Bourdieu terms "symbolic capital" (Gudeman 2001: 470). But Gudeman's definition of "community" begs a key question: if reciprocity requires a pre-existent community and is never contained within it, then how are communities formed? What principles create communal bonds? Later in his essay Gudeman calls a family a community; but if this is so, then his previously-cited assertion must be false, since reciprocity – at least the so-called "generalized" form as described by Sahlins – certainly obtains within many families at some times. Despite leaving these unanswered questions, Gudeman's essay illuminates the problematic nature of reciprocity, which, he declares, is "not the core of society but its expression. ... [It is] neither a primitive isolate nor the atom of society but its badge." Hence, "if the gift is an unstable or uncertain category that is only because it is 'about' uncertainty itself" (2001: 473).

In other words, some gifts are given altruistically and others are not, and the nature of a transaction may change while it is in progress, or from one prestation to another. It is thus essential to keep in mind that, as Parry reminds us, "Mauss repeatedly stresses a *combination* of interest and disinterest, of freedom and constraint, in the gift" (1986: 456; emphasis in original). Indeed, as both Alain Testart and Derrida point out, if we define the gift as something given without the need for reciprocation, Mauss never discusses the gift at all (Testart 1998: 97; Derrida 1992: 24). Testart further suggests that reciprocity is not at all universal, and that we may represent it more adequately only by distinguishing between various forms of sanction. He proposes a scale running from the least to the most coercive forms of sanction, and further divides them into two groups. In the first group are gifts, which are acts "of someone who provides something without demanding a return." At the highest end of this group are charitable donations, for which there is no reciprocal obligation; next come invitations to friends, wherein we recognize a feeling of obligation but no sanction; and finally potlatch ceremonies, which involve a social but not a legal sanction. The second group includes transactions that are clearly obligatory: the *kula*, in which a donor can seize from the donee a *kula* object; creditor/debtor relations in Western societies, where a creditor can seize goods or garnishee wages; and creditor/debtor relations in some pre-colonial African societies, where a creditor can seize the person and enslave him or her (Testart 1998: 103–4). Although it is not difficult to criticize Testart's categories – for example, there clearly *is* an implicit sanction for failure to reciprocate invitations, since in doing so one risks the loss of friendships and a consequent reduction of social capital – his work invites us to refine our definitions of reciprocity. If we do not, writes Testart, we "blur all the difference between gift and exchange" – the very difference we had hoped to assess (1998: 104).

In a densely argued essay first published in 1972 and recently translated into English, Rodolphe Gasché, in the spirit of Derrida, critiques the principle of reciprocity by deconstructing its tropes. Mauss, he argues, regularizes and tames reciprocity by using the figure of the circle (1997: 106). In so doing, he seeks to "master the originary ambiguity" in gift transactions: if one examines the circle, one realizes that it actually undermines Mauss's delineation of three obligations. That is, the donor of an originating gift would have to be located not on the wheel of circulation but on an immobile point barely touching the circle. Hence, an original donor would not be part of the cycle of exchange because he or she could not be reciprocating. But if reciprocity is primary, then one cannot first give without at the same time reciprocating (1997: 111). And if this latter is true, then the circle of giving is merely economic, a perfect cycle of gift and counter-gift in which the first prestation is "always already a counter-prestation" (1997: 111). To explain the donor's gift as a reciprocation is to bring him or her into the circle and thereby eliminate any motive or sanction other than reciprocity and desire for repayment. By this model, there can be no first gift at all. For Gasché as for other theorists, the deeper problem lies in the fiction of the individual self: if the circle of reciprocity exists regardless of the motives of individual givers, then the fixed point of departure – the beginning of the circle – disappears; if the autonomous individual exists prior to the circle of reciprocity, then gifts are merely a disguised form of debt. (Derrida presents these paradoxes in slightly different terms, as we will see below.) In figuring the gift as a circle, then, Mauss reduces it to an economic exchange.

If we accept the trope of the circle, there seems no way out of this dilemma. But perhaps the error lies not in the gift, but in our poetics. Alain Caillé thus submits a different metaphor: the spiral. Caillé suggests that, since the original gift introduces something that was not there before, it cannot be *merely* reciprocal. Further, reciprocity explains why things are given back, but not why one would give back *more* than one receives (Godbout 1998: 132–3). Behind the principle of reciprocity, Caillé concludes, lurks the specter (as Antonio Callari calls it in Chapter 12 of this volume) haunting all accounts of the gift: economism. Until we remove the gift from this shadow, declares Caillé, "we cannot hope to study what lies behind the obligation to reciprocate without seeing a primitive form of the law of book-balancing equivalence, a prefiguring of mercantile reciprocity governed by the law of tit-for-tat, or the first rough versions of contracts" (Godbout 1998: 130). I would go further: to discover the true nature of the gift, we must redirect our gaze from reciprocity toward other principles and motives. When we do, a different set of norms emerges, a set founded upon spontaneity rather than calculation, upon risk instead of reciprocity, upon altruism in place of autonomy.[4]

The essays in the first section of this volume similarly question conventional views of the range and power of reciprocity. They begin the work of dismantling the implicitly economistic underpinnings of conventional gift theory. In his opening essay, James Laidlaw focuses upon the practices of Jain renouncers in India to demonstrate persuasively that a truly free gift – that is, one unencumbered by obligation and expectation of reward – not only exists, but also partakes of certain characteristics, such as impersonality, that are usually associated with commodity exchange. Indeed, the social importance of *dan* – the ritual gifts he examines – lies precisely in the fact that they do not create obligations. Next, Yunxiang Yan extends the analysis presented in his book *The Flow of Gifts* (1996) by scrutinizing asymmetrical gifts in rural China. In contrast to Mauss's contention that in such relations power flows to the donor, Yan demonstrates how the opposite may be true: power flows unilaterally toward the recipient. Finally, Lee Anne Fennell outlines two characteristics of modern gift exchange that further allow us to reconceive reciprocity: illiquidity and empathetic dialogue. The conversion of cash into illiquid objects, she argues, is aimed at abolishing both the appearance and the existence of calculation. Further, selecting or creating a gift requires donors to engage in an imaginative exercise whereby they empathize with and share recipients' preferences. Fennell's contribution suggests that gift exchanges help to erase boundaries between individuals and to confirm relationships based upon empathy rather than expectation of return. All three of these essays, then, challenge traditional conceptions of balanced reciprocal exchange and the economistic assumptions that underwrite them

"Everything speaks"

Recent anthropological work on the gift has emphasized another principle, one that Mauss acknowledges but never names: inalienability. Mauss does distinguish between different forms of property. Certain objects, he suggests, never move outside of the family, and when they are handed down are surrounded by rituals of great solemnity; these possessions are never really transferred at all, but only lent (1990: 43). Such objects, never fully dissociated from their original owners, are thus said to be *inalienable*: they speak in the specific voice of a person, family, clan or tribe. Chris Gregory and the late Annette Weiner have elaborated on this distinction in their important books. Since I discuss inalienability in detail in my other contribution to this volume, I will merely sketch their ideas here. Inalienable possessions serve as the foundation of the gift system for Gregory, who expands the distinction between alienability and inalienability into an ambitious theory in which gifts and commodities embody two vastly different social systems and visions of identity.[5] For Weiner, inalienable possessions reveal that exchange is predicated upon a universal paradox: "how to *keep-while-giving*" (1992: 5); they thus embody the inherent duality of the gift, which is disinterested and interested at once. In order to understand the nature of gift objects, we must juxtapose them with objects withheld from exchange. Weiner emphasizes the power of inalienable possessions to function as a "force against change" by authenticating origins and kinship histories (1992: 9, 33), and goes so far as to claim that inalienable possessions represent "absolute value" (1992: 42). For Weiner, what motivates reciprocity is really its "reverse – the desire to keep something back from the pressures of give and take" (1992: 43).

Maurice Godelier's recent study, *The Enigma of the Gift* (1999), extends Weiner's discussion of inalienability through a reinterpretation of Mauss. Re-evaluating *hau*, Godelier holds that the inalienability of the gift – that is, its association with a specific person – impels the return gift. If some power lies in the thing itself, it is merely the embodiment of "the relationship which binds it to the person of the giver" (1999: 44). Furthermore, Godelier argues, Mauss (and many of those who followed him) failed to grasp an essential distinction between ownership and possession. In certain rituals – the *kula* among them – an object may be possessed by different hands but is never relinquished by the original owner; indeed, the more temporary possessors an object has, the greater its value for that first owner. Gifts retain the personhood of their primary owner; thus it is not the object but the owner's identity that drives the object to be returned. Such objects speak in one voice only.

More significantly, Godelier seeks to reinstate the primacy of a fourth obligation that Mauss recognized but did not develop, one that has since been neglected, he argues, to the detriment of anthropology: the obligation to make gifts to gods (1999: 13). By excluding sacred objects from his analysis, Godelier claims, Mauss unintentionally fostered the illusion that exchange was the be-all and end-all of social life, thereby paving the way for the more sweeping secularizations of Lévi-Strauss and his inheritors (Godelier 1999: 69). From this fourth obligation Godelier traces the hierarchical effects of gift giving: since the gods can never be fully repaid, those humans who give the most are elevated to quasi-godlike status (1999: 30). The core principle behind gift exchanges therefore lies in the double nature of gift objects, which are simultaneously "substitutes for sacred objects and substitutes for human beings" (1999: 72). Thus, gift objects are caught between the "inalienability of sacred objects" – those gifts from the gods, heirlooms and kinship markers inextricably linked with tribal or social identities – and "the alienability of commercial objects" – things freely exchanged for profit (1999: 94). Gifts are thus double-voiced, speaking now in the voices of ancestors or divine beings, and now in the neutral tones of mere merchandise.

In contrast to Lévi-Strauss and other anthropologists who describe gift practices in terms of their homological relationship with broader semiotic exchanges, Godelier derives them from myth. For him, then, the gift is religious before it is legal or linguistic; in other words, it is not essentially symbolic but essentially imaginary (1999: 106). Inalienable objects are regarded as such because they constitute an inextricable part of a clan's identity, and thus permit a synthesis of the real and the imaginary, of the secular and the sacred (1999: 120, 138). And yet this synthesis depends upon something else: the concealment of the fact that human beings invent the stories of their beginnings. Sacred objects – inalienable possessions – give us back our own laws, mystified and idealized and therefore brooking no disagreement (1999: 174). "Everything speaks" but some things speak louder than others. Through such privileging, the social imaginary creates a divine sanction for human practices. Hence, the foundation of gift practices in "primitive" societies (and, I would add, in modern societies as well, although here it is more deeply buried) is the need at once to disclose and to deny the superhuman origins of culture. Inalienable objects are sacred because they are said to have been given to humans by gods or ancestors; and yet they require a certain opacity as to their origin in order for society to preserve itself and the myths that engender its identity (1999: 137).

Gifts, then, embody the doubleness of all societies, in which there must be both sacred and profane things, both objects freely exchanged and objects preserved from exchange. To put it another way, we might say that gift practices tell conflicting narratives: on the one hand, they expound a narrative of transfer and exchange, of hierarchy, aspiration, and freedom from history; and on the other, they retell a narrative of continuity with nature and the past, a story of human interconnectedness and humility before the transcendental. It is this second narrative that has too often been ignored in Western accounts of gift practices, and that any fully satisfactory theory of the gift must seek to restore.

The gift in history

For his part, Mauss urged his readers to recognize the power of the past and to learn from it. Indeed, much of part three of *The Gift* comprises a historical argument in which Mauss traces an evolution from the system of total prestations that characterized archaic societies to modern societies where the market has supplanted the gift.[6] Mauss seeks to write a "prehistory of our *modern* kind of legal and economic contract" (Parry 1986: 457): a narrative of decline and fall from a world where prestations dominate to one where market and gift are radically divorced. Yet Mauss concludes that vestiges of the archaic principles remain in modern gift practices; hence, "[c]harity is still wounding for him who has accepted it," and "things sold still have a soul" (1990: 65, 64). In his conclusion, Mauss calls for a return or at least a reconsideration of these practices, urging readers to become more conscious of their connectedness with others.

Later gift theorists have offered other versions of this history. For example, Helmuth Berking, focusing on Germanic cultures and relying heavily on the theories of René Girard, derives modern gifts from the rituals of food distribution performed by ancient hunters. "Before giving, taking and reciprocating, there is slaughtering, taking and distributing," writes Berking (1999: 52). Rites of distribution sacralized killing and reinforced hierarchy, so that the giving of food became associated with the role of clan chief. As a result, the gift became deeply affiliated with sacrificial practices. According to Berking, the sacred aura that still surrounds gifts finds its origin in primordial violence (1999: 50–70). "Gift exchange and exchange sacrifice belong together, just as the logic of sacrifice is from the beginning inherent in exchange, and the logic of exchange in the sacrifice" (1999: 72).[7]

As a result of the sacralization of food distribution, argues Berking, many of our current gift practices and norms revolve around host/guest relations: the history of the guest is nothing less than a "complete miniature of the anthropology of giving" (1999: 82). The guest functions as the quintessential stranger whose arrival throws everyday practices into question. Thus the stranger is treated as a demigod, but hospitality removes his or her strangeness and thereby reinforces the positive social practices of the host(s). Hence "strangers who might be happily mistreated with impunity are turned into representatives of the ideal values of one's own group, to be handled with respect, restraint, and ritual distance" (1999: 92). Hosts practice with guests what they have learned in dealings with the gods, thus enabling societies to perform the key transition from religion to civility. In his influential study, Lewis Hyde offers a similar analysis by way of the sanctions on usury, suggesting that Old Testament doctrines permitting usury only outside of the clan were countered by gifts to strangers, which turned others into brothers. The later separation of gift and market, he suggests, is thus accompanied by an inner division in which each man "has a civil and a moral part," and "the brother and the stranger live side by side in his heart" (1983: 125). The result, for Hyde, is an erosion of the potential for gift giving in civil society, where exchanges instead tend increasingly toward the neutral "balanced reciprocity" described by Sahlins (Hyde 1983: 136).

When the shift from a gift to a market system occurred in Europe is unclear; most theorists trace a gradual shift in the early Modern period, culminating sometime in the eighteenth century. No matter where they mark the dividing line, these histories generally describe a trend that runs this way: "as the economy becomes progressively disembedded from society, as economic relations become increasingly differentiated from other types of social relationship, the transactions appropriate to each become ever more polarized in terms of their symbolism and ideology," so that now gifts are normally given "with the sole objective of cementing social relations" (Parry 1986: 466–7).[8] Perhaps more important than the commonalities in these historical narratives are their moral conclusions. Virtually all gift theorists echo Mauss, who exhorts us to put back into the "melting pot" all "these concepts of law and economics that it pleases us to contrast: liberty and obligation; liberality, generosity and luxury, as against savings, interest and utility" (1990: 73). Indeed, in the final pages of his monograph Mauss seems to forget what he previously emphasized – that gifts within the system of total prestations were obligatory – to wax nostalgic, claiming that in ancient times "individuals … were less sad, less serious, less miserly, and less personal than we are. Externally, at least, they were or are more generous, more liable to give than we are" (1990: 81).[9] Only by emulating them, he declares, will modern humans "succeed in substituting alliance, gifts and trade for war, isolation and stagnation" (1990: 82). It is easy to scoff at Mauss's rueful romanticizing. But placing his work in its historical context – he wrote in the years between two bloody conflicts that tore Europe apart and left millions dead – should give us pause. Have the dominant ideologies of the twentieth century offered more beneficent ways of living? Have they helped to produce more ethically sound human beings, or have they rather increased the disparities between those who have much and those who have little?

The ethics of giving

Historical foundations

To answer, or at least press beyond, these questions we must turn to a different set of theorists and a different history, one deriving not from anthropology but from philosophical ethics. Two traditions (not always in harmony) prevail in philosophical thinking about the gift: the Judeo-Christian and the Greek.[10] The essays in the second section of this volume investigate these ancient and early modern religious and philosophical writings, from which our contemporary questions draw. First Charles H. Hinnant, focusing on the patriarchal writings of Genesis, shows that even in the earliest biblical texts, gift practices do not adhere to the strict division between the familial and extra-familial forms of reciprocity and exchange outlined by Sahlins and others. Indeed, the gift is treated – both in the events and by the later redactors – as a hybrid form that blends kinship and commodity exchanges.

Hinnant focuses less on the theological than on the social underpinnings of the gift. Theologically, the Judeo-Christian tradition tends to treat all exchanges as versions of the unremittable debt that humans owe to God for the gift of life; all other gifts – whether between kin, between strangers, or between individuals and their own communities – are simply faint echoes of this original endowment. Beyond this, however, the Christian tradition, with its founding narrative of sacrifice and redemption, departs from the Jewish. Christian morality depends upon an ethics of intention wherein the "unreciprocated gift becomes a liberation from bondage ... a denial of the profane self, an atonement for sin, and hence a means to salvation" (Parry 1986: 468). Hence the most noble acts of charity emulate the grace that God dispenses to sinners through Christ's death and resurrection.

Parry goes on to observe, however, that the Christian ideology of the gift encourages a radical separation between this world and the world to come, resulting in a "*contemptus mundi* which culminates in the institution of renunciation, but of which the charitable gift – as a kind of lay exercise in asceticism – is also often an expression." Free gifts become the "purchase price of salvation" (1986: 468). Perceiving gifts in this way exemplifies the *ressentiment* that Nietzsche so savagely criticized, in which people practice good works only to buy a ticket to heaven. Still, whether actual Christians think in so calculating a way seems debatable, and this formulation further begs the question of whether gifts are really given without expectation of reward. In contrast, Natalie Zemon Davis argues that, in the Christian rituals practiced in sixteenth-century France, God was never seen to be "obliged" or "grateful" for charitable gifts given in His name; rather, Catholic rituals such as the mass were undertaken with the hopes of appeasing God and inviting mercy (2000: 105). Such rites established for early modern Christians a "model of close gift reciprocity between humans and God" (2000: 109). Nevertheless, Christian – especially Protestant – morality does seem to encourage the same separation of persons and things upon which market exchange depends; perhaps, then, the "ideology of the pure gift may thus itself promote and entrench the ideological elaboration of a domain in which self-interest rules supreme" (1986: 469). That is to say, the ethic of intention is a corollary of the belief in individual salvation. It seems no accident, then, that the emergence of the bourgeois ideology of gift giving occurs nearly concurrently with the Reformation, which rejects priestly intervention for the primacy of the individual's freely chosen relationship with God. If the foregoing caricatures Christian morality to some degree, it nevertheless exposes certain key problems of the gift: the relationship between gift giving and individual choice and autonomy; the difficulty of removing calculation from charitable actions or religious ceremonies.

Greek thought on gifts probably commences with Aristotle's *Nicomachean Ethics*. In contrast to the Christian tradition, which emphasizes charity, sacrifice and atonement, Aristotle's ethics revolve around political and social standards: friendship, nobility, magnanimity. Aristotle's vision of the "magnanimous" person shapes a political philosophy in which, as Vincent Pecora has shown, the household or *oikos* becomes the model for the polis. Martha K. Woodruff, in the second essay in this section of the present volume, invites a reconsideration of Aristotle's categories as a needed supplement to the modern gift ethics that come to us by way of Nietzsche's "gift-giving virtue." Woodruff argues that Nietzsche's praise for the gift giver creates a dilemma: if everyone emulates Zarathustra in giving excessively, who is left to receive? For Woodruff, Aristotle's description of the friend as "another self" provides an alternative not only to Nietzsche's vision of friendship as competition and challenge, but also to modern conceptions of identity. Aristotle's ethics imagines identity as socially defined, and thus contests the models of autonomous selfhood prevalent in Christian ethics and neoclassical economics. Aristotelian friendship, she argues, combines the seemingly conflicting claims of self-interest and altruism.[11]

Nietzsche's praise for magnanimity and wariness about debt may have derived in part from an earlier writer who exerted a powerful influence upon Anglo-American thought: Ralph Waldo Emerson.[12] In his brief 1844 essay on gifts, Emerson not only recognizes but recommends the affiliation that Mauss described between persons and their presents, declaring that "the only gift is a portion of thyself. Thou must bleed for me" (Emerson 1997: 26). Such a sacrifice, however, demands an equivalent return, one that the recipient may find onerous. Thus the champion of self-reliance admits that "we do not quite forgive a giver. The hand that feeds us is in some danger of being bitten" (1997: 26). Gifts, Emerson suggests, invade our privacy and demolish our carefully constructed autonomy. The gift is thus a dangerous phenomenon because it involves risk: the risk that one may give without reciprocation; the risk that one may accrue burdensome obligations; the risk that one may never be able to repay a gift; the risk of the loss of freedom. Emerson thus astutely introduces several problems to which later writers on the gift have repeatedly turned: those of gratitude, autonomy, and chance.

In both strains of the Western tradition, generosity and gratitude are represented at once as powerful motivators and as possibly unattainable ideals. In Europe these traditions converge in the Enlightenment, when modern bourgeois identity was constructed along with the ideology of the market. In her essay in this volume, Eun Kyung Min discovers a respect for generosity in an unlikely source from this period: Adam Smith, a writer usually viewed as the chief codifier of modern conceptions of self-interest. Smith's ethics, Min demonstrates, describes gratitude as an interiorized form of commerce in which justice is administered by the authority of "impartial spectators" we create in our own minds. Thus Smith's moral commerce, built upon the key principle of gratitude, is a hybrid construction lying somewhere between the market and the gift.

Perhaps the best known modern discussion of gratitude is that of Georg Simmel, who declares that gratitude is the very foundation of social behavior, the "moral memory of mankind" (1996: 45); without it, society would break apart. Echoing Emerson, however, Simmel also acknowledges the less welcome aspects of gratitude: once one receives a gift, he or she is forever under a coercion to reciprocate. The first gift, for Simmel, can never really be returned, for it has a "freedom which the return gift, because it is *that*, cannot possibly possess" (1996: 47; emphasis in original). Further, Simmel speculates, there has probably never been a reciprocal interaction that was precisely equal. Thus gratitude is irredeemable, and inevitably generates or solidifies power inequities between givers and receivers (1996: 48). And yet, not only do we continue to give gifts, but such giving constitutes perhaps the fullest expression of what it means to be human, embodying a "beauty, a spontaneous devotion to the other, an opening up and flowering from the 'virgin soil' of the soul" that at once forges social connections and enacts one's true freedom (1996: 47–8). Gratitude is both beautiful and dangerous.

Contemporary treatments of the gift revolve around these problems of freedom and autonomy, calculation and spontaneity, gratitude and generosity, risk and power. These questions of the gift are indeed simultaneously ethical questions about the nature and range of obligations; philosophical questions about the nature of human subjectivity; moral questions about the possibility and range of altruism; psychological questions about choice and freedom; and literary questions about our self-representations – about the truth and elasticity of our narratives. Thus all of the thinkers discussed so far address perhaps the primary truth about the gift: its essential ambiguity. Gifts at once express freedom and create binding obligations, and may be motivated by generosity or calculation, or both. Beneath them all lies the unexpressed question, which is perhaps the most fundamental question of all: do gifts exist in the real world, or are they unattainable ideals?

Present impossibilities

This is the question asked in the most influential recent philosophical inquiry into gifts, Jacques Derrida's *Given Time: I. Counterfeit Money* (1992).[13] Derrida has little to say about the actual practice of gift giving; as usual his concern is rather with sign systems, with those superfluities and paradoxes involved in systems of meaning. Heavily influenced by Nietzsche, Derrida's writings on the gift conform to his long-term project of exposing the aporias of rational thought, of teasing out the differences and deferrals that inevitably result from the gap between representations and what they represent. Thus Derrida seeks to complicate the relationship between the gift and what he calls, after Georges Bataille, the "restricted" economy of reciprocity. He defines the gift as "that which, in suspending economic calculation, opens the circle so as to defy reciprocity or symmetry … and so as to turn aside the return in view of the no-return." His premise is paradoxical: the gift is impossible; indeed, it is "*the* impossible. The very figure of the impossible" (1992: 7). Why? Because a gift must be given freely, generously, without the expectation of reward. And yet, at the moment that one even conceives of a certain transaction as a gift, or even conceives of giving something, the thought itself presupposes some reward. The gift is "annulled each time there is restitution or countergift," and there is inevitably countergift even in the conception (1992: 12). In fact, neither giver nor recipient may even register that there has been a gift, because to do so cancels it: once the donor recognizes that he or she has given a gift, or is thinking of giving a gift, he or she immediately pays him- or herself "with a symbolic recognition, to praise himself, to approve of himself, to gratify himself" (1992: 14; see also Jenkins 1998: 84).

Like Pierre Bourdieu, whose work I take up below, Derrida suggests that temporal deferral is the essence of the gift. Giving a gift requires forgetting, so that "there could be a gift only at the instant an effraction in the circle will have taken place, at the instant all circulation will have been interrupted and *on the condition* of this instant" (1992: 9; emphasis in original). As Tim Jenkins interprets it, a gift could exist "only as the paradoxical instant where time tears apart" (1998: 84). But how can one forget at the very moment that one intends? How can we fail to recall that we have given a gift, when, as we have noted, gift relationships depend for their existence upon our creation of stories about our transactions and relations? Here, then, is Derrida's double-bind: "Mauss reminds us that there is no gift without bond, without bind, without obligation or ligature; but on the other hand, there is no gift that does not have to untie itself from obligation, from debt, contract, exchange, and thus from the bind" (1992: 27).

Although he nibbles, gnaws, ruminates upon and recycles this paradox throughout the length of *Given Time*, Derrida never finds his way out of this aporia. Of course, he doesn't wish to; his aim is rather to expose the limits of rationalism and empiricism, as well as to probe the limits of previous analyses of the gift. The closest he comes to breaking through this logical stalemate occurs near the end of *Given Time*, where he presages, in different terms, the concepts stressed by sociologists such as Godbout and Caillé: the gift "must let itself be structured by the aleatory; it must *appear* chancy or in any case lived as such, apprehended as the intentional correlate of a perception that is absolutely surprised by the encounter with what it perceives" (Derrida 1992: 122). A gift must be unforeseeable and forgotten; "there must be chance, encounter, the involuntary, even unconsciousness or disorder, and there must be intentional freedom, and these two conditions must – miraculously, graciously – agree with each other" (1992: 123). A gift without intention, however, is not a gift but an accident. Here Derrida gestures ambiguously toward what other theorists state more plainly – that the gift involves risk and spontaneity. Harnessed to his faith in reason, Derrida may exaggerate the miraculousness of behaviors that human beings perform every day. Indeed, what seems truly impossible here is not actual gift giving but Derrida's elaborate, complicated version of it.

There are at least two flaws in his rendering. The first is a simple error of description: Derrida's premise is based upon a straw man. Surprisingly, for a philosopher whose entire career has been devoted to overturning conventions and undermining Cartesian selfhood, he adheres to an ideology of the "perfect gift" that, as we have seen, rests upon the belief in the autonomous Western self who chooses rationally and unconstrainedly. Derrida notes that Mauss "speaks of everything but the gift" (1992: 24), but in fact, as we have observed, Mauss clearly recognizes its inherent duality – that it is *both* disinterested and interested at once. Derrida's conundrum, in contrast, is binaristic. The gift is obviously not "impossible," because, in fact, people *do* give, both choosing to do so and responding to the recipient's perceived expectations, while calling what they do giving a gift. *Pace* Derrida (and Bourdieu), human beings are quite capable of simultaneously entertaining conflicting ideas about their behavior. Moreover, the "disinterestedness" in a particular gift may disappear and reappear during the course of one or more transactions. Second, as Philip Mirowski suggests, Derrida seems to equate intention and calculation (2001: 447). One may decide to give a gift, and even reason carefully about the selection, without also calculating expected rewards. Gift givers may also improvise, as when a husband decides on the spur of the moment to buy his wife flowers. Although later he may consider the blessings he might receive in return, in the moment of decision he need not have calculated at all. Spontaneity is a sufficient but not a necessary cause for giving gifts, but incorporating it is a necessary precondition for an adequate definition of the gift.[14]

Derrida's "forgetting" closely resembles Bourdieu's concept of "misrecognition"; each of them leads to the conclusion that giving gifts involves bad faith, that we lie to ourselves by choosing to ignore or forget our calculation of self-interest; that the pleasure we gain in giving gifts is just self-gratification. Although his own analysis of the gift betrays related flaws (as discussed below), Bourdieu has recently pointed to the requirements for transcending these Derridean double-binds: "it is not possible to reach an adequate understanding of the gift without leaving behind both the philosophy of mind that makes conscious intention the principle of every action and the economism that knows no other economy than that of rational calculation and interest reduced to economic interest" (1997: 234). For Bourdieu, the gift is "an act situated beyond the opposition between constraint and freedom, individual choice and collective pressure, distinterestedness and self-interest" (1997: 236). To understand the gift we must employ what Keats called "negative capability": the capacity to entertain conflicting thoughts or interpretations without seeking to resolve them neatly. Gifts expose the truth that human behavior and the stories with which we dramatize it are more flexible than the rational theories with which we attempt to account for it. The meanings of the gift, in short, expose the limitations of our categories. Hence, more adequate descriptions of its meanings will require that theorists become flexible enough to embrace and emulate the gift's own elasticity.

The sociology of the gift

Good and bad gifts

Current social thought, which maps and explores the territories where gifts operate, may move us toward such flexibility. Sociologists have gathered a wealth of information to assess whether contemporary human beings are indeed, as Mauss charges, less generous, less socially bound, and more miserly than "primitives." However, two different interpretations of gift practices coexist uneasily in sociological discourse. In one camp are those adhering to what Aafke Komter dubs the "moral cement" approach. These theorists emphasize the unifying effects of gift giving, gifts' capacity to forge or solidify social bonds. In the other camp are those who stress the ways that gifts can be used to acquire and exercise power; these writers emphasize inequality and social disintegration (Komter 1996a: 107).

In the first group we find sociologist David Cheal, who uses data gleaned from Canadian communities to argue that gifts participate in and create what he terms a "moral economy": "a system of transactions which are defined as socially desirable … because through them social ties are recognized, and balanced social relationships are maintained" (1988: 15; see Chapter 12 of this volume for further treatment of Cheal's work). Cheal espouses the gift system; yet in his theory gifts never really threaten the dominant market economy partly because for him (as for Hyde) the gift is an economy of small groups (Cheal 1998: 16; Hyde 1983: 89). In contrast to the neutralized exchanges of the marketplace, for Cheal gifts contribute to what he (unfortunately) calls "love culture," because in giving gifts transactors empathize with each other and see the world through another's eyes (Cheal 1996: 105). However, Cheal does not stress, as does Lee Anne Fennell, the dialogic aspects of gift giving and receiving, whereby the selves interacting in such transactions are also reconfigured through them. Thus he ends up limiting both the range and the value of the gift and risks trivializing what he attempts to endorse.

Komter's research reveals similar findings. She concludes that, despite most givers' belief that they are acting altruistically, balanced reciprocity remains the most common paradigm for gift transactions, and that mixed motives – both generosity and a desire to be recognized – generally characterize both gift givers and receivers (1996a: 110, 117). Contemporary gift giving is, we see again, decidedly ambivalent. One reason may be that, as Berking suggests, nowadays people who give feel the need to justify themselves in terms of the dominant ideology of self-interest. For example, let's say I invite a new colleague over to my house for dinner. I clean the house, prepare a costly dinner, buy new place-mats, and purchase expensive wine. Why do I unproductively spend resources which I could use to increase my wealth and comfort? I could argue that I want to make the acquaintance feel welcome, to treat her as I would wish to be treated if I were she. But Berking discovered that many Westerners would frame their motives differently. To the question, "Why did you invite the friend?" they answer, "Because it gives me self-fulfillment: I can increase my self-esteem, feel rewarded, and perhaps create good will and obligations that I can exploit in the future" (1999: 145). Contemporary Westerners are so uncomfortable with communalism and altruism that we tend to re-explain our generosity as self-interest. In such cases, our stories fail to account for the complexity of our motives. Instead we remold connected selves into isolated consumers, and replace collective obligations with individualist gratifications.

In the second camp are those for whom collective obligations are sources of power, or what Bourdieu dubs "symbolic capital." We might call this The *Godfather* Paradigm: when I give more to you or perform extravagant favors for you, I both enhance my prestige and engender deep obligations. This, of course, is the principle behind the potlatch. In contemporary societies, as Barry Schwartz observes, personal gifts may likewise be hostile or presumptive: because a gift is imbued with the identity of its giver and codifies the giver's perception of the recipient(s), to accept a gift is to allow someone else to impose that version of self upon you (1996: 70). Such gifts may indeed be "offers you can't refuse." Likewise, to refuse a gift – if the offer can be refused – is to reject the identity imposed as well as the tendered relationship it involves. Theorists such as Schwartz demonstrate that gift exchanges not only promote reciprocity but also protect hierarchies.

Let's use another story to exemplify some of the nuances in reciprocal exchanges. A longstanding friendship between couples is waning: the couples find they have fewer and fewer interests in common and have neglected to maintain the social exchanges – invitations, conversations, jokes – that nourish friendships. Yet Couple A insists upon continuing to give extravagant birthday presents and ceremonial gifts to Couple B. Couple B feels obligated to reciprocate, but invariably grumbles and procrastinates in doing so. Because of their gifts, Couple A continues to ask for favors, such as the use of Couple B's car, and still keeps borrowed CDs for months, while also resenting the implied disrespect in Couple B's delays. Finally Couple B does not return a phone call, and fails to reciprocate for a birthday present. Here the refusal of reciprocity sends a clear signal that may create a hostility as persistent as the Godfather's extorted gratitude. Not so clear, however, are the accompanying signals: Will Couple A understand Couple B's implication that they find Couple A's "gifts" to be manipulative? Or will they just accuse them of ingratitude? Is Couple B accusing Couple A of extortion when in fact they are merely inconsistent? Is Couple A seeking to outdo Couple B in extravagance because they feel diminished by Couple B's loss of interest in the relationship? The parties in this relationship are telling conflicting stories and living by conflicting interpretations of their reciprocal exchanges and the balance of power. This case highlights the fact that reciprocal exchanges are not always friendly, even among friends. Indeed, taken to its furthest expression, the "norm" of reciprocity may encompass vengeance, in which repayment for a service rendered or not rendered becomes violent or destructive. This is the gift as poison. But even within relationships that remain generally amicable, gifts can generate exploitation, manipulation, and a battle for control. Thus one fears that the friendship described above will end only when one of the couples denounces the other.

Gender

Theorists in both camps agree that women still dominate gift rituals. For Cheal, gift giving is an essential component of a "feminized ideology" of love (1996: 97). Godbout and Caillé similarly declare that the gift is "the special domain" of women (Godbout 1998: 36), and Lewis Hyde proposes that gifts comprise a "female property" (1983: 103). Hyde fails to emphasize, however, the other meaning of his phrase: the degree to which females *are* or *have been* the property of males. Lévi-Strauss argues, in fact, that historically women have not just given gifts but have *been* gifts, and indeed that the exchange of women by men constitutes the very origins of culture (1997: 24).[15] The source of this affiliation between gift and gender may lie in the historical separation of spheres, whereby males operate in the wider marketplace of commodity and price and leave the domestic realm to women. French feminists such as Hélène Cixous have suggested that the "feminine" economy is essentially connected with the gift, and that this economy provides a needed libidinal alternative to the intrinsically "male" economy of debt (1981: 48–55). Such questionable essentialism aside, the more common feminist response has been to interpret women's association with gifts as a sign of oppression: that is, women have greater freedom and power in a domain that is ultimately trivial; furthermore, by fostering the illusion of control, this condition prevents women from seeking more authentic pathways to power. Yet another interpretation is possible: that women use gifts to establish and confirm networks of social obligation that engender true social influence. Who benefits, then, from the affiliation between women and gifts? Is it a sign of impotence or of power appropriated?

Komter outlines four possible ways that women's role in gift exchanges could be related to power. This affiliation may: (1) create asymmetrical power in favor of men; (2) generate equivalent reciprocity, whereby each gender benefits equally; (3) produce asymmetrical reciprocity in favor of women; or (4) engender a condition of alternating asymmetry, in which women and men profit in turn (1996b: 124). In the first model, gift giving is presented as involuntary labor that confirms women's position of inferiority. Men disdain these transactions because they are insignificant. In the second model, women's gifts and the social interconnections they establish create an alternate economy equivalent to that of males (1996b: 126). In many societies, for example, women perform the essential rituals surrounding birth and death, and these symbolically rich functions are just as indispensable to the smooth functioning of society as male trade. In the third model, women actually show their superiority in matters of emotion through the giving and receiving of gifts; they also establish deeper and longer-lasting friendships, thereby promoting social stability and support through female bonding. In the fourth model, models one and three alternate: women and men benefit equally, if in different ways and at different times, from women's status as greater gift givers (1996b: 129). Komter concludes that model four best describes social reality, and it seems true that women's affiliation with the gift economy offers important benefits for both genders.[16]

But it is not clear how this conclusion avoids the pitfall of tacitly approving a separation of spheres that seems inevitably to ascribe a higher value to market transactions than to gifts. To accept a rigid gendering of the gift, that is, may ensure that gifts remain beyond the pale of mainstream economic thought and activity, and that the moral economy dominated by women will continue to be marginalized. Thus for Komter women's gift giving is involved in a fundamental paradox:

> on the one hand, their gift exchange may be considered a powerful means of reconstituting social identities and of keeping social relationships alive. ... On the other hand, in giving much to others, women incur the risk of losing their own identities, given their unequal societal and economic power compared with men.
>
> (Komter 1996b: 130–1)

Here again the gift is understood as an ambiguous phenomenon, both embodying the connectedness that fosters social strength and cohesion and enacting a form of disenfranchisement, an "alternate" economy, that is granted value only after the fact, as a tributary of the channels where real power flows.

Two economies

The consideration of separate spheres is related to another question of the gift that has been posed repeatedly in sociological studies: are current gift practices a continuation of ancient ones, or do gifts represent something entirely different for us than for the ancients? These historical alternatives imply different degrees of separation between the domains of home and work: if the gift is something different for us than for ancient people, this condition seems to be both a cause and a result of the increasing divorce between the domestic realm and the realm of business. In contrast, if contemporary gift practices are merely evolved versions of ancient ones, then the two realms interpenetrate in a myriad of ways. The problem with the first formulation is, as Alan Smart has noted, that it ends up trivializing or ghettoizing the gift; yet the second interpretation threatens to dissolve differences and offer weak resistance to economistic explanations (Smart 1993: 389).

Still, the second alternative seems intuitively true. For example, let's say I buy produce from a man who brings fruit and vegetables into the neighborhood in his truck. Although his prices are generally lower than those in supermarkets, quite often his grapes are soft and his oranges dry. One could argue that the transactions retain a vestige of the gift because the man delivers to our home; they involve a personal relationship as well as an economic one. An economist might argue, in contrast, that we are simply calculating costs: the value we receive from home delivery and lower prices outweighs the risk that his produce will be stale. Thus we are simply getting more for our money. But this explanation fails to account for what is most important in this relationship. We continue to give him our custom, not for convenience's sake (since we visit the supermarket every week, it would actually be more convenient to buy produce there than to leave a note for him), but because over the years we have come to know and respect this man. A small businessman, we feel, needs our custom more than the supermarket chain does; perhaps more importantly, his personal attention contrasts starkly with the gleaming, sterile ambience of the supermarket. His presence and good humor make the world seem a friendlier place. Consequently, his fruit and vegetables seem less alienated; because our beans were *his* beans, they seem more natural, as well. And although we pay full price for the produce, because it carries our grocery man's stamp it bears a kind of weak inalienability. Here, then, the domain of the gift and the sphere of the market cross paths and may converge. Nevertheless, this relationship remains an exception to the way that we purchase virtually all other products, for there is no hint of the gift when we line up at the local Giant.

The separation and interaction between these realms and their accompanying objects – gifts and commodities – constitutes the major theme of James Carrier's recent study. Carrier provides a nuanced treatment of this separation and suggests that different models of gift exchange bring with them different models of selfhood. He shows how the ideology of the "perfect gift" – in which gifts are seen as unconstrained and unconstraining – emerges from, and may foster, economism (1995: 149; I discuss this further in Chapter 12). That is, conceiving that the desire to give gifts issues from some "pure" impulse of generosity and entails no obligation really assumes that gift givers are the same disinterested, autonomous individuals found in economists' models. Accordingly, in this view presents are "transubstantiated in a kind of reverse fetishism of commodities," losing their past – that indissoluble attachment to persons that Mauss articulated – to act as fungible expressions of fleeting encounters (Carrier 1995: 166). Contemporary depictions of gifts as free and unconstrained merely import the autonomous self of neoclassical economics into another terrain. Although the ideal of the "perfect" or free gift is very rarely carried out in practice, the ideology remains, and may prevent donors and recipients from understanding their own motives and actions. We feel guilt that our gifts are sometimes given with strings attached, and pretend that we alone are altruistic; as a result, we trip on the kind of logical paradoxes presented by Derrida: "pure" gifts are impossible, yet we continue to give something that we call gifts. Gifts and commodities, or gift transactions and market relations, are thus for Carrier "polar terms that define a continuum along which one can place existing transactions and friendships" (1995: 190). They overlap. Thus we need a richer description of identity, something akin to what Carrier dubs the "situated self," in order to define subjects not as trapped by but as produced by the web of relationships that gifts promote. Although Carrier himself cannot give up his investment in the autonomous individual, he does demonstrate the difficulty of reconceiving selfhood, as well as the dangers inherent in an uncritical championing of the gift as a pure ideal of free, unconstrained giving.

Jacques T. Godbout and Alain Caillé similarly define the gift as the embodiment of a "system of relationships that is strictly social, in that these relations cannot be reduced to factors of power or economic interest" (Godbout 1998: 13).

But the gift fails to play the major role in society that it could. Why? For three reasons: because the gift is defined as the antidote to the market, and is thus "burdened with the impossible task of embodying absent hope and the lost soul in a soulless world" (1998: 165); because the gift requires a break with both ideologies of self-interest and Nietzschean egoism; and because, as we have seen, modernity prides itself on a ferocious individualism that mistrusts selflessness (1998: 16–17). According to Godbout and Caillé, family life nourishes the gift by creating support mechanisms, by compelling reciprocal services, by linking generations through inalienable possessions, and by performing gift rituals such as weddings (Godbout 1998: 48). But this definition assumes the separation of spheres. Thus, while Godbout and Caillé's ratification of the gift rebuts neoclassical analyses of the family (such as Gary Becker's), their retention of the radical separation of gift and market once again restricts the gift's range and deepens the very rift whose existence they lament.

They attempt to escape this problem by analyzing what they call "the gift to strangers." These are not Berking's host-guest relations, although they may derive from them. Instead they are referring to support groups such as Alcoholics Anonymous, in which strangers (and the carefully preserved anonymity of such groups is designed to maintain that "strangeness") give each other the gifts of sympathy and conversation, and to charitable organizations, which connect individuals through usually anonymous gifts to those in need (Godbout 1998: 64–77). The phenomenon of "gifts to strangers" is "quintessentally modern" because these presents are not circumscribed by primary obligations such as family or friendship (1998: 77). The "gifts to strangers," unlike the kin-based gifts in earlier societies, depend for their efficacy on a degree of impersonality.

Godbout and Caillé outline other features that characterize the modern gift as well, but the most important of these is spontaneity (Godbout 1998: 96–7; cf. Caillé 2001: 34). This feature, too often neglected in gift theory, is a signpost toward a possible route out of the dilemma of self-interest. The gift, as Gudeman aptly notes, is a "probe into uncertainty" (2001: 467): a giver never truly knows whether he or she will receive anything back. Giving must therefore be to some degree its own reward. But two problems attend this phenomenon. The first is what Godbout and Caillé dub the "Dale Carnegie paradox": in order to win friends and influence people, one must treat them respectfully and act spontaneously sincere. When one sincerely cares for others, one finds oneself receiving rewards of respect and compassion in return. Thus habitual gift givers end up cultivating sincerity. Yet to cultivate sincerity would seem to ensure insincerity; likewise, "practicing spontaneity" seems oxymoronic (Godbout 1998: 79–80). The second problem is a social paradox. Gifts should be given spontaneously. But people value them so much that they tend to make them obligatory in certain circumstances, and creating such obligations seems to deny the gift its essence, its voluntary quality (1998: 142). The Dale Carnegie paradox resembles Derrida's impossibility, which rests, as I have suggested, upon a mistaken notion of how gifts really operate, and upon a binaristic way of thinking that gifts render inadequate. The second paradox also seems founded upon an erroneous definition. As we have seen, Mauss emphasized that gift practices in "primitive" societies were *simultaneously* obligatory and disinterested. As I have suggested, modern gifts function similarly: they are at once disinterested, in that no return is specified, and interested, in that a return exists nonetheless. Givers feel rewarded *by the very act of giving*, whether or not they receive something tangible back. Moreover, gifts may be either spontaneous or calculated, or both. Indeed, even an obligatory gift may involve spontaneous moments during part of the process of procuring and giving.

The question of the gift is thus a question of categories, and we fail to account for them adequately if our classifications remain rigid. The question of the gift is also a question of value. Gifts may have exchange-value: we buy commodities for a certain price, and receivers may also evaluate them in terms of that price. "Why did they bring such a cheap wine?" the hosts privately complain after the guests leave. "I guess they don't think much of us." Gifts may also have use-value: granddad receives a bathrobe for Christmas because he needs a warm wrap to prevent getting chilled after a shower. But something is left out of this analysis, something that Godbout and Caillé term "bonding-value" (Godbout 1998: 173). A giver isn't just proving her magnanimity or generosity; she is spending time and thought, hypothesizing about mutually interacting representations of herself and her recipients. Yet this term scarcely solves the problem. How is bonding value to be measured? Have we just renamed Mauss's *hau*? Who ascribes the value to the transaction, and what happens if the parties assign conflicting values to the object or relationship? Bonding-value begs the question.

Despite their inability to produce fully persuasive paradigms, Godbout and Caillé succeed admirably in demonstrating (sometimes inadvertently) how gifts trouble our categories. One reason for this condition is what they call the "rule of the implicit" (Godbout 1998: 186), an "active and conscious refusal of explicitness on both sides" during a gift transaction (1998: 187). We cherish this rule, they conclude, to "preserve or introduce an element of risk … an uncertainty, an indeterminacy," an "element of play," into our social interactions (1998: 187–8). But all of this would appear to a rationalist as nothing but hypocrisy. These "implicit" norms are just a collective lie whereby givers pretend not to gain from what they give and receivers act as though gifts are bestowed for their own good, rather than for the feeling of magnanimity or the promise of reward the giver gets. We all know the rules, and the rules are that nobody may announce the rules.

In simplified terms, this is the position of Pierre Bourdieu, who has written one of the most influential recent sociological treatments of gift practices. For Bourdieu, the gift is one of those risky strategies that "owe their infinite complexity to the fact that the giver's undeclared calculation has to reckon with the receiver's undeclared calculation" (1997b: 204). He thus seeks a "logic" of social practice (actually a theory to account for that logic) that depends upon flexible conceptions of the distinctions between what people say and how they act; these unspoken assumptions and implicit norms he calls the "habitus."

There is often, if not always, a tension between what an "objective" observer might determine to be the underlying beliefs and rules of a social practice and how the players themselves think of it. The sociologist, argues Bourdieu, should not attempt to achieve some speciously "objective" standpoint, but rather to inhabit the minds of the players, to think of it as they do.

Perhaps Bourdieu's key insight regarding the gift concerns the importance of time: the gift is a system in which obligations are constantly deferred. This deferral of repayment, he argues, allows transacting parties to "forget" that obligations exist. "The interval inserted between the gift and the counter-gift is an instrument of denial which allows a subjective truth and a quite opposite objective truth to coexist" (1997b: 200). The subjective truth is that we give without expecting a reward; the objective truth is that the giver and receiver are calculating benefits. Thus "the functioning of gift exchange presupposes individual and collective misrecognition of the truth of the objective 'mechanism' of the exchange, a truth which an immediate response brutally exposes" (1997b: 198). The passage of time allows the collective lie to be forgotten and permits the deferral of obligations that camouflages the expectation of reward as altruism.

The word "misrecognition," however, exposes the major flaw in Bourdieu's ingenious theory. What is the difference between a misrecognition and a recognition? The "mis" is inserted by that same "objective" observer whom Bourdieu wishes to unseat. Indeed, his description of these phenomena suggests that we *mis*understand our own habits, that we all believe a lie. The truth would expose gifts for what they "really" are – disguised economic transactions. Bourdieu constantly criticizes economism, arguing that it fails to capture the nuances of transactions as perceived by the actors, that it "annihilates the specificity located precisely in the socially maintained discrepancy between the 'objective' reality and the social representation of production and exchange" (1997b: 206). And yet his description falls victim to such economism by implying that the economic truth is the most basic one.

This problem is exposed in another of Bourdieu's major contributions to social theory: his suggestive but somewhat confusing codification of various forms of non-economic capital.[17] These include "symbolic capital," defined as "prestige and renown attached to a family and its name" (Bourdieu 1977: 179); "social capital," which refers to "obligations ... and the advantages of connections or social positions, and trust"; and "cultural capital," which is embodied or institutionalized knowledge or expertise (see Smart 1993: 392). Gift giving generates and enhances these non-economic varieties of capital: landed aristocracy enrich their symbolic capital through endowments and trusts; a local businessperson creates social capital by giving low-interest loans to neighbors, and so on. But in fact Bourdieu's various forms of "capital" are all derived from economic capital. As he admits, when a society refuses to recognize the naked truth of self-interest it converts economic capital into symbolic capital, which, therefore, is merely denied or "misrecognized" or transubstantiated economic capital (Bourdieu 1997b: 210–11). Indeed, for Bourdieu, the "transformation of any given kind of capital into symbolic capital ... is the fundamental operation of social alchemy (the paradigm of which is gift exchange)" (1997b: 219). Just as the underlying truth of gift exchange is a "fiction" of disinterest that masks calculation, so other forms of capital are generated through the social repression of an ugly economic truth. Gift exchange is just a euphemism (1997b: 218) for calculation. As in Freud's theory of the unconscious, in which the disguising of unpleasant psychological truths permits them to subsist in more palatable forms, Bourdieu's social unconscious just dresses naked competition in designer clothing.

Bourdieu has responded to charges of economism by claiming that in using "capital" he means to posit not identities but a series of homologies: they are not precisely the same, but have similar structures, and emerge from the same sources (1990: 111). But as Amy Koritz and Douglas Koritz suggest, Bourdieu wants simultaneously to deploy "the rhetorical and explanatory power of economic metaphor while denying that a fundamental identity between 'homologous' structures is implied by that rhetoric" (Koritz and Koritz 1999: 411). If economic capital does not underlie these other forms, if "capital" is merely an explanatory metaphor, why not choose a different set of metaphors (1999: 415)? Bourdieu's terms, while not explicitly endorsing economic explanations, "offer too little resistance" to them (Koritz and Koritz 1999: 415). In a later essay Bourdieu responds to the charge of economism by renaming the collective "misrecognition" involved in gift exchange a "lie," and by redescribing the system of rewards and recognition in symbolic capital as a "market" (1997a: 232, 233). Obviously, these responses description don't rebut the charge of economism so much as reinforce it.[18]

Better than Bourdieu's overlapping categories is Alan Smart's description of gift exchanges as "contingent performances" (1993: 405). As I have observed, gift practices do not follow rules; they seep outside of our categories. Gift exchanges are like games, or a form of social theater in which shifting relationships are dramatized, created, dissolved. To suggest that the players "misrecognize" their own motives is to misunderstand the aleatory and ludic qualities that make the game worth playing. As Godbout and Caillé note, something in the gift resists rational delineation. Gift practices are uncertain, risky, sometimes spontaneous, and often pleasurable. Thus, as Russell Belk points out, one essential aspect to genuine gifts is their capacity to surprise and delight (1996: 67); this feature, in turn, seems a consequence of the risk and spontaneity involved in giving. Any theory that does not make room for the flux of contingency, for spontaneity, risk and shifting roles, is doomed to wind up in the dustbin.

What can we salvage, then, from sociological accounts of the gift? Quite a bit. (1) *Disinterestedness*. Gifts are disinterested not because there is no return, but because what comes back often violates or transcends the rules of mercantile equivalence (Godbout 1998: 183). We may receive less, monetarily, than we give; yet the impulse to give does not necessarily depend upon any assurance that we will receive equal value in return. One gives to loved ones, furthermore, *because* they are loved ones. One is interested in the others' happiness before one's own. (2) *Risk.* I may receive nothing; the recipient may refuse the gift; in selecting, buying and giving, I may impoverish myself emotionally or financially. The idea of "bonding-value" will not account for these losses, but the term at least gestures towards the rewards of such contingent interaction. The idea of the gift must include the risk of loss. Indeed, *pace* Derrida, a gift may not be a gift at all unless it *is* known as such, and unless the donor is "capable of appreciating the reality of loss and risk" (Caillé 2001: 34). (3) *Spontaneity.* People sometimes give without thought of the consequences; we are sometimes caught up in the moment. Any adequate description of gift practices must acknowledge this performative aspect of the gift, because without that acknowledgment we have no response to the reductive explanations of economists and cynics. (4) *Pleasure.* Giving gifts – like receiving them – produces pleasure that is not merely a result of expecting a reward. Gifts reward precisely because in thinking about another person's happiness one is at once fully free and free from freedom. To put it another way, giving is pleasurable precisely insofar as it is *not* egoistically motivated: liberation occurs in relinquishing considerations of individual benefit, in affirming a commitment to caring for another person. (5) *Superfluity.* This term describes the gift in several respects. First, giving and receiving gifts, as Cheal points out, is often a "redundant" activity: gifts received may not be what we need, or even want. Many times they are luxury items whose meaning is more social than monetary. But even if the gift does fulfill a need, giving a gift in reciprocation is not the same as paying a debt: we may give more, not because we want to generate greater obligations (although we may) but because the nature of the social practice encourages and sometimes requires it. Second, both donors and receivers in gift transactions usually find themselves concerned with others during the gift sequence, even if either or both *also* think at some point in terms of self-interest. Fennell's article dubs this condition "empathetic dialogue," but, as I have observed, the dialogue need not be empathetic. Yet even giving a hostile gift requires that one think outside the bounds of one's own needs and wishes. Thus the gift threatens the sanctity of the rational, autonomous individual and his calculation. Giving and receiving gifts permits individuals to lose their autonomy to a ritual or activity that nobody can entirely control. I'll return to this idea below.

Clearly, then, gift practices disclose essential questions about social life: definitions of identity and subjectivity; tensions between individual autonomy and collective obligations; the nature or kinds of risk involved in deciding to give; the overlaps and distinctions between rationality and spontaneity; and, perhaps above all, the limits of rationality itself. Yet no matter how we measure and analyze the gift, something seems to elude our grasp. Something lies outside our attempts to corral the gift into categories. This is the third way that the question of the gift involves superfluity: as Caillé puts it, the gift "affirms participation in the universe of 'without cause'" (2001: 37). We might tentatively propose, then, that the essence of the gift is superfluity itself.

The gift and artistic commerce

General economy

The best sociological explanations of gifts succeed in troubling the categories, but even they seem either to trivialize them by limiting their range or redescribing them economistically, or to fail to follow up the implications of their own premises. Missing from all of these accounts is that key fourth term so compellingly discussed by Godelier: the deep affiliation between gifts and the sacred.[19] This affiliation underpins much of the writing of Georges Bataille, the French erotician and sociologist whose work inspired Derrida's important early writing on gift issues. Bataille is the bridge between Mauss and Derrida, as well as an important link between sociology and literary theory (Pecora 1997: 251). His 1933 essay, "The Notion of Expenditure" (*dépense*) and his later treatise *The Accursed Share* (*La Part maudite*) outline a radical view of human society based upon expenditure. Extrapolating from such rituals as the potlatch, Bataille proposes the existence of a "general economy" that violates Western norms of production, acquisition, saving, and reciprocity. For Bataille, human beings subsist not in order to save, but to "accede to the insubordinate function of free expenditure" (1985: 129). This economy of expenditure includes all moments of liberation from acquisitive labor, including gambling, gifts, games, festivals and the arts, and especially all varieties of sacrifice. Extended to the problem of representation, the "general economy" encompasses whatever lies outside of systems of meaning: it is a name for the very idea of superfluity. For Bataille as for Simmel, the gift is the highest expression of human freedom because it liberates givers and receivers from ego boundaries and rationality. As the pure embodiment of *dépense*, the gift underwrites Bataille's entire vision of social life. In his later work, however, Bataille emphasizes the generative power of sacrifice, which paradoxically creates value by "destroying that which it consecrates" (1988: 58), thus producing meaning and health out of expenditure and loss.

Unfortunately, Bataille's intriguing ideas are plagued by a central incoherence. He sometimes suggests that expenditure comprises an orgy of freedom from which nothing is recovered. Thus it would equal absolute loss. But at other times he states that the extravagant losses in the potlatch are merely converted into prestige or rank (1988: 68–9).[20] As Pecora observes, Bataille's "general economy" makes sense only if one accepts his radical division between economic and symbolic capital (Pecora 1997: 249), a distinction that, Frow notes, boils down to little more than clever "sleight of hand" (Frow 1997: 118). More compelling – and more important for our purposes – than Bataille's inconsistencies is his association of expenditure with art. For Bataille, the word "poetry" must be applied to "the least degraded and least intellectualized forms of the expression of a state of loss" (1985: 120): "poetry" refers to whatever expresses an impulse toward the gift. Poetry, like sacrifice, creates value out of expenditure, turning loss into gain.

This Bataillean idea inspires most literary criticism employing gift theory. For literary critics, gift theory offers an alternative to the rampant commodification of art, and contests the neo-Marxist perception of literary and artistic production as just mystified capitalist production. For literary critics, the gift raises questions that go to the heart of the creative process: does art have a value separate from its exchange-value? How is art related to the sacred? Can the creation and reception of art works be best understood as a form of gift giving or gift exchange? In sum, for literary and art critics, gift theory seems to promise the possibility of reenchanting the world.

Erotic economy

Such reenchantment is celebrated in the most influential literary study of the gift, Lewis Hyde's 1983 book, *The Gift: Imagination and the Erotic Life of Property*. A wholehearted champion of the "moral cement" approach, Hyde barely acknowledges that gifts can also widen power differentials or promote hostility. For Hyde, the gift is an "emanation of eros," a "binder of many wills" (1983: 22, 35). Hyde also adheres (at least for most of his book) to the "two economies" approach: his gift economy is distinct from the market economy inasmuch as gifts erase boundaries whereas market exchanges solidify them (1983: 61). Gifts create bonds by constantly staying in motion; dissolving the separation of transactors and encouraging the sharing of objects, they function as "anarchist property," as "property that perishes" (1983: 84, 8). Hyde's eloquent endorsement of erotic commerce has a strong appeal to writers and scholars who feel threatened by the encroachment of market rhetoric and paradigms into every corner of social and professional life. Nevertheless, Hyde's exaggeration of the "erotic" qualities of gift exchange and his blindness to the complexities of power renders his version somewhat romanticized and one-dimensional.

More persuasive than Hyde's social theory are his explorations into what he calls the "commerce of the creative spirit." His thesis in this portion of his book is that art participates in the gift insofar as it operates as an agent of transformation and regeneration (1983: 47). Hyde's artist does not will his or her works, but receives them: he or she is placed in a "gifted state" and, having entered that state, is compelled to "make the work and offer it to an audience. The gift must stay in motion. 'Publish or perish' is an internal demand of the creative spirit" (1983: 146). To treat the products of the imagination as gifts, he declares, "ensures the fertility of the imagination" (1983: 148), because the artist who (quoting Rilke) engages in a "continuous squandering of all perishable values" (Hyde 1983: 150), can "reproduce the gifted state" in his or her audience. The artist makes his or her audience grateful and therefore eager to pass on the gift. The work of art, then, is the highest expression of the spirit of the gift; it serves as a "bond, a band, a link by which the several are knit into one" (1983: 153). Indeed, art impels a "transcendent commerce, the economy of recreation, conversion, or renaissance" (1983: 193): the artist is renewed by immersion in the grateful state, and the reader or viewer repays that gratitude by tendering the gift of attention. This transformation of the recipient not only repays the gift but passes it on to others. Hyde caps this theoretical manifesto with scintillating readings of Walt Whitman's and Ezra Pound's poetry.

It is easy to see why Hyde's celebration of creative commerce has vitalized so many literary critics: he makes creation and interpretation sound noble, even holy; he provides a powerful defense of the moral and social value of art; he captures what, for many critics, was the original motive for their choice of profession – those exhilarating moments of gratitude and awe engendered in the encounter with beauty. He also depicts artists and critics as valiant defenders of aesthetic value and truth hedged about by philistine merchants. Alas, his analysis is fraught with problems, not the least of which is his emulation of Mauss's nostalgia for an unfallen world and his notion that something in the gift itself makes it special. Moreover, it is not quite true (or not only true) that gifts are "anarchist" property, or belong to nobody: as we have seen, gifts retain a vestige of inalienability and thereby encourage connection because in some sense they are *never* really passed on, but retain the imprint of the original giver. Whoever reads a book with close attention or masters a piece of music incorporates some of that artist's identity, insight, or skill. In this regard, art works are gifts that never cease to belong to the first owner: they are property that *never* perishes.

Further, as Charles Rzepka observes, Hyde's notion of creative commerce tends to "mystify the real origins of literary work in labor" (Rzepka 1995: 53): the artist isn't just "given" inspiration; she has to work for it by thinking, revising and reworking what has been written or produced, and by submitting it to an audience. Further, "matching labor for labor [for example, reading for writing] is not the same as bestowing it or its products upon another, or reciprocating that bestowal" (1995: 56). That is, it is not at all clear how reading or viewing a work of art "repays" the artist. Aren't the reader's rewards actually directed inward? One might also question the assumption that what a reader owes to or gains from a writer is comparable to the obligation attached to a material boon. Rzepka concludes that the relationship between author and reader is not that of gift-*exchange* but of "gift-*giving* or sacrifice, a one-sided relationship in which the 'gratitude' of the receiver is an index of the ineradicable nature of the debt he has incurred" (1995: 58; emphasis in original). But here Rzepka responds to Hyde's mystifications with some of his own: like a true Romantic, Rzepka elevates the author to a god to whom poor readers are mere supplicants. On the contrary, a text is, after all, nothing but dormant words until a reader activates it. Isn't the writer, then, actually indebted to the reader? One might even claim that a truly alert and appreciative reader increases the value of a text by exposing what wasn't previously apparent in it and conveying those insights on to other readers. Second, both Hyde and Rzepka conflate the biological person who writes with what Foucault calls the "author-function," that "principle of thrift in the proliferation of meaning," a principle made of words alone (Foucault 1979: 159). The reader responds to this presence by conversing with it. The gift, if there is one, is not to the author but to the author-function activated by collaboration between author and reader. Finally, one questions whether this commerce should be best understood as a gift or as a debt, especially since authors are always readers first, and thus are not merely "given" their generic and cultural forms, but inherit them from earlier writers and readers. An author is influenced by previous authors, and these intertextual relations may be as fruitfully analyzed through tropes of interest and debtorship as through metaphors of the gift.[21]

Interpretive economy

Nevertheless, literary critics, stimulated by Hyde's work and lately by Derrida's, have found in gift theory a ready set of paradigms for both practical and theoretical scholarship. Several different approaches have appeared. The first type focuses on the gifts or gift exchanges depicted within a text. Thus, for example, Ronald Sharp (1986) has illuminated the friendship between Antonio and Bassanio in Shakespeare's *Merchant of Venice* by applying principles drawn from Mauss and Hyde, and Steven Dillon (1992) has treated the relationship between femininity and generosity by analyzing the gift objects found in several novels by George Eliot. A second approach, taking its cue from Hyde, unpacks the relationship between author and audience by examining how language functions within a gift economy. At its best this type of criticism incorporates discussions of actual gift practices either in the societies portrayed or in the society within which a text has been read. Thus, for instance, Robert Bjork has joined stylistic analysis, medieval language philosophies, and modern theories about gifts in premarket societies to reach a deeper understanding of the way speech functions as a gift in *Beowulf* (1994: 993); similarly, Britton J. Harwood (1991) has delved into medieval representations of largesse to expose the ways that *Sir Gawain* embodies and challenges the social and religious values surrounding gift exchanges. Others have scrutinized relationships between or among authors to explore affiliations between gift practices and intertextuality (see, for example, Modiano 1989). Others investigate the style(s) of a particular text to explore analogies or homologies between "economies" of form and economies of social life. Thus, for example, a given text might be said to manifest "generosity" or "expenditure" if it exhibits a tendency toward floridness, parody, and so on. Still others synthesize several approaches, as for example when the present writer discussed the gift systems in both Homeric Greece and turn-of-the-century Ireland, and then combined these data with a treatment of James Joyce's stylistic extravagance in the "Cyclops" episode of Joyce's *Ulysses*, in order to suggest how Joyce's work operates within a system of power differentials and representational excess that epitomizes, on several levels, a gift economy (Osteen 1995: 250–77).

The bulk of literary criticism (whether performed by literary scholars, sociologists, or historians) employing gift theory treats pre-modern or early modern texts – not surprisingly, given the historical shift from gift-dominated to market-dominated economies outlined above.[22] Unfortunately, despite the signal influence of the gift in philosophy and literary theory, much of the practical criticism using those theories has been inadequately conceived. Too many critics are content simply to "apply" mechanically the paradigms of Hyde, Derrida, Mauss or Bataille without acknowledging the limitations and blind spots in each, and without attempting to blend literary explication and broader social analysis. Many literary critics treat the gift only as a useful metaphor rather than as a material practice. The result has been a good deal of work that replicates the worst tendencies in Hyde and Derrida but without their eloquence or subtlety.

The literary essays making up the third section in this volume avoid these pitfalls by combining social analysis, theory, and sound practical criticism. First, Jacqui Sadashige trains her attention on the poetry of Catullus to show how the sentimentality expressed therein points to new forms of post-imperial masculine subjectivity. By examining Catullus's representation of both gift objects and friendship, she sheds new light on the emergence of the modern idea of commodification. Nicoletta Pireddu's fascinating exploration of the career of Italian modernist Gabriele D'Annunzio finds in him an earlier exponent of a sacrificial poetics that presages Bataille's general economy. For D'Annunzio the gift operated as both a tangible ceremonial object and a principle of collective ritual founded upon expenditure. In D'Annunzio's later work, Pireddu shows, he imagined in art a form of dissipation and destruction beyond giving, one that depicted pleasure as a non-exchangeable form of productivity no longer lacerated by the distinction between gift and debt. Anthony Fothergill reads the gift exchanges in Joseph Conrad's story "Karain: a memory" through the lenses of Walter Benjamin and Georg Simmel to disclose how the material transfer it portrays is finally secondary to the non-material values – particularly faith and friendship – symbolically attributed to it. Fothergill's essay offers another way to view the relations between storyteller and audience as a gift. Finally, Stephen Collis employs the longstanding literary and personal affiliation between the poets H.D. and Robert Duncan to investigate the ways that literary influence conforms to Mauss's three obligations to give, receive and reciprocate, and then to question the use of gift exchange to represent forms of literary exchange, including influence.

Posing new questions

The essays in this volume not only exemplify how social and anthropological theory may inform literary criticism; they also demonstrate the need for sharper and more refined theory that steers clear of both the Scylla of sentimentality and the Charybdis of economism. Such theory must above all remain anchored in social practice. To build this bridge, however, requires that scholars from diverse disciplines converse much more than they do now. In this regard, two gaps appear in the foregoing discussion. First, the discipline of economics seems conspicuously absent from a topic that seems to lie well within its purview. Second, theorists in sociology often seem to be speaking a different language from philosophers such as Derrida. Indeed, sociologists often scorn philosophers' abstractions, which seem remote from any sense of how human beings actually give and receive gifts. Conversely, sociological work too often marshals enormous amounts of information that merely re-establishes what was already obvious. The flaw here is not overripe abstraction but impoverished theory. Thus the essays in the final section of this volume seek to address and perhaps fill each of these gaps by analyzing the deficiencies of gift theory itself.

The first gap is, in fact, relatively easy to explain: I have been silent about economics because economics has been almost totally silent about the gift. How can scholars in the humanities and researchers in the social sciences engage in dialogue if one side remains mute? As I note in my other essay in this volume, economic theory is so wedded to the twin sisters of market rhetoric and utility maximization that it seems unable to imagine any other potential partners. Admittedly, self-interest is a powerful explanatory tool. Indeed, as Amartya Sen observes in his now-famous essay, "Rational Fools," one can "define a person's interests in such a way that no matter what he does he can be seen to be furthering his own interests in every isolated act of choice" (1996: 151). So-called "rational choice" theory, however, limits explanations to individual decisions, as if human beings don't also care about other human beings, and as if every scintilla of value and pleasure in such choices can be quantified. Sen distinguishes between two ways of thinking that might counter, or at least supplement, this ideology. The first he terms "sympathy," which occurs when a person's well-being is psychologically dependent upon someone else's welfare (1996: 153). This idea resembles Fennell's concept of "empathetic dialogue" and the term I offered above, "distinterestedness." For example, a parent feels devastated when her child is injured or seriously ill, and may risk health and poverty to find proper medical care. One can, of course, argue that such feelings are in an important sense egoistic: the parent will feel guilty if her child fails to recover; her self-image is closely tied to the child's health, and so on. The other concept, which Sen calls "commitment," seems even more useful. When one chooses an action because of some moral principle that one believes will actually yield a lower level of personal welfare than an available alternative, one is exercising "commitment" (1996: 154). As Sen observes, "commitment" drives a wedge "between personal choice and personal welfare, and much of traditional economic theory relies on the identity of the two" (1996: 155).

What do these ideas have to do with the gift? Let us adduce some examples. When I give my spouse a gift I believe that she will like, I may be anticipating some reward: not just personal satisfaction, but the kind of daily goodwill and returned favors that one spouse routinely gives to another. No "commitment" here. However, when I volunteer to deliver food or medicine to sick people, I not only risk contracting their illnesses, but give time and energy that I could have spent working or playing music. Such gifts to strangers – which Godbout and Caillé describe as one of the triumphs of modern gift culture (1998: 64–78) – contest economistic explanations. Or let's say my brother-in-law chooses, at his own risk, to donate a kidney to me. He certainly gains a feeling of satisfaction, perhaps even of heroism, from doing so; but it would be difficult to argue that such a reward is equivalent to the pain and risk he endures from undergoing the transplant surgery. The fact is, my brother-in-law's desire for me to live – because he loves me, because he feels that I have done nothing to deserve this pain, because he wants to challenge fate, whatever the reason – is stronger than any other factor, including his desire to avoid pain and death. That's commitment.[23] Such choices are not merely rational, and they are not made in a vacuum. The problem with the ideology of self-interest and what Berking calls the "programmatic exclusions" of market rhetoric (1999: 132) is that they reduce human motives and behavior to a one-dimensional set of rules. Indeed, moral judgments made on the basis of cost-benefit analysis are not really moral judgments at all; they are just counting coins.

The inadequacy of economistic thinking to account for gift giving may be seen in famous economist Kenneth Arrow's response to Richard Titmuss's 1972 book, *The Gift Relationship: From Human Blood to Social Policy*. To put it briefly, Titmuss contrasts American blood banks (where, at the time, blood was purchased) with British ones (which used donations only), concluding that a regime permitting donation alone is not only healthier and more cost effective but actually fosters altruism. Responding to Titmuss's book, Arrow wrote: "like many economists, I do not want to rely too heavily on substituting ethics for self-interest. ... Wholesale usage of ethical standards is likely to have undesirable consequences. We do not wish to use up recklessly the scarce resources of altruistic motivation" (1975: 22). Is altruism a "resource"? Why must it be scarce? Arrow's use of economic language and principles to discuss ethical choices reveals both his unexamined assumptions (that altruism can be quantified like, say, cattle futures) and the rigidity with which even great economists sometimes apply them.

Moreover, as I suggest in Chapter 12 of this volume, such thinking relies on an attenuated notion of selfhood. As Margaret Radin has argued, the commodified personhood underpinning neoclassical economics is a "thin" theory of self, because nothing in it "is intrinsic to personhood but the bare undifferentiated free will," and everything else is alienable (1996: 62). Along with its ideological counterpart, market rhetoric, it fosters an "inferior conception of human flourishing" that fails to account for significant ways in which human beings interact with each other and with objects. A thicker theory of the self would recognize that "much of the person's material and social context [lies] inside the self, inseparable from the person" (1996: 62). Such a "contextual personhood" (1996: 60) is implicit in gifts, whereby individuals are understood in terms of what Marilyn Strathern calls their "enchainment" with others (1988: 139). Thus we return to the idea of superfluity. That is, we cannot understand the gift if we persist in the idea that gifts are given and reciprocated by autonomous individuals. The superfluity that I earlier posited as an essential quality of the gift applies to personhood as well, because in giving and receiving we expand the self, paradoxically, by firmly attaching it to social relations. In so doing we render economic concepts of loss and gain inadequate.

Economists have recently begun to reconsider the question of the gift. In an important recent essay, distinguished economist Philip Mirowski analyzes the deficiencies of both gift theory and economists' explanations of it.[24] For Mirowski, while the gift has been "constitutive to any number of anti-neoclassical social theories in the twentieth century," every one has eventually been "vanquished" as social theory. The reason, Mirowski continues, is that "the modern concept of 'the 'gift' is itself incoherent." He predicts that "all further attempts to capitalize on the gift will go the way of their predecessors, and worse, attempts to base social theory upon it actually serve to strengthen the neoclassical orthodoxy" (2001: 433–4). The crux, for Mirowski, is that the concept of the gift depends upon the specification of invariants but also "corrodes and undermines" such invariants (2001: 451). That is, gifts attempt to transcend the system of monetary value while also presupposing some monetary structure; thus, without money, there is no "outside" to which to escape (2001: 454). Hence, gift theory relies upon the very dichotomy that it seeks to disrupt, and therefore remains vulnerable to devastating incursions by neoclassical economics (2001: 451).

This is a powerful and incisively shaped critique. Mirowski is certainly wrong, however, when he claims that "every aspiring theorist of the gift in economic anthropology end[s] up dispirited and dejected" (2001: 441); Godelier's and Laidlaw's recent work are enough to rebut that assertion. A more significant problem with Mirowski's argument is that he demonstrates precisely the difficulty in thinking outside of binaries that I alluded to above. As we have noted, the gift tends to erode any dam we try to build around it. Thus, the fact that the gift beckons us to think about value both in terms of money and beyond money demonstrates not its incoherence but its elasticity; the incoherence lies rather in theoretical categories too rigid to account for it. Thus, Antonio Callari, in his contribution to the present volume, uses Mirowski's essay to explore the ramifications of the gift for the very idea of disciplinarity. The gift, he suggests, inevitably opens economic reason to ethical and political questions, and thus casts doubt on the notion that economics is a self-contained discipline. Further, the value of the gift as an intellectual category is, Callari argues, precisely that it dissolves borders, and thus challenges any construction of society itself as bordered. The gift functions like a ghost haunting economics and calling it to break down walls. In his "addendum" to Callari's essay, Jack Amariglio suggests that the gift is not the only phenomenon defined by incertitude; in fact, the very notion of exchange is always uncertain, depending as it does on fluid and fragile subjectivities and negotiations. In this sense, "the gift" may be the name we give to the omnipresent excesses that erode the alleged self-determination and certainty of all exchange.

The second gap noted at the beginning of this section – the increasing distance between gift theory and social practice – is addressed in Andrew Cowell's concluding essay. Surveying French cultural theory since Mauss, Cowell shows how each theorist has been complicit with the binary logic he or she has sought to contest. Perhaps the most egregious absence in the recent history of the gift, Cowell argues, is the body, which was in the Middle Ages a key sign that distinguished gifts from other transactions. As a result of the neglect of the body – particularly the body in pain – the gift has been converted into a floating signifier representing nothing more than a rueful nostalgia for a lost order. Only by reattaching theory to its physical and social meanings, Cowell suggests, can we flesh out and revivify these increasingly empty abstractions.

Such a move is only possible, however, through the kind of interdisciplinary dialogue that this volume incorporates and aims to inspire. *The Question of the Gift* has been prepared with the belief that the only way to gain a fuller understanding of the gift is to expand, rather than narrow our focus, and to encourage experts from disparate fields to engage with each other. Scholars from different disciplines must now emulate the practices they study: that is, we must participate in critical exchanges. These essays are just a beginning. Literary criticism and theory must go further in joining social analysis, anthropological research, ethical exploration, and textual exegesis. Producing more sophisticated gift-based literary criticism will not only enrich literary studies; it will also help to provide sociologists, philosophers, anthropologists and historians with richer stories and metaphors, stronger historical exempla, and more complex descriptions of personhood and social forms. In return for its gifts to these other disciplines, literary criticism and theory will benefit from becoming better informed about social practice and better versed in social and anthropological theory. Such encounters will not take us further from literature; rather, they will help us discover new riches, form new paradigms, and create more refined and detailed renderings of how art represents and shapes human behavior. Moreover, by employing social and anthropological theories to study artistic commerce – whether it concerns authors and other authors, authors and texts, authors and readers, or texts and the marketplace – we will generate a deeper understanding of the place of literature in society, while at the same time promoting a more ethical social life. Finally, and most importantly, melding literary criticism to social and theoretical theory will help us all to ask better questions about the gift, and to use these questions to engender better human beings. Such exchanges will demand that scholars and scientists participate in the spirit of the gift: they will require that we accept risk and danger and reject ossified disciplinary and conceptual constructions, with the ultimate goal of creating the kind of elastic, engaged and expansive theories worthy of the gift's own communion and delight.

Notes

1   Ian Cunnison's 1967 translation reads: "What is the principle whereby the gift has to be repaid? What force is there in the thing given which compels the recipient to make a return?" The problems with Cunnison's translation are well known (see, for example, Parry 1986: 455, 456, 469). Though Cunnison's translation is far more readable, W.D. Halls's (1990) is more accurate. I will therefore use Halls's translation unless otherwise specified. However, I will employ the untranslatable term "prestations" rather than Halls's unsatisfactory approximation, "services."

2   As Vincent Pecora observes, this equation of "the magical element in a system of gifts with a supplementary signifier in systems of thought is [also] a crucial one for post-structuralist literary theory" (1997: 50).

3   Some theorists, including, most recently, Pecora, conflate this spirit with Marxian commodity fetishism. As I suggest in Chapter 11 of this volume, the phenomenon Mauss limns here is quite different from this Marxist idea.

4   In his later essay Caillé himself emphasizes the principles of spontaneity and risk (2001: 34–5).

5 Gregory's theories have endured much criticism. See, for example, Mirowski, who argues that Gregory's distinction ends up being circular (Mirowski 2001: 445). Laidlaw, in the present volume, further demonstrates how Gregory's definitions become "counter-intuitive" and lead to the conclusion that in giving a gift one is not really giving anything away. See also Frow (1997: 121–7).

6 Gudeman (2001: 462) notes that Mauss employs an Aristotelian genealogy; Pecora suggests that Mauss was Aristotelian not only in method but in content, arguing that the distinction Mauss finds in Roman law between *familia* and *pecunia* (see Mauss 1990: 49–50) "parallels Aristotle's distinction between *oikonomike* and *chrematistike*" (Pecora 1997: 226).

7 Berking thus provides an anthropological and historical foundation for Simmel's claim that all value is "the result of a sacrifice" (Simmel 1990: 84–5).

8 Other histories of the gift that follow these outlines include those of Carrier (1995: 39–105), Godbout and Caillé (Godbout 1998: 101–67), and Hyde (1983: 109–40). In her important recent study, Natalie Zemon Davis offers a partial exception to the usual pattern by arguing that:

> there is no universal pattern of evolutionary stages, where a total gift economy dwindles to occasional presents. Rather, gift exchange persists as an essential relational mode, a repertoire of behavior, a register with its own rules, language, etiquette, and gestures. The gift mode may expand or shrink … but it never loses significance.
>
> (2000: 9)

She stops short, however, of suggesting that the gift "register" threatens or even challenges the dominance of the marketplace in modern society.

9 Mirowski claims that this dual thesis – "that the gift is not what it at first seems, obscuring the calculus of power and aggression which lay just beneath the surface; but, per contra, the gift is an earlier and kindlier, gentler form of economic organization" – is "what allows anyone to walk away from *The Gift* taking whatever" he or she wants from it (2001: 440). Although Mirowski exaggerates the range of interpretations one might draw from Mauss, his analysis points to the way Mauss falls victim to the same ambivalence that has plagued most later theorists.

10 Robert Bernasconi even suggests that the seemingly unsolvable problems within the gift can be traced to the conflicts in these competing traditions (1997: 269).

11 Aristotle's friend – that "other self" – resembles Davis's "second model" of alliance and obligation, in which the interactions of friends approach "fusion or boundarylessness" (Davis 2000: 111). For a more detailed treatment of Nietzsche's gift ethics, see Shapiro 1997: 274–7; Schrift 2001.

12 For a discussion of Nietzsche's debt to Emerson, see Shapiro 1997: 277–81; Stack 1992. For a more general treatment of Emerson's thoughts on gifts and their relation to a broader "economy of expenditure," see Grusin 1988.

13 Although Derrida has been exploring questions of the gift since as far back as his essay "From restricted to general economy," which grapples with Georges Bataille's writings on expenditure and potlatch, *Given Time* (1992) summarizes and synthesizes his thinking on these issues.

14 Related critiques of Derrida's treatment of the gift include those of Jenkins (1998), Caillé (2001), O'Neill (2001), and in this volume, Callari and Cowell.

15 Several important anthropological studies emphasizing the role of women's work in the formation of culture have recently challenged Lévi-Strauss's analyses. See, for example Rubin 1975, and especially Strathern 1988 and Weiner 1992. A few literary critics have analyzed literary depictions of women's role in gift transactions. See, for example, Osteen 1997 as well as Kay 1995 and Dillon 1992.

16 Here Komter is indebted to Marilyn Strathern, for whom the key concept in the gift economy is the "enchainment" of persons in social networks. (See Strathern 1988:

139ff.) It should be noted that some of Cixous's later work seems to draw back from the essentialism of "Castration or decapitation" (1981). See, for example, Cixous 1990: 156.

17 Alan Smart very helpfully clarifies the differences among Bourdieu's various types of "capital." As he notes, "there is too much overlap" among the various forms for anyone to use them efficiently without amendation (Smart 1993: 392). Although Smart pinpoints significant differences, I would be hard-pressed to distinguish between, say, "symbolic" and "social" capital in certain circumstances. Suffice it to say that these forms of capital blur together much of the time; their value is primarily as analytic tools, not as a template with which to describe real behavior.

18 For a similar critique of Bourdieu, see Caillé 2001: 24–8.

19 In *The Gift of Death* (1995), something of a sequel to *Given Time* (1992), Derrida does probe the interrelationships among gifts and the sacred.

20 For other critiques of Bataille's system, see Pecora 1997: 248–9; Smith 1988: 135–41. For an extensive sympathetic treatment of Bataille's thought, see Richman 1982, which is especially helpful on the Mauss–Bataille connection.

21 An example of such an analysis may be found in Osteen 1995: 215–49.

22 Other examples of scholarship in early modern or pre-modern texts include that of Thieme (1998), Kay (1995), Burnett (1993), West (1996), Donahue (1975) and Hill (1982). Gift-based criticism of twentieth-century texts has been sparse: in addition to my own work, see the scholarship of Herring (1992), Segal (1998) and Pecora (1997).

23 Godbout and Caillé discuss organ donation as a major form of the modern gift. In such acts of donation, they suggest, "people do not behave in accordance with utilitarian postulates. They do not calculate but act completely outside this explicative model" (1998: 90). See also Caillé 2001: 36–8.

24 Mirowski also offers a helpful and witty analysis of Arrow's response to Titmuss. What truly upsets Arrow, notes Mirowski, is the possibility that "gift-giving, *if it exists*, could outperform the market in any way" (2001: 437; emphasis in original).

References

Arrow, Kenneth. "Gifts and exchanges." In Edmund S. Phelps (ed.) *Altruism, Morality, and Economic Theory*. New York: Russell Sage Foundation, 1975, pp. 13–28.

Bataille, Georges. *The Accursed Share: An Essay on General Economy*. Trans. Robert Hurley. New York: Zone, 1988.

—— "The notion of expenditure." In Allan Stoekl (ed.) *Visions of Excess: Selected Writings 1927–1939*. Trans. Allan Stoekl, with Carl R. Lovitt and Donald M. Leslie, Jr. Minneapolis: University of Minnesota Press, 1985, pp. 116–29.

Belk, Russell W. "The perfect gift." In Cele Otnes and Richard F. Beltramini (eds) *Gift-Giving: A Research Anthology*. Bowling Green, OH: Bowling Green State University Popular Press, 1996, pp. 59–84.

Berking, Helmuth. *Sociology of Giving*. Trans. Patrick Camiller. London: Sage, 1999.

Bernasconi, Robert. "What goes around comes around: Derrida and Levinas on the economy of the gift and the gift of genealogy." In Alan D. Schrift (ed.) *The Logic of the Gift: Toward an Ethic of Generosity*. New York and London: Routledge, 1997, pp. 256–73.

Bjork, Robert. "Speech as gift in *Beowulf*." *Speculum* 69 (1994): 993–1022.

Bourdieu, Pierre. *Outline of a Theory of Practice*. Trans. Richard Nice. Cambridge: Cambridge University Press, 1977.

—— "A reply to some objections." *In Other Words: Essays Toward a Reflective Sociology*. Trans. Matthew Adamson. Cambridge: Polity, 1990, pp. 106–19.

—— "Marginalia – some additional notes on the gift." In Alan D. Schrift (ed.) *The Logic of the Gift: Toward an Ethic of Generosity*. New York and London: Routledge, 1997a, pp. 231–41.

—— "Selections from *The Logic of Practice*." In Alan D. Schrift (ed.) *The Logic of the Gift: Toward an Ethic of Generosity*. New York and London: Routledge, 1997b, pp. 190–230.

Burnett, Mark Thornton. "Giving and receiving: *Love's Labour's Lost* and the politics of exchange." *English Literary Renaissance* 23 (1993): 287–313.

Caillé, Alain. "The double inconceivability of the pure gift." *Angelaki: Journal of the Theoretical Humanities* 6.2 (August 2001): 23–38.

Carrier, James G. *Gifts and Commodities: Exchange and Western Capitalism since 1700*. London and New York: Routledge, 1995.

Cheal, David. *The Gift Economy*. New York and London: Routledge, 1988.

—— " 'Showing them you love them': gift giving and the dialectic of intimacy." In Aafke Komter (ed.) *The Gift: An Interdisciplinary Perspective*. Amsterdam: Amsterdam University Press, 1996, pp. 94–106.

Cixous, Hélène. "Castration or decapitation?" *Signs: Journal of Women in Culture and Society* 7 (1981): 41–55.

—— *Reading with Clarice Lispector*. Ed. and trans. Verena Andermatt Conley. Minneapolis: University of Minnesota Press, 1990.

Davis, Natalie Zemon. *The Gift in Sixteenth-Century France*. Madison: University of Wisconsin Press, 2000.

Derrida, Jacques. *Given Time: I. Counterfeit Money*. Trans. Peggy Kamuf. Chicago: University of Chicago Press, 1992.

—— *The Gift of Death*. Trans. David Wills. Chicago: University of Chicago Press, 1995.

Dillon, Steven. "George Eliot and the feminine gift." *Studies in English Literature* 32 (1992): 707–21.

Donahue, Charles. "Potlatch and charity: notes on the heroic in *Beowulf*." In Lewis Nicholson and Dolores Warwick Free (eds) *Anglo-Saxon Poetry: Essays in Appreciation for John C. McGalliard*. Notre Dame, IN: University of Notre Dame Press, 1975, pp. 23–40.

Douglas, Mary. "No free gifts." Foreword. In Marcel Mauss *The Gift: The Form and Reason for Exchange in Archaic Societies*. Trans. W.D. Halls. New York and London: Routledge, 1990, pp. vii–xviii.

Emerson, Ralph Waldo. "Gifts." In Alan D. Schrift (ed.) *The Logic of the Gift: Toward an Ethic of Generosity*. New York and London: Routledge, 1997, pp. 25–7.

Foucault, Michel. "What is an author?" In Josue V. Harari (ed.) *Textual Strategies: Perspectives in Post-Structuralist Criticism*. Ithaca: Cornell University Press, 1979, pp. 141–60.

Frow, John. *Time and Commodity Culture*. Oxford: Clarendon Press, 1997.

Gasché, Rodolphe. "Heliocentric exchange." Trans. Morris Parslow. In Alan D. Schrift (ed.) *The Logic of the Gift: Toward an Ethic of Generosity*. New York and London: Routledge, 1997, pp. 100–17.

Godbout, Jacques T. with Alain Caillé. *The World of the Gift*. Trans. Donald Winkler. Montreal: McGill-Queen's University Press, 1998.

Godelier, Maurice. *The Enigma of the Gift*. Trans. Nora Scott. Chicago: University of Chicago Press, 1999.

Gouldner, Alvin W. "The norm of reciprocity." In Aafke Komter (ed.) *The Gift: An Interdisciplinary Perspective*. Amsterdam: Amsterdam University Press, 1996, pp. 49–66.

Gregory, C.A. *Gifts and Commodities*. London and New York: Academic, 1982.

—— "Kula gift exchange and capitalist commodity exchange: a comparison." In Jerry W. Leach and Edmund Leach (eds) *The Kula: New Perspectives on Massim Exchange*. Cambridge: Cambridge University Press, 1983.

Grusin, Richard A. "'Put God in your debt': Emerson's economy of expenditure." *PMLA* 103 (1988): 35–44.

Gudeman, Stephen. "Postmodern gifts." In Stephen Cullenberg, Jack Amariglio, and David F. Ruccio (eds) *Postmodernism, Economics, and Knowledge*. New York and London: Routledge, 2001, pp. 459–74.

Harwood, Britton J. "*Gawain* and the gift." *PMLA* 106 (1991): 483–99.

Herring, Phillip F. "James Joyce and gift exchange." In R.M. Bollettieri Bosinelli, Carla Marengo Vaglio and Christine Van Boheemen (eds) *The Languages of Joyce: Selected Papers from the 11th International James Joyce Symposium, Venice, 12–18 June 1988*. Philadelphia: John Benjamins, 1992, pp. 173–90.

Hill, John M. "Beowulf and the Danish Succession: gift-giving as an occasion for complex gesture." *Medievalia et Humanistica* 11 (1982): 177–97.

Hyde, Lewis. *The Gift: Imagination and the Erotic Life of Property*. New York: Random, 1983.

Jenkins, Tim. "Derrida's reading of Mauss." In Wendy James and N.J. Allen (eds) *Marcel Mauss: A Centenary Tribute*. New York: Berghahn, 1998, pp. 83–94.

Kay, Sarah. "Contesting 'romance influence': the poetics of the gift." *Comparative Literature Studies* 32 (1995): 320–41.

Komter, Aafke. "The social and psychological significance of gift giving in the Netherlands." In Aafke Komter (ed.) *The Gift: An Interdisciplinary Perspective*. Amsterdam: Amsterdam University Press, 1996a, pp. 107–118.

—— "Women, gifts and power." In Aafke Komter (ed.) *The Gift: An Interdisciplinary Perspective*. Amsterdam: Amsterdam University Press, 1996b, pp. 119–31.

Koritz, Amy and Douglas Koritz. "Symbolic economics: adventures in the metaphorical marketplace." In Martha Woodmansee and Mark Osteen (eds) *The New Economic Criticism: Studies at the Intersection of Literature and Economics*. New York: Routledge, 1999, pp. 408–19.

Lévi-Strauss, Claude. "Selections from *Introduction to the Work of Marcel Mauss*." In Alan D. Schrift (ed.) *The Logic of the Gift: Toward an Ethic of Generosity*. New York and London: Routledge, 1997, pp. 45–69.

Mauss, Marcel. *The Gift: The Form and Reasons for Exchange in Archaic Societies*. Trans. W.D. Halls. London and New York: Routledge, 1990.

—— *The Gift: Forms and Functions of Exchange in Archaic Societies*. Trans. Ian Cunnison. New York: Norton, 1967.

Mirowski, Philip. "Refusing the gift." In Stephen Cullenberg, Jack Amariglio, and David F. Ruccio (eds) *Postmodernism, Economics, and Knowledge*. New York and London: Routledge, 2001, pp. 431–58.

Modiano, Raimonda. "Coleridge and Wordsworth: the ethics of gift exchange and literary ownership." *The Wordsworth Circle* 20 (1989): 113–20.

O'Neill, John. "The time(s) of the gift." *Angelaki: Journal of the Theoretical Humanities* 6.2 (August, 2001): 41–8.

Osteen, Mark. *The Economy of* Ulysses: *Making Both Ends Meet*. Syracuse: Syracuse University Press, 1995.

—— "Female property: women and gifts in *Ulysses*." In Jolanta W. Wawrzycka and Marlena G. Corcoran (eds) *Gender In Joyce*. Gainesville: University Press of Florida, 1997, pp. 29–46.

Parry, Jonathan. "*The Gift*, the Indian gift, and the 'Indian gift.'" *Man* (N.S.) 21 (1986): 453–73.

Parry, Jonathan and Maurice Bloch (eds). *Money and the Morality of Exchange*. Cambridge: Cambridge University Press, 1989.

Pecora, Vincent P. *Households of the Soul*. Baltimore: Johns Hopkins University Press, 1997.

Radin, Margaret Jane. *Contested Commodities*. Cambridge: Harvard University Press, 1996.

Richman, Michele H. *Reading Georges Bataille: Beyond the Gift*. Baltimore and London: The Johns Hopkins University Press, 1982.

Rubin, Gayle. "The Traffic in Women: Notes on the 'Political Economy' of Sex." In Rayna R. Reiter (ed.) *Toward an Anthropology of Women*. New York and London: Monthly Review Press, 1975, pp. 157–210.

Rzepka, Charles J. *Sacramental Commodities: Gift, Text, and the Sublime in De Quincey*. Amherst: University of Massachusetts Press, 1995.

Sahlins, Marshall B. *Stone Age Economics*. Chicago: Aldine, 1972.

Schrift, Alan D. (ed.). *The Logic of the Gift: Toward an Ethic of Generosity*. New York and London: Routledge, 1997.

—— "Logics of the gift in Cixous and Nietzsche." *Angelaki: Journal of the Theoretical Humanities* 6.2 (August, 2001): 113–23.

Schwartz, Barry. "The social psychology of the gift." In Aafke Komter (ed.) *The Gift: An Interdisciplinary Perspective*. Amsterdam: Amsterdam University Press, 1996, pp. 69–80.

Segal, Alex. "Secrecy and the gift: Paul Auster's *The Locked Room*." *Critique* 39 (1998): 239–57.

Sen, Amartya K. "Rational fools: a critique of the behavioral foundations of economic theory." In Aafke Komter (ed.) *The Gift: An Interdisciplinary Perspective*. Amsterdam: Amsterdam University Press, 1996, pp. 149–63.

Shapiro, Gary. "The metaphysics of presents: Nietzsche's gift, the debt to Emerson, Heidegger's values." In Alan D. Schrift (ed.) *The Logic of the Gift: Toward an Ethic of Generosity*. New York and London: Routledge, 1997, pp. 274–91.

Sharp, Ronald A. "Gift exchange and the economies of spirit in *The Merchant of Venice*." *Modern Philology* 83 (1986): 250–65.

Simmel, Georg. "Faithfulness and gratitude." In Aafke Komter (ed.) *The Gift: An Interdisciplinary Perspective*. Amsterdam: Amsterdam University Press, 1996, pp. 39–48.

—— *The Sociology of Georg Simmel*. Ed. and Trans. Kurt H. Wolff. New York: Free Press, 1950.

—— *The Philosophy of Money*. Second edition. Ed. David Frisby. Trans. Tom Bottomore and David Frisby. New York: Routledge, 1990 [1907].

Smart, Alan. "Gifts, bribes and *Guanxi*: a reconsideration of Bourdieu's social capital." *Cultural Anthropology* 8 (1993): 388–408.

Smith, Barbara Herrnstein. *Contingencies of Value: Alternative Perspectives for Critical Theory*. Cambridge: Harvard University Press, 1988.

Stack, George J. *Nietzsche and Emerson: An Elective Affinity*. Athens: Ohio University Press, 1992.

Strathern, Marilyn. *The Gender of the Gift: Problems with Women and Problems with Society in Melanesia*. Berkeley: University of California Press, 1988.

Testart, Alain. "Uncertainties of the 'obligation to reciprocate': a critique of Mauss." In Wendy James and N.J. Allen (eds) *Marcel Mauss: A Centenary Tribute*. New York: Berghahn, 1998, pp. 97–110.

Thieme, Adelheid L.J. "Gift giving as a vital element of salvation in *The Dream of the Rood*." *South Atlantic Review* 63 (1998): 108–23.

Titmuss, Richard. *The Gift Relationship: From Human Blood to Social Policy*. London: Allen and Unwin, 1971.

Weiner, Annette B. *Inalienable Possessions: The Paradox of Keeping-While-Giving*. Berkeley: University of California Press, 1992.

West, William N. "Nothing as given: economies of the gift in Derrida and Shakespeare." *Comparative Literature* 48.1 (1996): 1–18.

Yan, Yunxiang. *The Flow of Gifts: Reciprocity and Social Networks in a Chinese Village*. Stanford, CA: Stanford University Press, 1996.

Part I
Redefining reciprocity

1   A free gift makes no friends

James Laidlaw

The notion of a "pure" or "free" gift has been largely neglected in anthropology. Malinowski employed it in *Argonauts* (1922: 177–80), but in *Crime and Custom* (1926: 40–1) he accepted the objections put forward by Mauss in the *Essai sur le don* (1990: 73–4), and discarded it. Following Mauss, anthropologists have mostly been interested in gift giving as a way in which enduring social relations are established and maintained. It seemed to Mauss, and has seemed to anthropologists since, that a genuinely free gift – one, as we say, with no strings attached – would play no part in the creation of social relations, for it would create no obligations or connections between persons; and therefore, even if such a thing existed, it would be of no serious interest to anthropology.

Accordingly, little attention has been paid to the free gift. The most sustained discussion has been Jonathan Parry's writings on the gifts in India known as *dan*.[1] Parry has shown that these are unreciprocated, and has related the pure-gift ideology which governs them to the existence of a developed, commercial economy and an ethicized salvation religion (1986: 466–9).

However, there is a still inadequately explained relation between this and Parry's other major observation about *dan*, which is that it brings misfortune (1994: 130–1). From the north-Indian village of Pahansu, for example, Raheja (1988) describes how *dan* diverts misfortune from donors to recipients. Gujars, described as the dominant caste, specialize in this diversion, and make gifts to hereditary clients, including Brahmin priests, barbers, sweepers, washermen and others. Gifts to wife-taking affines have a similar effect (1988: 153). In Parry's own ethnography from Banaras, misfortune, illness, and even death among funeral priests and their families are attributed to gifts received from pilgrims and mourners. In contrast to the generally benign profits of commerce, *dan* brings with it moral and physical corruption, and is likened to a sewer (1989: 69). It is said to carry the donor's sin (*pap*, *dosh*), inauspiciousness (*ashubh*, *amangal*), misfortune (*kasht*), and/or impurity (*ashuddh*).[2] What kind of a free gift is that?

The apparent paradox in this ethnography – that pure gifts should be so dramatically harmful – can, I think, be resolved. The first step is to reject the view, whose most influential exponent is C.A. Gregory, that gifts are the logical opposite of commodity exchange, and are necessarily personal, reciprocal, and socially binding. Malinowski's original intuition deserved a better defense than he realized: a comprehensive conspectus of exchange transactions requires the category of non-reciprocal free gift.

Because the free gift has, as we shall see, a paradoxical and self-negating character, it may be that convincing institutional enactments of it are at best rare; but on the other hand all the major world religions include institutions of great importance that at least aspire to it. I shall consider a particular case of *dan* that comes remarkably close to being a truly free gift. It enables us to resolve the interpretive puzzle presented by the existing ethnography on *dan*, and in so doing to shed light on the general character of the free gift: the fact that it does not create obligations or personal connections is precisely where its social importance lies. The *dan* in question is the giving of alms to Shvetamber Jain renouncers.[3]

Giving and grazing

The followers of Shvetambar Jainism in India consist of between 2 and 3 million lay people and a few thousand celibate renouncers. The latter have no property, and rely on alms from lay families for their limited personal possessions: clothes, prayer books, and alms bowls. These they carry as they travel between villages and towns, walking barefoot, usually staying in spartan rest houses attached to Jain temples. Justly famed for their asceticism, they follow a daily routine of ritualized confessions, prayer, study and preaching, punctuated by extended fasting and other austerities.

The ultimate goal of the renouncer's life is spiritual purification and salvation (*moksha*). As in other Indic religions, the soul is believed to be polluted by *karma*, the effects of previous actions (also called *karma*), which Jains tend to talk of as matter attached to and weighing down the immaterial soul. Sinful actions (*pap*) result in *karma* that is more harmful and difficult to remove than that resulting from good actions (*punya*), but although acts of merit are steps towards purification, even good *karma* must be removed before it can be achieved. Removing *karma* accumulated over many lives requires the heat of austerity (*tap*) to burn it from the soul. In these generally sinful times, it is impossible to achieve purification during a single lifetime, but the injunction to ascetic self-sacrifice is powerful for lay Jains as well as for renouncers.

A guiding principle in the pursuit of purification is non-violence (*ahimsa*), which includes limitations on diet. Since Jain tradition holds that not only animals but also plants and even bacteria have immortal souls, all eating and preparation of food involves violence, and there are elaborate rules for how to keep this violence to a minimum. Practising Jains are invariably vegetarian, most refrain from a range of vegetables believed to contain many life forms, and many follow more elaborate restrictions about the preparation of food and when it may be consumed. Renouncers follow exacting versions of these restrictions, and so must anyone who wishes to give them alms.

Most days around noon, as Jain families finish preparing lunch, renouncers go out, usually in pairs, to collect alms. They do not ask for food. They make their way along streets where Jain families live – never following the same route on consecutive days – pausing as they go near the doorways of houses and waiting to be invited in. The process is called *gocari*, or grazing. Like grazing cows, renouncers wander unpredictably and turn up unexpectedly. From each household they take so little that the donors will hardly notice the loss, just as a cow eats only the top of the grass without pulling up the roots and damaging the plant.[4]

Giving *dan* is the paradigmatic religious good deed (*punya*), and lay families are actively keen to give alms to renouncers. In practice, people often keep a lookout and call renouncers into their homes. Sometimes they even go to a rest house in advance, hoping to invite them back home. Strictly, this is against the rules, and even if they do end up going where they are asked, renouncers never explicitly agree, because they are supposed to arrive unexpectedly. This norm has two aspects. Accepting an invitation would obligate them and compromise the detachment and autonomy essential to their pursuit of personal spiritual purification. In addition, the renouncer is not only an object of religious veneration, but also, as a by-definition, an uninvited guest (*atithi*), the paradigmatic test in folklore of someone's true generosity. Sometimes the right to be first to give alms to a newly ordained renouncer is auctioned to the highest bidder, the money paid (which is also *dan*) going into religious funds.

On entering a house, renouncers are taken to receive their food directly from the family cooking pots. They will enter the kitchen only if it is clean, with no prohibited foods (butter, onions, garlic, potatoes, etc.) in evidence. Cooking must have finished – the stove not being lit is the accepted sign for this. Family members place food in the renouncers' alms bowls, generally trying to ensure that they give some of each of the dishes in their meal, and attempting to persuade them to accept as much as possible. The renouncers respond with a litany of refusal: "No! Less of that. Not so much. Stop!" The family emphasizes that all the ingredients are pure and natural, that it has all been prepared at home, and that there is plenty and they ought to take more.

This all generally ends with the renouncers jamming down the lids of their alms bowls. They offer no thanks and make no positive comments on the food. At this point, as a way of emphasizing that enough is enough, they often also call out the benediction, *dharm labh*. It is ambiguous, meaning both "May you receive the fruit of good conduct," and "May your adherence to good conduct increase."[5] They also sometimes say this as they enter the house and, invariably, as they leave it, and always in a brusque and perfunctory manner. They then move on to another house and go through the same procedure there. They are not allowed to accept an entire meal from just one household, or to accept food from the same families day after day.

The image of grazing is important, but one must not be misled. Jain renouncers are not like the cow that picks its way through an Indian town or village, eating what it finds as it goes. They are not collecting leftovers. That is why they must collect alms before lay families eat. The food they take would have been eaten by the family, who are therefore renouncing (*tyag*) part of their meal, even if the portion is so small they will not feel the loss of it. And only food which has been purposefully given, carefully and in the prescribed manner, is acceptable. Unlike Buddhists and some Hindus, Jains consistently deny that alms given to their renouncers are *bhiksh* – that which is given to a beggar. Jain renouncers do not beg, and what they receive is, in theory at least, a spontaneously offered gift.

The food collected is taken back to the rest house and mixed with that brought by other members of the group. It is all combined into a single mass and eaten out of public view. No one should feel hungry and be encouraged to eat as a result of seeing them do so. If they did, then the sin of their eating would be borne by the renouncers. In addition, it is important that no one comment on the type or quality of food that he has received, so that no donor is either praised or criticized because of what he or she has given.

No real gifts in anthropology

Probably the most widely cited recent analysis of the gift in anthropology has been Gregory's opposition between gift and commodity exchange. He emphasizes that gifts and commodities create different kinds of debt and therefore different kinds of relationships between transactors. Gifts belong to and reproduce "the social conditions of the reproduction of *people*" within a clan or kinship-based social order; commodities belong to "the social conditions of the reproduction of *things*" in a class-based division of labor (1980: 641; emphasis in original). These two systems of social relations may coexist in the same society (such as contemporary Melanesia), but they work in logically opposed ways. Gift exchange is "exchange of inalienable objects between people who are in a state of reciprocal dependence that establishes a qualitative relationship between the transactors," whereas commodity exchange is "exchange of alienable objects between people who are in a state of reciprocal independence that establishes a quantitative relationship between the objects exchanged" (1982: 100–1). Even more symmetrically, gift exchange consists of "relations between non-aliens by means of inalienable things," whereas commodity exchange consists of "relations between aliens by means of alienable things" (1997: 53).

Gregory's emphasis on the way transactions can create obligations and social relations is of course valid and interesting. The most common complaint one sees is that his contrast between gift and commodity is "overdrawn," but if the contrast is a valid one, it ought to be counted a virtue that he articulates it so clearly. The problem seems to me rather that it is incorrectly formulated. It is a mistake to insist that reciprocity and non-alienation are not just observable features of some relations created through gift transactions, but are defining features of gifts as such. According to Gregory, only transactions that show these features count as gifts (1997: 65). This analysis obscures rather than illuminates the question of how gift giving can create the very effects Gregory is interested in. And what in Mauss is an exploration of the paradoxical character of the gift becomes, in Gregory, a flawed and counter-intuitive definition.

We can see that it is counter-intuitive because it rules out good examples of gifts: the more so the more intuitively prototypical they are. The toy I give to my friend's child is ruled out if it is not reciprocated (because I have no children of my own, say). My donation to charity is ruled out if I seek no recognition for myself. The drink I buy you becomes more of a gift (rather than less) if I feel entitled to drink some of it myself! Thus the set of processes and relations identified in this definition is not the set denoted by the English word "gift"; and the same is true of its equivalents in other Indo-European languages, including that of Gregory's own informants in India. It is striking that he makes no use of his analysis, though it is restated and defended at the beginning of *Savage Money* (1997), when he turns later in that same book to a description of how Jain families in central India extend their kinship and trading networks (1997: 163–210), even though gifts, at marriage and other times, certainly play a part in this process. And Gell (1992) suggests that even for Melanesia the idea that we have only given something when we retain ownership rights over it is distinctly counter-intuitive.[6]

These curious features of Gregory's analysis follow from the fact that he reads Mauss, and also Melanesian ethnography, in terms derived from Marx. This is quite explicit. He intends to enlist the anthropological tradition into an alliance with Marxist political economy against neoclassical economics (Gregory 1982: x, 1997: 42). But Mauss, as we shall see, is not a suitable recruit for this particular draft. Marx's notion of surplus value is logically tied to his essentially metaphysical (and also Romantic) view that value is "really" derived exclusively from labor, which the worker is assumed "naturally" to own. The fact that labor is commodified, so that the worker is alienated from his labor, is what makes possible the alienation of the product in commodity exchange. When Gregory claims that the gift is not alienated he is saying that just those ownership rights violated in commodity exchange are preserved and reinforced in the gift: hence the elegant variations and inversions in his definitions.

Mauss is invoked in support of this notion of inalienability, and indeed Mauss does speak of enduring connections between givers and things given. But Mauss's talk of the intermingling of (previously separate) souls and persons with things (1990: 20) is a quite different line of thought – one that ought to lead us to think, if of anything in Marx, of fetishism. The connections Mauss is talking of are not ultimately derived from labor value, as they are in Marx, and are therefore not restricted to relations between producers and things they have made. And Mauss does not conceptualize them as ownership rights. When Gregory rejects the ethnographic interpretation given by Gell, he does so on the basically *a priori* grounds that if a gift giver were genuinely to lose what he or she gave, then this would be an alienation "of the type that occurs when Marx's proletarian walks home without his surplus-value after a hard day's work in the factory" (1997: 79). Thus the conceptual yoking of the gift to Marx's analysis of the commodity presents a clear choice. Either there is alienation of ownership, in which case, as Gregory rightly observes, the recipient of a gift would be expropriating the donor, and this (as well as being implausible) would mean that the supposed specificity of capitalist exploitation would evaporate; or else there is no alienation in the gift. It is the latter possibility that Gregory insists upon, even though it implies that in giving a gift you are not really giving anything away.

The effect is that Gregory's definition attempts to tidy away the basic paradox at the heart of the idea of a gift. I shall next try to describe what that paradox is and how the Jain institution of *dan* so nearly overcomes it, before showing how a perception of this paradox lies at the heart of Mauss's essay, and helps to explain why and when we find harmful free gifts in India.

The impossible idea of a gift

What is the basic, irreducible idea of a gift? One party makes over something of his or hers to another. There is no "price," and there is no recompense. It is given, and that is that. This is such a simple idea that anyone might have it, and there is no reason to suppose that there has ever been a society in which nobody has ever sought to enact it. But if we reflect on what would need to be the case for a pure and incontestable example to occur, then it emerges as deeply para-doxical. This theme is explored in an illuminating way by Derrida in *Given Time* (1992), and, without any broader philosophical or ontological commitments, I shall draw here on what he says (see also the excellent discussion in Jenkins 1998).

Derrida asks: What are the conditions implicit in the idea of a gift? What has to be the case to prevent us from questioning whether a transaction is really a free gift? He suggests four conditions. (1) First, there can be no reciprocity. It must not be in return for something else, either past or anticipated. A return would enter into or establish an economic cycle – calculation, interest, measure-ment, and so on – and make it part of an interested exchange. (2) To prevent this, therefore, the recipient must not recognize the gift as a gift, or him- or herself as recipient of one, which would lead to a sense of debt or obligation. (3) Similarly, the donor must not recognize the gift, since to do so is to praise and gratify oneself, to "give back to himself symbolically the value of what he thinks he has given" (1992: 14). (4) Lastly, and as a result of the foregoing, the thing cannot exist as a gift as such. As soon as it appears "as gift" it becomes part of a cycle and ceases to be a gift. So, Derrida suggests, we cannot even speak of a gift without making it disappear. "The simple identification of the passage of a gift as such, that is, of an identifiable thing among some identifiable 'ones,' would be nothing other than the destruction of the gift" (1992: 14). In sum then, "[f]or there to be gift, it is necessary that the gift not even appear, that it not be perceived or received as gift" (1992: 16).

This basic perception of paradox is a useful insight. However unalloyed we postulate the motivating intention to be, an indubitable gift, as an actual event in the world, is difficult to envisage. I do not wish to follow Derrida very far, however, down his never-ending (and probably historically and culturally specific) regress through ever more acute hermeneutic suspicion – "[the donor or donee] must also forget it right away (*à l'instant*) and moreover this forgetting must be so radical that it exceeds even the psychoanalytical categoriality of forgetting" (1992: 16). The basic paradox, implicit in the very idea of a gift and therefore present wherever it occurs, is enough for social arrangements to have to grapple with.

Here and elsewhere (e.g., 1978: 251–77), Derrida uses the term "economy" in a very broad sense. It refers not just to the circulation of goods and services, but also beyond that to the circulation of time, or rather to the way in which, through the medium of time, events and actions are related causally to each other. This "economy" is the world of common sense and everyday experience, but within it, Derrida concludes, a gift is impossible. There could only really be a gift if we could suppress any sense of the cyclical or of repetition in time. The routine transitivity of actions in time, according to which my giving to you implies that you receive from me, would have to be overcome. There could only be a gift, that is to say, on condition that the flow of time were suspended.

A gift that is given, but not received

In the light of Derrida's analysis, we can see the rules governing the Jain alms giving as an institutionalized attempt to overcome almost exactly the problems he identifies: to nullify the reasons why there cannot be a gift, and so to make one of the alms giving. The requirements that call for this are clear. Jain renouncers must obtain the food they need to sustain life without breaching the insulation from "the economy" that is the precondition and point of their spiritual enterprise. The result does not exactly match Derrida's free gift – if he is right, of course, it never could – but perhaps it comes as close as we can fairly expect a practical solution ever to get to resolving an existential paradox. Let us then retrace Derrida's main points, in reverse order, to see how Jain alms giving holds back the "inevitable" transition from gift to economic exchange.

(4) Householders make a gift of food, and renouncers receive and consume it, but both linguistically and in terms of how it is treated, everything is done to undermine the idea that "there is a something" given by the donor and received by the recipient. The word "food" (*khana*) is never used for what renouncers eat. It is called *gocari*, after the process of collecting it. Householders even avoid using the verb "to give" (*dena*). There is no question that giving alms is a *dan* – if you ask the average Jain about *dan*, along with the funding of temples and provision for the needy, this is what he or she will mention – but it is disrespectful to use the word in this context, as it seems to equate renouncers with mere recipients of charity. A common indirection is to speak of "placing" something in the alms bowl. More formally, the act is referred to as *baharana*. This word seems to be used only by Jains, and its etymology is unclear, but the likeliest derivation is from the causative form of a verb for "to fill." That renouncers are given something to eat ought to remain unspoken.

Not only language separates what is given from what is received. When renouncers go from house to house, the food collected is added to the same bowls. It is brought back to the rest house and handed over to the most senior renouncer, who then combines it with that collected by others from the group. All this *gocari* is mixed together in one mass. Partly this is done as an austerity, because renouncers should not savor the separate tastes of different dishes; but also, and inseparable from this, it effectively subsumes each family's individual offering.

The family making the gift strives to ensure that what they give is singularly theirs. They press the renouncers to accept all the dishes in the family meal, and on occasions when they try to invite renouncers home, they often prepare some time-consuming dish, which one might normally buy pre-prepared from the market. But this personal substance, closely identified with the donors, although it is what they give, is not what the renouncers receive and consume, which is instead an anonymous and undifferentiated substance. Derrida comments that we cannot speak of a gift without making it disappear. Here, the gift as object is made to disappear once it has been given, so that there is no longer the same "it" of which to speak.

(3) Derrida suggests that a gift which the donor recognizes as such ceases to be a gift. We should distinguish two possible sources of this recognition: identification of the other as the beneficiary of one's largesse on the one hand, and of oneself as donor on the other. While the Jain practice does effectively prevent the former, it actually, and as a result, emphasizes the latter. Even if donors were allowed to witness the food being eaten, they could not see their gift being enjoyed, for it is no longer there as such. Any gratification donors feel as a result of making their gift – and there can be no doubt that they do – cannot derive from there.

This alms giving, like other instances of *dan* (see Biardeau 1976: 27; Parry 1980, 1986; Strenski 1983) is ideologically identified with sacrifice; but the size of the sacrifice any donor can make is restricted – in theory to the point where it becomes indiscernible. No experience of hardship for the donors, which might give rise to a sense of personal indebtedness and obligation, should result.

This point is preserved even in competitive auctions for the right to give *dan*. There, although donor families commit large sums of money to temple funds in order to be able to make their gift, it remains the case that the gifts renouncers receive are the same small quantity of simple food, or their simple cotton robes or wooden alms bowls (which are of negligible monetary value). In these instances, the donors are able to play a role of public benefactor and patron, funding the buildings and activities that lie at the center of the local Jain community and therefore using their donations, in classic Maussian fashion, to augment their honor and standing; but in what happens between them and the renouncers, no such dynamics are set in motion. Instead, however much they pay for the privilege, what they give remains the same minimal contribution, received and consumed with studied indifference. One may actually say of this gift that, for the donors, it is their own thought that counts. What is salient is not the receiving of their gift, or any indebtedness or obligation that could arise from it, for this is elided, hidden and effectively denied, but rather their own thwarted attempts to give to the limit of their capacity (*yatha shakti*). The sense of the self as giver, therefore, is emphasized, in the absence of any corresponding emphasis on the gift being received.

(2) As for the recipients, the food they eat cannot appear to them as the gift of someone in particular, because different donors' contributions are merged. What they receive is depersonalized, being something they have gathered from among the laity. They need not then, in Derrida's terms, recognize the gift as gift.

They know that their food was not made especially for them. This is why they must leave most of each dish to be consumed by the family, and why they are not allowed to take food from a kitchen where cooking is still going on. If food were subsequently cooked to replace what they had taken, then it, and the sin attaching to it, would effectively be theirs. The same would be true if they were ever to express a liking for any particular kind of food, and someone later made that dish with the intention of giving it to them. It would then be a gift for them, and in accepting it they would be entering into the economy of temporal and causal connections. They would be the cause of *karma* – causing actions in the world, and therefore guilty of sin.

(1) Therefore – to bring us back to Derrida's starting point – there is no reciprocity. Renouncers are specifically forbidden to express pleasure at the food offered, to offer any thanks, or even to be diverted into general conversation, especially where, as is sometimes the case, they know the lay family quite well. The whole procedure is completed as quickly as possible, and in a generally abrupt and business-like manner. A renouncer may not give, and a donor family may not receive anything in return for the food donated – not even, as we have seen, praise or blame for its quality.

However, although donors receive nothing back from the renouncers, or indeed from anyone else on their behalf, it is generally held that they will benefit from being the giver of the gift. This is where the alms giving differs from Derrida's impossible pure gift. The recipient is spared the obligations that arise from receiving, but the givers have still given. Making a *dan* is meritorious, an act of *punya* or good *karma*. As such, it is expected, by an entirely impersonal process over which no one has any influence, to bring its own reward, although one cannot know when or in what manner the resulting good fortune will come. It may be in a future life, and indeed in Jain religious stories, this is typically the case (see Balbir 1982). Everyone agrees that this only happens if the *dan* is unreciprocated, because otherwise it would not really be *dan* at all, but part of the give-and-take of worldly life.

There is not a complete escape from paradox, however, because Jain teachers, like their Hindu counterparts (Parry 1986: 462, 1994: 128), insist that if even an unreciprocated gift is motivated by the desire for merit, then none will result. A good gift is given without desire. It is not premeditated and prompted by neither reverence (*bhakti*) nor compassion (*daya*) for the recipient. In line with Derrida's reasoning, even self-congratulation is a "return" and invalidates the gift. This seems to be the one aspect of the impossibility of the gift that the rules and formal arrangements of the Jain alms giving cannot circumvent. It is left as a matter between the donors and their own desires and intentions.

In any case, any good *karma* the donor receives does not come from the recipient. The imagery (as in Buddhism) is that renouncers are a "field of merit": fertile soil where a good action will bring forth a good reward (Williams 1963: 149–66). The more virtuous the renouncer, the greater the merit in making a gift to him or her. But renouncers do not give the merit; it is the natural result of the donor's good action. The biblical image fits so well that Jain teachers often use it: as you sow so shall you reap.

It follows therefore that the *dharm labh* benediction is not, as it might appear, itself a return for the gift of food. As mentioned above, it is ambiguous, and can be interpreted either as the wish that donors will enjoy the fruits of their good action, or as an injunction to further and greater religious observance. On the second reading, although rather terse and formulaic, it could be regarded as a gift, but the sense in which this might be so needs careful specification.

Exchange out of time

As is the case in Hinduism and Buddhism, over the centuries Jain teachers have shown great interest in gifts. They have laid down rules about how they should be given and received,[7] and developed numerous classifications of types of gift (Williams 1963: 149–66). The most prominent today is the following:

1   *abhay dan*   a gift of fearlessness
2   *supatra dan*   a gift to a worthy recipient
3   *anukampa dan*   a gift given out of compassion
4   *ucit dan*   a gift given out of duty
5   *kirti dan*   a gift given to earn fame

These gifts are listed in descending order of virtue. The last three are self-explanatory, and include any *dan* given for the specified motives. Acting from compassion, especially spontaneous identification with the needs or sufferings of a stranger, is better than regular giving to those for whom one has responsibility. And this in turn is better than giving in order to appear generous or compassionate. This last (*kirti dan*), because it is motivated by vanity, is not a *dan* at all, but rather a sin.

The first two categories are less transparent, because they are special ways of naming specific practices. *Abhay dan* is the teaching of Jain religion, and therefore basically synonymous with preaching by renouncers. Jain teaching – on the immortality of the soul, the possibility of liberation, the value of non-violence – delivers one from fear, especially fear of one's own death. Lay Jains, if they actually save someone's life, perform a pale reflection of this *abhay dan* (its merely material form), but in its essential form it is the preserve of renouncers. *Supatra dan* constitute gifts to Jain renouncers, including offerings before statues in Jain temples. They are the highest form of *dan* a lay person can make, to the only really worthy recipients.

Abhay dan and *supatra dan* thus have in common that they are specifically concerned with Jain soteriology. They are the two forms of gift which make

Jainism possible, and are therefore on a higher ethical level than the ordinary give-and-take of worldly life, where your intentions are what differentiate one kind of gift from another. They belong to a different ethical realm from the three lower kinds of gift, because their *raison d'être* is the pursuit of escape from *samsar* – the cycle of death and rebirth – and so the achievement of permanent cessation of embodied temporal existence. (This is undoubtedly a distant objective for the laity, but one which religious practice such as this insistently invites them to pursue.) If, as Derrida suggests, the condition for a pure gift is that the flow of time be suspended, then we may note that this is exactly the condition of transcendence and salvation to which *abhay dan* and *supatra dan* are oriented. They stand in opposition to what Derrida calls "the economy." But although, as free gifts, they would only really be possible outside *samsar*, the point of Jain tradition is to try as nearly as possible to instantiate them in the temporal world.

Now even though *abhay dan* is only metaphorically a gift (in both its material and essential forms nothing is actually given), it is possible to imagine it and *supatra dan* as making up a system of exchange. In the case of Theravada Buddhism, Ivan Strenski has argued persuasively that gifts given by lay Buddhists to renouncers, and the mostly ritual services which are provided by renouncers to lay Buddhists, constitute a system of generalized exchange. He notes that this system rests on the fact that *dan* is an unreciprocated gift, ideologically close to sacrifice, and on a firm rejection of reciprocity between particular lay Buddhists and particular monks.[8] Departing somewhat from Lévi-Strauss himself, Strenski (1983) argues that although what it binds together is conceptualized as consisting of just two entities (the laity and the *sangha*), the system can be regarded as generalized exchange because it is brought about by a great multiplicity of unreciprocated gifts between multifarious lay families and monks. No donor binds the recipient of his or her gift with an obligation to return. Each, in giving, must take the speculative risk on which generalized exchange depends (Lévi-Strauss 1967: 265) – that a return will come from elsewhere.

The same applies in the Jain case, where what the laity give to the renouncers can be counterposed to the teaching and example given by the latter. The imaginative abstraction that enables one to see things this way – from the time of lived experience to the long-run of what Lévi-Strauss calls structural or "reversible" time – is one that Jains themselves also make. If the participants are imagined not as particular lay families and particular renouncers, but as the abstract orders of laity and renouncers, then Jain society consists of these entities and the relation between them that is produced and sustained by a patterned exchange of gifts.[9]

So even though Jain society rests in this way on a system of exchange, it is a system made up, in real lived time, of unreciprocated gifts, and the collective entities which make it up are different in kind from the parties involved in the gifts. No one is motivated to make a gift of food "in return" for the teaching renouncers give or the example they represent. Householders seek to maximize their gift out of devotion and the desire to perform a good *karma*, and so gain merit. For renouncers, the priority is to avoid anything that compromises their autonomy.

These apparently conflicting purposes are mutually reinforcing (see Laidlaw 1995: 314–23). The renouncer's surly indifference encourages the importunate generosity of the donor. The latter's persistence enables the renouncer to exercise exemplary restraint, and yet still emerge from the encounter with enough to eat. So insofar as there is calculation and even agonistic competition in how both parties behave, this is not governed by considerations of reciprocity (not even by Sahlins's oxymoronic positive or negative reciprocity). There is no attempt to calculate equivalence, or to balance or outdo the other, and no sense in which what is given is conditional on a return.

In all these respects, it is therefore reasonable to say that *supatra dan* is a free gift. It is a specific institutionalized cultural elaboration of that simple but inherently paradoxical idea: an attempt to give it a real existence in practice.[10] It should not only be a voluntary expression of positive sentiments, an unreciprocated sacrifice of something closely identified with the giver; it should also create no debt or obligation, indeed no social relation at all between giver and recipient.

Why should anyone go to all this trouble not to create social relations? In the Jain case the *raison d'être* lies, as Parry anticipates, in a radically soteriological religion. Reciprocal relations between lay Jains and renouncers, unlike the out-of-time exchange of *abhay dan* and *supatra dan*, would preclude the transcendence of temporal causal relations (*samsar* or Derrida's "economy"), and the achievement of unending spiritual perfection (*moksha*).

The idea of a gift in *The Gift*

What is the relation between the free gift and what we may call the Maussian gift, one that creates social relations? It has been often observed that Mauss's celebrated essay on the gift is about many things, but that on the face of it gifts as such are not among them. He goes out of his way to say that some things Malinowski thought to be so are not in fact free gifts, and explicit discussion of anything that might be is virtually non-existent (see Testart 1998: 97; see also Derrida 1992: 24). This is not because the idea of a gift is peripheral to Mauss's essay; on the contrary it is because implicit invocation of it is central to the construction of the argument.

Mauss's essay traces the genealogy of the most important concepts in commercial exchange (1990: 4). It assembles, in Parry's words, an "archaeology of contractual obligation" (1986: 457). The gifts of the title are the forerunners of today's market transactions; they are the way the market operated before its more characteristic instruments (such as money, formal contracts, and self-interest) had developed. This is a story that embraces all of human history, for "the market is a human phenomenon that, in our view, is not foreign to any known society" (Mauss 1990: 4). There never was a "natural" economy of production for use. The essay tells a story of how contractual obligation grew out of the binding of the recipient to the giver that takes place by means of the gift, and of how the qualities of gifts that made that possible have been progressively (but not entirely) stripped away and replaced during the course of social evolution.

The evolutionary argument in Mauss has been well brought out by Parry (1986). The origins of the gift are lost to us, but even the most ancient forms we know of are already complex (Mauss 1990: 36). The story is one of simplification, as the modern forms of gift and commodity are progressively disaggregated from this original complex whole. The free gift is an idea that has developed and been more clearly articulated as the commodity economy has developed. The articulation has been pioneered (this is a point made more by Parry than by Mauss in *The Gift* although it is implicit in some of his other writings) by the world religions. But this distinction between the free gift and the commodity is not only an historical product, which Mauss's essay describes; it is also a logical tool that Mauss uses in making his argument. That argument proceeds by a sort of rhetorical double movement, one that is repeatedly applied to all of the major examples he uses along the way.

Mauss tells us on the one hand that the transactions he describes "take the form" of gifts. He never elaborates on what exactly this implies, except for the repeated use of expressions such as "free," "disinterested," and "generous." So the point is that although these transactions are serious politics and serious economics – he insists again and again on their size and importance – they are "given as" free gifts. The complementary move is where Mauss says that their gift-like quality notwithstanding, they are always also obligatory. Sometimes Mauss opposes the appearance of the free gift to a reality of obligation (1990: 3); elsewhere, and increasingly as the essay proceeds, he speaks of a combination of these characteristics (1990: 33, 65, 68, 73).

So these transactions both are and are not free gifts. Mauss can only really make the argument because the idea of what a real free gift would be is left unexamined. The reader's understanding of it is tacitly invoked. Because the invocation is implicit, and because the idea of the gift is, as Derrida has shown us, unstable and paradoxical, it can be made to work in two quite contrary ways at once.

Our idea that a real gift is free, beneficent, and unconstrained supplies the moral content, not reducible to utilitarian self-interest, required for Mauss's Durkheimian account of sociality – the non-contractual moral content that makes contract possible. Mauss finds this ethnographically expressed in the widespread idea that a part of the giver's soul or self is embodied in the given thing: that "by giving one is giving *oneself*" (1990: 46; emphasis in original). He explicates this idea with reference first to the Maori notion of the *hau*, although as Parry (1986) has plausibly suggested, he may have derived it from his reading of Indian texts. He then emphasizes the same idea in the other cases he examines (Mauss 1990: 43–4, 46, 58–9, 62). The reader irresistibly recognizes his or her own belief that a real gift is personal: that, as Emerson puts it in an essay cited (though for another reason) by Mauss, "The only gift is a portion of thyself" (Emerson 1995: 257). Thus Mauss's explanation for how gifts can have the capacity to create the moral basis of sociality mobilizes our everyday understanding of what a pure gift would be.

On the other hand, he also mobilizes our knowledge of the less elevated calculation – the "polite fiction, formalism, and social deceit" (Mauss 1990: 3) –

which our time-bound gift giving necessarily involves. Among us, as much as in his "archaic" examples, gifts and invitations are required by custom, and must be returned with the same or more (1990: 65–6); and we too make generous gifts in order to lord it over others (1990: 75). In particular, Mauss's account of the way reciprocity is demanded by considerations of honor (1990: 37–9) accords with the normally veiled and tabooed aspects of calculation and one-upmanship that we know are reflected in our giving and receiving of hospitality and other gifts. Thus Mauss invites us to see that these things, which we have thought of as improprieties or offenses against the "spirit of the gift," are in fact in perfect accord with it. He commends the gift-exchange systems described in the body of his essay to the attention of a modern readership because of their capacity to generate peace and social cohesion, as well as prosperity (1990: 25, 32–3, 34, 82–3). They are an invitation to us to turn back the clock, and pull back from what he rather snobbishly describes as the emerging "tradesman morality" (1990: 65). As Sahlins writes, "If friends make gifts, gifts make friends" (1972: 186). Mauss's explanation of how they do this depends equally on the calculation and competition we know to be at work in competitive exchange and on the freedom and generosity implied by the idea of a free gift. Gifts evoke obligations and create reciprocity, but they can do this because they might not: what creates the obligation is the gesture or moment that alienates the given thing and asks for no reciprocation.

Derrida remarks, "The truth of the gift ... suffices to annul the gift" (1992: 27). This self-annulment is recapitulated in Mauss's essay. Although he could only develop his analysis of exchange systems by means of the concept of the gift, by the end of it (Mauss 1990: 72–3), he is wondering whether the essay has really been about gifts at all. He remarks that because the objects are not really given freely and givers are not really disinterested, the words "present" and "gift" do not properly apply to them.

Mauss's essay therefore works by playing on the paradoxical and self-negating character of the gift. His explanation of reciprocity depends on invoking features of both the free gift and its negation, which is frankly interested exchange. Bourdieu's critique of Lévi-Straussian structuralism is therefore genuinely Maussian when he makes the point that even in highly regularized reciprocal exchange the "pretense" of freedom and spontaneity maintained at the time of giving is just as real as the "out of time" fact of reciprocal exchange. An objectivist analysis (such as Gregory's) that sees only the latter loses the ability to explain how it can come about. If the gift were not voluntary, and therefore uncertain, at the time of giving, then the pattern of reciprocity, however inevitable it might seem in retrospect, would not arise as it does (Bourdieu 1977: 3–9).

To take the argument we find in Mauss, with its careful exploitation of the paradox of the gift, and to replace it, as Gregory does, with a definition of the gift as necessarily reciprocal, is to deprive ourselves of Mauss's central insight. For Mauss, friend-making gift exchange is not opposed to but rather an embryonic form of commodity exchange, and its principles are still to be found, though attenuated, in modern commerce. It is located on the logical and phenomenological trajectory between pure gift and commodity, which are therefore shown to be genetically related and mutually constitutive. The self-negating free gift is present, even if only for a moment, in the transactions that make up systems of reciprocal gift exchange. Without the free gift, we only have part of the picture.

Pure poison?

If we now turn back to the Indian practices that seek to instantiate the free and unreciprocated gift, how are we to account for the dangers associated with it? In Parry's most comprehensive discussion (1994: 119–48), he concludes that the perils of *dan* are a cultural idiom in which norms of reciprocity and interdependence are expressed. Priests in Banaras suffer because they receive but do not give *dan*, so contravening the norm of reciprocity (1989: 77, 1994: 134).

They should not reciprocate directly, but they should be givers of *dan* in their turn. Then the poison they receive would also be passed on harmlessly. In the case of *dan* to affines, a family who receives *dan* with their daughter-in-law will typically make similar gifts at their own daughter's marriage. There is an open-ended cycle of Lévi-Straussian generalized exchange that keeps the poison in motion. But since the Banaras priests depend on gifts for their subsistence, they are only ever recipients. Flow and circulation stop. As Parry puts it, the sewer becomes a cess pit.

Parry considers another possible solution to their predicament. They subscribe to the widespread idea that ideally a Brahmin is a this-worldly representative of the renouncer (1994: 123; see also Heesterman 1964; Fuller 1984: 49–71). If, like an ideal Brahmin, they performed their rituals correctly and practiced austerities, they could consume the impurities they receive by burning them away through asceticism. But they do not know the rituals well enough or practice serious asceticism, and so they suffer.

Comparison with the Jain case suggests that neither of these points quite gets to the heart of the matter. The practical problem of being dependent on *dan*, and therefore not being able to give it oneself, can be resolved or at any rate glossed over with just a little semiotic ingenuity. Jain renouncers are daily dependent on alms but are also givers of *dan*, albeit in a non-material currency. The "gift of fearlessness" costs them nothing in material terms. Some version of this idea must be available to the Banaras priests. The fact that they do not adopt it suggests that it would not solve the problem, and indeed it does not do so for Jain renouncers. Neither does the latter's asceticism. As we have seen, Jain renouncers still have to take elaborate precautions in the way they accept *dan*, or they too would be afflicted by their donors' misdeeds. The danger is present, but the rules help them to avert it.

In Pahansu, recipients of *dan* are also said to digest it by means of heat. Brahmins perform austerities, mostly by reciting *mantra*s. Other castes, who do not, are said to generate heat through "the simple activities of householdership (*grihasthi*): grinding, husking, churning, and sexual intercourse, and so forth" (Raheja 1988: 91). In other words, no one has to do anything he or she would not be doing anyway, which hardly seems like evidence of a very afflicting poison. Thus not being able to dispose of poison received with gifts is not the most fundamental problem. Although Raheja (1988: 34) cites Parry's account of Banaras (1980) and says that the reluctance to receive *dan* in Pahansu is caused by similar fears, there is no indication in her ethnography of anyone allegedly suffering anything, other than that very dominance of the Gujars of which these transactions are the symbolic performance. This contrasts with the Banaras priests, whose gifts keep them in "a perpetual state of moral crisis" (Parry 1994: 123). Why is the *dan* given to priests and renouncers so much more dangerous in the first place? How are these dangers averted by the renouncers and not by the priests?

It should be emphasized that these possibilities of moral and biological miscegenation are not limited to *dan*. The theme of social contact and inter-dependence as morally entangling is extraordinarily prominent in South Asian social life. The whole elaborate ideology of caste is predicated on the idea that this can occur through physical contact, propinquity, and transactions not restricted to *dan* (Dumont 1980; Marriott 1968, 1976). Cooked food and cloth are powerful media for the flow of bio-moral qualities between persons, even when they are bought and sold, or given as non-*dan* gifts (see Appadurai 1981; Bayly 1986). Detached parts of the body, such as hair and nails, can be conduits of spiritual and personal qualities, as can sexual fluids. Moreover, such bio-moral contact is not always poisonous. Successful marriage depends on a propitious mixing of bio-moral substance (see Daniel 1984) . Blessings from deities and holy men are given in similar ways (Babb 1987). Substances being pooled, shared, or mixed, with consequent changes in the physical and spiritual condition of those involved, is therefore common in other kinds of transactions and interactions. The "poison in the gift" is not some unique or mysterious substance found only in gifts; it lies in the dangers attendant on social interaction in general: demeaning or demanding connections, debts and obligations to do things for other people's benefit.

So if there is anything distinctive about *dan* it is not that it carries poison; nor is it the case that afflicting others is peculiarly what *dan* is for. Nowhere in the ethnography is giving *dan* described as an act of aggression whose point is to harm recipients. Even at its most selfish, the point is to do oneself good. It is this hope on the part of donors to rid themselves of their own misdeeds that seems to be distinctive, but it is not guaranteed. Where it fails – where recipients are unworthy, or put their gifts to immoral purposes – donors can be afflicted by new misfortunes. The two parties become, as Parry notes, like moral Siamese twins, sharing the evil consequences of each other's misdeeds (1986: 69, 1994: 122, 132).

For most people, the dangers of social interdependence are bound to be double-edged. Treat your affines with caution, even suspicion, but you do need and want to have affines. Try to avoid importunate demands from your acquaintances, but make your own demands on them. Receiving *dan* and incurring obligations are only unambiguously bad things for those who aim at non-reciprocity, which means renouncers, and all those, like many Brahmins and especially Brahmin priests, whose social status depends on their claim to resemble renouncers.

It is therefore unsurprising that these are precisely the dangers that the rules governing the Jain *supatra dan* all work to prevent. The donor and the renouncer must not become morally entangled and responsible for each other's actions. Insofar as this *dan* succeeds in being a free gift, such entanglement is indeed prevented, because no social obligations are created by the transaction. Food is given (though it is something else that is received) without anything else changing: no obligation, reciprocation, mutuality or sociality comes into being. Indeed, even if they know each other, the parties behave as strangers in the transaction.

This social distancing is an important aspect of *dan* that derives from its character as a free gift. Raheja notes that people in Pahansu say that *dan* is only given to those who are "other"; but she notes also that these same recipients are described as "one's own people" when they are recipients not of *dan* but of reciprocal gifts (1988: 212; see also 1995). I suggest that the recipient's being "other" is less a precondition than a result of *dan*, which counteracts the mutuality established by Maussian gifts. In the case of *supatra dan* this is crucial, because everyday mutuality would be fatal to the renouncer's project of detachment and purification.

So priests in Banaras suffer not because they contravene the (putatively universal) norm of reciprocity, but because they contravene the norm of nonreciprocity: the ideal that governs the free gift they are supposed to be receiving, and one to which, as aspirant quasi-renouncers, they are supposed to subscribe. They are bad recipients (*kupatra*) of *dan*. In contrast not only to Jain renouncers but also Brahmins and others in Pahansu, they do not fulfil the requirement (Parry 1994: 122) of being unwilling to receive it. And in general they behave in such a way that, whatever their donors do, they turn a free gift into an interested exchange. Parry gives a vivid description of the inventive, persistent, and at times by turns deceitful and vituperative haggling that Banaras priests employ in arguing up the *dan* they are offered (1994: 139–48). They operate a sophisticated cartel system to prevent competition between them from exerting downward pressure on the price of their services (1994: 75–90). No wonder there is widespread skepticism, which they themselves share, about the value-for-money of what they provide.

Drawing on Gold's ethnography of pilgrims from Rajasthan, Parry puts forward an ingenious argument for why pilgrimage priests' rapacity might contribute to their patrons' religious experience: it allows them to feel what it is like to give "to the limit of one's capacity," which is often cited as a feature of a good *dan* (1994: 119–22). But it is equally intrinsic to a good *dan* that one's gift be spontaneous and generous, and these virtues are precluded by the priests' conduct. They complain and ask for more no matter how generous the gift they are offered. It is true, as Parry says (1994: 139–42), that bargaining is often found in ritual (including *dan*), and is not restricted, as some have thought, to commodity exchange. But there is all the difference in the world between, on the one hand, donors competing with each other for the right to make a gift or haggling because recipients are reluctant to accept, and, on the other hand, haggling between reluctant donors and grasping recipients that in effect creates a price for the service offered in return. It is surely not just Western mores, as Parry implies (1994: 142), that would regard the latter as at best a parody of a gift. Everything he himself tells us of the ideology of *dan*, as these priests understand it, points to the same judgment.

The first part of an answer to the question of "Whence the poison in the gift?" is therefore that it is not poisonous for everyone or in all situations. This is clear in the classical texts which, where they mention such dangers, do so in the context of *dan*'s being performed incorrectly. What the Jain case makes clear, then, is that *dan* is not the problem – the cause of a unique kind of peril – but on the contrary a solution, though admittedly a highly elusive one. It is a transaction that can, if performed correctly, be free of a peril otherwise highly prevalent in this social and cultural environment. In a world in which the mixing of persons and things, which Mauss describes as happening in gift exchange and which Gregory misdescribes as "inalienability," actually occurs very readily all the time, the point of a free gift is to prevent it.

Dan should be an alienated and non-reciprocal free gift. In practice, it can at best approach this ideal, because the ideal itself is impossible (which is why the texts are full of warnings). Sometimes this failure does not matter all that much. For the recipients of Gujars' gifts in Pahansu, it rubs salt into a wound. Receiving *dan* dramatizes their subordination to the Gujars, and this is reflected in their grudging acceptance of it. The Gujars, on the other hand, aware that they are regarded as a recent, upstart and very uncertainly dominant caste, seem, from Raheja's account, to find this petty humiliation of their subordinates inexhaustibly gratifying.

The matter is more serious for people – paradigmatically renouncers but also those who model themselves on renouncers – who aspire not to dominance but to detachment and social separation (see Fuller 1988; Parry 1994: 264–71). For Jain renouncers this concern is definitional of their whole way of life. In *gocari*, they can more or less entirely overcome the impossibility of a free gift, and they receive without incurring any debts. For Banaras priests there seems to be a contradiction.

Here it is relevant that although many of these priests are known as Mahabrahmins ("great brahmins"), in fact most people deny that they are Brahmins at all. Their contact with death means they are regarded as hardly different from untouchables. Like the Gujar "dominant" caste of Pahansu, they claim a high status that is denied by many others, which probably explains, in both cases, why *dan* is such a salient concern. The Banaras priests subscribe to the theory that their status derives from being quasi-renouncers, and their assertion of this status is as vehement as their detractors' denials are contemptuous;

but the plain fact is they are not actually renouncers. And even as priests go, they conform poorly to the ideal. They need to maintain their homes and families, and renunciatory detachment is a luxury they can ill afford. It is tempting to read their flagrant subversion of the ethics of *dan* as a gesture of defiance against a standard they cannot possibly meet. At any event, and at base, if they are poisoned by a gift, that is because they have asked for it.

Conclusion

The point that a free gift has no power to bind was recognized, according to Pollock and Maitland (1898: 213), from the earliest period in English law. No court would uphold gratuitous gifts or enforce gratuitous promises. From this arose the custom that the giver of a gift should receive in return some valueless trifle, just enough to make an exchange and therefore a legally valid transaction. *Dan* takes the opposite course: by remaining a resolutely free gift it remains free of obligation.

While the concept of a "pure gift" has often been dismissed as naive and unsociological, that of a "pure commodity" has been shown more latitude. Carrier (1995), in a general discussion of commodity exchange, makes the point that commodities are fungible. He then notes that this is not always equally so. Works of design, art and craft are not interchangeable one for another, and it matters by whom they were made; yet they are exchanged as commodities. However, he continues, "these qualifications do not contradict the point that commodities are impersonal. Instead they show that not everything that we buy and sell is a pure commodity" (1995: 29). Similarly, not all that we give and receive is a pure gift. I have suggested that almost nothing ever could be. But in so far as the Jain case is a guide, it suggests that impersonality, if it is a feature of the commodity (which seems reasonable enough), is equally a feature of the free gift, rather than being, as incautious reading of Mauss has led us to expect, a dimension along which these two kinds of transaction are opposed. No doubt this fact explains why religious charity and philanthropy in all the great religions have repeatedly rediscovered the supreme value of the anonymous donation, only to find that time and again donors have been more attracted to the benefits of the socially entangling Maussian gift, which does make friends.

Notes

This paper began as a talk given to the Anthropological Theory seminar at the London School of Economics in January 1999. I am grateful to Fenella Cannell for her invitation to the seminar, and to the participants for stimulating questions and observations. I am grateful to those who read and commented on subsequent drafts of the paper: Alan Babb, Marcus Banks, Susan Bayly, Barbara Bodenhorn, John Cort, Paul Dundas, Chris Fuller, Caroline Humphrey, Jonathan Mair, Jonathan Parry, Marilyn Strathern and Helen Ward. I am grateful also for comments from the editor and readers of the *Journal of the Royal Anthropological Institute*.

1 Others who have discussed the free gift include Sahlins (1972: 185–276) and Carrier (1995: 145–67). Others who have observed that *dan* is unreciprocated and ideologically

a free gift include Tambiah (1970: 213), Trautmann (1981: 278–93), and Strenski (1983).

2 See also Heesterman 1964; Shulman 1985; Trautmann 1981. Raheja would exclude impurity from this list, but for counter-arguments see Parry 1991.

3 To be more precise, the example is that of the Shvetambar Murtipujak Khartar Gacch Jains, as I have observed it, mostly in the city of Jaipur, since 1983.

4 Another image used by the Jains (Lalwani 1973: 3; Laidlaw 1995: 305) and also by Hindus (Parry 1980, 1994: 122) is of the bee who gathers pollen from the flower without damaging the plant.

5 The purpose is to call attention to themselves so that everyone of the opposite sex, including small children, will be careful not to violate their celibacy rules by coming too close.

6 Jain teachers have agreed. The tenth-century Digambar author Amitagati wrote that if a giver continues to regard what he has given as his own property all his possessions will be stolen from him by his sons or wives or by thieves (Williams 1963: 154).

7 Contemporary practice is most influenced by the *Dashavaikalika Sutra*, which is studied by all Shvetambar renouncers. See Lalwani 1973.

8 Carrithers (1983) has pointed out that in practice, because Buddhist monks have often lived sedentary lives among their lay followers, relations of reciprocity have tended to develop, and this has been one of the motivations for reformist movements of forest-dwelling monks (see also Tambiah 1984). While Jain history has also seen schismatic movements and reforms along similar lines, the itinerancy of Jain renouncers has meant that the Jain case has more consistently resembled Strenski's (1983) model.

9 Jains would deny any implication that the two gifts might be of equal value. It is also relevant that renouncers are not obliged to offer the opportunity of giving them gifts, but on the contrary to fast as much as possible and eat rarely.

10 Of course it is not the only possible way this might be done, and it may be contrasted, for example, with the paradigm of the "perfect present" that Carrier (1995: 145–67) finds expressed in contemporary Euro-America.

References

Appadurai, Arjun. "Gastro-politics in Hindu South Asia." *American Ethnologist* 8 (1981): 494–511.

Babb, Lawrence A. *Redemptive Encounters: Three Modern Styles in the Hindu Tradition*. Berkeley: University of California Press, 1987.

Balbir, Nalini. *Danastakakatha: recueil Jaina de huit histoires sur le don*. Paris: Collège de France, 1982.

Bayly, C.A. "The origins of swadeshi (home industry): cloth and Indian society, 1700–1930." In Arjun Appadurai (ed.) *The Social Life of Things*. Cambridge: Cambridge University Press, 1986, pp. 285–321.

Biardeau, Madelaine. "Le sacrifice dans l'hindouisme." In Madelaine Biardeau and Charles Malamoud (eds) *Le sacrifice dans l'Inde ancienne*. Paris: Press Universitaires de France, 1976, pp. 80–154.

Bourdieu, Pierre. *Outline of a Theory of Practice*. Trans. Richard Nice. Cambridge: Cambridge University Press, 1977.

Carrier, James G. *Gifts and Commodities: Exchange and Western Capitalism since 1700*. London: Routledge, 1995.

Carrithers, Michael. *The Forest Monks of Sri Lanka: An Anthropological and Historical Study*. Delhi: Oxford University Press, 1983.

—— "The domestication of the *sangha*." *Man* (NS) 19 (1984): 321–2.

Daniel, E. Valentine. *Fluid Signs: Being a Person the Tamil Way*. Berkeley: University of California Press, 1984.

Derrida, Jacques. *Writing and Difference*. Trans. Alan Bass. London: Routledge, 1978.

—— *Given Time: I. Counterfeit Money*. Trans. Peggy Kamuf. Chicago: University of Chicago Press, 1992.

Dumont, Louis. *Homo Hierarchicus: The Caste system and Its Implications*. Revised edition. Trans. Mark Sainsbury, Louis Dumont and Basai Gulati. Chicago: University of Chicago Press, 1980.

Emerson, Ralph Waldo. "Gifts." In Tony Tanner (ed.) *1844. Essays and Poems*. London: Everyman, 1995, pp. 256–9.

Fuller, C.J. *Servants of the Goddess: The Priests of a South Indian Temple*. Cambridge: Cambridge University Press, 1984.

—— "The Hindu pantheon and the legitimation of hierarchy." *Man* (NS) 23 (1988): 19–39.

Gell, Alfred. "Inter-tribal commodity barter and reproductive gift-exchange in old Melanesia." In Caroline Humphrey and Stephen Hugh-Jones (eds) *Barter, Exchange and Value*. Cambridge: Cambridge University Press, 1992, pp. 142–68.

Gold, Ann Grodzins. *Fruitful Journeys: the Ways of Rajasthani Pilgrims*. Berkeley: University of California Press, 1988.

Gregory, C.A. "Gifts to men and gifts to gods: gift exchange and capital accumulation in contemporary Papua." *Man* (NS) 15 (1980): 626–52.

—— *Gifts and Commodities*. London: Academic Press, 1982.

—— "Kula gift exchange and capitalist commodity exchange: a comparison." In Jerry W. Leach and Edmund Leach (eds) *The Kula: New Perspectives on Massim Exchange*. Cambridge: Cambridge University Press, 1983, pp. 103–17.

—— *Savage Money: The Anthropology and Politics of Commodity Exchange*. Amsterdam: Harwood Academic, 1997.

Heesterman, J.C. "Brahmin, ritual, and renouncer." *Wein. Z. Kunde Süd-Ostasiens* 8 (1964): 1–31.

Jenkins, Timothy. "Derrida's reading of Mauss." In Wendy James and N.J. Allen (eds) *Marcel Mauss: A Centenary Tribute*. Oxford: Berghahn, 1998, pp. 83–94.

Laidlaw, James. *Riches and Renunciation: Religion, Economy, and Society among the Jains*. Oxford: Clarendon Press, 1995.

Lalwani, K.C. *Arya Sayyambhava's Dasavaikalika sutra*. Delhi: Motilal Banarsidass, 1973.

Lévi-Strauss, Claude. *The Elementary Structures of Kinship*. Revised edition. Trans. J.H. Bell, J.R. von Sturmer and Rodney Needham. Boston: Beacon Press, 1967 [1949].

Malinowski, Bronislaw. *Argonauts of the Western Pacific*. London: Routledge, 1922.

—— *Crime and Custom in Savage Society*. London: Routledge, 1926.

Marriott, McKim. "Caste ranking and food transactions." In Milton Singer and Bernard S. Cohn (eds) *Structure and Change in Indian Society*. Chicago: Aldine, 1968, pp. 133–71.

—— "Hindu transactions: diversity without dualism." In Bruce Kapferer (ed.) *Transaction and Meaning*. Philadelphia: Institute for the Study of Human Issues, 1976, pp. 109–42.

Mauss, Marcel. *The Gift: The Form and Reason For Exchange in Archaic Societies*. Trans. W.D. Halls. London: Routledge, 1990 [1925].

Parry, Jonathan P. "Ghosts, greed, and sin: the occupational identity of the Benares funeral priests." *Man* (NS) 15 (1980): 88–111.

—— "*The Gift*, the Indian gift and the 'Indian gift.'" *Man* (NS) 21 (1986): 453–73.

—— "On the moral perils of exchange." In Jonathan Parry and Maurice Bloch (eds) *Money and the Morality of Exchange*. Cambridge: Cambridge University Press, 1989, pp. 64–93.

—— "The Hindu lexicographer? A note on auspiciousness and purity." *Contributions to Indian Sociology* (NS) 25 (1991): 267–85.

—— *Death in Banaras*. Cambridge: Cambridge University Press, 1994.

Pollock, F. and F.W. Maitland. *The History of English Law Before the Time of Edward I.* Second edition. Volume 2. Cambridge: Cambridge University Press, 1898.

Raheja, Gloria Goodwin. *The Poison in the Gift: Ritual, Prestation, and the Dominant Caste in a North Indian Village*. Chicago: University of Chicago Press, 1988.

—— " 'Crying when she's born, and crying when she goes away': marriage and the idiom of the gift in Pahansu song performance." In Lindsay Harlan and Paul B. Courtright (eds) *From the Margins of Hindu Marriage*. New York: Oxford University Press, 1995, pp. 19–59.

Sahlins, Marshall. *Stone Age Economics*. Chicago: Aldine, 1972.

Shulman, D. "Kingship and prestation in South Indian myth and epic." *Asian and African Studies* 19 (1985): 36–79.

Strenski, I. "On generalized exchange and the domestication of the *Sangha*." *Man* (NS) 18 (1983): 463–77.

Tambiah, S.J. *Buddhism and the Spirit Cults in North-east Thailand*. Cambridge: Cambridge University Press, 1970.

—— *The Buddhist Saints of the Forest and the Cult of Amulets*. Cambridge: Cambridge University Press, 1984.

Testart, Alain. "Uncertainties of the 'obligation to reciprocate': a critique of Mauss." In Wendy James and N.J. Allen (eds) *Marcel Mauss: a Centenary Tribute*. Oxford: Berghahn, 1998, pp. 97–110.

Trautmann, Thomas R. *Dravidian Kinship*. Cambridge: Cambridge University Press, 1981.

Williams, R. *Jaina Yoga: a Survey of the Mediaeval Sravakacaras*. London: Oxford University Press, 1963.

2 Unbalanced reciprocity

Asymmetrical gift giving and social
hierarchy in rural China

Yunxiang Yan

In his 1925 classic Marcel Mauss raises the fundamental question of gift giving: "What force is there in the thing given which compels the recipient to make a return?" (1967: 1). Since then, the obligation of return has remained a primary concern in the anthropology of the gift, and scholarly accounts have been developed along two theoretical models, namely, the spirit of the gift and the principle of reciprocity.

Mauss establishes the first model by resorting to the Maori concept of *hau* – a mystic power that lies in the forest and in the valuables given by one person to another. The *hau* always wishes to return to its place of origin, but can only do so through the medium of an object given in exchange for the original gift. Failure to return a gift, therefore, can result in serious trouble, including the death of the recipient. It is the *hau* in the gift, Mauss asserts, that forces the recipient to make a return, and he calls this "the spirit of the gift" (1967: 8–9).

Mauss's preoccupation with the spiritual significance of the *hau* in the gift was criticized by many anthropologists who viewed gift giving as an important mode of economic exchange and social communication. Malinowski argues that the binding force of economic obligations lies in the sanction that either side may invoke to sever the bonds of reciprocity. One gives because of the expectation of return and one returns because of the threat that one's partner may stop giving. All rights and obligations are "arranged into well-balanced chains of reciprocal services" (Malinowski 1962: 46). Even among the Maori people, Raymond Firth notes, the notion of reciprocity (locally called *utu*) is a key drive to social interactions (1959: 412, 419–20; see also MacCormack 1982: 287). Through his well-known tripartite division of exchange phenomena – generalized reciprocity, balanced reciprocity, and negative reciprocity – Marshall Sahlins demystifies the "spirit of the gift" and reinforces the accountability of the principle of reciprocity (1972: 191–210). Today many ethnographic studies interpret gift giving in terms of the principle of reciprocity, so much so that reciprocity has become something of a cliché (see MacCormack 1976).

The spirit of the gift – the classic theme in Mauss's book – was revitalized during the 1980s. Rather than continuing Mauss's interpretation of the Maori *hau*, many anthropologists have employed the notion of inalienability to explain the existence of spiritual, non-utilitarian ties between giver and recipient and used it to criticize the reciprocity model for its overemphasis on economic rationality defined by Western values (see Damon 1982, 1983; Gregory 1980, 1982; Liep 1990). Weiner's recent book (1992), in which she asserts Mauss is right about the Maori *hau*, is an exception. Weiner argues that there is a close connection among the *hau*, the person and valuables (*taonga*) such as cloaks, fine mats, and shells; because of this connection, valuables gain their own identity and become inalienable possessions; hence the obligation of return (1992: 46–56). Partially based on Weiner's theory, Maurice Godelier's (1999) work focuses on sacred objects that are not exchangeable and argues that the secret of gift exchange lies in the authoritative conferral of power associated with the sacred objects.

Although the spirit model and the reciprocity model explain the original motive for returning a gift differently, scholars of both schools agree that gifts always obligate the recipients to return gifts, and that a failure to return a gift puts the recipient at a disadvantage. Based on this shared assumption, most students of the gift also agree that in the game of gift exchange the donor gains prestige and power by transforming the recipient into a debtor. In situations where unbalanced transactions occur, gifts usually pass downward in the social hierarchy because giving is prestigious. In other words, it is the obligation of return, regardless of the motive, that generates and sustains the superiority of the donor. Hence Chris Gregory concludes that the superiority of the gift giver is "a feature that is common to gift exchange systems all over the world" (1982: 47; see also Befu 1966–7; Raheja 1988; Sahlins 1972; A. Strathern 1971; Vatuk and Vatuk 1971).

Is the superiority of the gift donor truly universal? Ethnographic evidence from a Chinese village shows that although expressivity and reciprocity play prominent roles in most gift-giving activities, there is also a type of asymmetrical gift that flows up the ladder of society. In this particular type of gift-giving relationship, the recipient not only ignores the obligation of return but also remains superior to the donor. The absence of reciprocity and the superiority of the gift recipient thus pose a double challenge to the existing anthropological theory of the gift. In the following pages, I will first examine the one-way flow of gifts from lower to upper social strata within the Chinese socialist hierarchy that was established after 1949. Next I will discuss the social-cultural mechanisms that sustain such unilateral gift giving. Finally, I will conclude the chapter by explaining why the Chinese case reveals features so strikingly different from earlier studies.

My case study is based on fieldwork that I carried out in 1991, 1997 and 1999 in Xiajia village, a farming community with a population of 1,500, in Heilongjiang province, northeast China.[1] In Xiajia village, as in most rural communities in China and some other East Asian societies as well, for each major family ceremony that they host villagers always write a gift list – a document that records the names of the gift givers as well as a description of all gifts received. Families carefully keep these gift lists and use them for future reference when reciprocal gifts are to be offered. From a researcher's point of view, a gift list may serve as a repository of data on the changing nature of interpersonal relations and as a social map that vividly displays *guanxi* networks. In my 1991 fieldwork, I collected 43 gift lists based on a stratified selection of households, containing a total of 5,286 individual gift transactions. More data were collected on subsequent field trips in 1997 and 1999. There are 22 types of gifts, more than half of which are given and received in the context of family ceremonies, such as weddings and funerals. All but three types of these gifts are what I refer to as "expressive gifts," which are ends in themselves and often reflect a long-term relationship between a giver and a recipient. The remaining three can be called "instrumental gifts," which are offered for a utilitarian purpose and ordinarily indicate a short-term relationship between the two parties. Both expressive and instrumental gifts are exchanged between social equals and across the boundaries of social strata. What is to be examined in the present chapter is the type that is given upwardly along the social ladder without the expectation of immediate return of goods, favors or services from the recipient. The obligation of return and the superiority of the donor, it should be noted, do apply to other types of gift exchange in Xiajia village (for details see Yan 1996: 43–73).

Imbalance in gift exchange

During my fieldwork, many villagers complained that they had to offer so many gifts that giving had become unaffordable. While complaining about the huge expense, they tried to convince me that they were not stingy; on the contrary, they made efforts to be generous in gift exchange. As a result, more than half of the Xiajia households needed 500 *yuan* or more for a year's expenses on gifts, nearly one-fifth of the average household annual income (Yan 1996: 76–9). When discussing the economic burdens of gift exchange, most villagers maintained that they had given more gifts than they had received.

If so many villagers gave more gifts than they received, where did these gifts end up? In other words, are there some people who receive more than they give? According to ordinary villagers, the answer is "Yes, the cadres."[2] They attributed the recent increase of gift-giving activities to ulterior motives by cadres. As a schoolteacher in Xiajia put it:

> These days people make every effort to host ceremonies and receive gifts. The more criticism there is of the "gift-giving wind" in newspapers, the stronger it blows. Why? Because the wind comes from above. All the new customs [of gift giving] are created by cadres and other people above, because they can receive gifts but they don't worry about returning them.

However, when I asked the same question to the village cadres, they all denied that they had ever failed to return gifts to villagers. A cadre maintained: "That would make me a shameless person, a person who is ignorant of human feelings and morality. Nobody wants to do such a stupid thing to hurt one's own reputation." Yet some of these local cadres went on to complain about their superiors for the same reason: they offered gifts to state officials in the township or the county government, but the latter did not return the gifts.

Inspired by my informants' ambiguous and often contradictory answers, I conducted a special survey on the balance of gift exchange. I discerned that the asymmetrical flow of gifts was determined by two factors: the cycle of family development and the social status hierarchy. The former was a universal process that every family underwent and thus did not attract much attention or complaints from Xiajia villagers. The latter causes asymmetrical gift giving only when a disparity in social status exists between the donor and the recipient, and, in this context, some people (mostly cadres) indeed did receive gifts without fulfilling the obligation to return them.

Operating within the kinship system, there is a type of gift called *xiaojing*, which literally means "filial piety and respect." A *xiaojing* gift is given by a junior person to a senior kinsman or kinswoman during special occasions, with no expectation of a return gift. In fact, the reverse order is considered improper in inter-generational gift giving.[3] Such unilateral, upward gift giving symbolizes the junior person's gratitude and respect to the elder and, hence, the more gifts one receives, the more prestigious one becomes. It is common for an older villager to make a show of a gift recently given by his son (daughter, nephew or other junior kinsman), and enjoy hearing the public's appreciative comments. In this connection, the one-way flow of gifts serves to restate the kinship rank between the two generations in symbolic terms.

A type of *xiaojing*-like gift giving is also found in public life between subordinates and social superiors. According to older informants, before the 1949 Revolution gift exchange outside the web of kinship was rare and few villagers had connections with important figures in the outside world. The most common type of inter-strata interactions was found between landlords and tenants. All informants agreed that tenants had to show respect to their landlords by giving gifts during ceremonial occasions or during the lunar New Year. The landlord, however, usually did not make return gifts directly; instead, he might offer benefits to the tenants in daily life, such as allowing the tenants' children to pick up the remaining grain in the field after the harvest, or holding a banquet at the end of the year. When the tenants hosted ceremonies, the landlord might send a representative and offer a gift, but he did not personally come unless a special relationship had developed between the two parties.[4] To explain the absence of the landlord at the ceremonies, my informants referred to the difference in "face." They explained that the landlord's face was bigger than that of the tenants, so a gift presented by a representative of the landlord was already considered an honor.

After the 1949 Revolution, especially during the collective era (1956–83), a new social hierarchy was established and quickly replaced the dominant role of kinship in social life. Through its agents (the cadres) at the grassroots levels, the power of the Communist Party and the state penetrated every corner of village society and turned the previous social order upside down. As I have described elsewhere (Yan 1992), social life during the collective era was far from "egalitarian," and the collectives were no less hierarchical than the pre-Revolutionary communities. The socialist hierarchy system in Xiajia village consisted of six status groups, with the cadres at the top and the so-called "four bad elements" at the bottom, namely, those who were assigned the class labels of "landlord," "rich peasant," "counterrevolutionary" and "rotten element."

The most noticeable impact of this new system of social hierarchy on gift exchange was that the unilateral, upward flow of gifts became more elaborate in public life. Unlike during the pre-Revolution period, this new pattern involved almost every villager, due to the intensity of state intervention in village life and the day-to-day exercise of cadre power. Unilateral gift giving mainly took two forms: from villagers to cadres; and from lower rank cadres to their superiors.

Many informants recalled that when the cadres hosted family ceremonies, almost all the villagers went to show their respect by presenting gifts, even though not everyone had previous gift-exchange relationships with the leaders. But when the villagers hosted ceremonies, only those who were close to the cadres or enjoyed higher social status could expect a return gift. Many ordinary villagers could only hope to have the cadres attend the after-ceremony banquets, without expecting to receive gifts. Given the much lower standard value of gifts during the collective era (0.5 to 1 *yuan* on average), it seems to me that what cadres mostly cared about was the significance of receiving, rather than the economic value of the gifts.

At the surface, the upward, unilateral gift giving during the collective era was not compulsory, and subordinates seemed to present gifts to superiors of their own free will. The secret was that in most cases villagers, and, as we shall see below, cadres in lower positions, would not send invitations to their superiors when they hosted weddings or other celebrations, regardless of the previous gifts they had given to the latter. By refraining, they helped their superiors avoid the obligation of returning gifts. In a close-knit rural community, information about family ceremonies cannot be missed, and superiors can easily learn about such events. If a superior wants to develop a more intimate relationship with a subordinate, he may come to present a gift even without invitation. In other words, the mechanism is designed to protect the superiors at the expense of ordinary villagers.

Moreover, the superiors were aware of the driving force behind this kind of gift giving and thus did not think of themselves as falling into the position of debtor. Unlike the landlords or other patrons during the pre-Revolution era, cadres often did not reciprocate gifts and pretended not to know about the imbalance of transactions between villagers and themselves. A recent example is a dispute between a cook nicknamed "big bread Zhao" and his leader, deputy party secretary Lin of the township government. Although Zhao had continually offered gifts to Lin for years, Lin did not make any return gift when Zhao hosted a wedding for his son. As some villagers commented, Lin probably never took Zhao's previous contributions into serious consideration, because there were so many gifts from below.[5] I once asked a friend about the obvious decrease in the number of guests (less than thirty people) recorded by the gift list of his second wedding, for I wondered whether it had anything to do with the fact it was a second marriage. He regarded my speculation as nonsense and told me that when he married in 1977 for the first time, his elder brother was a powerful cadre. Many people attended his wedding and they had come, without invitations, not for his or his father's sake, but to flatter his brother. These guests did not show up when he remarried in 1985, because his brother had fallen from power due to decollectivization. When I asked how he repaid these guests' gifts, he said, "for those sycophants, I gave them shit! Who cares about them! They are not my *renqing* [indebtedness in personal relations] and I am not responsible for their ulterior gifts." In this case alone several dozen people lost both their gifts and their social credit.

When I transcribed the gift lists I discovered an interesting incident of what Sahlins calls "negative reciprocity," in which one party received but did not fulfil the obligation of repayment. In this case, an ordinary villager presented a gift of 5 *yuan* to a cadre, which was recorded on the latter's gift list of 1979, but I could not find the return gift from the latter in the former's 1989 records. When I alluded to the imbalance to the cadre and his wife during an informal interview, his wife explained that since there was no previous gift-giving relationship between the two families (which implies that the villager's motivation was to flatter the leader), and since the villager's family ceremony was performed ten years later, she forgot to return the gift. Later she argued that her husband had done some favor for the villager before the gift giving, so the villager had presented a gift to express his gratitude and balance the "debt." Whatever the reason, the hidden message she conveyed was indifference, which reflects the attitude of superiority of cadres toward their subordinates.

As a result of this kind of unbalanced flow of gifts between villagers and their leaders, village cadres usually possess the largest networks of personal relations and have the most lavish celebrations. After decollectivization and other reforms in the early 1980s, which to a great extent broke the cadres' monopoly over resources, some villagers stopped presenting gifts to their leaders. And interestingly enough, because of the changes in power relations and the political environment in general (see Yan 1995), in recent years cadres have paid more attention to cultivating good relations with the villagers, and have become more mindful of returning their share in gift exchange. However, the difference in guest numbers remains, which vividly illustrates the disparity in social status and prestige between subordinates and superiors. According to my survey in 1991, the number of gift givers in ordinary villagers' family ceremonies varied from fewer than 100 to 200; in contrast, the number of guests attending cadres' ceremonies usually exceeded 300. In a 1997 case, the top leader in the village received gifts from 662 guests during his son's wedding, and the smallest monetary gift was one of 20 *yuan*. No wonder many informants complained that cadres could make a fortune simply by holding family ceremonies to extract gifts from ordinary villagers.

The second form of unilateral gift giving in the socialist hierarchy is found among cadres themselves. Due perhaps to the importance of political allies and the influence of superiors, the upward flow of gifts has long been practiced within the bureaucratic system of traditional China. A folktale may well illustrate how, in popular perception, officials are engaged in upward gift giving. It is said that when a county governor's birthday was approaching, the officials in the county government gathered to discuss what kind of gifts they should present to their superior. Finally, the smartest official among them proposed: "Since the governor was born in the year of mouse, why not give him a golden mouse as a birthday gift?" They all agreed and presented a golden mouse to the governor. The governor was very happy and said: "Let me tell you a little secret. I will celebrate my wife's birthday next month. She was born in the year of cow."

As between villagers and their leaders, the village cadres offer gifts to their superiors in the township government or at higher levels when the latter host family rituals, but they do not expect their superiors to give return gifts. For instance, the village party secretary told me that in 1990 he calculated his expenditures for gift giving and found the total to be over 2,600 *yuan*. This was extremely high in comparison with other families, the main reason being his upward gift giving. According to Han, since he had become a principal cadre in Xiajia in 1981, he had continually presented gifts to most cadres in the township government. But when he hosted a wedding for his second son, only lower-rank cadres attended. He emphasized that he did not send invitations to the cadres in township government, for he did not want to remind them of obligations from below. Yet his superiors never forgot to let him and other lower-rank colleagues know the dates of their own ceremonies. He recalled that he had attended the wedding of the son of the current vice-governor of the county, which lasted four days; the third day was reserved especially for village cadres from all over the county. During the banquet, he and several friends made fun of themselves, saying that they were called upon to endow the vice-governor's family ceremony.

Sometimes, hierarchical gift giving among cadres may take a more compelling form. In a case I witnessed, Mr. Su, a retired government official who grew up in Xiajia, formally invited all five cadres in Xiajia to attend his youngest son's wedding in the town seat. According to my informant, Su had an obvious ulterior motive – to accumulate monetary gifts and to make a show of his prestige. Su had stopped maintaining gift-giving relations with most villagers in Xiajia after he left the village in the early 1950s. "This man knows nothing about human feelings," said my informant,

> he should not have forgotten his natal home and fellow villagers in the first place, no matter how big he has become. Besides, without previous interactions and good feelings with us, how could he possibly think about asking us to present gifts. But he did. It's really a shame!

Nevertheless, in spite of all the complaints, my informant still decided to attend the wedding and make his contribution. Why? He told me that Su's second son was currently in charge of an important office in the local government. It would not be wise to refuse the invitation, because it might be taken as a sign of disrespect. "That would be the last thing I wanted. Keeping up a good relationship with your superiors is, you know, the key to keeping your rice bowl [i.e., one's job]."

This informant was not the only one to rationalize his decision – all the other village cadres did the same thing, hoping to maintain good relationships with Su's second son. It is obvious that both sides made rational calculations, taking social hierarchy into consideration. On the one hand, Su had considered his second son's influence when he sent invitations to the village cadres with whom he did not have previous relationships of gift exchange. On the other hand, the village cadres reacted in a similarly rational way, by trying to manipulate the game in their favor. They took advantage of the occasion to cultivate good relationships with a superior (Su's second son). But at the same time, they complained about Su's behavior, which to a certain extent relieved them of their emotional distress and helped them to justify their actions.

Unbalanced reciprocity and the reproduction of social hierarchy

As indicated at the beginning of this chapter, most anthropologists share the assumption that unilateral gift giving eventually leads to an increase of power and prestige for the donor. Many ethnographic studies suggest that what appears to be the operation of a unilateral, asymmetric principle is in fact governed by a rule of symmetric reciprocity (see Malinowski 1962, 1984; Mauss 1967). As Sahlins notes: "In primitive society social inequality is more the organization of economic equality. Often, in fact, high rank is only secured or sustained by o'er-crowing generosity: the material advantage is on the subordinate's side" (1972: 205). If a gift does not bring back a similar gift in the strict sense, there must be some invisible counter-gifts to restore the balance, such as political control over the recipient or a gain in prestige for the donor (see, for example, A. Strathern 1971: 10). Thus "the aim of the capitalist is to accumulate profit while the aim of the 'big man' gift transactor is to acquire a large following of people (gift-debtors) who are obligated to him" (Gregory 1982: 51).

The tributary gifts given by commoners to chiefs, however, constitute an exceptional case of upward, one-way giving. Malinowski noticed that the chief sometimes owed a *kula* gift to a commoner, but never vice versa. "In the inland Kula, the determining factor is the relative social position of the two partners. Gifts are brought to the man of superior by the man of inferior rank, and the latter has also to initiate the exchange" (Malinowski 1984: 473). But this one-way giving is, many anthropologists argue, balanced in the long run by the chief's ceremonial display and redistribution of material goods. Leach points out that "although an individual of high-class status is defined as one who receives gifts (e.g., 'thigh-eating chief') he is all the time under a social compulsion to give away more than he receives. Otherwise he would be reckoned mean and a mean man runs the danger of losing status" (1954: 163). In Sahlins's model, this is called "pooling" or "redistribution," and "*pooling is an organization of reciprocities, a system of reciprocities* – a fact of central bearing upon the genesis of large-scale redistribution under chiefly aegis" (1972: 188; italics in original). Here the anthropological discourse of the gift comes full circle: a chief's authority and status are achieved by giving rather than receiving, just as in the case of big-man society (see Gregory 1982: 55).

Anthropologists are not alone in emphasizing the universal superiority of the gift donor. Most sociological studies of social exchange focus on the process by which the initial unbalanced exchange generates a differentiation of power and leads to an obligation of unilateral compliance. According to Richard Emerson (1962, 1972), exchange relationships are based on predicated dependence of two parties upon each other's resources. To the extent that A is unwilling voluntarily to surrender a resource desired by B and is able to use this resource to force, coerce, or induce compliance upon B, A is said to have power over B. As George Homans notes, "Men are powerful when many want what they, the few, are able to supply or many fear what they, the few, are able to withhold" (1974: 197). Moreover, if A can monopolize all the resources B needs, A will make B dependent on A's power in a "power-dependence relationship," as referred to by Emerson. The central theme here is that unilateral giving establishes superordination, which in turn balances the initial imbalance in exchange relationships. Thus Peter Blau maintains: "A person who gives others valuable gifts or renders them important services makes a claim for superior status by obligating them to himself" (1964: 108).

It is precisely on this issue that the Xiajia case challenges the generalizations of previous theories. As far as the material flow of gifts is concerned, unilateral giving in Xiajia reveals four features: (1) gifts are given by subordinates to superiors without the expectation of an equal return; (2) due to the pyramidal structure of the social hierarchy, the number of donors exceeds that of recipients, which leads to an accumulation of gifts at the upper levels; (3) recipients remain socially superior and powerful, even though they fail to return the gifts; and (4) the repeated one-way flow of gifts creates an institutionalized imbalance in exchange values between adjacent social strata, which in turn is regarded as another sign of status differences. All of these features seem to conflict with existing sociological and anthropological theories of social exchange.

An obvious and direct answer to the question of why Xiajia is so different lies in the simple fact that Xiajia village represents a different type of society than those that predominated in earlier studies of social exchange. Most anthropological analyses of gift exchange are based on observations of social life in relatively "simple" societies, where the local economy and social relations have only marginally or incompletely been affected by the penetration of a political state (see Sahlins 1972: 188). In contrast, sociological theories of social exchange focus mainly on interactions in modern, industrial societies, which are characterized by democratic political systems, social stratification based on economic classes, and a free market economy. Obviously, Xiajia does not resemble either of these models. In the past five decades, Xiajia village, like other communities in China, has been under the strict control of a centralized, powerful state. Xiajia residents have lived under a planned economy with a system of state redistribution, and have witnessed the establishment of a new, socialist status hierarchy. It is not surprising, then, that existing theories of social exchange do not fit the reality of life in Xiajia.

In studies of state socialism, it has been widely recognized that the party-state's power and authority is based on its monopoly over resources and opportunities, which is maintained and reinforced by the new ruling class of cadres (Djilas 1957; Szelenyi 1978). Such a monopoly leads to citizens' dependence upon officials for the satisfaction of material needs and social mobility, a social phenomena characterized as a form of "organized dependency" by Walder (1983, 1986). It is the redistribution of resources that constitutes the integrative principle of the socialist economy and establishes a vertical relationship between redistributor and producer (see Kornai 1986; Szelenyi 1978; Nee 1989).

At the level of village society, grass-root cadres are in charge of the redistribution system and thus can compel villagers to depend on the resources under their control. By resources, I refer to those materials and services that are needed or desired by villagers, including economic, political and sociocultural resources. During the collective era, Xiajia villagers worked under the supervision of cadres and their basic needs were fulfilled annually by the collectives. In terms of economic resources, cadres controlled villagers by distributing basic grain rations, assigning daily work, supervising the development of family sidelines and granting social welfare.[6] Government restrictions on rural–urban migration further confined villagers within the collectives and thereby increased the power of the local cadres. During the radical period, villagers also had to ask for leave from the cadres for all social activities outside the collective, such as visiting relatives or going to nearby marketplaces. Unlike the landlords in the pre-Revolution period, the cadres were completely in charge of people's daily lives by redistributing basic resources and opportunities.

In such a power-dependence relationship (see Emerson 1962, 1972), the cadre's superior status and power ruled out the possibility of equal exchange. As a redistributor, a cadre may have felt free of the obligation to return a gift to his subordinates, because the latter depended on the resources he controlled and thus failure to return did not affect the mutual relationship. By the same token, a village cadre's gift did not obligate his superiors either, because the latter provided the necessary protection and connections for the former to remain in power. In other words, the obligation of reciprocal repayment, which is the basis of all forms of gift giving, according to Mauss, was overshadowed by the existing inequality of social status between the two parties. The received structure of social relations neutralized obligations of reciprocity. As Blau notes: "Unilateral giving produces status differences between former peers, but once superior status is securely grounded in the social structure its occupant can demand unilateral services without endangering his superordinate position" (1964: 110).[7]

Furthermore, as the resources controlled by the cadres often cause competition in upward gift giving among the dependent villagers, the latter's gifts are devalued, or in anthropological terms, their gifts to the leaders are of a lower rank. The gifts in ceremonial situations are considered the obligatory dues villagers owe to cadres, not the potential sociocultural debt that one must pay back. Gift giving in this hierarchical context works only as a passive strategy adopted by the subordinates to protect themselves from being discriminated against by their superiors.

As indicated above, upward gift giving symbolizes the subordinates' respect and loyalty to their superiors and also reflects the latter's authority and popularity among their subordinates. Cadres often compare with one another the number of guests who attend their family ceremonies, and take this to indicate their authority and achievement. Thus, one's failure to present a gift could be interpreted as an offense to the leader; because of the public nature of ceremonial exchanges, this offense would be taken very seriously and personally. The same is true of the relationship between village cadres and their superiors, except that in this case the donor's personal loyalty matters more to the recipient, due to needs for alliances in politics and the desire for career achievement in the bureaucracy. There are many ways by which cadres can express their anger toward those who fail to fulfill the obligation to give gifts, such as giving a bad job assignment in collective work or, in the case of the bureaucracy, withdrawing support for the cadres in inferior positions. The possibility that their relationship with their superiors will deteriorate already constitutes a negative sanction upon subordinates and is sufficient to keep them engaged in upward gift giving. That is why the majority of people continue to offer gifts to leaders, even though no specific return can be expected.

The negative sanction inherent in hierarchical giving is also reflected in the cadres' reactions to guest attendance. An informant who is a ritual specialist told me that when a small household (that of an ordinary villager) holds a wedding or other ceremony, the host usually takes note of every guest in attendance, and when checking the gift list after the ritual, he/she is interested in who has attended the ritual. In contrast, a cadre or other high-status person can hardly greet the guests. When checking the gift list, a cadre tries to determine who did not attend and why. My informant commented that as a ritual specialist he has more responsibilities when he manages ceremonies for big households, because the hosts are interested only in entertaining the honorary guests and leave the rest to him and his assistants. Clearly, unlike ordinary villagers who appreciate the attendance of guests as a favor, cadres (or their superiors) take gifts from below for granted, and therefore only want to know who has not attended the ritual.

Interestingly, while decollectivization and market-oriented reforms reduced the power of village cadres to a great extent and thus freed ordinary villagers from the obligation of unilateral gift giving, some individuals managed to monopolize the new opportunities in the post-Mao reform era and became newly designated gift recipients. For instance, in the late 1980s, through family connections a villager obtained a lucrative position to supervise the local milk collection station for a dairy factory jointly owned by the Nestlé Company and a Chinese partner in the county seat. Within a few years raising milk cows became a major business for many Xiajia villagers. As the local station was the only place where they could sell their milk, a new power-dependence relationship emerged between the milk collector and the dairy farmers, in which the former had monopoly power to determine the quality and hence the selling price of the latter's product.

When the productivity of the local dairy farms exceeded the demands of the milk-processing factory in the late 1990s, a quota system was enforced whereby each dairy farmer was allowed to sell only a certain amount of fresh milk to the factory. The unsold milk became worthless to the farmers because there was no second local buyer, and they could not transport fresh milk to distant cities due to the lack of special equipment to keep the milk fresh. Their only solution was to try to sell more to the local station, which gave the local collector even more power. When the local collector hosted family ceremonies in 1996 and 1998, a large number of unexpected gift givers who previously had no gift-exchange relationship with the host offered generous monetary gifts. Competition was so stiff that some gift givers simply registered their gifts by their milk-selling account numbers instead of by their own names. As several informants told me, if a dairy farmer failed to present a gift on such an occasion, the milk collector could easily hurt the farmer's chances to sell milk once and for all. This is why some farmers used their account numbers to register their gifts, highlighting the link between their gifts and the opportunity to sell milk to the station. Some dairy farmers also offered extra cash or other instrumental gifts directly to the milk collector outside the context of the family ceremonies, because they wanted to bribe the latter for more opportunities. This case shows that as long as resources are monopolized and a hierarchy is established between two parties, unilateral, upward gift giving will be created in the village community, even under conditions of commodity production and a market economy.

There are some positive rewards for upward gift giving, but only when subordinates go beyond conventional gift giving to establish a special relationship with their superiors. Quite often other forms of social exchange must be involved, such as consistently providing personal services to the leaders or offering valuable instrumental gifts in return for favors. In these cases, the social superiors may use their positional power to redistribute resources in favor of these gift givers, thereby converting gift exchange into general social exchange. As in many other places in China, Xiajia residents describe this kind of social exchange as an effort to "cultivate personal connections" (*la guanxi*), and the term *guanxi* in this context has a more negative meaning than in its common usage.[8]

In cases of instrumental gift giving, although the inferior's gift is eventually repaid by his/her superiors, it is not repaid in kind. Rather, superiors repay the gifts through exercising their positional power, by arranging a job assignment or career promotion. Unlike the case of material gifts, the offering of instrumental resources does not incur a loss of resources in direct proportion to the amount given. The cadres are supposed to distribute the resources they control anyway; what is different is to whom they distribute the favors, and for what profits. More importantly, after the transaction, the previous hierarchical relations between the two parties remain, and are perhaps accentuated by an increase in the superior's personal wealth.

Lebra suggests that "each culture provides mechanisms which keep within a limit the tension generated in the mutual constraint between symmetry and asymmetry" (1969: 130). The gift giver's disadvantageous position in a hierarchical context is balanced by two distinguishing notions in Chinese culture. First, the emphasis on nominal status and role difference in Chinese culture provides unilateral gift giving with a legitimate foundation. Until the 1949 Revolution, loyalty, filial piety, chastity and righteousness (*zhong, xiao, jie, yi*) were promoted as the most important moral characteristics for human beings in Chinese culture and, among them, filial piety was particularly emphasized in village life. The display of respect, obedience and devotion to one's parents and elder kinsmen as well as to social superiors was positively rewarded by village society as good behavior. By the same token, failure to be filial could ruin one's credit in other domains of social life. For instance, the Chinese believed that "an unfilial son is also a bad businessman who fails to pay his parents' old age insurance" (L. Yang 1957: 302). As a result of the glorification of filial piety and loyalty, "the mere position of a ruler or a parent guaranteed his privilege to receive respect and service from his subject or son" (L. Yang 1957: 308). After 1949, although filial piety in domestic life was severely attacked by the Communist Party, its extension in public life was transferred into a new political norm called "absolute compliance to the Party's leadership." As in the pre-Revolution era, the position of a village cadre provides a legitimate basis for receiving respect and gifts from the villagers.

Second, the notion of social face (*mianzi*) plays a subtle yet important role in perceptions of unilateral gift giving. Defined as "a function of perceived social position and prestige within one's social network" (Hwang 1987: 961), social face is always attached to those who are in the upper ranks or higher positions. When they receive gifts from their subordinates, their acceptance of the gift itself is believed to render face to the inferior gift givers. Unlike moral face (*lian*), which refers to basic moral characteristics, social face "can be borrowed, struggled for, added to, padded – all indicating a gradual increase in volume" (Hu 1944: 61). One of the ways to increase the volume of one's social face is to connect oneself with powerful and well-known people as much as possible, because personal connections are considered part of one's resources and prestige. It is common for villagers to flaunt the fact that they have attended the family ceremony of a powerful person and have started a gift-giving relationship with such a person. Although an ordinary villager cannot expect to receive a return gift from a superior recipient, he or she can use the latter's acceptance of the gift as his or her own social capital. By so doing, one hopes to increase the volume of one's own social face and then in turn to enjoy respect and gifts from those of lower status.

A typical example in this regard is the chain of upward gift giving among local cadres. When a cadre offers a unilateral gift to his superior, he can expect similar gifts from below (either from lower-rank cadres or ordinary people) as compensation. In addition, because of his close connections with his superiors, he may gain a more compelling force over his subordinates. As a popular saying captures: "the big fish eats small fish, the small fish eats tiny shrimp" (*dayu chi xiaoyu, xiaoyu chi xiami*). Such a reciprocal chain of unbalanced exchanges goes beyond the dyadic relationship between giver and recipient, and involves at least a third party in the hierarchy in order to realize symmetrical reciprocity. Lebra categorizes a similar practice in Japanese society as "lineal transferred reciprocity" (see Lebra 1975: 559–60).

Concluding remarks

To sum up, the Xiajia case demonstrates that in a hierarchical context unilateral giving does not necessarily generate power or create superiority on the part of the donor. On the contrary, the previously existing social hierarchy may overshadow the reciprocal obligation inherent to the gift and free the recipient of superior rank from falling into debt to the donor. Furthermore, when the social superior's power and superiority are based on a monopoly of resources, the subordinates' gifts become obligatory dues, with unilateral gift giving serving to express subordination and the respect of inferiors to their superiors.

Under certain circumstances, gift givers of inferior status may obtain rewards by two forms of hierarchical exchange: by cultivating a clientist relationship or by the granting of favors from one's superiors. In either form the transaction is no longer gift exchange in its original sense. Gift exchange, by definition, should be like-for-like and be more expressive than instrumental. As Marilyn Strathern notes, gift exchange differs from barter in the sense that "people [are] exchanging things which they did not need" (1992: 169). However, if someone wants to use a gift as a means of attracting other resources, one has either to make an investment with ulterior motives alone in advance or present a gift that is valuable and seductive to the recipient. Here the convertibility of gifts to favors or services may balance the unequal distribution of resources between some individuals but not among the entire population. Because of this, certain individuals are able to move up the ladder of the social hierarchy while the structure of the ladder remains unchanged. In this sense, while the existing social hierarchy shapes unilateral gift giving, each action of unbalanced exchange also helps to reproduce the social hierarchy.

The Chinese case is not actually unique. In South Asia studies, several anthropologists have explored the Indian notion of giving without expectation of material return. Vatuk and Vatuk observe the asymmetric gift-giving relationships in the context of the caste hierarchy: "Persons of low castes, particularly if they are also in an economically subordinate position *vis-à-vis* the donor, are generally not expected to return the gifts they receive from their superiors, and in such cases these gifts may be classified as *dan* and thus meritorious" (1971: 217). Both Parry and Raheja argue that because the gift of *dan* serves to transfer the dangerous and demeaning burden of death and the impurity of the donor to the recipient, the institutionalized pattern of gift flow from the dominant caste to subordinate castes creates a mode of cultural domination (see Raheja 1988: 28,

31, 248). Following Mauss, Parry interprets the absence of reciprocity in the Indian *dan* in terms of the "evil spirit" of the gift. But by so doing, he actually challenges Mauss's original argument that the spirit of the gift elicits a return gift. Realizing this difficulty, Parry writes: "Where we have the 'spirit,' reciprocity is denied; where there is reciprocity there is not much evidence of 'spirit.' The two aspects of the model do not hang together" (1986: 463).[9]

Here the commonality shared by the Chinese and the Indian cases lies in the overwhelming power of social hierarchy over the obligation of return (or reciprocity) in unequal gift-giving relations across the boundaries of social groups. Unlike in individual-centered, highly mobile and industrialized societies where people can choose not to engage in hierarchical gift giving with their social superiors, the Chinese and Indian villagers are locked into the game by an institutional arrangement – the collectivization system in China and the Jajmani system in India. A noticeable difference between the two is the direction of the gift flow. In India, the *dan* gift unilaterally flows downward along the social ladder because it is believed to carry an "evil spirit," while in China the unilateral, *xiaojing*-like gift always represents prestige and power and thus goes in the other direction in the hierarchical context. Yet in both cases those in the lower strata of the society are forced to sacrifice themselves in gift exchange for the benefit of those of higher social status. The absence of a return gift, therefore, indicates the absence of social equality and justice.

Two further implications can be drawn here. First, inter-strata gift exchange, like many other social interactions across the boundaries of social groups, is determined by and in turn reinforces the existing structure of inequality and power. This aspect of the gift has largely been overlooked in most existing studies, which may have something to do with our easy acceptance of the obligation of return, or the universality of reciprocity. Second, in both China and India, the asymmetrical flow of gifts represents only one type of gift-giving activity, albeit an important type that challenges current anthropological generalizations. This means that different types of gifts may be exchanged in accordance with different principles. The more complex the social relations, the more complicated the gift principles may become. Therefore, when one studies gift exchange in a highly differentiated society where many types of gifts coexist and some gifts flow across boundaries of social strata, neither the spirit of the gift nor the principle of reciprocity alone can provide a satisfactory answer to the question of the gift. One must unpack the rich meanings of the gift in relation to the complexity of the social processes in the localized context, because, after all, the gift itself is also a social construction.

Notes

1 For a brief history of the village, see Yan 1996: 22–42.
2 Here, the word "cadre" refers to officials in village government who are appointed by the upper-level government yet are paid by public funds of the village. From 1956 to 1983, Xiajia villagers, like villagers all over China, were organized into collectives where cadres had great influence on the everyday life of ordinary members of the

collectives. The collectives were dismantled as part of the economic reforms at the end of 1983, and both the number of cadres and the power they held were reduced significantly. For details on cadre–villager relations in Xiajia village, see Yan 1995.

3 However, elders offer gifts to juniors in the form of *yasui* money (the "Happy New Year gift") during the lunar New Year, but the recipients must be non-adults, or at least unmarried.

4 The landlord–tenant relationship can involve warmth and intensity as well as other emotional responses. Fried regards the well-developed, personalized interactions between landlords and tenants as an "institutionalized technique by which class differences are reduced between non-related persons" (1953: 101).

5 It is interesting to note that some villagers blamed Zhao for sending the invitation in the first place, because they believed that it should have been completely up to the cadre to decide whether a return gift would be made. For detailed discussion of the case, see Yan 1996: 133–6.

6 For a detailed discussion of how cadres in the collectives controlled villagers by controlling and redistributing resources, see Oi 1989, especially pp. 132–42.

7 Interestingly enough, Blau makes this statement to explain tributary gifts to the chief, which, in his perspective, constitute upward one-way gift giving. But in order to support his general assumption that giving generates power, he takes this as "a notable exception to the principle that unilateral giving establishes superordination" (1964: 110).

8 For detailed discussions on the Chinese notion of *guanxi* (social connections or networks), see Kipnis 1997; Yang 1994; Yan 1996.

9 Japan may provide another example in this connection. For instance, Lebra (1969) questions the "equivalent return" in reciprocal relations by examining the repayment of Japanese *on* gifts (benevolent favors from superiors). She demonstrates that, given the hierarchical context of Japanese society, the gift-donor who is in a subordinate position can never balance the gift received from a superior. In "An Alternative Approach to Reciprocity" (1975), Lebra further argues that the exchange aspect of reciprocity is characterized by two strains: one toward symmetry and the other toward asymmetry, and she offers a more inclusive model of reciprocity which includes extra-dyadic relations.

References

Befu, Harumi. "Gift-giving and social reciprocity in Japan." *France-Asie* 21 (1966–7): 161–77.

Blau, Peter M. *Exchange and Power in Social Life*. New York: John Wiley, 1964.

Damon, F.H. "Alienating the inalienable." Correspondence. *Man* (NS) 17 (1982): 342–3.

—— "What moves the Kula: opening and closing gifts on Woodlark Island." In Jerry Leach and Edmund Leach (eds) *The Kula: New Perspectives on Massim Exchange*. Cambridge: Cambridge University Press, 1983, pp. 309–42.

Djilas, Milovan. *The New Class: An Analysis of the Communist System of Power*. New York: Praeger, 1957.

Emerson, Richard M. "Power-dependence relations." *American Sociological Review* 27.1 (1962): 31–41.

—— "Exchange theory." In J. Berger and M. Zelditch (eds) *Sociological Theory in Progress*. Boston: Houghton Mifflin, 1972, pp. 38–57.

Firth, Raymond. *Economics of the Zealand Maori*. Wellington, New Zealand: Government Printer, 1959.

Fried, Morton. *The Fabric of Chinese Society*. New York: Praeger, 1953.

Godelier, Maurice. *The Enigma of the Gift.* Trans. Nora Scott. Chicago: University of Chicago Press, 1999.

Gregory, C.A. "Gifts to men and gifts to God: gift exchange and capital accumulation in contemporary Papua." *Man* (NS) 15 (1980): 626–52.

—— *Gifts and Commodities.* London: Academic, 1982.

Homans, George. *Social Behavior: Its Elementary Forms.* New York: Harcourt Brace Jovanovich, 1974.

Hu, Hsien-chin. "The Chinese concept of face." *American Anthropologist* 46 (1944): 45–64.

Hwang, Kwang-kuo. "Face and favor: the Chinese power game." *American Journal of Sociology* 92 (1987): 944–74.

Kipnis, Andrew. *Producing Guanxi: Sentiment, Self, and Subculture in a North China Village.* Durham: Duke University Press, 1997.

Kornai, Janos. *Contradictions and Dilemmas: Studies on the Socialist Economy and Society.* Cambridge: MIT Press, 1986.

Leach, Edmund. *Political Systems of Highland Burma.* London: Athlone, 1954.

Lebra, Takie Sugiyama. "Reciprocity and the asymmetric principle: an analytical reappraisal of the Japanese concept of *On.*" *Psychologia* 12 (1969): 129–38.

—— "An alternative approach to reciprocity." *American Anthropologist* 77 (1975): 550–65.

Liep, John. "Gift exchange and the construction of identity." In Jukka Siikala (ed.) *Culture and History in the Pacific.* Helsinki: The Finnish Anthropological Society, 1990, pp. 164–83.

MacCormack, Geoffrey. "Mauss and the 'spirit' of the gift." *Oceania* 52 (1982): 286–93.

—— "Reciprocity." *Man* (NS) 11 (1976): 89–103.

Malinowski, Bronislaw. *Argonauts of the Western Pacific.* Prospect Heights, IL: Waveland, 1984 [1922].

—— *Crime and Custom in Savage Society.* Paterson, NJ: Littlefield, Adams, 1962 [1926].

Mauss, Marcel. *The Gift: The Form and Functions of Exchange in Archaic Societies.* Trans. Ian Cunnison. New York: Norton, 1967.

Nee, Victor. "A theory of market transition: from redistribution to markets in state socialism." *American Sociological Review* 54 (1989): 663–81.

Oi, Jean. *State and Peasant in Contemporary China: The Political Economy of Village Government.* Berkeley: University of California Press, 1989.

Parry, Jonathan. "*The Gift*, the Indian gift, and the 'Indian gift'." *Man* (NS) 21 (1986): 453–73.

Raheja, Gloria G. *The Poison in the Gift: Ritual, Prestation, and the Dominant Caste in a North Indian Village.* Chicago: University of Chicago Press, 1988.

Sahlins, Marshall. *Stone Age Economics.* New York: Aldine de Gruyter, 1972.

Strathern, Andrew. *The Rope of Moka.* Cambridge: Cambridge University Press, 1971.

Strathern, Marilyn. "Qualified value: the perspective of gift exchange." In Caroline Humphrey and Stephen Hugh-Jones (eds) *Barter, Exchange and Value, an Anthropological Approach.* Cambridge and New York: Cambridge University Press, 1992, pp. 169–91.

Szelenyi, Ivan. "Social inequalities under state socialist redistributive economies." *International Journal of Comparative Sociology* 1 (1978): 61–78.

Vatuk, Ved Prakash and Sylvia Vatuk. "The social context of gift exchange in North India." In Giri R. Gupta (ed.) *Family and Social Change in Modern India.* Durham, NC: Carolina Academic Press, 1971, pp. 207–32.

Walder, Andrew. "Organized dependency and cultures of authority in Chinese industry." *Journal of Asian Studies* 43.4 (1983): 51–76.

——— *Communist Neo-Traditionalism: Work and Authority in Chinese Industry*. Berkeley: University of California Press, 1986.

Weiner, Annette. *Inalienable Possessions: The Paradox of Keeping-While-Giving*. Berkeley: University of California Press, 1992.

Yan, Yunxiang. "The impact of rural reform on economic and social stratification in a Chinese village." *Australian Journal of Chinese Affairs* 27 (1992): 1–23.

——— "Everyday power relations: changes in a North China village." In Andrew Walder (ed.) *The Waning of the Communist State: Economic Origins of Political Decline in China and Hungary*. Berkeley: University of California Press, 1995, pp. 215–41.

——— *The Flow of Gifts: Reciprocity and Social Networks in a Chinese Village*. Stanford: Stanford University Press, 1996.

Yang, Lien-sheng. "The concept of 'pao' as a basis for social relations in China." In John K. Fairbank (ed.) *Chinese Thought and Institutions*. Chicago: University of Chicago Press, 1957, pp. 291–309.

Yang, Mayfair Mei-hui. *Gifts, Favors, Banquets: The Art of Social Relationships in China*. Ithaca: Cornell University Press, 1994.

3 Unpacking the gift

Illiquid goods and empathetic dialogue

Lee Anne Fennell

Introduction

In Western cultures dominated by market exchange, the gift is a conceptual misfit. The voluntary, unilateral act of bestowing something of value on another "has always posed a challenge to self-interest models of human behavior" (Frank 1992: 319). Perhaps not surprisingly, a tremendous scholarly emphasis has been placed on the role of reciprocity and exchange in gift giving (Mauss 1990; Blau 1964: 88–114; Baron 1989: 194–8; Rose 1992: 298–308). In this essay, I argue that notions of reciprocal exchange cannot adequately explain the practice of gift giving as it exists in modern Western societies. The shortcomings of the exchange account of gift giving can be seen most clearly when one considers personal gifts between individuals. Such gifts are the focus of this essay.[1] Gift giving in this context undeniably generates benefits for both donor and recipient, but it does so in a manner qualitatively different from that in other exchange transactions. I focus on two related characteristics of gift giving – illiquidity and empathetic dialogue – to explore these unique contributions of the gift.

I begin with the observation that the prototypical Western gift involves the intentional conversion of a generalized medium of exchange – cash – into an illiquid object, based upon imperfect information about the preferences of the intended recipient. The conversion of money into a difficult-to-sell object would be nonsensical as an opening move in a market exchange, given the high probability that the item selected will have less economic value to the recipient than would the original cash (Waldfogel 1993; E. Posner 1997: 572). Moreover, the expected reciprocation would likewise take the form of an illiquid good chosen under conditions of relative ignorance. Such a cumbersome and wasteful exchange transaction would seem to be unthinkable in an economically advanced society with well-developed markets and a generalized medium of exchange. Nevertheless, gift giving persists as an institution, complete with unwritten rules and conventions that are followed with remarkable consistency (Caplow 1984). What we need is a new vocabulary for understanding gift giving as it is practiced in modern Western societies. Instead of attempting to conflate gift giving and market exchange, such a vocabulary would focus on the characteristics of gifts that set them apart from ordinary commodities.

Two characteristics of gifts are particularly salient in this context – the illiquidity that gifts exhibit, and the empathetic dialogue that they embody and perpetuate. An examination of gift-giving practices shows that gifts are not treated as ordinary commodities, but are instead intentionally withdrawn from the stream of commerce. A gift's former commodity status is overwritten by layers of personal meaning and symbolically effaced through such measures as wrapping and removal of price tags (Belk 1993: 90; Carrier 1995: 174–5). This process of decommodification reinforces and contributes to the illiquidity of gifted items.

I posit that this illiquidity, which casts doubt on the treatment of gift giving as a utility-maximizing market exchange, also provides the key to understanding the human utility functions actually served by gift interactions. Such illiquidity becomes not only explicable but indispensable when gift giving is cast not as a market transaction, but as a specialized form of communication (Caplow 1984: 1320–2). Because an illiquid object carries far more communicative potential than cash, gifts of money are often deemed unacceptable (Webley *et al.* 1983; Douglas and Isherwood 1979: 58–9; Eisenberg 1997: 845). I argue that money cannot be a successful gift in the absence of some explicit or implicit limitations on its use. Illiquidity, whether inherent in the gifted object or socially constructed through the conditions and relationship giving rise to the gift, is essential to the performance of the gift's communicative function.

Next I consider the nature and function of the specialized communication effected through gift interactions. I suggest that in the idealized gift situation, this communication can be conceived as an empathetic dialogue between donor and recipient that can deepen and sustain the parties' relationship. In selecting a suitable gift, the donor puts herself in the place of the recipient and tries to determine not what the recipient would purchase for himself, but what the recipient would most want to receive from this particular donor. The recipient, in turn, imaginatively recreates the donor's empathetic efforts in selecting the gift (Cheal 1988: 63). Through the operation of this empathetic dialogue, a gift can gain "sentimental value" above and beyond the market value of the underlying commodity. However, lack of empathetic imagination on the part of either party can cause the gift to fail, as can manifestations of imaginative exercises inappropriate to the relationship.

I conclude by exploring the human utility functions served by gift giving. These, I suggest, are closely linked to the notion of empathetic dialogue. The giving and getting of gifts taps into certain desires that are rarely discussed by scholars: the desire to identify with another; the desire to have one's true preferences divined by another (when those preferences may not even be clear to oneself); the desire to surprise and to be surprised. The communicative ritual of gift giving also serves game-theoretic purposes, acting both as a signaling device to transmit perceptions and intentions regarding the relationship, and as a screening mechanism that discourages the continuation of relationships in which empathetic dialogue between the parties is absent or untenable.

Reconsidering the exchange model of gift giving

The model of the self-interested, mutually advantageous market transaction is pervasive in our culture (Radin 1987: 1859–63). The gift, taken at face value, is a purely gratuitous unilateral transfer that cannot easily be assimilated into this framework (Rose 1992: 298). Theoretical approaches that emphasize the reciprocal nature of gift giving seem to provide an attractive means of reconciling this apparent anomaly. Gifts, such theories suggest, are not really gratuitous at all (Rose 1992: 298–302). The gift interaction is instead presented as a type of exchange, a slow-motion value-for-value transaction (Bourdieu 1977: 171, quoted in Appadurai 1986: 12). Although the law treats gifts differently from the way it treats exchanges, other disciplines typically equate the two (Baron 1989: 194).

The idea that successful gifts can generate returns for the giver is uncontroversial, at least if one adopts a sufficiently broad definition of what counts as a return. For example, non-material or intangible goods may be involved in the gift interaction (Baron 1989: 195). In return for a gift, a donor might receive appreciation, gratitude, affection, loyalty, love, respect, power, status, understanding or simply the knowledge that she has pleased another person. Jacques Derrida has more broadly asserted that the mere perception of a gift as a gift by either the donor or the donee generates a symbolic return that effectively cancels the gift (1992: 13–14). The fact that people generally "get something" out of the gifts they give does not, however, demonstrate that gift giving can be meaningfully or accurately equated with a market transaction. The reciprocal exchange model, for all its conceptual elegance, simply cannot be squared with gift-giving practices in modern Western society (Camerer 1989: S181).

The model's lack of explanatory force becomes apparent when one considers the gift's typical incarnation as an illiquid item that was purchased for cash by the donor expressly for the purpose of gift giving. A completely liquid commodity would enable the recipient to pursue most efficiently her optimal consumption pattern, and would also respect her autonomy as a consumer (Mack 1989: 209). Thus, other things being equal, one would expect a rational recipient to value cash more highly than any other item which could be bestowed on her.[2] We find support for this intuition in Joel Waldfogel's (1993) study of the valuation of gifts by Yale undergraduates. Waldfogel found that students judged the economic value of the Christmas gifts they received to be significantly lower than the amount of money spent to purchase them, resulting in a "deadweight loss."[3] If a gift interaction is characterized as an exchange, the conversion of a liquid asset into an illiquid one would seem most irrational. It is costly to the donor and needlessly reduces the value transferred to the recipient, thus also reducing the expected return to the donor.

A deeper problem lurks just behind this matter of illiquidity. I have just suggested that a donor could maximize her own return, as well as the utility of the other party, by giving cash. However, a cash-for-cash "exchange" would be utterly pointless. Giving cash as the first half of an exchange would seem to make more economic sense, but only if one could specify what one would then receive in return. In a gift setting this would be impossible, yet in the marketplace it could be handled with great efficiency. So why resort to gift giving at all, if exchange is really the point?

In cultures without a well-developed monetary system, the reciprocal provision of goods in-kind clearly serves an economic function. Marcel Mauss suggests that the gift-reciprocation cycles found in Polynesia, Melanesia and certain Native American economies of the American Northwest constitute "the market as it existed before the institution of traders and before their main invention – money proper" (1990: 4; see Camerer 1989: S181). Money stores value over time, rendering in-kind trades based on temporal exigencies obsolete, and it provides each consumer with the most efficient means possible of directly pursuing her individual consumption goals. Markets, furthermore, provide an efficient means of matching buyers and sellers. Where money and markets are available, reciprocal in-kind transfers are both unnecessary and wasteful from an economic standpoint. Incurring costs to convert cash into illiquid gift items is an extraordinarily clumsy and ineffective way of seeking to satisfy one's preferences, as no conceivable reciprocal gift can match the efficiency of simply taking one's cash into the marketplace.

This question of motivation is pointedly raised by Eric Mack, who ponders why he chose to purchase a hand-selected sweater for his wife's Christmas present rather than giving her a gift certificate or an envelope filled with cash (1989: 209–10). The choice of the sweater appears irrational in economic terms; the envelope of cash would have been "the alternative that would most fully have economized on my shopping time while also most fully preserving her consumer sovereignty" (1989: 209). The explanation for such gift-giving behavior is not obvious, nor can it be found by examining ordinary market transactions. The expectation of a reciprocal gift does not offer a credible motive. A gift is given with full knowledge that the recipient will not simply hand back the cash value of the item, nor even the (presumably lower) cash equivalent of the recipient's subjective valuation of the item. Instead, the recipient, if she chooses to reciprocate at all, will herself convert liquid resources into another illiquid item to transfer back to the original donor. Both parties usually spend additional resources on extras such as giftwrapping and gift cards, and sometimes even plan celebrations to showcase the gift giving. These also are pointless and inexplicable from the narrowly economic perspective of economic exchange.

Unless one looks beyond conventional notions of economic valuation, Waldfogel's notion of a "deadweight loss" associated with ritualized rounds of gift giving appears quite apt. David Cheal's suggestion that reciprocal gifts could effectively cancel each other out, yielding no net benefit to either party (1988: 13), does not put the matter nearly strongly enough. Claude Lévi-Strauss's assessment of the Christmas gift exchange as "a vast and collective destruction of wealth" (1969: 56) is closer to the mark. If one focuses exclusively on the exchanged items as commodities, it is apparent that a donor cannot expect to break even by purchasing a gift for a friend, and would be much better off simply keeping the cash in her pocket (E. Posner 1997: 572). People are clearly not in the game for the commodity value of the items exchanged; they must have powerful alternative motivations to counterbalance the economic losses they incur by engaging in gift giving.

One might protest that focusing on the actual items exchanged misses the point entirely. For example, Jane Baron maintains that "gift-exchange can be characterized as a non-commodity market which functions in the affective realm in much the same way as commodity markets function in the conventional economic realm" (1989: 197). In other words, one might argue that people are only nominally trading objects, and that the real exchange is taking place in the realm of the emotions. The question then becomes whether the market metaphor is a helpful way of conceptualizing what is actually happening between the parties when they give each other gifts. Putting aside the question of whether it makes any sense to think of people "trading" emotions with each other in a market-oriented manner, it is unclear why such emotional trades would be accompanied by illiquid gift items. If the gift items are completely superfluous, then their presence in a market exchange would be most odd. If they are part of the value being exchanged, then the question of their illiquidity reappears.

The market metaphor simply cannot adequately account for the intentional illiquidity of gift items. Plainly, something more is going on. To understand what that might be, it is worthwhile to consider the ways in which gifts are set apart from ordinary commodities.

Gifts and wrappings

Modern gift objects usually begin their lives as commodities (Appadurai 1986: 13–16). The giver, in selecting, purchasing and giving a gift, effectively removes the item from the stream of commerce. This gift-selection and gift-giving process "singularizes" the item so that it is no longer a fungible commodity (Kopytoff 1986: 73–7), though it may remain eligible for eventual return to commodity status (Appadurai 1986: 13–16). Thus, the gift can be thought of as a good so thoroughly wrapped in layers of personal involvement and sentiment that it has at least temporarily lost its identity as an article of commerce. The item chosen may itself be well suited to this extra-commercial role: "By having presents be frivolous, luxurious or otherwise special, they are distinguished from the concern for ordinary utilities that leads people to purchase commodities more routinely" (Carrier 1995: 174).

The literal wrapping of gifts in brightly colored paper and bows serves to symbolize this overlay of sentiment and to set the item apart from the ordinary stream of commerce (Carrier 1995: 174–5; Searle-Chatterjee 1993: 184–5). Giftwrap thus communicates "the personal bond between the giver and the gift, and the magical function of the gift" (Lévi-Strauss 1969: 56). As Caplow found in his study of Christmas giving in Muncie, Indiana ("Middletown"), there is virtually absolute compliance with what he terms "The Wrapping Rule" (1984: 1310–11). The removal of the price tag may likewise serve as a ritual cleansing of marketplace influences (Belk 1993: 90). Even gifts of money are almost always camouflaged with a gift card or placed within a special gift container, such as an ornate box (Searle-Chatterjee 1993: 185; Zelizer 1994: 105–7).

Despite such wrappings, once a present is opened, its status as a former and potential article of commerce is readily apparent. Yet invisible layers of "giftness" arising out of the relationship in which the gift was given still distinguish it from an ordinary commodity. These attributes give gift items sentimental value above and beyond the cash value of the item in question. If these intangible "wrappings" are stripped away, the gift becomes a mere commodity again that may be reintroduced into the stream of commerce. This can happen in several ways. First, the recipient may simply reject the intangible sentiment that accompanies a gift. If the recipient refuses to accept the gift, the giver may then attempt to return the item to the place where it was purchased for a refund. Or the recipient may flagrantly violate the gift nature of an item by immediately reselling it like any other commodity (Eisenberg 1997: 844). A gift may also lose its sentimental "wrappings" if it is stolen or lost; a thief or finder interested only in its resale value will readily reintroduce it into the flow of commerce. The emotional packaging of a gift may simply wither away as those directly implicated in the relationship which gave rise to it die or forget the gift's origins. Many of the personal items found in estate sales doubtless fall into this category.

More dramatically, a gift's "wrappings" may be torn away when the underlying relationship that gave the gift its meaning is dissolved or destroyed. The result is often that the former gift is reintroduced into the marketplace. For example, in the movie *La Promesse*, a young boy who has been forced to act against his conscience by his despicable father decides to sell a ring which his father has given him and which is identical to a ring worn by the father. The price named by the merchant is obviously lower than the boy expected, yet the boy agrees to the sale with hardly a murmur. The relationship that the ring represents no longer holds value for the boy, he can tolerate the loss necessary to convert the ring into cash. Indeed, the ring in its present form is morally toxic; the boy is well rid of the thing, at whatever price.

Although former gifts may be returned to the stream of commerce in such cases, it is apparent that gifted items are not intended to confer wealth on the other party in the manner of an ordinary commodity. Instead, the intent is to add richness and depth to the recipient's life, and by extension, to the donor's life as well. A better way of conceptualizing the giving of gifts is as a specialized form of symbolic communication, complete with its own linguistic rules (Caplow 1984: 1320–2). Viewed in this light, a gift acts primarily as a vehicle for dialogue between the parties rather than as a commodity in its own right (Douglas and Isherwood 1979: 62). The reciprocal gift replies to the prior gift. If the value of the prior gift is roughly matched, that is a function of the recipient's desire to give an appropriate gift within the context of the dialogue rather than an attempt to pay for the prior gift or wipe out a debt. Yet the transferred objects are far from irrelevant. Instead, they serve as "markers" or "tie-signs" that link the giver and the recipient to each other and provide evidence about their relationship (Douglas and Isherwood 1979: 74–5; Cheal 1988: 22, citing Goffman 1971: 194–9). Significantly, the communicative capacity of gifts stems from the very illiquidity that makes implausible a "market exchange" explanation for modern gift giving.

Illiquid goods in a cash economy

Gifts lack the "pure potentiality" of money (Simmel 1990: 218). They are not intended for resale on the open market, nor are they designed to make the recipient wealthier in monetary terms. A tribal saying related by Lewis Hyde remains apt: "One man's gift must not be another man's capital" (1983: 4). Usually the illiquidity is a direct function of the item given. Gifts are often tangible objects for which there is no adequate secondary market. Sometimes, as with gifts of food, drink or entertainment, the illiquidity is virtually absolute. The item must be enjoyed by its recipient, given to another person immediately or discarded altogether (Hyde 1983: 8). Gift certificates allow the recipient some degree of choice, but are still quite illiquid since they specify the store from which the gift must be selected (Zelizer 1994: 109). Likewise, the ability to exchange an item for a different size or color merely converts the original gift into a different illiquid object or into the relatively illiquid potentiality of store credit.

In contrast, other types of "voluntary" transfers, notably bribes, kickbacks, blackmail payoffs and "protection" money, are usually marked by the extreme liquidity of the transferred commodity. While other commodities are sometimes used, the anonymity and impersonality of cash is usually preferred in such transactions (Simmel 1990: 384–9; Noonan 1984: xxi). This tendency suits the nature of the transaction. As Simmel explains,

> Money, more than any other form of value, makes possible the secrecy, invisibility and silence of exchange. By compressing money into a piece of paper, by letting it glide into a person's hand, one can make him a wealthy person. … Its anonymity and colourlessness does not reveal the source from which it came to the present owner: it does not have a certificate of origin in the way in which, more or less disguised, many concrete objects of possession do.
>
> (1990: 385)

When one's purposes are illicit, a silent, secretive transaction that leaves behind no traces is ideal (Noonan 1984: 697). With a gift, these priorities are reversed. One wishes to give an object that will speak to the recipient and that will be strongly and permanently identified with the donor and the relationship. Because they are uniquely linked to the donor and to the donor's relationship with the recipient, gifted objects are non-fungible and literally irreplaceable, even when a physically identical replacement is available on the open market (Carrier 1995: 28).

The need for human interactions involving non-fungible items is undoubtedly heightened in a modern cash-based economy characterized by a multitude of anonymous, indifferent market transactions. Today's market transactions usually involve an end-user who is separated by thousands of miles and many intermediaries from the manufacturer or producer, with money and goods passing between buyers and sellers in a far more alienated and impersonal manner than was the case prior to the eighteenth century (Carrier 1995: 74–83). Thus Ralph Waldo Emerson's essay, "Gifts" (1983), expresses reservations about the effects of rising commercialism on gift giving, finding it "a cold, lifeless business when you go to the shops to buy me something, which does not represent your life and talent, but a goldsmith's" (1983: 536; see also Carrier 1995: 147–8).

Because few modern givers can manage to make their own gifts, the representation of self must be achieved through the process of choosing a gift. James Carrier observes that shopping allows individuals the opportunity to "transform things from a part of the indifferent mass of commodities in the store to the special things that reflect the shopper and the social relations in which the shopper is located" (1995: 178). Retailers may attempt to facilitate this process of appropriation by presenting goods as if they have been specially hand-crafted or uniquely designed with a particular type of recipient in mind. This is one variation of the strategy noted by Appadurai, which "consists in taking what are often perfectly ordinary, mass-produced, cheap, even shoddy, products and making them seem somehow (in Simmel's sense) desirable-yet-reachable" (1986: 55). Such pitches are attractive, despite their transparency, because they suggest that the items embody the kind of detailed knowledge of an individual that is present in the best of gift giving.

Cash is often unacceptable as a personal gift (Webley *et al.* 1983; Douglas and Isherwood 1979: 58–9; Eisenberg 1997: 845). If gifts are primarily valued for the imaginative effort that goes into choosing them and the communicative weight that they carry, the shortcomings of a monetary gift are obvious. Hazel Anderson, the subject of one of David Cheal's case studies, articulates the point perfectly in discussing her gifts to elderly people: "I never give them money because it's the thought of me choosing something for them and me thinking of them that is significant to them. And even if it's little, if it's cookies I bake, that's way more important to them than giving them the money" (Cheal 1988: 63). Webley *et al.*'s study of the gift-giving preferences of undergraduate students, and the gift-receiving preferences of their mothers, supports this intuition. The students indicated an overwhelming preference for purchasing a hand-selected gift for their mothers rather than giving a check (1983: 227). When mothers were asked what gift they would most like to receive from their offspring, they again expressed an overwhelming preference for hand-selected gifts (1983: 235).

There are, of course, some circumstances in which money can be an acceptable gift (Burgoyne and Routh 1991; Carrier 1995: 172–3). Burgoyne and Routh's study found that money may appropriately be used for intrafamilial gifts from older relatives to younger ones, but never from members of younger generations to their elders. Among peers within a social circle, however, a gift of money is considered vulgar (Douglas and Isherwood 1979: 59). Money would be deeply offensive as a gift between romantic partners, as it unavoidably evokes the anonymous and indifferent exchange involved in prostitution (Simmel 1990: 376–7). An exception to this would obtain if the money could be clearly earmarked for a particular personalized use, such as a plane ticket to visit the donor.

This "earmarking" exception points to a larger observation: where money is deemed an acceptable present, there are always implicit or explicit constraints on what it may be used to purchase. Viviana Zelizer's study of monetary gifts in the years between the 1870s and 1930s (1994: 71–118) supports this principle, and gifts of money continue to carry restrictions today. In some settings, the intended use of the gifted money is self-evident. The ritual of "presentation" at weddings, practiced by the Winnipeg families in David Cheal's study, involves gifts of money that are calculated to cover the cost of the wedding celebration itself (Cheal 1988: 133–4). In settings where the donor's expectations are not apparent, it is generally agreed that a monetary gift has failed if it is simply deposited into the recipient's bank account and spent on humdrum everyday expenses such as gasoline, stamps and paper towels (Zelizer 1994: 84, 111). Significantly, many recipients of monetary gifts are young children who would otherwise have few opportunities to make selections for themselves and who would not be in a position to use the money for ordinary household expenses. Instead, the gift of money invites the recipient to realize her emerging preferences, to "go pick out something you like." There may also be implicit limits on the types of items one can appropriately purchase with gifted money (Zelizer 1994: 111–12). A young person receiving a gift of money from a teetotalling aunt could not, without violating the spirit of the gift, use it to finance a drinking binge.

All gifts of money, if they are successful, involve a socially constructed element of illiquidity. Gifted money, as distinguished from charity or the provision of basic financial support, is to be earmarked for something special. The "wrapping" of gift money in a gift card and the ritual of presenting it to the recipient along with written or spoken expressions of love and goodwill set it apart from the ordinary mass of money sitting in the recipient's bank account. The convention of writing a thank-you note describing the use made of a monetary gift helps to enforce this implicit illiquidity (Zelizer 1994: 111, 116). Even when a recipient is in dire financial straits, it would be highly unacceptable to write a thank-you note pointing out the money's utility in staving off eviction or starvation. Instead, a recipient might describe the article of clothing, the book, the amusement park tickets or the flowers purchased with the gifted money. In so doing, the recipient allows the donor to participate imaginatively in her life much as if a hand-selected gift had been given.

Empathetic dialogue

As explored in this essay, a true gift embodies and perpetuates empathetic dialogue between giver and recipient, facilitating and documenting each party's imaginative participation in the life of the other.[4] The donor's exercise of empathy and imagination in selecting an appropriate gift is answered by the recipient's empathetic identification with the donor's gift-selection efforts. Such empathetic dialogue is intrinsically valuable as a form of communication between parties, and is also instrumental in developing significant relationships.

This feature is notably absent in other transfers of illiquid goods, such as in-kind payments of food stamps to welfare recipients, used property donated to a charity or store credit bestowed upon a complaining customer. Because such transfers typically do not involve the giver's empathetic identification with the recipient's true desires, their illiquidity serves only to restrict the recipient's exercise of autonomy. In the case of in-kind payments to welfare recipients, the interference with autonomy is quite intentional. By specifying what can and cannot be purchased with public assistance, donor-taxpayers communicate their doubts about the decision-making capacities of the recipients (R. Posner 1998: 511). As Alan Schrift observes, our society "views public assistance to its least advantaged members as an illegitimate gift that results in an unjustifiable social burden" (1997: 19). Taxpayer-donors react to this perceived illegitimacy by attaching conditions and restrictions that reduce the value of the benefit to the recipient and stigmatize the transfer (Piven and Cloward 1987: 85–7).

In contrast, a true gift engages both giver and recipient in empathetic mutual identification, the giver seeking to fulfill the recipient's true preferences and the recipient envisioning the giver's imaginative effort in selecting and giving the gift. To choose a gift, the donor imaginatively puts herself in the position of the recipient, seeking to discern preferences of which the recipient may not even be fully aware. The donor's task is not to determine what the recipient would purchase for himself with an equivalent amount of cash, but to divine what the recipient would most wish to receive as a gift within the specific framework of the relationship. People wish to receive gifts that appropriately reflect the relationship as well as the individual identities of the donor and recipient. In selecting a gift, the donor must also take into account certain higher-order preferences held by the recipient – preferences about preferences (Sunstein 1989: 285; McCloskey 1998: 32; Hirschman 1984). This requires considerable insight into the dynamics of the recipient's evolving identity. For example, a recipient without any current appreciation for jazz might nevertheless wish to become the kind of person who would enjoy jazz. Such a person would view a jazz collection as a particularly insightful gift, because it would demonstrate the donor's recognition of the recipient's interest in a specific form of self-transformation.

Most people also have a positive preference for being pleasantly surprised by a gift. A good gift is something like an act of recognition, in which the donor makes her knowledge of the recipient known to the recipient, who in turn may come to recognize something new about herself, or the donor, or the relationship. The desire to surprise and to be surprised arises out of this deeper desire to know and be known by another. It is impossible to go out into the marketplace and surprise oneself with an unexpectedly apt gift, and equally foolhardy to hire a stranger to do the surprising. The experience of a perfect surprise – a gift both wholly unexpected and wholly suitable – is possible only when one engages in a gift interaction with a person who is reasonably aware of one's preferences and who is willing to expend imaginative effort in choosing a gift (E. Posner 2000: 53; Camerer 1988: S193–4).

When a gift succeeds, the material object stands as a place marker for the empathetic dialogue that accompanied it (see Douglas and Isherwood 1979: 74). In this way, objects can gain sentimental value and a status that transcends the marketplace. Because of the sentimental wrappings that set gifts apart from ordinary commodities, gifted items may be valued at either more or less than fair market value. The emotional valence of a gift is not apparent from an examination of the gift object in isolation; rather, the gift serves a "totemic" function, triggering a stream of emotional associations (Eisenberg 1997: 844). As the term "sentimental value" suggests, these associations can add positive value to an item, perhaps causing it to be assessed at far more than its replacement value. For example, the narrator of Laurence Sterne's novel *A Sentimental Journey* (1987) describes his attachment to a relatively valueless horn snuffbox given to him by a monk: "I guard this box, as I would the instrumental parts of my religion, to help my mind on to something better: in truth, I seldom go abroad without it; and oft and many a time have called up by it the courteous spirit of its owner to regulate my own" (1987: 44).

The obverse side of sentimental value explains why a person might refuse an item of positive monetary value that has been offered gratis (Eisenberg 1997: 844–5). The argument that the gift implicitly obligates the recipient to respond in kind provides only a partial reason, for a recipient could ignore this obligation and the giver would have no legal recourse. It is instead the desire to cut off an unacceptable or inappropriate empathetic dialogue that prompts the refusal of gifts. For example, a young woman who receives a gift of lingerie from a man she barely knows would probably feel compelled to reject the gift, even if the clothing would otherwise please her (see Zelizer 1994: 99–100). The refusal may be only partly due to a fear that the man would demand some sort of repayment for his generosity. The intuition that using such garments would be deeply inappropriate stems primarily from the empathetic dialogue that would thereby be reinforced and perpetuated. In wearing the lingerie, the woman would be forced to recall the man's selection of the items for her, doubtless prompted by his imaginative projection of the woman wearing the items. Worse, the woman would be aware of the man's awareness that she retained the items and was at times wearing them, further prompting his continued acts of imaginative participation in her life.

Even the most well-intentioned donor may make serious errors in choosing gifts by failing to predict accurately the type of gift that the recipient would want to receive from her. Whether due to misperceptions about the relationship or lack of information about the recipient's preferences, such miscalculations can result in valueless or even repugnant gifts (Cheal 1988: 13). Alternatively, the recipient may misunderstand the empathetic import of the gift and misgauge the imaginative work involved in its selection. For example, a donor might select sweat socks in order to accentuate and celebrate the recipient's athletic tendencies. In picking out the socks, the giver might envision the recipient wearing them on early morning jogs, the extra-thick cotton providing optimal cushioning as he bounds along a scenic stretch of pavement. The recipient, on the other hand, might be extremely sensitive about foot odor and might view the gift as an insulting suggestion that he change his socks more frequently. He might bitterly chalk up the selection of extra-thick socks to the donor's calculations as to the quantity of sweat produced by his malodorous feet.

The potential for misunderstanding is great, just as it is in any conversation. Indeed, the misimpression created by a gift may be especially difficult to correct. If a recipient observes the convention of expressing gratitude for the gift, the donor may not even be aware that a misunderstanding has taken place. However, the iterative nature of gift interactions provides opportunities for clarification and restatement. Moreover, even when a donor's communicative intent is properly conveyed through a gift, the other party's response is by no means a foregone conclusion. As in a conversation, the possibilities are virtually limitless, and the potential for pleasant surprises and disappointments are also quite palpable. The conversation may continue, or there may be long silences, whether comfortable or uncomfortable. The work of the gift may be accomplished only years or decades later, after all opportunity to continue a dialogue with the original giver has been lost. In such instances, the empathetic dialogue may be continued in other directions by, for example, passing the gift along to one's own children.

Understanding gift giving as a specialized form of conversation provides a richer and more convincing explanation for reciprocity than accounts based on exchange can provide. As Camerer explains,

> gift giving will often be reciprocal (though not always), because gifts are meant to spur investments that are reciprocal. However, the reciprocity involved here is very different from the reciprocity that is so important in anthropological accounts. Potential mates or partners hope courtship gift giving is reciprocal, because in my model it takes two people to make a relationship. In the anthropological accounts, reciprocity is important because gifts are like loans rather than signals.
>
> (1988: S183)

The "reciprocal investments" of which Camerer speaks are personal investments in relationships. In an ideal relationship, reciprocal gifts will provide vehicles for an ongoing empathetic dialogue between the parties. When gifts are not given, are given inappropriately, or are not reciprocated, it may mean that one party's investment in the relationship is inappropriate or missing. This potential for gifts to provide meaningful cues as to a relationship's viability is the subject of the next section.

Signaling and screening

Gift giving, like any dialogue, is both iterative and interactive. The actions of each party are determined in part by the prior actions (and expected future actions) of the other party. Gift giving can thus be thought of as a type of game interaction, with the parties making discrete moves according to a ritualized pattern (Cheal 1988: 121). Thinking of gift giving in game-theoretic terms does not mean that the parties are acting in a cold or calculating way. On the contrary, the giving and getting of gifts can foster communication and empathy between the parties. Unlike tit-for-tat business arrangements in which each apparent favor is repaid by another of equal value (Frank 1992: 323–4), the moves made by parties in a gift interaction relate to larger emotional stakes that far transcend the value of the items exchanged. The two related concepts of signaling and screening are particularly relevant in this context (Camerer 1988; E. Posner 1997: 579–82).

In game interactions, each player's moves will be in part determined by what he expects the other player to do. For example, if one party can believably convey a willingness to cooperate, then the other party is more likely to make a cooperative move. The problem with simply telling the other party that one intends to cooperate is that this information cannot be verified. Signaling occurs "when those who possess nonverifiable information can convey that information in the way they choose their actions" (Baird *et al.* 1994: 123; see Frank 1988: 96–113). The old adage "actions speak louder than words" reflects the intuition that such action-based signaling is considered more reliable than a non-verifiable representation. Likewise, the expression "talk is cheap" reflects the problem with representations that are not backed by a personal investment from the person making the communication.[5] Gifts act as powerful signals because of the time, effort and thought that they are usually believed to represent – factors that indicate a real investment in the message the gift is conveying (Camerer 1988: S195; E. Posner 2000: 53).

In the gift context, the non-verifiable information in question usually relates to the donor's perception of the recipient, the donor's feelings for the recipient, or the donor's intentions for the relationship. For example, proclamations of eternal love and statements of intent to marry are notoriously unverifiable, but a gift of a diamond engagement ring is generally accepted as a reliable signal of intent. The reason the ring works so well as a signal relates partly to the cultural meaning assigned to it, but also to the relatively large commitment of resources it embodies. Jewelers cleverly frame this financial commitment in terms of labor, suggesting that men spend two months' salary on an engagement ring (see Camerer 1988: S194). Presumably, nobody would devote two months of hard work to something unless he was truly serious about it.

While it is possible that someone could give a diamond engagement ring without the requisite level of sincere emotion behind it, the signal satisfies what Robert Frank terms "the costly-to-fake principle" (1988: 99–101). According to Frank, "[f]or a signal between adversaries to be credible, it must be costly (or, more generally, difficult) to fake" (1988: 99). It may seem odd to cast a romantic couple as "adversaries," but the "costly-to-fake" signal is necessary in that context precisely because there is a significant risk that the partners' interests may not be in alignment. Camerer discusses the stereotypical formulation of the situation, in which the expensive gifts of an "earnest young suitor" serve to differentiate him from the "lusty bachelor" (1988: S183).

Signaling takes place with smaller gifts as well. One may doubt the sincerity of an apology, but one is more likely to credit an apology accompanied by flowers or foods that are favorites of the recipient because of the signaling involved in taking time, effort and money to select or prepare the gift. Likewise, the practice of regularly giving gifts to a family member on her birthday and at Christmas more persuasively signals one's interest in the recipient and one's desire to remain involved in her life than would an oral or written statement to the same effect (see Douglas and Isherwood 1979: 75). Parents may signal their understanding and appreciation of their children's unique interests and talents by selecting gifts that fit each specific child. For example, a father's gift of art supplies to his daughter might signal his intent to support and foster her interest in the visual arts. While it may well be "the thought that counts," thoughts are not only unverifiable, but also often inarticulable. A gift or a card may be a crutch in signaling one's thoughts, but it is a socially useful one.

"Screening" is in many ways the converse of signaling. According to game theory, "[s]creening takes place when the uninformed players can choose actions that lead informed players to act in a way that reveals information" (Baird *et al.* 1994: 123). The action chosen by the uninformed player in this interaction may represent a simple calling of the other player's bluff, or it may involve construction of a situation in which the other player is forced to make a choice of some sort. For example, a woman who demands an expensive diamond engagement ring before she will take seriously a promise to marry may be able screen out suitors who might otherwise lie about their intentions. She may also, intentionally or unintentionally, screen out the insolvent and those who are repelled by materialism.

Screening in gift interactions rarely takes the form of such a simple ultimatum, however. Instead, it often inheres in the building of a relationship in which gift giving would ordinarily be expected in some specified situation. The recipient's own past gifts to the putative donor may be instrumental in creating such a situation. For example, if a woman picks out a special gift for her friend's fortieth birthday – say, skydiving lessons – she may expect her friend to reciprocate with a similarly suitable gift when her own fortieth birthday rolls around. This circumstance is not necessarily the result of an acquisitive nature; rather, it may be the desire to continue the empathetic dialogue nurtured by the earlier gift. All the same, the arrival of the second woman's fortieth birthday is significant. If her friend forgets the birthday altogether, or if she gives something inexpensive and mundane, such as a potted plant, the relationship may well be threatened. If the friend chooses something that suggests she is not particularly aware of her friend's individual preferences and interests – such as tickets to see a long-running musical that the other finds utterly banal – it may trigger a reconsideration of the relationship.

While it may well seem childish to allow any relationship's fate to turn on the specific items given and received as gifts, the signaling and screening functions performed by gifts have clear social utility. Interestingly, failed gifts as well as successful ones are essential to these signaling and screening processes. These mechanisms help people to determine where relationships are going and whether they are worth pursuing or continuing, and may prompt the abandonment of relationships in which the capacity for empathetic dialogue between the parties is stunted or absent. This is socially significant, for mutual empathy and identification are indispensable to stable relationships.

Conclusion

People enter gift interactions for reasons unrelated to ordinary market exchange. The market itself provides a most efficient means of matching consumers with desired goods, making resort to illiquid gift items inexplicable and unnecessary in the context of economic exchange. Because market-oriented terms cannot describe the gift's function, we require alternative conceptual formulations to illuminate the gift's unique role. Two features that set the gift apart from ordinary market transactions – illiquidity and empathetic dialogue – offer the basis for such a new vocabulary. The gift's illiquidity and potential for facilitating empathetic dialogue offer opportunities for meaningful human connection that market exchange cannot provide.

However mass-produced and materialistic modern gifts may seem, they remain indispensable to the emotional and social lives of human beings. Words cannot fully convey all the sentiments that people wish to share. Half in desperation and half in hope, we reach out to the objects at hand. We giftwrap these items, plucked from the stream of commerce, layering them with individualized sentiment and meaning. When the effort is successful, the result is a true gift that can create or solidify a relationship of mutual identification and empathy.

Notes

1 My use of the term "gift" in this essay denotes only social or personal gifts, and excludes many other categories of gratuitous transfers, such as donations to charities, bonuses and gifts given to employees by their employers, gifts between business associates, gifts of financial support, and transfers of assets upon or in anticipation of death. Gift giving in these other contexts presents somewhat different sets of motivations and characteristics, some of which have been analyzed elsewhere (e.g., E. Posner 2000: 49–67; Katz 2000: 7–14; Rose 1992: 303–5).

2 However, it is possible that a donor could select a gift that a recipient would actually prefer over the equivalent cash, because markets are imperfect and consumers are not uniformly informed about the goods that are available (or even about their own preferences) (Waldfogel 1993: 1330; Camerer 1988: S194, n. 13).

3 Waldfogel's methodology and conclusions have been criticized (Solnick and Hemenway 1996; Eisenberg 1997: 846, n. 63). Significantly, his survey respondents were directed to disregard any sentimental value associated with the gifts they received (Waldfogel 1993: 1331), a fact that significantly limits the value of his conclusions (Eisenberg 1997: 846).

4 This is, of course, an intentionally idealized image of the gift. For example, I do not discuss humiliating or manipulative "gifts" – not because I think such elements are non-existent, but because I do not think that they align with our culture's

understanding of the term "gift." Empathetic dialogue provides a benchmark by which the success of a gift *as a gift* may be assessed. As I discuss later in the essay, gifts given without some minimal level of empathy and imagination are likely to fail; thus gifts act as signals to assist people in ordering their relationships with others.

5   "Cheap talk" does not present a problem, however, when neither party has an incentive to be untruthful (Farrell and Rabin 1996).

References

Appadurai, Arjun. "Introduction: commodities and the politics of value." In Arjun Appadurai (ed.) *The Social Life of Things: Commodities in Cultural Perspective*. Cambridge: Cambridge University Press, 1986, pp. 3–63.

Baird, Douglas G., Robert H. Gertner and Randal C. Picker. *Game Theory and the Law*. Cambridge, MA: Harvard University Press, 1994.

Baron, Jane B. "Gifts, bargains, and form." *Indiana Law Journal* 64 (1989): 155–203.

Belk, Russell W. "Materialism and the making of the modern American Christmas." In Daniel Miller (ed.) *Unwrapping Christmas*. Oxford: Clarendon Press, 1993, pp. 75–104.

Blau, Peter M. *Exchange and Power in Social Life*. New York: Wiley, 1964.

Bourdieu, Pierre. *Outline of a Theory of Practice*. Trans. Richard Nice. Cambridge: Cambridge University Press, 1977.

Burgoyne, Carole B. and David A. Routh. "Constraints on the use of money as a gift at Christmas: the role of status and intimacy." *Journal of Economic Psychology* 12 (1991): 47–69.

Camerer, Colin. "Gifts as economic signals and social symbols." *American Journal of Sociology* 94 (1988): S180–S191.

Caplow, Theodore. "Rule enforcement without visible means: Christmas gift giving in Middletown." *American Journal of Sociology* 89 (1984): 1306–23.

Carrier, James G. *Gifts and Commodities: Exchange and Western Capitalism since 1700*. London: Routledge, 1995.

Cheal, David. *The Gift Economy*. London: Routledge, 1988.

Derrida, Jacques. *Given Time: I. Counterfeit Money*. Trans. Peggy Kamuf. Chicago: University of Chicago Press, 1992.

Douglas, Mary and Baron Isherwood. *The World of Goods*. New York: Basic Books, 1979.

Eisenberg, Melvin Aron. "The world of contract and the world of gift." *California Law Review* 85 (1997): 821–66.

Emerson, Ralph Waldo. "Gifts." *Essays and Lectures*. New York: Literary Classics, 1983, pp. 535–8.

Farrell, Joseph and Matthew Rabin. "Cheap talk." *Journal of Economic Perspectives* 10 (1996):103–18.

Frank, Robert H. "The differences between gifts and exchange: comment on Carol Rose." *Florida Law Review* 44 (1992): 319–27.

—— *Passions Within Reason: The Strategic Role of the Emotions*. New York: Norton, 1988.

Goffman, Erving. *Relations in Public: Microstudies of the Public Order*. New York: Basic Books, 1971.

Hirschman, Albert O. "Against parsimony: three easy ways of complicating some categories of economic discourse." *American Economic Review* 74 (May 1984): 89–96.

Hyde, Lewis. *The Gift: Imagination and the Erotic Life of Property*. New York: Random House, 1983.

Katz, Robert A. "Can principal-agent models help explain charitable gifts and organizations?" *Wisconsin Law Review* 20 (2000): 1–30.

Kopytoff, Igor. "The cultural biography of things: commoditization as process." In Arjun Appadurai (ed.) *The Social Life of Things: Commodities in Cultural Perspective.* Cambridge: Cambridge University Press, 1986, pp. 64–91.

La Promesse. Videocassette. New Yorker Films Artwork, 1998 [1996].

Lévi-Strauss, Claude. *The Elementary Structures of Kinship.* Revised edition. Trans. James Harle Bell, John Richard von Sturmer and Rodney Needham. Boston: Beacon Press, 1969.

Mack, Eric. "Dominos and the fear of commodification." In John W. Chapman and J. Roland Pennock (eds) *Nomos XXXI: Markets and Justice.* New York: New York University Press, 1989, pp. 198–225.

Mauss, Marcel. *The Gift: The Form and Reason for Exchange in Archaic Societies.* Trans. W.D. Halls. New York: Norton, 1990.

McCloskey, Deirdre N. *The Rhetoric of Economics.* Second edition. Madison: University of Wisconsin Press, 1998.

Noonan, John T. Jr. *Bribes.* New York: Macmillan, 1984.

Piven, Frances F. and Richard A. Cloward. "The contemporary relief debate." In Fred Block, Richard A. Cloward, Barbara Ehrenreich and Frances Fox Piven(eds) *The Mean Season: The Attack on the Welfare State.* New York: Pantheon, 1987, pp. 45–108.

Posner, Eric A. *Law and Social Norms.* Cambridge: Harvard University Press, 2000.

—— "Altruism, status, and trust in the law of gifts and gratuitous promises." *Wisconsin Law Review* 1997 (1997): 567–609.

Posner, Richard A. *Economic Analysis of Law.* Fifth edition. New York, Aspen, 1998.

Radin, Margaret Jane. "Market-inalienability." *Harvard Law Review* 100 (1987): 1849–1937.

Rose, Carol M. "Giving, trading, thieving, and trusting: how and why gifts become exchanges, and (more importantly) vice versa." *Florida Law Review* 44 (1992): 295–317.

Schrift, Alan D. "Introduction: why gift?" In Alan D. Schrift (ed.) *The Logic of the Gift: Toward an Ethic of Generosity.* New York: Routledge, 1997, pp. 1–22.

Searle-Chatterjee, Mary. "Christmas cards and the construction of social relations in Britain today." In Daniel Miller (ed.) *Unwrapping Christmas.* Oxford: Clarendon Press, 1993, pp. 176–92.

Simmel, Georg. *The Philosophy of Money.* Ed. David Frisby. Trans. Tom Bottomore and David Frisby from a first draft by Kaethe Mengelberg. Second edition. London: Routledge, 1990 [1907].

Solnick, Sara J. and David Hemenway. "The deadweight loss of Christmas: comment." *American Economic Review* 86:5 (1996): 1299–1305.

Sterne, Laurence. *A Sentimental Journey Through France and Italy.* Ed. Graham Petrie. London: Penguin, 1987 [1768].

Sunstein, Cass R. "Disrupting voluntary transactions." In John W. Chapman and J. Roland Pennock (eds) *Markets and Justice: Nomos XXXI.* New York: New York University Press, 1989, pp. 279–302.

Waldfogel, Joel. "The deadweight loss of Christmas." *American Economic Review* 83:5 (1993): 1328–36.

Webley, P., S.E.G. Lea and R. Portalska. "The unacceptability of money as a gift." *Journal of Economic Psychology* 4 (1983): 223–38.

Zelizer, Viviana A. *The Social Meaning of Money.* New York: Basic Books, 1994.

Part II

Kinship, generosity and gratitude

Ethical foundations

4 The patriarchal narratives of *Genesis* and the ethos of gift exchange

Charles H. Hinnant

"*What rule of legality and self-interest, in societies of a backward or archaic type, compels the gift that has been received to be obligatorily reciprocated,*" asks Marcel Mauss quite early in his classic *Essai sur le don* (Mauss 1990: 3; italics in original). The very familiarity of the question serves very well to introduce a discussion of what the gift is about and whether the Hebrew Bible might have anything to contribute to our understanding of the subject. For, essentially, Mauss never doubts the assumption that subtends his question. That is, he proceeds on the view that "total services and counter-services are committed to in a somewhat voluntary form by presents and gifts, although in the final analysis they are strictly compulsory, on pain of private or public warfare" (1990: 5).

This passage is famous for identifying the primary motivation underlying the threefold obligations of giving, receiving and reciprocating gifts between groups in non-market societies. Yet, however plausible – indeed, however compelling – we may find Mauss's argument, there is at the same time one difficulty with it. That is his penchant for posing the alternatives of gift exchange and private and public warfare in the starkest possible terms:

> In all the societies that have immediately preceded our own, and still exist around us, and even in numerous customs extant in our popular morality, there is no middle way: one trusts completely, or one mistrusts completely; one lays down one's arms and gives up magic, or one gives everything, from fleeting acts of hospitality to one's daughter and one's goods.
>
> (1990: 81)

The problem with such an argument seems obvious enough. As a vision of the processes of exchange in non-market societies, it excludes any consideration of a middle way – that is, of situations in which one might not lay down one's arms or trust the other party in an exchange relation completely. Such a consideration will lead us to an analysis of the pressures and resistances that might impede the processes of gift exchange without actually disrupting these processes or that might contribute to the transformation of gift relations, not into private or public warfare, but rather into hybrid situations that fail to conform in all respects to the Maussian pattern or incorporate aspects of commodity exchange. In making this assertion, I do not wish to minimize the reality, importance or difference that gift exchange brings to non-European societies, or to deny that trust plays a decisive role in its operation. What I shall argue is that we must not ignore what might prompt groups to adjust to changes in existing circumstances without completely abandoning the ethos of hospitality and gift giving. In other words, a viable model of gift exchange must portray both the activities peculiar to gift exchange and whatever places these activities in temporary jeopardy or contributes to situations in which the categories of gift and commodity exchange become distorted or even merge with one another.

Is it possible to examine a body of data that at one and the same time evokes the ethos of gift exchange and also acknowledges the clash of interests that might disturb its smooth functioning? There is at least one such body – the patriarchal narratives of Genesis (12–36) – in which the gift is used to establish a measure of reciprocity and yet where the relationship between individuals and groups continually threatens to undermine that reciprocity. For what is unique about these narratives is that the categories of patriarchal family and household are quite different from those in the aristocratic and classical tradition with which Mauss has sometimes been linked (see Pecora 1997: 46–7, 238). In the case of the family, for example, the Hebrew Bible lays great stress on the elements that endanger its integrity, an emphasis that is unnoticed in Aristotelian economics, where the unity and durability of the patriarchal *oikos* is simply taken for granted. Within the narratives of Genesis, quarrelsome families are sometimes seen as breaking apart and becoming ethnically distinct in subsequent generations, no longer accepting a common paternal authority who could intervene when mutual injuries occur. The result of the special categories of conflict imposed by the biblical view is to bring into the foreground a number of matters that fail to appear clearly in Mauss's analyses, in particular the instability of the gift-exchange process whenever it is beset by scarce resources or by clashes among the participating agents.

Now it should be said immediately that a chronological gap separates the events depicted in the patriarchal narratives and the final redaction of the texts. The practices that these texts portray may reflect the concerns of later editors rather than of the patriarchs themselves. Why then bother with the patriarchal narratives when, as some recent commentators have insisted, their perspective is more "literary" than "historical"?[1] The reason is that Mauss, unlike more conventional students of the discipline, relied from the very start upon literary as well as anthropological evidence. Moreover, even if one acknowledges a historical gap between the patriarchs and later storytellers and editors, one can still argue that the distance between the perspective of an exilic dispersion to Mesopotamia or post-exilic return to Palestine and our own era is sufficiently great to enable us to make meaningful generalizations about the practices depicted therein.

Although Mauss's essay is, by its very nature, more systematic and comprehensive than the biblical text, the ethos of the gift occupies a prominent place in the patriarchal narratives, for no family or kinship group is in a position to rely on goodwill alone to establish peaceful relations with another group. Gifts are not customarily used to elicit counter-gifts in the classic Maussian sense, however, or to assert power and precedence by establishing an obligation. Rather they are more likely to serve as a mechanism for resolving specific conflicts that have erupted in the past and that threaten to lead to warfare between families and kin groups in the future. When two households are bound by ties of kinship, a gift may help to paper over a long-simmering dispute. Thus the presents – mainly livestock – that Isaac's younger son, Jacob, prepares for the stated purpose of winning over his brother Esau's favor should be viewed not as an isolated incident, but rather in the context of their previous clashes. Esau, the first-born son, cannot reasonably be expected to forgive Jacob for having persuaded him to trade away his birthright (Genesis 25:29–34) or – in a cognate episode – for having stolen his father's "blessing" (27:4–45). The stakes could not have been more effectively dramatized than by what follows Esau's approach to Jacob's camp with four hundred men. Jacob prays to Yahweh, "Save me, I pray, from my brother Esau, for I am afraid that he may come and destroy me; he will spare neither mother nor child" (32:11).[2] As Esau and his men come closer, Jacob responds by putting "the slave-girls and their children in front, Leah with her children next, and Rachel and Joseph in the rear" (33:2), and then by "bowing low to the ground seven times as he approached his brother" (33:3).

The actual encounter fails to produce the kind of hostility that Jacob obviously fears and expects. But if it does not lead to an armed clash, it is still fraught with tension. Jacob remains suspicious and wary, even if it is obvious from Esau's kiss and embrace that he has already decided in advance to forgive his brother (33:4). Moreover, this is not the kind of situation in which a gift would necessarily have to be accepted, much less matched by a counter-gift. What the episode depicts is not the reciprocity that constitutes the norm of gift exchange, although the principle of reciprocity may be involved in Esau's reluctant decision to accept Jacob's rams, goats, cattle and donkeys, but an embrace designed to reestablish a torn fraternal bond. The focus on Esau's gesture almost serves to render Jacob's gift irrelevant, as Esau implies when he says: "I have more than enough. Keep what you have, my brother" (33:9). It is no great extension of the analysis to see in his embrace a rival and even superior counter-gift. Jacob's insistence that Esau accept the livestock that he brings to him tellingly illustrates the extent to which anxiety continues to infuse their relationship. In an attempt to overcome Esau's objections, Jacob uses a word for gift (*minhâh*) that can also refer to a tribute to a superior power:

> "No, please! If I have won your favor, then accept, I pray, this gift from me; for, as you see, I come unto your presence as into that of a god, and yet you receive me favorably. Accept this gift which I bring you; for God has been gracious to me, and I have all I want." Thus urged, Esau accepted it.
>
> (Genesis 33:10–11)

Part of the pathos of the encounter involves Jacob's attempt to repair the damage produced by his earlier actions. An account of these actions must contend with the fact that the narrative traces the source of the conflict between the brothers to a shift from the ethos of hospitality and gift giving to one of barter and hard bargaining. Within the realistic parameters of the patriarchal narratives, a brother who succeeds in persuading his sibling to trade away his birthright in an exchange of non-equivalents (in this case, a bowl of red broth) can only be seen as dissolving the obligations that bind one kinsman to another. It thus should not be surprising that this episode is made the basis for an etiological explanation in which the brothers are the eponymous founders of two neighboring and ethnically differentiated peoples – Israel and the Edomites. For the episode reflects the cultural understanding that in barter – which is assumed to involve tough negotiating and even chicanery – people bind themselves only temporarily when they consent to exchange with one another. Barter thus stands in sharp contrast to the mutuality that binds people inalienably within the household and family. Admittedly, the context in which Esau rushes in from the field and demands a helping of broth is intended to exemplify his self-absorption and complacency, but there is nothing unusual about his expectation that a brother would comply with his wishes. The episode thus takes the ethos that supposedly informs kinship relations and transforms the two siblings into distinct and rivalrous figures. Indeed, the narrative implies that both are competent to transact only if they are free and independent of one another, for only then will each be able to protect his own interests. Their willingness to bargain divides them one from another, and in completing the transaction, they seal that division and so create the expectation that they will transact in a similar way in the future. Nor is this a simple domestic matter, for in the introduction of barter into social relationships, one can trace the move from the torn loyalties of warring individuals and groups within the same household to the wider sorts of social strife and ethnonationalism implicit in the redactor's etiological explanation. Rather than being rooted in a primordial substrate of tribal identity, the principles of ethnic affiliation and conflict are here traced back to discord within the family.

Esau's acceptance of Jacob's gift reaffirms the kinship relationship – at least for the moment. But this does not mean that the two brothers have succeeded in reestablishing a stable and enduring bond. On the contrary, they disagree as to whether they should leave the encampment together or separately, thus disclosing the degree of uneasiness that still exists between them (33:12–17). Jacob's unwillingness to allow some of Esau's men to escort his family and flocks marks the persistence of his suspicions concerning his brother's intentions. Because kinship is a social relation of reciprocity and mutual assistance, the decision of the two brothers to go their separate ways is recognition that the relation has effectively come to an end.

From this perspective, it is a matter of course that gift exchange, as the dominating principle of a small-scale society, must color and infiltrate the occupations that subtend its immediate ambit of operation. Scholars generally assume that the activities of the biblical patriarchs can be defined in terms of their occupations as nomadic stockherders and pastoralists.[3] Yet this explanation, unexceptionable as far as it goes, does not quite get to the bottom of things. For it leaves unexamined the way in which these social (and never purely "economic") activities are called into being and modified to fit the requirements of particular contexts and political affiliations. Here I take my lead from those who argue that a mode of production cannot be understood in isolation from the customs and practices in which it is embedded and that any attempt to describe the nature of a social formation by paying heed only to the most visible aspect runs the risk of reductionism. In many ways, the patriarchal narratives also take for granted what we have tended to forget, namely that food-producing activities, especially in multi-ethnic settings, are tenuous collective projects, dependent on the different situations in which particular groups find themselves.

As presented in the biblical text, the situation of the patriarchs can best be described as that of an embattled minority. Threatened at once by internal dissensions within their households and by external clashes with larger and more populous neighbors, these leaders are depicted as conducting themselves with a wary circumspection. In this climate, as we have seen, gift exchanges become a means of resolving differences rather than of forging new alliances. The risks involved in such transactions are considerable and come into even sharper focus when the two groups are separated by a distance in ethnic affiliation. It is at this point that a gift may fail to achieve its desired goal. When Shechem, the Hivite, rapes Jacob's daughter, Dinah, his father, Hamor, offers Jacob an exchange of daughters, including Dinah, as a means of bringing the feud to an end, but the offer fails as Dinah's brothers, Simeon and Levi, enact a brutal reprisal (Genesis 34). Here the interval between giving and returning, the strategic use made of time and pacing in social interaction, becomes the means by which the brothers transform the sequence of gift and counter-gift into what Marshall Sahlins termed a mode of negative reciprocity (Sahlins 1972: 195–6). Gift exchange remains normative, however, for Jacob tells his sons:

> You have brought trouble on me; you have brought my name into bad odor among the people of the country, the Canaanites and the Perizzites. My numbers are few; if they combine against me and attack, I shall be destroyed, I and my household with me.
>
> (Genesis 34:30)

The two separate outcomes of the encounters between Jacob and Esau and Jacob and Hamor stand in sharp contrast to one another, yet they also reflect each other in various ways. For Hamor, the offer of an exchange of daughters contains many of the same elements as that planned by Jacob for his brother Esau. Just as Jacob's gift involved a sharing of livestock, so Hamor declares: "If you settle among us, the country is open before you; make your home in it, move about freely, and acquire land of your own" (34:10). Obviously Shechem's rape of Dinah represents a more violent act of appropriation than Jacob's earlier negotiation with Esau. Perhaps less obvious, however, is the way Shechem's subsequent behavior unwittingly parallels that of Jacob. In professing a desire for friendship, he sounds like an exaggerated version of Jacob: "I am eager to win your favor and I shall give you whatever you ask. Fix the bride-price and the gift as high as you like, and I shall give you whatever you ask; only give me the girl in marriage" (34:11–12).

The failure of Hamor and Shechem's offer to procure its desired end points to the problematic nature of gift exchanges in the patriarchal narratives. Because they are so often the product of disparities in status, power or kinship affiliation, very few of these exchanges can be separated from the fear of violence, the anguish of displacement or the nostalgia of exile. When an individual, family or clan as a whole is compelled to presume on the hospitality of a more powerful neighboring people, it is assumed that they must offer a propitiatory gift to the leader of that people. The three cognate episodes (12:10–13; 20:1–8; 26:6–16) in which a biblical patriarch, driven by famine, offers his wife disguised as a sister to a foreign ruler in exchange for flocks and herds are governed by this imperative. The plagues that the Lord subsequently inflicts on the Egyptian Pharoah and his household in the first episode can be seen as imposing an ethical limit on the norms governing this kind of transaction. Where exchange is not seen as a distinct, morally neutral domain, where it is embedded in society and subject to its moral codes, gift relations are unlikely to be represented as the antithesis of the bonds of kinship, and there is consequently something inappropriate about making a gift of one's wife as a part of such exchanges. Commentators have expressed bewilderment that divine punishment is visited in these episodes on the Pharoah or the king of the Philistines rather than on Abraham or Isaac,[4] but this highlights the fact that moral responsibility is an attribute of superior power, especially when the figure in question is placed in the position of a receiver rather than giver of gifts. The reprisals that the Pharoah and Philistine king are made to suffer are brought about by their failure to anticipate the possibility that the patriarchs' gifts might not be what they appear to be.

Mauss cites the ancient Germanic languages in which the word "gift" means both gift and poison to refer to the ambiguity inherent in the process of gift exchange (1990: 63). An awareness of this kind of ambiguity may lie behind Abraham's refusal of the gifts – in this case, booty – offered to him by the king of Sodom after the king has been defeated by Abraham in battle (Genesis 14:21–4). Because generosity is a kind of constraint, it places the recipient in a circumspect and responsive relationship to the donor, imposing upon him the necessity of distinguishing appropriate from inappropriate gifts. Or to put it somewhat differently, the patriarchal narratives focus on situations in which a leader might find himself obliged to reject rather than accept a gift.

The servile stratagems that Abraham and Isaac believe that they are forced to adopt toward superior rulers are the outcome of their anxieties concerning their position as aliens in a foreign country. Their renunciation of their wives, a form of sexual impotence, would thus, if perpetuated, come to symbolize a form of political impotence as well. When the patriarch or a member of his family is placed in the dominant position, by contrast, his conduct is presented as non-exploitative, innocent and even transparent. An instance of this romantic ideal-ization of the world of hospitality can be seen in the unstinting generosity that Abraham displays toward the three strangers at the terebinths of Mamre (18:1–8). Unaware that he is being tested by the Lord in this episode, Abraham reveals an anxious desire to please his guests:

> Sirs, if I have deserved your favour, do not go past your servant without a visit. Let me send for some water so that you may bathe your feet; and rest under this tree, while I fetch a little food so that you may refresh yourselves. Afterwards you may continue the journey which has brought you my way.
>
> (18:3–5)

Although Abraham does not seem to be in a privileged position from a material point of view, he does have at his command enough water and food to provide a modest welcome to his unknown guests. The importance attached to this kind of hospitality is reflected in the promise of a first-born son the Lord gives to Abraham and the until-then-barren Sarah in the next episode (18:9–15). Although the two events are not explicitly linked, the symbolic contrast between the Lord's gift to Abraham and Sarah in response to their generosity and His destruction of the inhabitants of the city of Sodom (19:1–29) illuminates the immense moral gap that separates the xenophobic hostility and violence of the latter from Abraham's loftier attitude of altruistic hospitality.

The kind of hospitality that Abraham displays at the terebinths of Mamre has traditionally been opposed in Western culture not to ethnic hatred and mob violence but rather to the much blander exchange relationship within which commodities are bought and sold. Commodity exchange, so the conven-tional argument runs, is diametrically opposed to gift exchange; impersonal rather than personal, it is largely drained of emotional content, whereas gifts are invariably personal and highly charged with symbolic significance. Commodity exchange presupposes an arrangement that allows one to alienate possessions; gifts are inalienable since they continue to belong in some sense to the person who originally possessed them.[5] Yet there are reasons to question the neatness of this polarity. As Maurice Bloch and Jonathan Parry have pointed out, "*our* ideology of the gift has been constructed in antithesis to market exchange" and "we cannot therefore expect the ideologies of non-market societies to reproduce this kind of opposition" (1989: 9). This is certainly true of the patriarchal narra-tives, where a mode of commodity exchange can sometimes function as an intermediate state between hospitality and the open conflict associated with domestic and tribal violence. One can see this kind of compromise logic at work, for example, in an episode in which Abraham purchases a grave from the Hittites for the now-deceased Sarah (Genesis 23:3–20). Even though Ephron, a Hittite, offers to give Abraham the land and a cave that is on it (23:11), Abraham refuses. Exploiting an ambiguity in the verb "to give" (*nattatî*) which can also mean "to sell," Abraham insists instead that he "give" Ephron "the price" of the land (23:13). The issue is whether an individual belonging to a minority group

feels free to risk the uncertainty inherent in gift exchange rather than to invoke
the legality and non-violence attendant upon commodity exchange. Abraham's
response, in effect, collapses the necessary interval between gift and counter-gift,
thus instituting what René Girard calls rapid reciprocity, an improvised form of
commodity exchange (cited by Godbout 1998: 33). Confronted by Abraham's
demand for a price, Ephron mentions a figure in passing as if it were a matter of
no importance: "Listen, sir: land worth four hundred shekels of silver, what is
that between me and you! You may bury your dead there" (23:15). But the
confusion here produces more than mere psychological tit for tat. Abraham's
strategy is more than symbolic; it also has the practical effect of creating a
temporary political framework in the relative absence of larger institutions.
Abraham's subsequent payment to Ephron is based on the value merchants
place upon four hundred shekels and is made "in the presence of all the Hittites
who had assembled at the city gate" (23:18). More than a simple counter-gift,
this payment involves calculations based upon money as a standard of value and
medium of exchange ("four hundred shekels of the standard recognized by the
merchants"; 23:16). Instead of creating a situation in which Abraham will
become indebted to Ephron (and the Hittites), his actions produce a ceremonial
framework in which the inequalities potentially inherent in the exchange of gift
and counter-gift will, he hopes, be neutralized.[6]

In other words, what might have taken the form of a gift is deliberately made
into a commodity transaction. Is there then a systematic difference between the
two kinds of exchange? It seems not; as many recent commentators have emphasized, commodity exchange can be part of an arrangement involving personal
relationships and commitments. Only the context determines the nature of the
exchange, and this context includes both the cultural relationships of a transaction and before whom the transaction takes place. From Abraham's vantage
point as well as our own, the exchange with Ephron is less morally perilous than
the arrangement it has replaced. That is because Abraham and his household
are thrust into a larger context where they are subject to certain domination. It is
this submissive and potentially dangerous bond from which the agreement liberates the patriarch.[7] Yet the transaction reveals traces of the gift-exchange pattern
from which it obviously emerged. The result in the context of this episode is a
hybrid situation in which there are two contrasting moralities at work, one
stressing solidarity, friendship and trust, the other individuality and a wary
caution.

A somewhat different variation of this kind of hybrid transaction can be
found in the episode in which Jacob promises to work seven years for Laban in
exchange for the hand of his young daughter Rachel (29:18–19). Money is not
involved as a standard of exchange here; rather, the transfer of a daughter
between transactors who will become mutually allied and related is transformed
through the activity of manual labor into a hybrid relation somewhere between
commodity and gift exchange. Jacob's initial willingness to work without
compensation reflects the ethos of kinship alliance and gift giving but Laban's
subsequent query is couched in terms that are practical and individualistic rather

than social. It is telling that he uses the rare word (*maskureteka*) for wage in a context where it appears distinctly premature: "Why should you work for nothing simply because you are my kinsman? Tell me what wage you would settle for" (29:15). Both Jacob's reply that he would work seven years in exchange for Rachel (rather than for a wage payment) and Laban's response, "it is better that I give her to you than anyone else," are still couched in the language of gift and counter-gift, of reciprocated labor exchange or bride-price rather than wage labor. Yet there is a certain Janus-like quality about this arrangement: on the one hand, it has created a stable and apparently lasting association in which Jacob can become part of Laban's household; on the other hand, it has constructed a situation in which either one of the parties to the agreement may confront the other as an opposing interest, looking to maximize his utility at the other's expense. From this point of view, Laban's covert substitution of his older daughter Leah in place of Rachel on the wedding night is the inevitable result of this bifurcated perspective. What permits Jacob and Rachel's subsequent flight with Laban's household gods (31:19–22) is his release from the bonds of reciprocity that tie together members of a family. The behavior of one who tries, like Laban, to exploit a close kin tie is obviously seen as inappropriate; it attempts to transform kin relations into the kind of transaction that assumes the autonomy of the agents involved.[8]

Despite Laban's real and obvious victimization of Jacob, there is a sense in which Jacob has never been passive, never been totally innocent of the power-play inherent in his demand for the hand of Laban's younger daughter. His willingness to work for Laban is misleading because it implies a disinterestedness that his passion for Rachel belies. This may be why the relationship between Jacob and Laban, much like the relationship between Jacob and Esau, fails to conform to the anthropological norm that close kin participate in gift exchange, while distant and non-kin enter into impersonal commodity relationships or resort to guile and even open violence (Sahlins 1972: 196). From the perspective of the patriarchal narratives, kin relations are never "pure," never divested of the characteristics of other kinds of relations.[9]

In spite of the existence of hybrid arrangements, virtually all exchanges are constructed as "gift" exchanges within the patriarchal narratives. This is essential if the gift is to retain its power as a constitutive element in the creation of peaceful relations between different groups. When Abraham learns that Abimelech's men have seized a well that he had excavated (Genesis 21:25), his first instinct is to reestablish his claim by going to the king and complaining openly. The edgy defensiveness of Abimelech's response – "I do not know who did this. Up to this moment you never mentioned it, nor did I hear of it from anyone else" (21:26) – reveals the limitations inherent in this approach. It is surely no coincidence that Abraham's subsequent "gift" of "sheep and cattle" to Abimelech is intended to reconfirm and solidify his relationship to the king. Asked by Abimelech why he had made such a gift, Abraham replies, "Accept these seven lambs from me as a testimony on my behalf that I dug this well" (21:30). Clearly, there is more at stake here for Abraham than a proof of his sincerity. His gift can be seen as a tacit purchase at the same time that it serves as a symbolically necessary act of political renewal. In this case, it is the market relationship that is resisted by a ceremonial pact which not only divests the transaction of moral neutrality but places it firmly in the context of a newly-invented tradition. To commemorate the pact, Abraham plants a tamarisk tree at the well and then invokes "the Lord, the Everlasting God, by name" (21:34).

The phrase "ceremonial pact" might be used to encompass transactions that are accompanied by ritual practices, be they the embrace of the two leaders, the planting of the tree, or the invocation of a deity. For an embattled group, the construction of an atmosphere of hospitality and gift exchange helps to establish a measure of social control in an implicitly hostile situation. The biblical patriarchs are presented as aspirants to future nationhood yet also as parties in potentially violent confrontations with pre-existing political structures and ethnic groupings. In contrast to the earlier seizure of the well, the embrace of Abraham and Abimelech establishes a stable and recognizable relationship. Indeed, the whole purpose of the ceremony is to ratify collectively the ownership of the land in question, for it is the pact that fixes the well once and for all with a name – Beersheeba – that denotes both what it is and what it will remain in the future (21:32). Abraham's ceremonial gift and pact are thus an attempt to prepare – symbolically at least – for his future life as an alien in the country of the Philistines (21:34).

To acknowledge the constructed aspect of this kind of ceremonial pact is to call into question the uniform, monolithic, even inevitable character of gift exchange. And it is also to recognize the element of tactical uncertainty involved in the specific exchanges of Genesis. There is nothing in the episode of Abraham and Abimelech to suggest that Abraham has decided what he is going to do in advance or that he knows what the outcome will be. Even when a gift is part of a deliberate strategy, moreover, there is still a considerable degree of uncertainty in the transaction. Thus when Abraham sends a servant bearing gifts to his kinsman Nahor in search of a wife for Isaac (24:1–62), it seems that the entire arrangement hinges upon the response of Nahor's granddaughter, Rebecca, to a request for water (24:12–14). The centrality of water-drinking in the patriarchal narratives is such that Rebecca's act of sharing becomes the justification for the servant's subsequent offer of counter-gifts – "a gold nose ring weighing half a shekel, and two bracelets for her wrists, weighing ten shekels of gold" (24:22). Pierre Bourdieu has described such transactions as the consequence of strategies generated from a habitus of shared dispositions (Bourdieu 1977: 3–71), but even this formulation seems too mechanical, for no habitus is really a set of dispositions from which characters can simply read off decisions and procedures. In the absence of laws and an overarching government, particular situations call for specific, even unique choices and decisions. Thus when we read that Abraham "had already in his lifetime made gifts to sons by his concubines and had then sent them away eastwards, to a land of the east, out of his son Isaac's way" (Genesis 25:6), we need not regard this act as necessarily emerging from a pre-existing body of practices.

One might be tempted to view these ceremonial exchanges as the reflection of an all-embracing ideology of the patriarchal family, but there is nothing in the model of the paternal household that can account for the ethnic violence these exchanges seek to allay. At stake are the bonds that supposedly knit the individual members of a family into a unit. In patriarchal societies, this bond is secure because of a pact between the two groups or families from which the individuals come. In the Graeco-Roman tradition, it is an axiom that this kind of patriarchal family is the basis of society. Asked by the stranger in Plato's *The Statesman*, "Is there much difference between a large household and a small-sized city, so far as the exercise of authority is concerned," Socrates answers "None." Cicero, in a similar manner, held that the family is "the foundation of civil government, the nursery, as it were, of the state" (cited by Schochet 1975: 20, 24). Refreshingly straightforward, this argument resolves none of the problems raised by the patriarchal narratives concerning the politics of the family and household: its internal divisions and precarious position in relation to other households and clans.

In fact, those critics who remain wholly within the idealizing terms of the classical formulation are unable to resolve these key dilemmas. In place of an argument for the familial origins of the polis, the patriarchal narratives substitute a vision in which the divided family becomes the basis for ethnic differentiation and conflict. The division begins early with the acquisition of slaves, servants and stockherds, as the family becomes a household. When this has taken place, the unit begins to approach not the "self-sufficiency" that epitomizes the household economy (*oikonomia*) for Aristotle but a condition of scarcity that brings one member of a family into competition with another member. Abram and Lot, for example, both possess "sheep and cattle and tents" but both discover that "the land could not support them together. They had so much livestock that they could not settle in the same district, and quarrels arose between Abram's herdsmen and Lot's" (Genesis 13:5–7). Their decision to separate is directly related to their affiliation: "there must be no quarrelling between us, or between my herdsmen and yours, for we are close kinsmen" (13:8). The next step then is the division of quarrelling family members into separate households, only one of which will be able to bear the privileged line of succession. In the last stage, the households become rivalrous communities, Israel and the Canaanites or Israel and the Edomites. Kinship rivalry and ethnicity thus feed each other, as households produce ethnic categories that in turn become the basis for future historical conflicts. Of course, not every nation mentioned in scripture can be traced back to divisions within the patriarchal families of Genesis. But it does seem fair to say that there are few examples of patriarchal households in Genesis that are free of the internecine conflicts that lead to later historical oppositions.

By relating ethnic conflicts to the family in this manner, the patriarchal narratives project a view of the political order as a kaleidoscope of different and conflicting cultures. This view distances itself from those who see tribes and nations as associations of kin groups, whether bound together by ties of language, tradition, religion or culture in general. In classical political wisdom, there is always a suggestion that kinship and geographical proximity are more cohesive than spatially separated affiliations. The model of the pre-political household activates this naturalism, largely because it overlooks the warring loyalties that characterize households in the biblical narratives. These households are being pushed not only by the threats to their survival from larger neighboring peoples but also by the pressures produced by apparently trivial events within the same family. The episode in which Noah's drunkenness and exposure provide the occasion for the cursing of his son Canaan, the ancestor of the peoples in whose land the Hebrews would settle (9:20–7), is a case in point. Nothing in the episode allows us to see the paternal *oikos* as the sole foundation of broader political arrangements.

Thus a central feature of the patriarchal narratives is a politics in which the family, the classic loci of socialization, also becomes the loci of ethnic differentiation and strife. For the insistence on the family as a potential source of conflict is a key element, as we have seen, in the etiological explanations of Genesis. It follows that small intimate collectivities, usually those based on kinship or its extensions, are the origin, not only of group sentiments that involve a sense of group identity but also of group divisions that imply a sense of cultural and ethnic difference. It should not be surprising to discover, therefore, that these sentiments can lead in two opposing directions, one toward hospitality and the gift, the other toward barter, money and commodity exchange. The result is a body of practices that escapes easy categorization, develops in unanticipated directions, and bends the categories of gift and commodity exchange, readily admitting their inadequacies and faultlines. It is quite probable that the narrative structure of Genesis – especially the enforced migration of Jacob's clan from Canaan to Egypt – reflects an implicit transition from a household economy based on gift exchange to a much broader, more complex society in which monetary transactions predominate (Genesis 37–50). The point is, however, that even the patriarchal narratives – so markedly different from the anthropological data that Mauss studied – represent a world in which the categories of gift and commodity exchange are acknowledged to be porous and unstable rather than fixed and rigid.

Notes

1 For the most radical formulation of the argument that the historical books of the Bible are literary, see Whitelam 1996. A balanced assessment of the question can be found in Iain Provan's "The historical books of the Old Testament" (Barton 1998: 198–211).

2 All references to the patriarchal narratives in my text are from the *Revised English Bible*.

3 For a review of the scholarship devoted to the study of the biblical Israelites as a nomadic society, see Lemche (1985: 84–163). Naomi Sternberg (1993) argues that marriage functions in the patriarchal narratives to establish an endogamous line of descent rather than to forge exogamous alliances with alien groups. A consideration of the ethos of gift exchange and hospitality in these narratives has not been a part of this tradition of scholarly investigation of Genesis.

4 Thus John H. Marks asks in his article on Genesis in the *Interpreter's Commentary* (Laymon 1971: 13): "But what of God's righteousness? Why does God affect with plagues the Pharoah rather than the craven Abraham?"

5 The *locus classicus* for this position can be found in Gregory.

6 Commentators have tended to interpret this episode as if it were being conducted from the start as a commodity transaction and thus have interpreted Ephron's offer as a mere gesture, intended to elicit Abraham's call for a price. E.A. Speiser, however, recognizes that "a gift was the last thing that would answer Abraham's need" (1964: 172), while Claus Westermann notes that the exchange "is carried out according to fixed forms, which reveals a cultural structure that prevented buying and selling from being reduced to a mere commercial transaction" (1987: 166).

7 Godbout (1998: 151) describes this kind of intermediate arrangement as a transition from an archaic to a modern economic system but places it in a later feudal context.

8 Westermann notes that "in Laban's case, what had been conduct governed by the ethics of family relationships turns into that of a man pursuing his own advantage, whose only purpose is to get maximum benefit from Jacob's labor" (1987: 206).

9 Thus Paula McNutt describes reciprocity as the primary system of exchange during the Iron Age, the backdrop for both the patriarchal era and the age of monarchy (1999: 72–3, 156–7). It must be said, however, that her theoretical discussion of reciprocity, which is couched in conventional terms, would not enable us to account for the conflicts that take place within the patriarchal narratives of Genesis.

References

Barton, John (ed.). *The Cambridge Companion to Biblical Interpretation.* Cambridge: Cambridge University Press, 1998.

Bloch, Maurice and Jonathan Parry (eds). *Money and the Morality of Exchange.* Cambridge: Cambridge University Press, 1989.

Bourdieu, Pierre. *Outline of a Theory of Practice.* Trans. Richard Nice. Cambridge: Cambridge University Press, 1977.

Godbout, Jacques T. with Alan Caillé. *The World of the Gift.* Trans. Donald Winkler. Montreal: McGill-Queen's University Press, 1998.

Gregory, Chris. *Gifts and Commodities.* London: Academic, 1982.

Laymon, Charles M. (ed.). *The Interpreter's One Volume Commentary on the Bible.* Nashville: Abingdon, 1971.

Lemche, Niels Peter. *Early Israel: Anthropological and Historical Studies in the Israelite Society before the Monarchy.* Leiden: Brill, 1985.

Mauss, Marcel. *The Gift: the Form and Reasons for Exchange in Archaic Societies.* Trans. W.D. Halls. New York: Norton, 1990.

McNutt, Paula. *Reconstructing the Society of Ancient Israel.* London: SPCK; Louisville: Westminster John Knox Press, 1999.

Pecora, Vincent P. *Households of the Soul.* Baltimore: Johns Hopkins University Press, 1997.

The Revised English Bible with the Apocrypha. London and New York: Cambridge University Press/Oxford University Press, 1989.

Sahlins, Marshall. *Stone Age Economics.* Chicago: Aldine, 1972.

Schochet, Gordon J. *Patriarchalism in Political Thought.* New York: Basic Books, 1975.

Speiser, E.A. *The Anchor Bible Genesis.* Garden City: Doubleday, 1964.

Sternberg, Naomi. *Kinship and Marriage in Genesis: a Household Perspective.* Minneapolis: Fortress Press, 1993.

Westermann, Claus. *Genesis: A Practical Commentary: Text and Interpretation.* Grand Rapids, MI: Eerdmans, 1987.

Whitelam, K.W. *The Invention of Ancient Israel: the Silencing of Palestinian History.* London: Routledge, 1996.

5 The ethics of generosity and friendship

Aristotle's gift to Nietzsche?

Martha Kendal Woodruff

The highest virtue is a gift-giving virtue, says Nietzsche. With this statement he evokes the generosity and vitality that belong to the morality of strength. The gift-giving virtue poses a challenge to the calculating, utilitarian measurement of gift exchange, suggesting instead the excess and over-abundance characteristic of the Nietzschean goal for future humanity, the *Übermensch*. But while Nietzsche's goals and values are oriented towards the future and anticipate postmodern motifs, they have ancient Greek sources. Nietzsche's gift-giving virtue harks back to Aristotelian generosity, and the *Übermensch* calls to mind the Aristotelian idea of "greatness of soul," *megalopsychia*.

Yet although Nietzsche has radicalized and modernized these elements of Aristotle's ethics, he has failed to develop another crucial element: friendship. The centrality of friendship in Aristotle's ethics, a topic of much recent interest, renders generosity continual and reciprocal. By contrast, the absence of ethical friendship in Nietzsche leads to an asymmetrical, even paradoxical, form of gift giving. The problem Nietzsche faces is that of receiving: if everyone practices the gift-giving virtue, who is receiving these gifts? If giving is a practice only of the strong, must receiving be a sign of servitude and a form of debt? While Nietzsche suspects that it must, Aristotle avoids the problem of debt with his vision of ethical friendship that allows for giving and receiving between equals. As I will argue in this paper, retrieving the Aristotelian ideas of generosity and friendship overcomes the problems Nietzsche encounters in the gift-giving virtue. At the same time, this retrieval offers an alternative to modern economically determined models of self and other.

Greek philosophy and tragedy influenced Nietzsche's thought so deeply that we could, with tongue in cheek, describe it as "the gift that keeps on giving." But, of course, like many significant gifts, this one has been received with ambivalence. On the one hand, Nietzsche might not have wanted to receive everything the Greeks had to offer, while on the other he might have been reluctant to acknowledge just how much he was indebted to them. Especially concerning the Socratic gifts to the tradition – theoretical optimism, excessive rationalism, hostility to the "merely imitative" arts – Nietzsche wants to keep his distance. Such gifts,

Nietzsche suspects, may well be *vergiftet*, poisoned by a distrust of art, illusion and the life instinct itself. Yet the promise of a "music-making Socrates," a tragic and artistic philosopher, makes a strong appeal to Nietzsche in the *Birth of Tragedy* (1967a). Even when opposing Socrates, Nietzsche remains entangled with him.[1] As he writes in an early work: "Simply to acknowledge the fact: *Socrates* is so close to me that I am almost continually fighting with him" (Nietzsche 1992: 127). Even when overturning the Platonic hierarchies (being over becoming, soul over body, reason over emotion), Nietzsche still remains indebted to these structures. Such gifts are not easy to refuse.

But while Nietzsche's struggles against "Socratism" and Platonism are well known, his relationship to Aristotle is less clear. At first glance it might seem hard to imagine two philosophers more strikingly different in style and tone than Aristotle and Nietzsche. But consider this double-edged comment from *The Gay Science*: "Giving all honor – and the highest honors – to Aristotle, he certainly did not hit the nail, much less on the head, when he discussed the ultimate end of Greek tragedy" (1974: II.80, p. 135). The tragic feeling, Nietzsche writes in *Twilight of the Idols*, "has been misunderstood as much by Aristotle as, especially, by our pessimists" (1997: §5, 91). In the realm of aesthetics, Nietzsche repeatedly rejects the Aristotelian idea of the "discharge" of pity and fear in *katharsis*.[2]

Why, then, does Nietzsche give "highest honors" to Aristotle? Why does Nietzsche elsewhere praise Aristotle as a soul "full of joyfulness and peace" (1982: V.424, p. 182)? What, if anything, has Aristotelian ethics given Nietzsche? On this point scholars disagree: Walter Kaufmann stresses that "Nietzsche's debt to Aristotle's ethics is … considerable" (1956: 329), while Bernd Magnus maintains that Nietzsche is indifferent to Aristotle's ethics (1980: 290). I find the former position more persuasive than the latter, although my interest lies less in proving a historical influence than in rediscovering Aristotelian resources for the ethics of generosity and friendship.[3]

That Aristotelian virtue ethics has recently enjoyed a renaissance makes even more important the question of how it relates to the Nietzschean revaluation of values, which is so influential for modern and postmodern thought. In *After Virtue* (1982), Alasdair MacIntyre poses Aristotle and Nietzsche against each other as an "Either/Or": "the defensibility of the Nietzschean position turns *in the end* on the answer to the question: was it right in the first place to reject Aristotle?" (1982: 111).[4] But this way of framing the question oversimplifies the problem: Nietzsche's scathing critique of Kantian and Christian morality does not preclude his revival of another ethical tradition, that of the Greek heroic-aristocratic virtues. Robert Solomon, contra MacIntyre, argues that "the basis upon which we could best reconceive of morality" would be "a reconsideration of Aristotle through Nietzschean eyes" (Solomon 1982: 114), a project I will begin to develop here. Heidegger, for his part, finds such deep continuities between the two thinkers that he makes this striking suggestion: "It is advisable that you postpone reading Nietzsche for the time being, and first study Aristotle for ten to fifteen years" (1968: 73).[5]

Whether or not Nietzsche fully realized it, I believe we can read the *Nicomachean Ethics* (Aristotle 1941a, 1982) as a classic example of the morality of strength, flourishing, and noble self-love that Nietzsche seeks to describe in works such as *On the Genealogy of Morals* (1967b), *The Gay Science* (1974) and *Thus Spoke Zarathustra* (1984). As Sheridan Hough writes, "Nietzsche realizes that this 'ethics of self-interest' is controversial, but he claims that it has ancient antecedents," most obviously in Aristotle (1997: 19). We might say that Aristotelian ethics is aristocratic in the original Greek sense that Nietzsche seeks to revive: it allows the best, *aristos*, to achieve the best life without guilt or bad conscience but instead with pride and "greatness of soul."

Eudaimonia thus anticipates *Frölichkeit*: Aristotle's understanding of happiness, as the well-being and thriving of the good life, may be interpreted as one of the highest forms of the Nietzschean will to power, the joy of life. That joy is a nobler form of power than aggression Nietzsche suggests with statements such as: the need to hurt others is "a sign that we are still lacking power, or it shows a sense of frustration in the face of this poverty," and further, "whoever is dissatisfied with himself is continually ready for revenge" (1974: I.13, p. 87; IV.290, p. 233). That happiness expresses power is a lesson Nietzsche learns from the Greeks: "the first effect of happiness is the *feeling of power*; this wants to *express itself*," he writes, adding that Greek philosophers believed that "their happiness was the best refutation of other ways of life" (1982: IV.356, p.166; IV.367, p. 168). But, as I will show, for Aristotle happiness essentially involves friendship, while for Nietzsche joy lies in creative strife or deep solitude. The absence of friendship raises problems for the gift-giving virtue. To retrace the connection between generosity and friendship, I will turn first to Nietzsche on the paradoxes of the gift, and then back to Aristotle for a different way of confronting them.

Nietzsche portrays generosity as indispensable to the morality of strength and the life of plenitude. In *On the Genealogy of Morals*, generosity manifests itself as the abundant ability to overcome one's enemies and oneself, to "forgive and forget": "To be incapable of taking one's enemies, one's accidents, even one's misdeeds seriously for very long – that is the sign of strong, full natures in whom there is an excess of the power to form, to mold, to recuperate and to forget" (1967c: I.10, p. 39). There is, then, more than an accidental connection between giving and forgiving: the power of self-overcoming informs both.

In *Thus Spoke Zarathustra*, generosity takes center stage: "the highest principle is a bestowing [*schenkenden*] virtue" (1984: 100). In its dramatic context, this section on the gift plays a pivotal role: as the last section of Part I, it unifies the teachings of this part and anticipates those to come. Here, for the first time, Zarathustra calls his followers disciples; this section echoes many of Jesus' speeches to his disciples, but at the same time inverts them.[6] This section is the only one in Part I to have subdivisions, each marked by a different message and mood: the first speaks of gift-giving, the second of the earth and of healing, the third of the teacher's warning to his pupils.

The gift-giving virtue is called an "unnamable virtue"; as Gary Shapiro suggests, this is because it cannot be calculated "from the perspective of the market" (1997: 275). There can be only images or parables (*Gleichnisse*) of such virtues. The image Zarathustra chooses is gold, inspired by the golden staff that his disciples have just given him: like gold, this virtue is "uncommon and useless, shining and mellow in lustre" (Nietzsche 1984: 100). Gold also evokes the sun, which at the beginning of the drama was said to give light and warmth with superabundance (Nietzsche 1984: 39). Beyond utility and calculation, the gift-giving virtue always gives of itself, like the glow of gold or the light of the sun. Just as Zarathustra brings humanity a gift, he urges his disciples to do the same: "You thirst to become sacrifices and gifts yourselves" (Nietzsche 1984: 100). Zarathustra teaches that only when both body and soul have become so full and overfull that giving is a sign of strength, only when "your virtue is insatiable in wanting to give" – only then do we approach a new set of values and a new self-ishness that is "healthy and holy." Such selfishness differs fundamentally from the grasping selfishness that only takes and does not give, "that selfishness of the sick" (Nietzsche 1984: 100). The two ways of giving and taking reveal two kinds of self. Human, or over-human, generosity finds its inspiration in nature, which gives to us freely and beautifully: "Behold, what abundance is around us! And it is fine to gaze out upon distant seas from the midst of superfluity" (1984: 109).

But as Nietzsche recognizes, this gift-giving virtue raises substantial paradoxes of its own: this giving is in fact a form of taking, in that it is "a thief of all values" (1984: 100). It takes everything into itself only to transform it and give it back again. By insisting that such giving is selfish, Nietzsche challenges both the Christian ideal of self-sacrifice and the modern dichotomy between altruism and egotism; as we will see, this move recalls the Aristotelian ideal of noble self-love. Whether in giving or in taking, in self-overcoming or in self-sacrifice, the self is always present. Even extreme giving is an act of self-assertion, in that "magna-nimity contains the same degree of egoism as does revenge, but egoism of a different quality" (Nietzsche 1974: I.49, p. 114). Again agreeing with Aristotle, Nietzsche holds that the giver stands in a position of power, while the receiver stands in a position of debt. As Zarathustra says: "Great obligations do not make a man grateful, they make a man resentful [*rachsüchtig*]" (Nietzsche 1984: 113). In the language of *On the Genealogy of Morals*, this feeling of owing a great debt fertil-izes the breeding ground for resentment and bad conscience.

Can those who practice a morality of strength, then, never *receive* gifts from others? Is the gift-giving virtue one-sided? Who could possibly give to Zarathustra or be his equal? But then again, do not even the givers *need* someone to receive their benefits, for how else could they practice their gift-giving virtue? The gift-giving virtue thus threatens to undo itself over the problem of receiving. As Zarathustra asks himself almost mournfully:

> "Which of us owes thanks? Does the giver not owe thanks to the receiver for receiving? Is giving not a necessity? Is taking not – compassion?" O my soul, I understand the smile of your melancholy: your superabundance itself now stretches out longing hands!
>
> (Nietzsche 1984: 239)

In the end, Zarathustra suffers from a strange poverty of over-generosity, exclaiming, "I do not know the joy of the receiver," "I should like to rob those to whom I give," and finally, "Oh wretchedness of all givers!" (Nietzsche 1984: 129). Just as night is the other side of day, such despair proves to be the other side of the joy of giving. Indeed, suffering from the tarantula's bite, Zarathustra even admits to the spirit of revenge generated by generosity: "Such vengeance does my abundance concoct; such spite wells from my solitude. My joy died in giving, my virtue grew weary of itself through its abundance!" (Nietzsche 1984: 129).[7] Is the gift-giving virtue, then, bound to end in the resentment of giving? Is the gift as such impossible?

Faced with the *aporia* of the gift, let us turn back to Aristotle's discussion of three interconnected virtues specifically concerned with giving and receiving. In the framework of the *Nicomachean Ethics*, the discussion of these virtues follows that of temperance and precedes that of the social virtues, culminating in justice. The first of these virtues concerned with money and honor is *eleutheriotes*, "generosity" or "liberality," a mean between wastefulness and stinginess with regard to spending wealth in the right ways. The generous person will prefer giving to receiving and will be reluctant to ask for aid, "for it is not characteristic of a man who confers benefits to receive them lightly" (Aristotle 1941a: IV.1.1120a34). Indeed, the generous person is more likely to go to excess in giving. Nevertheless, Aristotle complicates this portrayal of generosity by saying that it "resides not in the multitude of gifts but in the state of character of the giver, and this is relative to the giver's substance" (1941a: 1120b7–10). The gift of a slice of bread, for example, could be a generous act under certain conditions of shortage or poverty.

Generosity, then, cannot be quantified by amount but must be judged by character and context. Those who have inherited wealth are likely to be more liberal than those who have made it themselves. It is hard for a generous person to hold onto money, since "he is profuse in spending it and values wealth not for its own sake but as a means of giving" (1941a: 1120b10–18). But, significantly, Aristotle stresses that generosity must include the virtues of *both* giving and receiving: "the giving and taking that accompany each other are present in the same man" (1941a: 1120b34). Aristotle thus sidesteps the problem of receiving by incorporating it into the virtue of generosity.

Second, Aristotle discusses *megaloprepeia*, "magnificence," which, "as the name itself suggests," means "a fitting [*prepousa*] expenditure involving largeness of scale [*megethos*]" (1941a: IV.2.1122a23). This virtue entails civic and religious expenditure, on a grander scale than that of generosity, taking the form of "gifts and counter-gifts": "for the magnificent man spends not on himself but on public objects, and gifts bear some resemblance to votive offerings" (1941a: 1123a).[8] A poor person, Aristotle tells us, could be generous, but not magnificent (1941a: 1122a30). Further, magnificence demands an artistic sense of scale so as to avoid vulgarity: "The magnificent man is like an artist; for he can see what is fitting and spend large sums tastefully" (1941a: 1122a34). This intertwining of artistic terms with ethical standards anticipates Nietzsche's own approach.

Turning to the third and highest of Aristotle's virtues of giving, *megalopsychia*, we are faced with an array of translations. Literally "great souledness" or "greatness of soul," the term has come to us from the Latin as "magnanimity." More loosely, it has been rendered as "high-mindedness" or "self-respect." Rackham, the translator of the Loeb edition of *Nicomachean Ethics* (1982), suggests the term means "lofty pride and self-esteem rather than magnanimity or high-mindedness (in the modern sense of the word)" (1982: 213). As Magnus notes, the term is "without question best known to English speaking persons as 'pride'" (1980: 261). Given that pride in the Christian tradition is a sin, this translation is especially significant from a Nietzschean perspective. Aristotle's suggestion that pride and self-love can be virtues would have been attractive to Nietzsche in his ongoing battles against the Christian ethics of humility and self-abnegation.[9]

Aristotle stresses the asymmetry in the kind of giving practiced by the proud man:[10]

> He is the sort of man to confer benefits, but he is ashamed of receiving them; for the one is the mark of a superior, the other of an inferior. And he is apt to confer greater benefits in return; for thus the original benefactor besides being paid will incur a debt to him, and will be the gainer by the transaction.
>
> (1941a: IV.3.1124b)

Ralph Waldo Emerson puts the point simply: "You cannot give anything to a magnanimous person" (1997: 27). Such a proud person will appear aloof and arrogant to commoners, yet he is virtuous, autonomous and generous in the extreme. There are bodily signs of greatness of soul, such as a slow step and a deep voice (1941a: 1125a13). Everything about such a person will be on a grand scale: "for pride implies greatness, as beauty implies a good-sized body" (1941a: 1123b6). Once again, we should note the intertwining of aesthetic and ethical terms. Unlike the vain man, the magnanimous man truly deserves the great things he claims. Aristotle calls this greatness of soul "a sort of crown of the virtues; for it makes them greater, and is not found without them" (1941a: 1124a). Outspoken, honest and courageous, disdainful of anything petty or slavish, the proud man "must be unable to make his life revolve around another, *unless it be a friend*" (1941a: 1125a; emphasis added). With this remark, Aristotle suggests that pride overcomes itself in friendship.

Here lies the key to another kind of giving and receiving: that between friends. Aristotle devotes two entire books of his ethics to friendship [*philia*], its types, its ethical and political implications, and its necessity for the good life. Contrary to our modern assumption that friendship is a merely personal, private matter, Aristotle understands friendship as the thread that knits together the social fabric.[11] Friendship resembles and encourages justice; friendship is esteemed as "the greatest good of states" (1941b: II.4.1262b7), so much that "legislators seem to be more concerned about it than justice" (1941a: VIII.1155a23). Aristotle emphasizes our need for friendship in the strongest terms: "For without friends, no one would choose to live" (1941a: VIII.1.1155a).

Aristotle envisions friendship as a partnership and a way of life, in which "some drink together, others dice together, others join in athletic exercises and hunting, or in the study of philosophy, each class spending their days together in whatever they love most in life" (1941a: IX.11.1172a4–6). Of the three main types of friendship, revolving around utility, pleasure, or virtue, it is only in the last and highest type that giving and receiving are equalized: "This kind of friendship, then, is perfect … and in it each gets from each in all respects the same as, or something like what, he gives; which is what ought to happen between friends" (1941a: VIII.4.1156b). In order for friends to practice the virtue of generosity, they must have someone *towards whom* they can be generous: beneficence is "exercised chiefly and in its most laudable form towards friends" (1941a: VIII.1.1155a9). Each friend will be strong enough to receive without becoming indebted. The giving and receiving will thus be continual, reciprocal and recognized. This mutuality resolves to a large degree the paradoxes of Nietzsche's one-sided gift-giving virtue.

However, Aristotle's theory of friendship does recognize that not all gifts can or should be precisely repaid, even between friends. In legal arrangements, "if it is possible we must repay" (1941a: 1163a8). But in other cases, "where there is *no* contract of service," the gift may be so great that no direct repayment is expected or even possible:

> And so, too, it seems, should one make a return to those with whom one has studied philosophy; for their worth cannot be measured against money, and they can get no honor which will balance their services, but still it is perhaps enough, as it is with the gods and with one's parents, to give them what one can.
>
> (1941a: IX.1.1164b2–6)

Here Aristotle recognizes that some gifts cannot be returned or repaid. In fact, Aristotle defines the gift in the strict sense of the term as "a transfer that need not be returned" (1984b: 125a18).[12] This definition opens up the possibility of giving and receiving beyond calculation, beyond the economy of the marketplace.[13]

The perception that allows Aristotle to go beyond the calculation of gifts is the well-known idea of the friend as "another self [*allos autos*]" (1941a: 1166a31). For Aristotle, friendship stimulates both ethical and intellectual achievement. Only through cultivating friendships of virtue do we realize who we are by recognizing ourselves in the other. The human self, to become fully itself, demands an "other," not an anonymous or abstract other, but an equal, a friend. This relation suggests a far richer understanding of self and other than either a Cartesian model, dependent on an isolated self, or an economic model, dependent on competing self-interests.[14] While for Descartes self-knowledge is the easiest and most certain of all, and the existence of "other minds" remains doubtful, for the Greeks self-knowledge is the hardest task of all. Knowing others as friends helps us to know ourselves, as dramatically expressed in this passage from *Magna Moralia*:

> We are not able to see what we are from ourselves. ... As then when we wish to see our own face we do so by looking into the mirror, in the same way when we wish to know ourselves we can obtain that knowledge by looking at our friend.
>
> (Aristotle 1984a: 1213a15–24)

Friendship in the Aristotelian sense thus obeys the command of the Delphic oracle, "know thyself."

Although in friendships of utility we calculate our advantage and measure each gift, making such relationships "full of complaints," in the highest kind of friendship this calculation does not occur. In this case, we relate to our friends not as "calculating agents" but as reflections of ourselves, so that between those "who are emulating each other [in virtue] there cannot be complaints or quarrels" (1941a: 1162b8). Emulation [*zelos*] Aristotle defines as "a good feeling felt by good people," in contrast to envy. "Emulation makes us take steps to secure the good things in question; envy makes us take steps to stop our neighbor having them" ([1941c]: II.11.1388a35). As if anticipating the Nietzschean threat of "the spirit of revenge," Aristotle holds that friends "do not nurse grudges or store grievances, but are always ready to make friends again" ([1941c]: II.4.1381b5). Hence friends in the highest sense may engage in a respectful rivalry and try to outshine each other in virtue, but in doing so they benefit themselves and each other. As Suzanne Stern-Gillet writes, Aristotle, "for whom selfhood is a moral goal, can claim *both* that friendship benefits the agent *and* that it disinterestedly seeks the good of another" (1995: 173). By practicing the virtue of generosity, for instance, I benefit both myself and my friend. As we give to our friend, so we also give to ourselves.[15]

There is then no clear demarcation of where our self-love ends and our love of our friend begins: "In loving their friend they love what is good for themselves" (Aristotle 1941a: VIII.1157b33). How, one might ask, does Aristotelian self-love differ from the "bad love" of self that Nietzsche criticizes as stingy and grasping (1984: 87)? While such bad selfishness in fact *lacks* self-affirmation, ethical friendship *strengthens* it. Nietzsche thus agrees with Aristotle that the root of our relation to others is our relation to ourselves, and further that not all self-love is created equal because not all selves are equal. But while Nietzsche criticizes the bad love of self, Aristotle criticizes the love of a bad self. Good people, Aristotle insists, should be friends to themselves and love themselves best, while bad people should not: the former have unified and harmonious souls, while the latter are "rent by faction," so that "the bad man does not seem to be amicably disposed even to himself" (1941a: IX.4.1166b25). In ethical friendship, "the extreme of friendship is likened to one's love for oneself" (1941a: 1166b1). Indeed, the self-sufficiency of the happy life does not exclude but demands friendship, "for no one would choose the whole world on condition of being alone, since man is a political creature and one whose nature is to live with others" (1941a: 1169b18). Even the proud person finds a counterpart in the friend. Aristotelian friendship is neither altruistic nor egotistic in the conventional sense, but involves a different kind of inter-subjectivity.[16] Friendship allows for mutual self-actualization in a life of flourishing: "as his own being is desirable for each man, so, or almost so, is that of his friend" (1941a: IX.9.1170b8). Aristotelian friendship thus allows for rivalry in giving while avoiding resentment over receiving.

Aristotle and Nietzsche, in sum, have more to say to each other than we usually assume. Both endorse self-cultivation and a "this-worldly" understanding of ethics, in which life itself, not the promise of an afterlife, is the reward. Both follow an empirical approach and differentiate between types of human characters instead of stressing universal moral laws or a transcendent, timeless Good. The idea of the *Übermensch*, as I have suggested, bears a striking resemblance to the idea of *megalopsychia*: both terms suggest a level of humanity over and above the average, an excessive generosity of soul.[17] We might further interpret the life-affirming will to power as a gift from Aristotelian *eudaimonia*. As Solomon notes (1987: 118), Nietzsche's own listing of "the four cardinal virtues" – honesty, bravery, magnanimity and politeness – sounds distinctly Aristotelian (Nietzsche 1982: V.556, p.224). And as we have seen, the Aristotelian ideal of noble self-love anticipates the Nietzschean ideal of "the sound, healthy selfishness that issues from a mighty soul [*aus mächtiger Seele*]" (Nietzsche 1984: 208).

But while these similarities are striking, it is also important to recognize the major differences. For Aristotle, greatness of soul is still a social virtue, a mean between extremes, and a "crown of the virtues." For Nietzsche, by contrast, "social virtues" suggest the "herd mentality," and talk of the "golden mean" sounds too conformist. Aristotle is confident that there is a human function, namely reasoning, and that we can cultivate it in communities; Nietzsche views both claims skeptically. As Hough writes, "Aristotle emphasizes training, upbringing, the development of appropriate sensibilities, while Nietzsche urges each person to embrace his fated constitution in the necessary fashion" (1997: 22). Another major factor separating the two thinkers is modern historicism. Lampert, citing Aristotle as an antecedent for the gift giving virtue, rightly notes this difference: "Aristotle's praise of gift-giving lacks the historical dimension present in Zarathustra's teaching" (1986: 78). For Nietzsche, unlike Aristotle, gift giving paves the way to the future.

The different roles of friendship, and the correspondingly different conceptions of selfhood, help us understand the divergence of the two thinkers. On this point, perhaps Nietzsche has something still to learn from Aristotle. While Nietzsche admires the Greeks both for their noble friendship and for their noble competition, *philia* and *agon*, he develops the latter at the expense of the former. Nietzsche expresses deep respect for the ancient ideal of friendship and calls it "the highest feeling" when he retells the story of a Macedonian king who said of an anti-worldly Athenian philosopher: "I should honor his humanity even more if the friend in him had triumphed over his pride" (1974: II.61, p. 124). He recognizes in this ethical form of friendship a rare "kind of continuation of love [...] – a *shared* higher thirst for an ideal above them" (1974: I.14, p. 89). As Zarathustra says, the perception that "made the soul of a Greek tremble" was " 'You should always be the first and outrival all others; your jealous soul should love no one, except your friend' " (1984: 85). But Nietzsche radicalizes friendship to mean strife: the noble person reveres his enemies as friends. Such reverence serves as a "bridge to love. – For he desires his enemy for himself, as his mark of distinction" (1967c: I.10, p. 39). When Nietzsche refers to greatness of soul, he omits the possibility of friendship, writing that "*greatness of soul has nothing romantic about it,*" and "nothing at all amiable" (1968: 981). Hence he emphasizes the "incomprehensible loneliness" of the philosophers of the future, and interprets "solitude as happiness" (1968: 985, 993). For Nietzsche there seems to be no possibility of desiring a noble friend in the Aristotelian sense as another self.[18]

In the famous scene that concludes the gift-giving section in *Zarathustra*, the leader urges his disciples to lose their love of him to find themselves.[19] Only then will they truly become friends: "the man of knowledge must be able not only to love his enemies but also to hate his friends" (Nietzsche 1984: 103). To follow Zarathustra truly means not to follow him at all, because "one repays a teacher badly if one remains only a pupil" (1984: 103). Correspondingly, the friend is not another self but an intimate antagonist: "In your friend you should possess your best enemy" (1984: 83). As Zarathustra (and Nietzsche himself, we might add) knows only too well, any kind of love, like any kind of receiving, proves the most difficult, for "*Love* is the danger for the most solitary man, love of any thing *if only it is alive!*" (1984: 175; emphasis in original). While Zarathustra preaches friendship, saying, "may the friend be to you a festival of the earth and a foretaste of the *Übermensch*" (1984: 87), he does not practice it. Zarathustra suffers from melancholy precisely because he has not overcome his pride and found a friend, an equal, and so has not learned how to *receive* with strength and grace.

The Nietzschean gift-giving virtue, then, could strengthen itself by re-encountering the Aristotelian *give-and-take* virtue between friends. The gift of friendship is a gift that knows how to *receive*; it knows how to give presents and also how to forgive debt. When Zarathustra exclaims, "Oh solitude of all givers!" (1984: 130), could we not respond with the Aristotelian community of friendship? And when Nietzsche writes, "Alas my friends, we must overcome even the Greeks!" (1974: IV.340, p.272), could we not reply, "Indeed, *as* friends, we must overcome even Nietzsche's overcoming of the Greeks!"[20]

Notes

1 For more on Nietzsche's continuing entanglement with Socrates and Plato, see my article "The music-making Socrates" (Woodruff 2002). See also the recent studies by Kofman (1998), Nehamas (1998) and Zuckert (1996).

2 Whether this interpretation does justice to Aristotle on the tragic emotions would be the subject for another paper. I suspect that interpreting *katharsis* as discharge does not

in fact fully capture Aristotle's sense of the term, but instead depends on a dominant medicinal view made popular in the nineteenth century by Jacob Bernays. For Nietzsche's relation to Aristotle's *Poetics* and to Bernays, see Silk and Stern 1981. On the range of meanings of *katharsis*, see Nussbaum 1986 and Rorty's (1992) collection.

3 The young Nietzsche was interested enough in Aristotle to hold lectures on his work in 1867 and to express the intention (not fulfilled) of writing a dissertation on Aristotle; see Wingler 1976.

4 For a perceptive critique of MacIntyre's oversimplified opposition of Aristotle and Nietzsche, see Bernstein's "Nietzsche or Aristotle? Reflections on Alasdair MacIntyre's *After Virtue*" (1986).

5 In his lectures on Nietzsche, Heidegger asserts that Aristotle's doctrine of *energeia*, actuality or activity, has a great deal in common with the will to power, although Nietzsche did not realize it (Heidegger 1991: I.56).

6 The gift-giving virtue offers an alternative to Christian charity that preaches, "it is nobler to give than to receive." As Laurence Lampert writes, Christian "charity sacrifices the self for the lowly," while the Nietzschean "gift-giving virtue squanders the self for the great" (1986: 78). My overall reading of *Zarathustra* is indebted to Lampert's analysis.

7 Already in *Daybreak*, Nietzsche worries over "*the shame of those who bestow*": "It is so unmagnanimous always to play the bestower and giver and to show one's face when doing so!" It is better, he says, to give without showing one's face, as nature does: "here we at last no longer encounter a giver and bestower" (1982: 182).

8 In *Given Time*, Derrida cites these passages and states that for Aristotle, "the magnanimous man does not spend for himself but for the common good. ... There are different sorts of largesse, of gift, of present" (1992: 139).

9 Kaufmann goes so far as to assert that this concept of pride "apparently made a tremendous impression on Nietzsche whose opposition to Christianity can scarcely be seen in proper perspective apart from Aristotle's ethics" (1956: 329).

10 Within my exegesis of the *Nicomachean Ethics*, I follow Aristotle in speaking of "the proud man," since Aristotle does mean primarily a male person; but when applying Aristotle's ideas in my own arguments, I say "the proud person" and intend it more inclusively. Despite Aristotle's own statements on female inferiority, feminist philosophers have found much worthy of retrieval in Aristotle. For a feminist reading of Aristotelian pride and friendship, see Groenhout.

11 As MacIntyre writes, "For us the notion that friendship, company and a city-state are essential components of humanity is alien" (1982: 127). And as A.W. Price notes, a modern work that devoted a fifth of its chapters to friendship would seem "quaint," in part because "modern moral philosophy has become obsessed with one's obligations towards people one does not know" (1989: 159).

12 For more on this statement, and on the meanings of the Greek words for different kinds of gifts, see Benveniste 1997. Derrida, citing Benveniste, places special emphasis on Aristotle's statement: "The importance of this allusive citation is in truth beyond measure. It announces the link between the economy of the proper ... and the coming or coming-back of the event as restitution or beyond restitution, in the *Ereignis* or in the *Enteignis*" (1992: 81).

13 Robert Bernasconi, with such passages in mind, suggests that here "the gift, like the friendship from which it derives, has the character of an excess (*hyperbole*) such that it cannot be measured by any calculation of its value" (1997: 267).

14 Such a different self/other relation seems demanded by any new ethic of gift giving. As Alan D. Schrift writes: "To free ourselves from the oppositional logic of 'self vs. all others' might allow for our self-construction as something other than isolated and atomistic subjectivities" (1997: 20). Aristotelian friendship, I suggest, gives us resources for just such a project.

15 As Paul Schollmeier writes, "another self belongs to us, for we make other selves ours by helping them attain or retain their happiness. They become our work, so to speak" (1994: 3).

16 Even the term "inter-subjectivity" seems anachronistic, since Aristotle did not of course have a modern idea of subjectivity, but my point is to underscore the interconnection between self-love and love of others that occurs in friendship. Suzanne Stern-Gillet is right to say that "a reliance on the dichotomy of egoism and altruism seriously impedes the exegesis of Aristotle's treatment of primary friendship" (1995: 4).

17 As Solomon asks: "who is the *Übermensch* if not Aristotle's *megalopsychos*, the 'great-souled man' from whom Nietzsche even borrows much of his 'master-type' terminology" (1987: 115). But a more direct source of the idea of the *Übermensch* is Emerson's idea of the "Oversoul"; see Stack 1992.

18 In the *Politics of Friendship* (1997), Derrida complicates the possibility of friends in Aristotle, and of enemies in Nietzsche, by repeating the phrase Montaigne attributes to Aristotle, "Oh my friends, there is no friend" and by referring to a statement Nietzsche makes in *Human All Too Human*: "'Friends, there are no friends!' thus said the dying sage; 'Foes, there are no foes!' say I the living fool!" (Nietzsche 1996: 376). Derrida stresses that we are "obliged to respect at least, first of all, the authority of Aristotle's questions"on friendship (1997: 6) and that a rebirth of friendship means a new kind of justice.

19 As Lampert notes (1986: 73), this speech offers an exact contrast with Matthew 16:24: "Then Jesus told his disciples, 'If any man would come after me, let him deny himself and take up his cross and follow me.'"

20 I gratefully acknowledge the gifts of several friends in developing this paper: Victor Nuovo, Middlebury College, read the first draft and raised helpful questions; Alan D. Schrift, Grinnell College, included this paper in his panel on the gift at the International Association for Philosophy and Literature in May 1998; Dennis O'Brien, University of Rochester, suggested how to situate Aristotle's discussions; and James E. Berg, Iowa State University, greatly helped with the revisions of the final draft.

References

Aristotle. *Nicomachean Ethics*. Trans. W.D. Ross. *The Basic Works of Aristotle*. Ed. Richard McKeon. New York: Random House, 1941a, pp. 935–1112.

—— *Politics*. Trans. Benjamin Jowett. *The Basic Works of Aristotle*. Ed. Richard McKeon. New York: Random House, 1941b, pp. 1114–1316.

—— *Rhetoric*. Trans. W. Rhys Roberts. *he Basic Works of Aristotle*. Ed. Richard Mckeon. New York: Random House, 1941c, pp. 1318–1451.

—— *Nicomachean Ethics*. Trans. H. Rackham. Loeb Greek-English Edition. Cambridge: Harvard University Press, 1982.

—— *Magna Moralia*. Trans. S.G. Stock. *Complete Works*. Volume 2. Ed. Jonathan Barnes. Princeton: Princeton University Press, 1984a, pp. 1868–1921.

—— *Topics* and *Magna Moralia*. *Complete Works*. Ed. Jonathan Barnes. Princeton: Princeton University Press, 1984b, pp. 167–277.

—— *Poetics*. Trans. Stephen Halliwell. Chapel Hill: North Carolina University Press, 1987.

—— *Rhetoric*. Trans. John Henry Freese. Loeb Greek–English Edition. Cambridge: Harvard UP, 1991. [Greek text only]

Benveniste, Émile. "Gift and exchange in the Indo-European vocabulary." Trans. Mary Elizabeth Meek. In Alan D. Schrift (ed.) *The Logic of the Gift: Toward an Ethic of Generosity.* New York: Routledge, 1997, pp. 33–42.

Bernasconi, Robert. "What comes around goes around: Derrida and Levinas on the economy of the gift and the gift of genealogy." In Alan D. Schrift (ed.) *The Logic of the Gift: Toward an Ethic of Generosity.* New York: Routledge, 1997, pp. 256–73.

Bernstein, Richard J. "Nietzsche or Aristotle? Reflections on Alasdair MacIntyre's *After Virtue." Philosophical Profiles.* Philadelphia: University of Pennsylvania Press, 1986, pp. 115–40.

Derrida, Jacques. *Given Time: I. Counterfeit Money.* Trans. Peggy Kamuf. Chicago: University of Chicago Press, 1992.

—— *The Politics of Friendship.* Trans. George Collins. New York: Verso, 1997.

Emerson, Ralph Waldo. "Gifts." In Alan D. Schrift (ed.) *The Logic of the Gift: Toward an Ethic of Generosity.* New York: Routledge, 1997, pp. 25–7.

Groenhout, Ruth. "The virtue of care: Aristotelian ethics and contemporary ethics of care." In Cynthia A. Freeland (ed.) *Feminist Interpretations of Aristotle.* University Park: Pennsylvania State University Press, 1998, pp. 171–200.

Heidegger, Martin. *What Is Called Thinking?* Trans. J. Glenn Gray. New York: Harper & Row, 1968.

—— *Nietzsche.* Volumes I and II. Trans. David Krell. San Francisco: Harper Collins, 1991.

Hough, Sheridan. *Nietzsche's Noontide Friend: The Self as Metaphoric Double.* University Park: Pennsylvania State University Press, 1997.

Kaufmann, Walter. *Nietzsche.* New York: Meridian, 1956.

Kofman, Sarah. *Socrates: Fictions of a Philosopher.* Trans. Catherine Porter. Ithaca: Cornell University Press, 1998.

Lampert, Lawrence. *Nietzsche's Teaching: An Interpretation of* Thus Spoke Zarathustra. New Haven: Yale University Press, 1986.

MacIntyre, Alasdair. *After Virtue: A Study in Moral Theory.* London: Duckworth, 1982.

Magnus, Bernd. "Aristotle and Nietzsche: *Megalopsychia* and *Übermensch.*" In David J. Depew (ed.) *The Greeks and the Good Life.* Indianapolis: Hackett, 1980, pp. 260–95.

Nehamas, Alexander. *The Art of Living: Socratic Reflections from Plato to Foucault.* Berkeley: University of California Press, 1998.

Nietzsche, Friedrich. *The Birth of Tragedy.* Trans. Walter Kaufmann. New York: Vintage, 1967a.

—— *Nietzsches Werke (Kritische Gesamtausgabe).* Ed. Giorgio Colli and Mazzino Montinari. Berlin: de Gruyter, 1967b.

—— *On the Genealogy of Morals.* Trans. Walter Kaufmann and R.J. Hollingdale. New York: Vintage, 1967c.

—— *The Will to Power.* Trans. Walter Kaufmann and R.J. Hollingdale. New York: Vintage, 1968.

—— *The Gay Science.* Trans. Walter Kaufmann. New York: Vintage, 1974.

—— *Daybreak.* Trans. R.J. Hollingdale. Cambridge: Cambridge University Press, 1982.

—— *Thus Spoke Zarathustra.* Trans. R.J. Hollingdale. London: Penguin, 1984.

—— "The struggle between science and wisdom." *Philosophy and Truth: Selections from Nietzsche's Notebooks of the Early 1870's.* Ed. and trans. Daniel Breazeale. Atlantic Highlands, NJ: Humanities Press, 1992, pp. 127–46.

—— *Human All Too Human.* Trans. R.J. Hollingdale. Cambridge: Cambridge University Press, 1996.

—— *Twilight of the Idols.* Trans. Richard Polt. Indianapolis: Hackett, 1997.

Nussbaum, Martha C. *The Fragility of Goodness.* Cambridge: Cambridge University Press, 1986.

Pakaluk, Michael (ed.). *Other Selves: Philosophers on Friendship.* Indianapolis: Hackett, 1991.

Price, A.W. *Love and Friendship in Plato and Aristotle.* Oxford: Clarendon, 1989.

Rorty, Amelie (ed.). *Essays on Aristotle's Poetics.* Princeton: Princeton University Press, 1992.

Schollmeier, Paul. *Other Selves: Aristotle on Personal and Political Friendship.* Albany: State University of New York Press, 1994.

Schrift, Alan D. "Introduction: why gift?" In Alan D. Schrift (ed.) *The Logic of the Gift: Toward an Ethic of Generosity.* New York: Routledge, 1997, pp. 1–22.

Shapiro, Gary. "The Metaphysics of Presents: Nietzsche's Gift, the Debt to Emerson, Heidegger's Values." In Alan D. Schrift (ed.) *The Logic of the Gift: Toward an Ethic of Generosity.* New York: Routledge, 1997, pp. 274–91.

Silk, M.S. and J.P. Stern. *Nietzsche on Tragedy.* Cambridge: Cambridge University Press, 1981.

Solomon, Robert C. *From Hegel to Existentialism.* Oxford: Oxford University Press, 1987.

Stack, George J. *Nietzsche and Emerson: An Elective Affinity.* Athens: Ohio University Press, 1992.

Stern-Gillet, Suzanne. *Aristotle's Philosophy of Friendship.* Albany: State University of New York Press, 1995.

Wingler, Henwig. "Aristotle in the thought of Nietzsche and Thomas Aquinas." Trans. Timothy F. Sellner. In James C. O'Flaherty, Timothy F. Sellner and Robert M. Helm (eds) *Studies in Nietzsche and the Classical Tradition.* Chapel Hill: University of North Carolina Press, 1976, pp. 33–54.

Woodruff, Martha K. "The music-making Socrates: Plato and Nietzsche revisited, philosophy and tragedy rejoined." *International Studies in Philosophy* 34.3 (2002): 135–54.

Zuckert, Catherine. *Postmodern Platos.* Chicago: University of Chicago Press, 1996.

6   Adam Smith and the debt of gratitude

Eun Kyung Min

> Men owe us what we imagine they will give to us. We must forgive them this debt.
>
> Simone Weil, *La pesanteur et la grâce* (1947)

What is the nature of Adam Smith's "moral economy"? I want to broach this question by examining Smith's discussion of the difficult "debt of gratitude" (1982: 79) in *The Theory of Moral Sentiments* (1982 [1759–90]).[1] How can gratitude help us understand what counts as a moral virtue, and why, in a commercialized market society? Smith writes that the "want of gratitude … cannot be punished," since "[t]o oblige [a man] by force to perform what in gratitude he ought to perform, and what every impartial spectator would approve of him for performing, would, if possible, be still more improper than his neglecting to perform it" (1982: 79).[2] Smith's postulate of a gift without equivalent that begets a permanent and unaccountable debt of gratitude thus has little to do with the exigencies of economic exchange or the consolations of justice. How can such a theory of gratitude contribute to an understanding of modernity?

To begin a reading of *The Theory of Moral Sentiments* with gratitude is to see immediately the self-acknowledged limits of Smith's first work. The difficulty of gratitude points out the irony of Smith's title and project, for what is distinctive about moral sentiments is that ultimately one cannot very well "theorize" about them or submit them to rules. On this point Smith is very clear:

> The rules of justice may be compared to the rules of grammar; the rules of the other virtues, to the rules which critics lay down for the attainment of what is sublime and elegant in composition. The one, are precise, accurate, and indispensable. The other, are loose, vague, and indeterminate, and present us rather with a general idea of the perfection we ought to aim at, than afford us any certain and infallible directions for acquiring it.
>
> (1982: 175–6)

Despite the familiar rhetorical blend here, we have a clear insistence on the disanalogy between moral and economic commerce. The rules of justice, like the rules of economy, work through an intentional "grammar" of motives and means: they "aim," "afford" and "acquire." Virtue, on the other hand, follows rules only in the sense of instancing standards and qualities we hold up as examples. When we intend virtue, that is, we are peculiarly unaided. Distancing virtue from the causal narratives of work and recompense, of deed and desert, Smith instead aligns virtue with aesthetic "composition" whose instruments remain unruly and mysterious to the "critics." In other words, just as critics can judge only the products, not the production, of literary labor, the moral theorist can give rules only "to correct and ascertain ... the imperfect ideas" we hold of virtue, not the rules by which we can infallibly act virtuously (1982: 176).[3]

It is important to see that what drives Smith's distinction between justice and virtue here is not a blanket skepticism toward the efficacy of moral discourse. It is rather Smith's careful distinction between "perfect rights" and "imperfect obligations" (Hont and Ignatieff 1983: 29)[4] – in other words, between the rights we can legally claim for ourselves as citizens among equals and the obligations we as virtuous individuals owe to our fellow-citizens. Like Hume, Smith circumscribes "precise, accurate, and indispensable" justice to our dealings in property (1982: 175). According to the story of economic progress that Smith tells in *An Inquiry into the Nature and Causes of the Wealth of Nations* (1981 [1776–89]), his second and best-known work, justice becomes a need only when the age of shepherds ushers in "inequality of fortune." Judicial authority is an invention of civil government that, in turn, "is instituted for the security of property" – that is, "instituted for the defence of the rich against the poor, or of those who have some property against those who have none at all" (1981: 236). Smith's project in *The Wealth of Nations* is to show how this protection of private property, originally aimed at defending the rich against the poor, ultimately *profits* the poor in commercial society.[5] In this sense, *The Wealth of Nations* is committed to justice over virtue: Smith sets a higher *political* value on the "universal opulence which extends itself to the lowest ranks of the people" (1981: 15) than on the monopoly on virtue held by the propertied elite in the civic virtue tradition.[6]

The Theory of Moral Sentiments, by contrast, is committed to virtue over justice. This difference in commitment, I submit, is not in itself a theoretical inconsistency.[7] Although the so-called "Adam Smith problem" has traditionally been defined in terms of a *conceptual* inconsistency between a market theory based on individual self-interest and a moral theory based on sympathy, *The Wealth of Nations* and *The Theory of Moral Sentiments* are committed to conceptually *complementary* forms of justice. As Smith explains in *The Theory of Moral Sentiments*, the kind of strict justice that can be violently enforced is negative (or "commutative," following Aristotle). It stipulates only that we must "abstain from doing [our neighbor] any positive harm" (1982: 269). There is, however, another kind of justice that consists in doing unto our neighbor all that he deserves:

> it is in this sense that we are said to do injustice to a man of merit who is connected with us, though we abstain from hurting him in every respect, if we do not exert ourselves to serve him and to place him in that situation in which the impartial spectator would be pleased to see him.
>
> (1982: 269)

The social virtues aim at this larger sense of positive, "distributive" justice, the doing unto others what is properly due to them.

At first sight, Smith's vision of the complementary relation between commutative and distributive justice appears profoundly realist. There is no question about which he considered more necessary:

> Society may subsist among different men, as among different merchants, from a sense of its utility, without any mutual love or affection; and though no man in it should owe any obligation, or be bound in gratitude to any other, it may still be upheld by a mercenary exchange of good offices according to an agreed valuation.
>
> (1982: 86)

This is why the idea of a "society of robbers and murderers" is a paradox for Smith: "If there is any society among robbers and murderers, they must at least, according to the trite observation, abstain from robbing and murdering one another" (1982: 86). By contrast, the society of merchants, unbound by gratitude, makes gratitude possible by making society possible. Gratitude, in this sense, is "the ornament which embellishes, not the foundation which supports the building, and which it was, therefore, sufficient to recommend, but by no means necessary to impose" (1982: 86). The move is familiar: justice and economy belong to the realm of the necessary; virtue lies beyond this realm of the necessitated, in the aesthetic realm of the "sublime and elegant in composition" (1982: 175). What is added here, however, is Smith's clear indication that the moral realm cannot be thought separately from the social. And the social, we discover, is *natural*. To return to the analogy: justice is the "main pillar that upholds the whole edifice ... the great, the immense fabric of human society, that fabric which to raise and support seems in this world," says Smith, "to have been the peculiar and darling care of Nature" (1982: 86).[8]

Consider the *natural* admiration of wealth and fortune:

> The rich man glories in his riches, because he feels that they *naturally* draw upon him the attention of the world, and that mankind are disposed to go along with him in all those agreeable emotions with which the advantages of his situation so readily inspire him. At the thought of this, his heart seems to swell and dilate itself within him, and he is fonder of his wealth, upon this account, than for all the other advantages it procures him. The poor man, on the contrary, is ashamed of his poverty. He feels that it either places him out of the sight of mankind, or, that if they take any notice of him, they have, however, scarce any fellow-feeling with the misery and distress which he suffers. He is mortified upon both accounts; for though to be overlooked, and to be dis-approved of, are things entirely different, yet as obscurity covers us from the daylight of honour and approbation, to feel that we are taken no notice of, necessarily damps the most agreeable hope, and disappoints the most ardent desire, of human nature.
>
> (Smith 1982: 51; emphasis added)

In *The Wealth of Nations*, it is the human "propensity to truck, barter, and exchange one thing for another" (1981: 17) that gives rise to wealth. This uniquely human tendency to engage in commerce, Smith carefully states, may be "one of those original principles of human nature, of which no further account can be given," but is *more probably* "the necessary consequence of the faculties of reason and speech" (1981: 17). Here we see Smith not only fully exploiting the double meaning of commerce but knitting the two senses of the word together through mutually binding narratives.[9] On the one hand, the social commerce (conversation, communication, association, interchange) we hold with one another gives rise to material commerce (buying, selling, bargaining, trucking and bartering). On the other hand, as we see in the passage above, the real consequence and joy of material commerce is the "attention" and "approbation" (1982: 51) it procures. As Smith puts it, the "purpose" of "all the toil and bustle of the world ... the end of avarice and ambition, of the pursuit of wealth, of power, and preheminence [sic]," the object of our emulative desire for "bettering our condition," is "to be observed, to be attended to, to be taken notice of with sympathy, complacency, and approbation" (1982: 52). The two meanings of commerce thus are *natural* origins and ends of each other. Hence the ambiguity: however much Smith's narratives emphasize process, desire, motion, exchange, they are grounded in a circular logic that gives his work the appearance of a formidable stasis.

The example of the rich man thus reads like (and has been read as) an apology for the status quo. But what kind of a status quo does Smith have in mind? Smith's analysis smacks less of adulatory belief in commercial progress than deference to a mythical paternalism – both of which E.P. Thompson calls "superstition."[10] When Smith rhetorically naturalizes our sympathy for the rich, however, he is not, by that gesture, simply endorsing it. As he puts it, "It is scarce agreeable to good morals, or even to good language, perhaps, to say, that mere wealth and greatness, abstracted from merit and virtue, deserve our respect" (1982: 62). In fact, Smith unambiguously states that "this disposition of mankind, to go along with all the passions of the rich and the powerful" (1982: 52) is grounded in "the abstract idea of a perfect and happy state" painted in the "delusive colours" of the imagination (1982: 51). Our belief in the "pleasures of wealth and greatness" is quite simply a "deception" that "nature imposes upon us" (1982: 183). Smith's rich man and poor man in *The Theory of Moral Sentiments*, in other words, are fictions that form an intrinsic part of the way we imagine ourselves. As Smith's contemporary Edmund Burke would similarly have claimed, our need and desire to see ourselves as others see us involves a natural, prejudicial acceptance of "the distinction of ranks, and the order of society" (1982: 52). Smith's striking move here is to posit that imagination, rather than experience, forms and guides our dispositions to act.[11] Being creatures of habit, we have an imaginative need for hierarchy and order. This is what grounds our standards of judgment and, at the same time, *naturally* (or as Smith puts it, "in the nicest manner" ([1982: 184]) "rouses and keeps in continual motion the industry of mankind" (1982: 183). Nature, in this regard, is simply another name for the harmonizing force Smith, in another context, calls the "invisible hand" (1982: 184).[12] The invisible hand, we might say, harmonizes *forward*, first by instilling in us an ardent, industrious desire to emulate the rich and the great, then by commuting new, individual property into common wealth, independently of individual intention. The rich man, "without knowing it, advance[s] the interest of the society" because his wealth employs, pays, sustains the poor (1982: 185). The deceptive, sympathetic imagination harmonizes *backward*, by rooting our moral responses in old social practices that, to borrow Pocock's phrase, "anchor commerce in history" (1985: 210). Imagination thus obviates, or rather endlessly defers, the question of origins and motives in Smith's work. Translating prejudice into profit and history into nature, it supplies the dynamic link between the past and the future.

Gratitude is an interesting test of Smith's theories because it touches on so many of the important Smithian themes: it is rooted in an ancient political practice, involves the exchange of goods, is relevant for justice, and carries pre-eminent moral value ("the duties of gratitude ... are perhaps the most sacred of all those which the beneficent virtues prescribe to us" ([1982: 174]). The now obsolete meaning of gratitude, "a grant or contribution made to the sovereign" (OED),[13] informs Smith's understanding of the grateful exchange, as the following discussion in *The Wealth of Nations* will show.

Noting that the administration of justice, necessary in all societies where disputes over property may arise, was never free of cost, Smith writes that justice was a profitable business for those who held the authority to administer it. According to Smith, the very institution of taxation originated in the practice of accompanying a petition for justice with a present. Predictably, the practice led to abuse, for "the person, who applied for justice with a large present in his hand, was likely to get something more than justice; while he, who applied for it with a small one, was likely to get something less" (1981: 237):

> When Agamemnon, in Homer, offers to Achilles for his friendship the sovereignty of seven Greek cities, the sole advantage which he mentions as likely to be derived for it, was, that the people would honour him with presents. As long as such presents, as long as the emoluments of justice, or what may be called the fees of court, constituted in this manner the whole ordinary revenue which the sovereign derived from his sovereignty, it could not well be expected, it could not even decently be proposed, that he should give them up altogether. It might, and it frequently was proposed, that he should regulate and ascertain them. But after they had been so regulated and ascertained, how to hinder a person who was all-powerful from extending them beyond those regulations, was still very difficult, not to say impossible. During the continuance of this state of things, therefore, the

corruption of justice, naturally resulting from the arbitrary and uncertain nature of those presents, scarce admitted of any effectual remedy.

(1981: 239)

What Smith calls "the arbitrary and uncertain nature of those presents" results from their function as symbols of gratitude. Whether given at the time of the petition or later, the private transaction of presents would seem to conflict with the public nature of the justice done. But this of course is a modern formulation. Why did gifts accompany the petitions for justice? Smith's invocation of nature again offers a clue. The original figure of natural authority for Smith is "the great shepherd or herdsman," respected for his wealth and the antiquity of his family, who "has a *natural* authority over all the inferior shepherds or herdsmen of his horde or clan" (1981: 235; emphasis added).[14] The proffering of gifts to the wealthy shepherd, then, is the natural corollary to the delegation of justice to him, since both wealth and authority naturally accrue to him. The proleptic gift in its origin is a symbolic reaffirmation of what is *naturally* due to the wealthy shepherd: wealth, honor, authority.[15]

What makes the transaction far trickier is what Marcel Mauss, in his important anthropological study of gift exchange, famously referred to as "the ancient morality of the gift, which has become a principle of justice" (1990: 18).[16] In *The Gift*, Mauss analyzes the mechanisms by which the gift "forges a bilateral, irrevocable bond" (1990: 59) between the donor and the recipient of the gift – a bond through which the donor exercises power over the recipient to the exact extent that the recipient understands that the gift is a "symbol of social life" (1990: 33). The "nature of the legal tie that arises through the passing on of a thing" is mythical, symbolic, imaginary (1990: 12), and for that reason all the more exacting. Since the gift is an expression of human solidarity[17] and involves the imagined oneness of a community, the failure to honor the tie is "to reject the bond of alliance and commonality" (1990: 13). Applying Mauss's insights to Smith's mythical narrative, we immediately see that the petitionary gift demands that the wealthy shepherd acknowledge his part in the symbolic transactions that accord him juridical authority over others. In other words, the gift is a reminder that the authority of the wealthy shepherd is authority that is naturally *given* to him by others. What is the lesson of Smith's story of the corruption of justice? It is not that the "all-powerful" man is morally fallible because he himself cannot be regulated and operates only on behalf of his own interests. On the contrary: it is that he is all too easily regulated by the very gifts he ought to regulate. The corruption, in other words, is not individual but communal. The gifts that are symbolically offered in the service of disinterested justice are hardly free. As Mauss writes, "the economy of the gift" is "burdened with consideration for people" (1990: 54). And so, in Smith's narrative, the gift procures the donor's, no less than the recipient's, interest. No wonder taxation was simpler, though also more corrosive to authority.

The modern dilemma of gratitude as Smith sees it follows the symbolic logic of the gift as evidenced in the origins of justice, with an important twist:

If your benefactor attended you in your sickness, ought you to attend him in his? Or can you fulfil the obligation of gratitude, by making a return of a different kind? If you ought to attend him, how long ought you to attend him? The same time which he attended you, or longer, and how much longer? If your friend lent you money in your distress, ought you to lend him money in his? How much ought you to lend him? When ought you to lend him? Now, or to-morrow, or next month? And for how long a time? It is evident, that no general rule can be laid down, by which a precise answer can, in all cases, be given to any of these questions. The difference between his character and yours, between his circumstances and yours, may be such, that you may be perfectly grateful, and justly refuse to lend him a halfpenny: and, on the contrary, you may be willing to lend, or even to give him ten times on the sum which he lent you, and yet justly be accused of the blackest ingratitude, and of not having fulfilled the hundredth part of the obligation you lie under.

(Smith 1982: 174)

This passage helps us understand the "arbitrary and uncertain" nature of the gifts discussed earlier (1981: 239). I have suggested that what makes the presents given to the wealthy shepherd ambiguous is the changeable balance between the power they give to and withhold from him, between his ability to regulate and his capacity to be regulated. The balance is decided not individually but through the complex of relations the wealthy shepherd has with his community. Here the difficulty appears more radical but, as I shall argue, harks as strongly back to gift exchange. Smith takes it as a "pretty plain rule" and "one which admitted of scarce any exceptions," that "as soon as we can we should make a return of equal, and if possible of superior value to the services we have received" (1982: 174). This rule, which we knowingly or unknowingly apply to ourselves, is the "overexpensive" rule of the gift (Mauss 1990: 54). It has nothing to do with the law of economic bargain.[18]

Then what is new about these questions? The wealthy shepherd, we imagine, could well have been asked to adjudicate between friends quarreling over a loan. The difference, to put it somewhat deceptively, is simply that there is no wealthy shepherd here. A third-person authority is notably absent from the picture. The wealthy shepherd has become internalized as Smith's famous impartial spectator, "the man within the breast" sitting at "the tribunal of [our] own consciences" (1982: 130), judging more justly than the shepherd, according to Smith, because he is paradoxically more dependent on the approbation of others. But the dependence implied in the judgments of the impartial spectator is notably different from the bonds of dependence authorized by the gifts for justice. The desire for approbation is natural in both cases because, as Smith says,

Nature, when she formed man for society, endowed him with an original desire to please, and an original aversion to offend his brethren. She taught him to feel pleasure in their favourable, and pain in their unfavourable regard. She rendered their approbation most flattering and most agreeable to him for its own sake; and their disapprobation most mortifying and most offensive.

(1982: 116)

Whereas the "others" in the story of the Greeks are actual members of a closed community headed by the wealthy shepherd, the "others" that the impartial spectator heeds are not actual bystanders and observers of our actions. They are imaginary, just as the impartial spectator is imaginary.[19]

A passage in the second edition of *The Theory of Moral Sentiments* helps us clinch the matter.[20] By learning to set up "*in our own minds* a judge between ourselves and those we live with," Smith writes,

> We conceive ourselves as acting in the presence of a person quite candid and equitable, of one who has no particular relation either to ourselves, or to those whose interests are affected by our conduct, who is neither father, nor brother, nor friend either to them or to us, but is merely a man in general, an impartial spectator who considers our conduct with the same indifference with which we regard that of other people.

(1982: 129n)

Like the wealthy shepherd, the father, the brother and the friend stand in very "particular relation" to the individual: they are representatives of an archaic order, where natural associations are built on "the force of blood" (Smith 1982: 222) and "normatively constituted by public roles and obligations" (Silver 1990: 1476).[21] The gifts for justice show that these associations are profoundly, *particularly* interested, and that judicial authority is founded on the strength of these interested relations. The imaginary, inner, impartial spectator, by contrast, seeks justice in the "still higher tribunal … of the all-seeing Judge of the world, whose eye can never be deceived, and whose judgments can never be perverted" (Smith 1982: 132). The justice of the impartial spectator, like that of God, is imaginary and "exact" (1982: 132).[22] That world will mete out "exact justice" where

> every man will be ranked with those who, in the moral and intellectual qualities, are really his equals; where the owner of those humble talents and virtues which, from being depressed by fortune, had, in this life, no opportunity of displaying themselves; which were unknown, not only to the public, but which he himself could scarce be sure that he possessed, and for which even the man within the breast could scarce venture to afford him any distinct and clear testimony; where that *modest, silent, and unknown merit*, will be placed upon a level, and sometimes above those who, in this world, had enjoyed the highest reputation, and who, from the advantage of their situation, had been enabled to perform the most splendid and dazzling actions.

(Smith 1982: 132; emphasis added)

What complicates this picture is the dilemma of the grateful person who does not know what gratitude exactly means, what gratitude exactly prescribes. In actual experience, impartiality always meets with inexactitude. The benefactor, Smith says, comes with "character" and "circumstances" (1982: 174). The "man within the breast" does not give us "distinct and clear testimony" even of our own merit. Something of the sense of this unknowable, intransparent, "modest, silent, and unknown merit" operates in Smith's questions concerning the man who does not know how to reciprocate the kindness of his benefactor and the trust of his friend. How is it that we can be grateful without repaying our debt? How is it that "you may be perfectly grateful, and justly refuse to lend him a penny," or return the debt tenfold "and yet be accused of the blackest ingratitude" (1982: 174)? Exactitude is not only imaginary; it is impossible in this world. This, I think, is the central paradox in Smith's moral vision of *distributive*, or total justice. Exactitude, in the form of the unity of virtue and justice, is what Smith's vision demands. But what Smith argues, at the same time, is not simply that fortune is a bad judge. That the impartial spectator and God do not give us rules means that inexactitude makes moral judgment and moral imagination possible. Let me unpack this thought.

The significance of the figure of God – the religious apotheosis of the wealthy shepherd, let us say – is not, as David Marshall would have it, that he plays the role of the "*deus ex machina*" (1984: 609), releasing us from our condition of always being, as it were, beheld and judged by others. In setting up an internal authority within our breasts, we do not thereby escape our "original desire to please" our "brethren" (Smith 1982: 116).[23] Time and again Smith emphasizes in *The Theory of Moral Sentiments* that "the chief part of human happiness arises from the consciousness of being beloved" (1982: 41), that "to be beloved by our brethren [is] the great object of our ambition" (1982: 225). Although D.D. Raphael has argued that "Smith's ethical doctrines are in fact a combination of Stoic and Christian virtues" (in his "Introduction" to Smith 1982: 6), Smith says quite clearly that "The plan and system which Nature has sketched out for our conduct seems to be altogether different from that of the Stoical philosophy" (1982: 292). His criticism of Stoicism could just as well be applied to what Hume calls the "monkish virtues" of Christianity:[24] Smith does not stand for "sublime contemplation" as our natural task in life (Smith 1982: 292). To endeavor "to enter into the views of the great Superintendant of the universe, and to see things in the same light in which that divine Being beheld them" (1982: 289) – this, for Smith, cannot mean, as he argues it meant for the Stoics, regarding as "the great business and occupation of our lives" (1982: 292) a perfect detachment and indifference to society. When Smith discusses the "indifference" of the impartial spectator (1982: 129n), then, this is not the indifference of the stoic who has mastered fortune by sublimating his desires and wants. What Smith does propose is the non-transparency of motives and action in the moral life (just as, in the doctrine of the invisible hand, he argues for the non-transparency of motives and outcome in the socio-economic life). However "arbitrary and uncertain" (1981: 239), the gifts for justice, by comparison, are transparent. They collude in a system of mutual benefits. In its cycle of "credit" (Mauss 1990: 36), each gift inherits and bestows, discharges and delegates, a debt that expresses the fullness of mutual understanding. By this I do not mean that the wealthy shepherd's choice is in all cases clear or inevitable, but that the carrying out of justice is tightly caught up in this cycle of debt. Modern gratitude, too, is caught in this cycle of debt, but without the certain reward of public understanding or even of exact self-understanding.[25]

The debt of gratitude is not communal in the old sense but personal – in some senses even more personal than love, says Smith.

> If the person to whom we owe many obligations, is made happy without our assistance, though it pleases our love, it does not content our gratitude. Till we have recompensed him, till we ourselves have been instrumental in promoting his happiness, we feel ourselves still loaded with that debt which his past services have laid upon us.
>
> (1982: 68)

This is why, for all his discussion of impartiality and indifference, Smith is ultimately a philosopher of attachment, a philosopher of personality. As Allan Silver has suggested, impartiality and indifference are virtues that Smith associated with a modern world of economic and social mobility in which personal relations came into new prominence. Smith's example of "the man who has received great benefits from another person," who, "by the natural coldness of his temper, feel[s] but a very small degree of the sentiment of gratitude" but "endeavour[s] to pay all those regards and attentions to his patron which the liveliest gratitude could suggest" (1982: 162), shows the difference between the proper but indifferent act of duty and *personal* gratitude. Such a man, Smith comments, will inevitably "fail in many nice and delicate regards" (1982: 162) that fall outside the purview of a stern duty. The husband who is "dissatisfied with the most obedient wife, when he imagines her conduct is animated by no other principle besides her regard to what the relation she stands in requires"; the parent who is disappointed in the son who "fail[s] in none of the offices of filial duty" but "wants that affectionate reverence which it so well becomes him to feel"; the son who feels the cold shoulder of the father who has "performed all the duties of his situation" yet has "nothing of that fatherly fondness which might have been expected from him" – all these figures illustrate the gap between exact duty and personal virtue. Their roles are traditional but their desires are personal. What counts as a duty in this realm of personality? It is the paradoxical duty not to follow duty: "we ought to reward from the gratitude and generosity of our own hearts, without any reluctance, and *without being obliged to reflect how great the propriety of rewarding*" (Smith 1982: 172; emphasis added).

I wish to end by reflecting on a most suggestive comment by Mary Douglas. In her Foreword to the English translation of Mauss's *The Gift*, she writes:

The gift cycle echoes Adam Smith's invisible hand: gift complements market in so far as it operates where the latter is absent. Like the market it supplies each individual with personal incentive for collaborating in the pattern of exchanges. Gifts are given in a context of public drama, with nothing secret about them. In being more directly cued to public esteem, the distribution of honor, and the sanctions of religion, the gift economy is more visible than the market. Just by being visible, the resultant distribution of goods and services is more readily subject to public scrutiny and judgments of fairness than are the results of market exchange. In operating a gift system a people are more aware of what they are doing.

(Mauss 1990: xiv)

In the moral realm where, as I hope to have shown, the logic of the gift operates, though with unexpected outcomes, Smith shows a penchant for the "secret" and silent reserves of virtue operating in the personal realm. The individual living in a society guided by the "invisible hand," where "every man thus lives by exchanging, or becomes in some measure a merchant" (1981: 27), enters an imaginative moral life of social exchange. Smith notes how tightly that exchange is tied to "public scrutiny" and "drama," the "distribution of goods and services," the rewards of honor, the comforts of religion. Smith's "moral economy," however, is distinguishable ultimately from both market economy and gift economy. To borrow Heinzelman's (1980) phrase, it is an "economics of the imagination."

Notes

1 An earlier version of this essay was first published in *Studies of English Languages and Cultures* 6 (Seoul, 1998). Six editions of *The Theory of Moral Sentiments* appeared in Smith's lifetime. The Glasgow edition collates all six editions of 1759, 1761, 1767, 1774, 1781 and 1790, but uses the heavily revised 1790 edition as the copy-text.

2 Gratitude is for Smith a form of "beneficence" and "Beneficence is always free, it cannot be extorted by force, the mere want of it exposes to no punishment" (1982: 78).

3 On the complex relations between aesthetics and political economy in Smith, see Guillory 1997, esp. 303–17.

4 Hont and Ignatieff (1983) persuasively argue that Smith owes this distinction to the natural jurisprudence tradition rather than the civic virtue tradition.

5 This is, of course, Smith's famous account of the paradox of commercial society – namely, that the "oppressive inequality" of commercial society nonetheless results in "the superior affluence and abundance possessed even by [the] lowest and most despised member of civilized society, compared with what the most respected and active savage can attain to." See " 'Early Draft' of *The Wealth of Nations*," quoted in Hont and Ignatieff 1983: 3–4.

6 Seligman (1995) provides a helpful contrast between the civic virtue tradition and the Scottish Enlightenment as represented in part by Adam Smith. Rooted in the political philosophy of ancient Greece and Rome, and more immediately associated with Machiavelli and Rousseau, the civic virtue tradition espouses a "community of virtue" where "the social good is defined solely by the subjugation of the private self to the public realm" (1995: 204). As Seligman warns, this is a slightly misleading

formulation, "for the boundaries, indeed the very definition of the public and private, are not only continually changing but, in the eighteenth century, were only beginning to emerge as a distinction worthy of thought" (1995: 204). Less forcefully put, the civic tradition, "predicated on the idea of the city, a 'closed' society or community of non-anonymous individuals," idealizes a community where the difference between the private and the public makes little political sense (1995: 211). For the citizen of the civic virtue tradition, as Pocock is right to emphasize, "property was both an extension and a prerequisite of personality" (1985: 103): only the propertied were held capable of public virtue. As we shall see, Smith also relates property to virtue, but property is a far less stable guarantor of virtue for Smith than it is in the civic tradition.

7   I maintain this point while acknowledging E.P. Thompson's insight that the "historical consequences" of Smith's separate treatment of virtue and justice have shown the practical inconsistency of these ethical ideals. Hardly assuming that Smith was "immoral" or "unconcerned for the public good," Thompson nonetheless argues that the political economy that Smith's work gave rise to "was disinfested of intrusive moral imperatives" (1993: 202).

8   Arguing that *The Theory of Moral Sentiments* is an apolitical text, Vivienne Brown has suggested that "the eclipse of polity [in *The Theory of Moral Sentiments*] was effected not by economy but by ethics; not by the superordinance of commerce, but by the pre-eminence of the moral analysis of TMS [*The Theory of Moral Sentiments*] which denied justice a place within a fully moral domain, excluded the development of a political personality, and accorded a lower moral status to the public as opposed to the private virtues" (1994: 211–12). Here I am arguing that Smith's moral argument fully depends on the existence of the socio-political realm: in this sense the greater necessity of justice must be thought together with the hierarchy of virtues.

9   As Peter France notes, "commerce" means "on the one hand, etymologically, buying, selling and exchange of goods, but on the other, metaphorically, social intercourse of all kinds, including one's dealings with God or with the opposite sex" (1990: 43).

10 Thompson writes, "It should not be necessary to argue that the model of a natural and self-adjusting economy, working providentially for the best good of all, is as much a superstition as the notions which upheld the paternalist model" (1993: 203). What Thompson means by "the paternalist model" is "a consistent traditional view of social norms and obligations, of the proper economic functions of several parties within the community, which, taken together, can be said to constitute the moral economy of the poor" (1993: 188). Thompson's concern is to show how this superstitious but not unpolitical faith in communal justice manifested itself in historical practices among the poor in eighteenth-century England. Smith's concern in *The Theory of Moral Sentiments*, by contrast, is to show how this "moral economy of the poor" coexisted with a profound imaginative fascination with the "oeconomy of the great" (1982: 183).

11 Smith's provocative example is the beheading of Charles I. "All the innocent blood that was shed in the civil wars," he writes, "provoked less indignation than the death of Charles I" (1982: 52). Our readiness to sympathize with monarchs is such that, "if experience did not teach us its absurdity," we would readily defer to them in all cases. Nonetheless, while "reason and philosophy" teach us that "kings are the servants of the people, to be obeyed, resisted, deposed, or punished, as the public conveniency may require, … it is not the doctrine of Nature" (1982: 53).

12 Cf. Cropsey: "With the use of an invisible hand, nature cajoles and compels us to society and virtue, to prosperity and humanity" (1979: 174).

13 In this very specific meaning, "gratitude" was a synonym for "benevolence" – "A forced loan or contribution levied, without legal authority, by the kings of England on their subjects. First so called in 1473 when astutely asked by Edward IV, as a token of goodwill towards his rule. Sometimes loosely applied to similar impositions elsewhere" (OED).

14 Smith considered "the Greek tribes" as part of "those nations of husbandmen who are but just come out of the shepherd state, and who are not much advanced beyond that state" (1981: 238).

15 In his discussion of "The semantics of money-uses," Polanyi (1968) notes that "exchange is not the fundamental money-use" in archaic and primitive societies. My discussion here fits well with what Polanyi describes as the "payment-use of money" in these societies where "payment was due alike from the guilty, the defiled, the impure, the weak and the lowly; it was owed to the gods and their priests, the honored, the pure, and the strong" (1968: 181). As Polanyi notes, such payments fed into a "self-maintaining institution": "Because the rich man is powerful and honored he receives payments: gifts and dues are showered upon him without his having to use power to torture and kill. Yet his wealth, used as a fund for gifts, would procure him a sufficiency of power to do so" (1968: 183).

16 The fuller context is the "theory of alms" in "the history of the moral ideas of the Semites": "Generosity is an obligation, because Nemesis avenges the poor and the gods for the superabundance of happiness and wealth of certain people who should rid themselves of it. This is the ancient morality of the gift, which has become a principle of justice. The gods and the spirits accept that the share of wealth and happiness that has been offered to them and had been hitherto destroyed in useless sacrifices should serve the poor and children" (Mauss 1990: 18). Smith's story of the origins of justice in gift giving does not give us a religious theory of alms, as in the passage cited above, but the same "logic of the gift" operates.

17 See Mary Douglas's foreword to Mauss's *The Gift* (Mauss 1990: x).

18 In Allan Silver's words, "Smith rejects the applicability of the exchange model, drawn from the impersonal market, to personal relations" (1997: 62).

19 As D.D. Raphael emphasizes, "The 'supposed impartial spectator,' as Smith often called him, is not the actual bystander who may express approval or disapproval of my conduct. He is a creation of my imagination. He is indeed myself though in the character of an imagined spectator, not in the character of an agent" (1975: 90).

20 This passage was added in the second edition of *The Theory of Moral Sentiments* (1767).

21 Allan Silver has argued that friendship in commercial society defines the realm of the personal very differently: commercial society enables relationships that are not "exclusivistic" (1990: 1484) but intimate. Although "personal relations are prevailingly defined and experienced in contemporary theory and culture as radically different from the impersonal relations of modern society," the impersonal character of modern encounters is precisely what enables personal exchange to take place (1990: 1475). This argument is fully present, according to Silver, in Smith's theory of impartiality. The friend that Smith mentions in the citation above is not this paradigmatic, modern, impartial friend, but a kind of friend-of-the-family, one in whom one can safely entrust the family's interest.

22 In calling divine justice "so comfortable to the weakness, so flattering to the grandeur of human nature," Smith gives it *imaginative* coherence that has nothing to do with the particulars of religious doctrine. In fact, he notes that "the distributions of rewards and punishments" in religious doctrine have been "too frequently in direct opposition to all our moral sentiments" (1982: 132). He cites as an example the pronouncements of Jean Baptiste Massillon, Bishop of Clermont (1663–1742), who argued that a single day of religious mortification was more deserving of reward in the eyes of God than a life of worldly merit. See Smith 1982: 133, n. 15.

23 As Vivienne Brown puts it, "the impartial spectator functions as the analogue of the divine Being, but here the point of distance and objectivity is rooted in a more socialized view of human nature rather than in the detached infinitude of the Stoic moral universe" (1994: 209).

24 Hume lists "celibacy, fasting, penance, mortification, self-denial, humility, silence, solitude." See Hume 1975: 270.

25 I am thus in agreement with R.F. Brissenden's point that *The Theory of Moral Sentiments* is striking for its "preoccupation with guilt and remorse, and with the sense of moral compulsion and obligation" (1969: 958). This preoccupation, I have argued, is significant for its deviation from rather than conformity to economic reason. Thus, while Dimock is correct to point out that "political economy had always been held up by its early advocates as a much-needed complement and corrective to the unstable field of morality" (an argument she derives from Hirschman), her suggestion that moral philosophy and political economy share "a common foundation, a quantifying foundation" of "commensurability" in Smith is highly disputable (Dimock 1996: 149).

References

Brissenden, R.F. "Authority, guilt, and anxiety in *The Theory of Moral Sentiments*." *Texas Studies in Literature and Language* 11.2 (1969): 945–62.

Brown, Vivienne. *Adam Smith's Discourse: Canonicity, Commerce and Conscience*. London: Routledge, 1994.

Copley, Stephen. "Introduction: reading *The Wealth of Nations*." In Stephen Copley and Kathryn Sutherland (eds) *Adam Smith's* Wealth of Nations*: New Interdisciplinary Essays*. Manchester: Manchester University Press, 1995, pp. 1–22.

Cropsey, Joseph. "The invisible hand: moral and political considerations." In Gerald P. O'Driscoll Jr. (ed.) *Adam Smith and Modern Political Economy: Bicentennial Essays on The Wealth of Nations*. Ames, Iowa: Iowa State University Press, 1979, pp. 165–76.

Dimock, Wai Chee. *Residues of Justice: Literature, Law, Philosophy*. Berkeley: University of California Press, 1996.

Douglas, Mary. "No free gifts." Foreword. In Marcel Mauss *The Gift: The Form and Reason for Exchange in Archaic Societies*. Trans. W.D. Halls. New York: Routledge, 1990.

France, Peter. "The commerce of the self." *Comparative Criticism: A Yearbook* 12 (1990): 39–56.

Guillory, John. *Cultural Capital: The Problem of Literary Canon Formation*. Chicago: University of Chicago Press, 1997.

Heinzelman, Kurt. *The Economics of the Imagination*. Amherst: University of Massachusetts Press, 1980.

Hirschman, Albert O. *The Passions and the Interests: Political Arguments for Capitalism before Its Triumph*. Princeton: Princeton University Press, 1977.

Hont, Istvan and Michael Ignatieff (eds). *Wealth and Virtue: The Shaping of Political Economy in the Scottish Enlightenment*. Cambridge: Cambridge University Press, 1983.

Hume, David. *Enquiries Concerning Human Understanding and Concerning the Principles of Morals*. Ed. L.A. Selby-Bigge and P.H. Nidditch. Oxford: Clarendon Press, 1975.

Ignatieff, Michael. "Smith, Rousseau and the republic of needs." In T.C. Smout (ed.) *Scotland and Europe, 1200–1850*. Edinburgh: J. Donald, 1986, pp. 187–206.

Marshall, David. "Adam Smith and the theatricality of moral sentiments." *Critical Inquiry* 10 (1984): 592–613.

Mauss, Marcel. *The Gift: The Form and Reason for Exchange in Archaic Societies*. Trans. W.D. Halls. New York: Routledge, 1990.

Mitchell, Harvey. " 'The mysterious veil of self-delusion' in Adam Smith's *Theory of Moral Sentiments*." *Eighteenth-Century Studies* 20.4 (1987): 405–21.

Pocock, J.G.A. *Virtue, Commerce, and History: Essays on Political Thought and History, Chiefly in the Eighteenth Century*. Cambridge: Cambridge University Press, 1985.

Polanyi, Karl. *Primitive, Archaic and Modern Economies*. Ed. George Dalton. Boston: Beacon Press, 1968.

Raphael, D.D. "The impartial spectator." In Andrew S. Skinner and Thomas Wilson (eds) *Essays on Adam Smith*. Oxford: Clarendon Press, 1975, pp. 83–99.

Seligman, Adam B. "Animadversions upon civil society and civic virtue in the last decade of the twentieth century." In John A. Hall (ed.) *Civil Society: Theory, History, Comparison*. Cambridge: Polity, 1995, pp. 200–23.

Silver, Allan. "Friendship in commercial society: eighteenth-century social theory and modern sociology." *American Journal of Sociology* 95.6 (1990): 1474–1504.

—— " 'Two different kinds of commerce' – friendship and strangership in civil society." In Jeff Weintraub and Krishnan Kumar (eds) *Public and Private in Thought and Practice: Perspectives on a Grand Dichotomy*. Chicago: University of Chicago Press, 1997, pp. 43–74.

Smith, Adam. *An Inquiry into the Nature and Causes of the Wealth of Nations*. Ed. R.H. Campbell and A.S. Skinner. Volume 2 of *The Glasgow Edition of the Works and Correspondence of Adam Smith*. Indianapolis: Liberty Fund, 1981 [Oxford: Clarendon Press, 1976].

—— *The Theory of Moral Sentiments*. Ed. D.D. Raphael and A.L. Macfie. Volume 1 of *The Glasgow Edition of the Works and Correspondence of Adam Smith*. Indianapolis: Liberty Fund, 1982 [Oxford: Clarendon Press, 1976].

Thompson, E.P. "The moral economy of the English crowd in the eighteenth century." *Past and Present* 50 (1971). Reprinted in *Customs in Common*. Harmondsworth: Penguin, 1993.

Part III

The gift and artistic commerce

7   Catullus and the gift of sentiment in republican Rome

Jacqui Sadashige

Catullus 12 (loosely translated)

Asinius Marrucinus, you're a real handy-man at dinner parties.
You lift our napkins when we are otherwise occupied.
Do you think this is funny? You have no clue –
It's an utterly tasteless and witless thing to do.
You don't believe me? Go ask your brother Pollio –
He'd gladly give a million for the goods you've lifted.
Now there's a man of substance and charm.
So, give me back my napkins,
Or expect 300 hendecasyllables.
Quite frankly, it's not the financial loss that bothers me.
They're actually a souvenir from my friends.
Fabullus and Veranius sent them to me –
Genuine Saetabian napkins from Spain. So you see,
I have to love them – just like I love my friends.

The poetry of Gaius Valerius Catullus, of which the above is an example, has long tantalized literary scholars. In part, the status of the Catullan corpus in the Roman literary canon has been occasioned by its own history. It is something of a truism that historians of ancient literature and culture possess insufficient evidence from which to construct a satisfying picture of the past. As a result, the scatterings of text we do possess can give the problematic impression that they are all exemplary and pivotal. Yet it can hardly be denied that certain Roman writers – for example, the comic playwright Plautus, whose career overlapped significantly with the Second Punic War – composed their works during periods charged with historical significance. Likewise, it is clear that other Roman writers, such as Vergil, exerted considerable influence on those who followed.

In the case of Catullus, we are both doubly blessed and doubly damned. We are doubly blessed inasmuch as Catullus's own works testify to the milieu in which he circulated and to his self-intended place in the development of Latin literature.[1] Included among his shorter poems are epigrams that announce his disregard for Julius Caesar and Marcus Tullius Cicero, probably the most celebrated advocate of the Roman Republic. Likewise, the specificities of his diction, choice of form, and literary models (often explicitly and self-consciously

deployed) mark him as a *neoteric*, a proponent of a new style of poetry characterized by its overt intellectualism and the eschewing of more traditional forms such
as epic. We are, however, doubly damned, since a part of the Catullan pose
entails constructing the writer's own self-importance. To pursue certain lines of
Catullan criticism would thus work merely to produce complicit readings of the
poems. That is, either to focus on narrow historical criticism – for example,
attempting to reconstruct the Republican political climate through Catullan
invective – or to restrict discussion strictly to literary history would result in a
more expansive articulation of what the text itself already claims. A more
productive line of inquiry would be to negotiate between the realms of literary
and extra-literary history and to inquire not so much about what Catullus has to
say, in the example above, about the value of linen napkins but about what his
poetic sentimentalization of the value of material goods can be made to say
when placed within the larger nexus of Roman culture. But before entering the
various realms of Roman politics, economics and the like that poem 12 lays
open, we must turn briefly to the place of Catullus in Latin literary history.

Scholars have identified Catullus as writing at a number of points of transition. Catullus wrote during that period of Roman political history in which the
old structures of the Republic, the Senate in particular, were beginning to
weaken. Civil war and the subsequent reign of L. Cornelius Sulla as dictator had
enfeebled the existing oligarchy through strife, legislation and proscription. The
formation of the first triumvirate in 60 BCE – essentially a private agreement to
work towards mutual political advantage – only served to erode further the
power of the Senate. In terms of literary history, Kenneth Quinn has situated
Catullus during the transition between "literature" as spoken performance and
"literature" as written text. Thus while neoteric compositions were marked by
specific diction, form, subject, models and style, Catullus's poetry appears further
to revel self-consciously in its own textuality, containing repeated references to
the tools of literary production such as writing tablets and bookstalls.[2] Finally,
several historians have suggested that a rise in expressions of sentimentality
towards wives and children in particular occurred during this same period (see,
for example, Evans 1991). Sources for this are found in epitaphs, the plastic arts,
literary descriptions, etc., and Catullus is cited as evidence of this phenomenon.

I will not argue that Catullus caused any of these shifts nor that his writing
provides the *terminus ad quem* or *a quo* for any phenomenon. I will, however,
suggest that there are links between a variety of these transitions that warrant
further investigation. For example, while neoteric poets undoubtedly derived an
aspect of their self-representation from specific Greek models, it is a curious fact
of Catullan love poetry that it is marked by what David Ross (1969) identified as
terminology culled from political alliance and what R. Lyne (1980) has
expanded to call the language of "aristocratic obligation." Thus, in poem 72, the
poet compares his love to that which a father feels for his sons or sons-in-law. In
reaction to such expressions of sentiment that may strike the modern reader as
odd, some readers have concluded that Catullan poetry is "about" finding or
creating a language to express romantic love. I return, at greater length, to the

subject of sentiment and its expression in the latter portions of this essay. Yet I would note for now that such an interpretation places too great a burden on sentiment or love itself both by granting it an essential and *a priori* existence and by identifying it as the singular condition for the production of Catullus's poetry. At the very least, poem 12, despite its apparent simplicity, hints at the complicated relationships among sentiment, value, materiality and social ties that existed in Roman culture.

In what follows I address what the poetic sentimentalization of value – specifically the value of a gift – means when placed within the doubled context of Roman imperial expansion and Latin literary expression. I argue that what we glimpse in Catullus's work is the emergence of a new and self-representedly sentimental subject. In contrast to the traditional rhetoric of upper-class (male) Roman self-presentation, the poet/persona here confesses to feelings of deep sentiment. The feelings, particularly in the case of poem 12, are occasioned by an attachment to foreign luxury items. Figures such as the historian Sallust and Cato the statesman held such items responsible for the weakening of Roman character. In contrast, while Catullus's speaker acknowledges the monetary worth of his linen napkins, he claims their value for him to be purely sentimental. In this way poem 12 recuperates the growing presence of and demand for foreign luxury goods in Rome. Rather than condemning their negative effects on Roman character, poem 12 harnesses them to affirm the habits and character of the elite. Hence the luxury napkins here bear no taint of indulgence, but have been transformed into a symbol of *amicitia*, the male–male bond underlying Roman social and political formation.[3]

It is not enough, however, to argue that Catullan poetry is "really about" sentimentality and its relationship to subjectivity. As much as poem 12 presents an attitude of financial disinterest common to much of his work, it also engages a complex nexus of political, economic and legal discourse. Two areas of Roman life in particular merit explication. In the first place, Catullus identifies the luxury item in question as a gift. Gifts, as I will show, occupy a curious place in the Roman legal system – not to mention the critical language of economic history. The gift's ambiguous position between economic transfer and expression of interpersonal relations is put to good use in poem 12, where its indeterminacy allows the poetic narrative to shift from monetary to sentimental value. In addition to their status as a gift, the linen napkins of poem 12 issue both directly and indirectly from Roman systems of provincial government and economic circulation. Thus this essay examines Roman political life and its role in the production of both linen and poetry. While I do begin and end with Catullus, and return repeatedly to poem 12, I do not do so in order to argue that Roman poetry or politics begins and ends with Catullus. On the contrary, I employ Catullus's poetry as a particular textual example with an identifiable historical and cultural context.

My essay aims at dismantling the still pervasive use of antiquity as "Western" modernity's social, economic and cultural Other. Specifically, I suggest that a historical and cultural dialogue within the spheres of Roman literature, law and politics complicates our picture of Western economic and cultural histories. Insight into the problematic nature of gifts in Roman culture promises to supplement the critical discourse surrounding commodity fetishism and its relationship to subjectivity. Catullus provides a striking example of a marked shift in economic conditions occurring at the same time as the appearance of a new form of cultural expression, all of which hints at a shift in subjectivity.[4]

Gifts in Rome

In the eyes of the ancient Romans, gifts were hardly disinterested objects, and a variety of measures existed to check their circulation. The benchmark for this was the *lex Cincia de donis et muneribus* of 204 BCE.[5] At base, the *lex Cincia* regulated financial transfers of two sorts. A special provision prohibited advocates from receiving payment – either in the form of prearranged fees or gifts – for pleading cases. Secondly, gifts below a certain (unknown) amount were permitted "between cognates up to second cousin, between *adfines* [relations by marriage], to any female cognate if the gift were intended as *dos* [dowry], and by a *tutor qui tutelam gerit* [legal guardian]" (Watson 1968: 229).

The ban on payment to advocates extends logically from the structure of Roman socio-political life. In the first place, the blatant acceptance of remuneration by a lawyer would violate a basic tenet of patron-client relations: that the relationship was one of mutual and voluntary loyalty. Allowing payment between patrons and clients would have recast the generosity, goodwill and protection of the patron as a commercial enterprise. More broadly, the self-presentation of the senatorial class dictated that its members not appear to engage in commercial activities.[6] It was, in short, "a fundamental belief of the Roman governing class, that a gentleman should live off the land, or at any rate seem to do so" (Crawford 1992: 54). One should not, however, gain the false impression that such gestures were or were intended to be wholly effective. Not only was the provision against payment to advocates "constantly reiterated" and even reenacted by Augustus, but both Tacitus (*Annales* XI. 5, 7) and Pliny (*Epistulae* V. 4, 9, 13) mention upper limits of gifts to lawyers (Crook 1967: 90). Such remarks suggest a conceptual shift by the Imperial period with the result that the gift could be classed, at least rhetorically, as separate from payment.

Gifts between spouses were quite another story. Despite the existence of the *lex Cincia*, gifts between spouses were nonetheless prohibited by custom during much of Roman history.[7] According to jurists, the prohibition was accepted "in order to prevent them [spouses] – not being moderate but with extravagant readiness towards one another in gift giving – from being despoiled by turns out of mutual love" (*Digest* 24.1.1).[8] The explanation – recorded some five hundred years after the fact – rings with uncharacteristic melodrama. While no one would assert that Roman marriages functioned solely as political or economic alliances, information gleaned from sources such as epitaphs, personal letters and works of literature or history emphasize more "functional" (as opposed to emotional) qualities such as fidelity, respect and marital harmony.[9] Further, Niall Rudd

(1981) has argued that the state of marriage was not wholly compatible with the qualities or features recognized as patently romantic (e.g., love at first sight) within Roman culture.

Given these less-than-passionate representations of Roman marriage, it makes immediate and obvious sense that legal historian J.A. Crook should assert, "The purpose of the prohibition was for the sake of family property, to prevent either party from parting with it to the other" (1967: 106).[10] While it seems doubtful that individuals born into a culture where dowry, inheritance and other transfers of property were strictly regulated and closely guarded would "despoil" family property even if given the opportunity, Crook's explanation nonetheless provides a comfortingly intellectual rationale. Although he does not directly address the language or sentiment of the juristic explanation, Crook accounts for the rule itself by supplying it with an underlying *economic* logic. Moreover, an economic explanation finds support in the laws themselves despite their dichotomous positions. The customary ban on gifts directly opposes the legal allowances made by the *lex Cincia*, but both rules nonetheless suggest that the Romans recognized the gift's potential for conveying economic value by transferring family property. The *lex Cincia*, in addressing both payment for advocacy and familial gifts, identifies familial gifts as exceptions within a larger class of financial transactions. Even the *Digest* concedes that gifts between spouses were banned in part to safeguard the reputation of both partners from the taint of "gold-digging": "So that marital harmony should not seem to have been brought about by money" (*Digest* 24.1.3).[11] Yet despite the obvious logic of an economic explanation, two caveats should give us pause.

In the first place, Pierre Bourdieu's charge that "economism is a form of ethnocentrism" (1997b: 205) suggests that to see through the cultural "misrecognition" of Roman law to its "true purpose" is to transform radically its inherent logic. For Bourdieu, the affront lies not only in the erasure of the cultural specificity of the archaic economy – for instance, the schizophrenia of its opposing written and unwritten laws – but in the "tacit acceptance of a certain number of principles of division, the emergence of which is correlative with the social constitution of the economic field as a separate field" (1997a: 234). In other words, scholars who leap immediately to the "economic truths" of the ancient world run the risk of imposing a cultural bias that reads antiquity as if it were modernity, of assuming not just the operation of a specifically capitalist logic of equal exchange (as opposed, for example, to the "illogic" of a gift economy), but the very existence of an economy in the modern sense. And it is this type of mistaken assumption that more recent ancient historians have sought to correct. Thus, for instance, Keith Hopkins has written:

> Until recently, scholars often used to write about the commercial foreign policies of small Greek states, and about the large industrial centers of the ancient world. These modernizing terms assumed a correspondingly high level of commercial and industrial activity, which now seems completely unjustified. ... In short, they assumed that there was an ancient economy,

> which was in some sense autonomous and which, like the economies of modern states, could plausibly be treated for most analytical purposes as separate from the polity and from society as a whole.
>
> (1983: xi)

In contrast to the modernizing model, recent scholars have laid stress on the circularly self-sufficient nature of many farms, districts, or regions. To the extent that one could speak of "an ancient economy," it was primarily agricultural. At the same time, "consumption cities" did exist.[12] It is in the model of the consumption city that Hopkins's emphasis on the inseparability of the economy from society in the ancient world becomes most clear. He writes, "In the classical world, urbanization was more a reflection of a cultural pattern than of economic growth; it was a reflection of where rich agricultural land-owners chose to live and of their culturally induced patterns of conspicuous consumption" (1983: xiii). Ancient towns and cities were not centers of production in any meaningful sense; their rise and growth was far more an indication of the central importance of status than of economic development.[13] The emphasis on culturally induced patterns of behavior and on the central importance of such codes suggests a reconsideration of Crook's economic rationale. One might, for instance, speculate that the rule against spousal gifts was not so much about safeguarding family property through the language of passion as about regulating expressions of passion through the more manageable medium of property. In any case, one would be hard pressed to view either property or passion as the rule's "object," while the autonomy of each remains doubtful. As already seen in the example of payment for advocacy, legal rules often existed quite independently of actual practice, and the significance of those rules often lay beyond the object in question and in their existence as discourse.

Before moving onto the second caveat, I should point out that Bourdieu's critique is actually doubled. At first glance, the charge against ethnocentrism appears wholly a question, in his words, "of knowledge" (1997a: 234). Ethnocentric scholars will produce inadequate bodies of information. But behind Bourdieu's intellectual critique lies a broader meditation on the cultural conditions of which such a "scholastic bias" is merely a symptom. The end point of his essay is not a particular model for non-ethnocentric analysis *per se* but rather a near plea for the politicizing of academic engagement, ultimately leading to a radical shift in the social economy. In sum:

> The purely speculative and typically scholastic question of whether generosity and disinterestedness are possible should give way to the political question of the means that have to be implemented in order to create universes in which, as in gift economies, people have an interest in disinterestedness and generosity, or, rather, are durably disposed to respect these universally respected forms of respect for the universal.
>
> (1997a: 240)

The wider implications of Bourdieu's argument are dizzying – at once inspiring and troubling in their recourse to notions of universal humanity. Although an extensive interrogation of Bourdieu's call for "generosity and disinterestedness" exceeds my aims here, I will return briefly to the question of value and interest at the close of this essay.

In addition to Bourdieu's admonitory "economism is ethnocentrism," the discourse occasioned by the prohibition of spousal gifts itself enjoins against adopting a wholly economic explanation. As already noted, both the *lex Cincia* and the customary ban on spousal gifts give evidence of the gift's ability to contain and convey economic value. This is, of course, if the laws are construed broadly. The *lex Cincia*, upon closer inspection, attempts to except familial gifts from payment even as it assimilates the two forms of financial transfer. Thus the ban on gifts between spouses suggests a certain indeterminacy, especially given the entry in the *Digest* regarding marital harmony in exchange for payment. As a result, rather than clarifying the nature of the Roman gift, the *lex Cincia* safeguards rhetorically cognate and affined relations from even the suggestion of social impropriety. Likewise the prohibition of payment to advocates does more to reinforce discursively the separation between patrons and clients and the nature of the relationship between them than it could ever effect in practice. Therefore, within Roman legal discourse, the gift represented a problematic category of transfer specifically on account of its indeterminacy. Gifts, in other words, could never merely be; they were incomplete without investigation into or explanations surrounding their contents, history, the giver, the recipient, etc. Ironically, however, such supplementary information seems to have complicated rather than clarified the nature of gifts in Rome. At the same time, a gift to one's spouse was not subject to the same set of pressures as was a gift to one's patron-lawyer. Gifts between spouses were discursively caught between various forms of property transfer and what seems like a move towards establishing various degrees of interpersonal intimacy; the systems of social power and self-presentation, on the other hand, competed with the realities of personal ambition to bear upon gifts to one's "superiors." Since various kinds of gifts were subject to their own forms of over- and indeterminacies, it is difficult to define a paradigmatic category of the gift in Roman culture or to identify the reason for the allowance or disallowance of a particular form of exchange susceptible to the title of a gift. Thus not only could gifts never simply be, but, given the perspective of later critical thinking on gifts, one might argue that gifts did not really exist in ancient Rome.

Gifts beyond the legal sphere

Thus far I have shown how the gift represented a problematic category in Roman legal discourse. While the *lex Cincia* and the customary ban on spousal gifts do not specify the kinds of gifts affected by law, anecdotal evidence shows, for example, that smaller gifts such as birthday presents between spouses were permitted. Not surprisingly, then, laws regarding gifts seem directed at the transfer of large sums of cash or their equivalent, such as real estate. This raises a number of questions. In the first place, we might wonder to what degree the indeterminacy of gifts in the legal realm affected the representation and giving of gifts in practice. Was there, for instance, an obvious difference between a gift of sentiment or gratitude and an illegal transfer or payment masquerading as a gift? The question is provocative, not least because it hints at a complex relationship between sentiment and finance. Logically speaking, suspicions about financial transfers could limit expressions of sentiment – presuming of course that Roman society could recognize a purported correspondence between magnitude of price and depth of feeling which, given the escalation in dowries, triumphs, honorary games, etc. over time, seems likely. We might also question whether prevailing sentiments affected gifts exchanged between persons other than spouses or patrons and clients or whether less pressure was brought to bear upon gifts offered in less "consequential" circumstances.

If we recall Catullus's poem, it becomes clear that he not only wrote within this context of discursively vexed gifts, but that similar pressures could bear upon gifts of disparate worth and between a variety of individuals. In particular, the speaker's apparent insistence on a difference between economic and sentimental forms of value suggests a similar indeterminacy surrounding gifts as financially and socially insignificant as a set of souvenir napkins exchanged between social equals. In this way, poem 12 appears to reinforce the problematic definition of gifts generated within the legal sphere and, likewise, suggests that such a definition reflects a broader cultural truth. But whereas the laws already cited deal with gifts broadly construed, Catullus's poem addresses a gift whose history and materiality, however fictive, are outlined with great specificity. At this point, then, we return to Catullus with closer scrutiny. For while the legal evidence suggests a desire to distinguish between the gift and some baser form of economic exchange, it is not at all clear how one might go about mapping that binary against or within the economic/sentiment dichotomy highlighted by Catullus. What is clear, however, is that sentiment – its expression, production and control – forms both the crux and the point of contact for these binaries. Not only does juristic writing identify an excess of sentiment as the underlying reason for the ban on spousal gifts, but Catullan self-fashioning entails the construction of a poet whose financial disinterest complements his sentimentality. It is easy to see, in literary terms, how Catullus's confessional and semi-private speaking voice provides a point of contact or transition between the young lovers of Roman comedy (whose feelings are more often assumed than expressed) and the fully elegiac personae of Tibullus, Propertius and still later writers such as Petrarch. Yet the fact that Catullus's emotional expressions find a parallel in the non-literary world of epitaphs and a basis in the objects of empire suggests that Catullan sentiment should not be regarded strictly as a literary development, but may indicate a broader shift in the formation and representation of subjectivity. With this in mind, I return to Catullus's gift: first, with an eye towards uncovering the historical and cultural details of its broadly fictive "biography," and second, to tease out the implications of that biography – both within the context of Roman imperial expansion and against the legal and theoretical permutations of the gift.

Sentimental subjects

As I mentioned at the outset, I believe that poem 12 deceives with its apparent simplicity. The nature of this simplicity lies in the reproduction, indeed the naturalization, of a familiar pose of the economically disinterested but sentimentally and culturally invested poet. Catullus adopts a similar pose, for instance, in poem 13. There he claims that his money purse is full of cobwebs but promises Fabullus that he "will dine well" (*cenabis bene*) provided that he (Fabullus) supplies the more obvious, material components of the dinner: food, wine, a girl, and even laughter. So pervasive is this trope to the body of Catullus's work that it has been identified as something of a governing theme: "Catullus is chiefly interested in formulating a special aesthetic creed for the neoteric artist. ... [T]he artist's instinct for what is right and fitting becomes a touchstone of true refinement" (Skinner 1981: 104, 105). In other words, the *cena* (dinner party) setting provides a motif through which notions of urbane cultivation and true friendship can be explored and expressed. The repeated adoptions of this position by the speaker (who is, for the most part, identified with the author) find their complement in poems that attack individuals engaging in self-serving and self-indulgent financial practices. Caesar, Mamurra and Furius are all castigated for their unethical spending in poems such as 26 and 29: "First you squandered your patrimony, then the Pontic booty, thirdly that of Spain" (Catullus 29.17–19).[14] T.P. Wiseman attributes the attitude taken in poems directed against men like Mamurra to a more traditional respect for obligations and fair transactions on the part of Catullus:

> Careless big spenders financed themselves by careless big plunder. ... Magnificence could regard itself as above the law. Hence Catullus' distaste for Mamurra, rich from the loot of successive campaigns and lording it through all the bedrooms of Rome. Oh yes, Mamurra was great all right – a great big prick!
>
> (1985: 105)

As Wiseman aptly points out, the profligate habits of a Mamurra or a Furius are often linked to the politics and policies of empire. Hence, not only does Catullus set the cultured and deep-feeling poet against a gamut of individuals marked by their unethical means of acquisition and spending, but he likewise suggests a similarly dichotomous positioning between poetic production and the work of Roman expansion and provincial government. In various ways, then, the polymetric poems reproduce repeatedly the dichotomies that underlie poem 12 – things versus relations, cost versus value, or materialism versus sentimentality. What is most significant for our purposes, however, is the links that are forged along each side of those binaries. As the speaker-poet repeatedly sets himself against a series of individuals, their petty theft, brutish manners and interest in mere cost come to be associated with the work of Roman imperialism.

Rome's acquisition of Sicily, Spain, portions of North Africa, and other parts of the Mediterranean in the wake of wars against Carthage and other powers resulted in a network of provinces that were governed by a regular rotation of provincial governors and their staff. Catullus himself worked in Bithynia under the *praetor* Memmius (c. 57–56 BCE), and the experience appears to have occasioned a number of poems (10, 28, 46, and probably 4 and 31). Generally, the institution of provincial government combined with a trade between Rome and its provinces to produce an influx of booty, foreign "products" (such as litter-bearers) and practices (such as Eastern religions) into Roman Italy.

The degree to which, starting in the third century BCE, Rome acquired territory and wealth can hardly be overstated.[15] Much of the money flowed in circuits outside of Rome; for example, provincial tribute funded the garrisoning of provinces. Yet vast sums also made their way into the hands of private citizens – especially to wealthier senators and equites – and in so doing enabled increases in conspicuous consumption. Such behavior, however, had its critics. I should make clear that statements about "conspicuous consumption" and similar practices address a specific segment of the Roman society. The city itself teemed with slaves, craftsmen, petty traders, etc. But much of the literary and historical record addresses the experiences of the most privileged members of Roman society. Thus, when I speak of vast increases in personal wealth, I am not suggesting an across-the-board increase in the standard of living. We should not, for instance, view Rome in terms of a "developing nation." Nevertheless, it seems clear that the acquisition of huge sums of money by private individuals could and did effect visible changes both in the narrow sphere of personal homes and in the public realms of games and triumphs. Despite the city's vast increase in revenues, Roman opinion appeared to remain divided on the subject of wealth, in part reflecting the tension between traditional modes of self-presentation and the changing, material reality. Thus while individuals extorted provinces in order to recoup liquid assets, the *lex Fannia* of 161 BCE stated that only one unfattened hen could be served on ordinary days. More than a trace of this "schizophrenic" attitude can be seen in the presentation of the napkins in poem 12.

Catullus's napkins, we are told, are made of the Saetabian linen, which, the Elder Pliny notes, was considered to be the best in Europe:

> In Germany the women carry on this manufacture in caves dug under-ground [the humidity is said to be favorable to the manufacture of linen]; and similarly also in the Alia district of Italy between the Po and the Ticino, where the linen wins the prize as the third best in Europe, that of Saetabis being first, as the second prize is won by the linens of Retovium near the Alia district and Faenza on the Aemilian Road.[16]
>
> (Catullus 19.9)

The quality of the linen, combined with the sum that Pollio is said to be willing to offer as compensation for the napkins' theft (*talentum*, an indefinite but large sum of money), identifies the linen napkins as a luxury product.

Despite Catullus's claims that he must love the napkins as a reflection of the love he feels for his friends, the repetitive specificity with which they are described – moving from the general "napkins" (*lintea*) to "genuine Saetabian napkins from Spain" (*sudaria Saetaba ex Hiberis*) – emphasizes their foreignness, even their Spanishness, more than any other quality. When more Saetabian napkins reappear in poem 25, again as the objects of theft, they are grouped with a Greek-styled *pallium* (cloak) and Bithynian *catagraphoi* (a term whose referent is unknown), creating an odd collection of souvenirs. By figuring the napkins as the objects of unexplained theft, poems 12 and 25 suggest their blanket desirability and, hence, the general appeal of "foreign" products. The degree to which one was expected to procure such things actually becomes the subject of poem 10, in which a bumbling persona claims, in order to impress the girlfriend of a friend, to have purchased litter-bearers while in Bithynia. The regularity with which such products of empire appear is in no way random, as the polymetric poems are actively engaged in exploring the subtler effects of imperial expansion – such as the way that tantalizing luxury products factor into the schematic of male friendship. While poems such as 12 appear to emphasize the personal attachments that underlie the speaker's ownership of the napkins, such poems also suggest that luxury items provided the most appropriate mark of that attachment.

The figuration of male–male socio-political associations in a set of linen napkins is striking in and of itself since, as already mentioned, such a move admits the role that foreign luxury items played in the self-presentation, in fact the construction, of Roman masculinity. Yet the implications of the treasured napkins range well beyond the specific recuperation of Roman "materialism." As I noted above, the very expression of emotion is, at this moment in Roman literary history, something of a novelty. More noteworthy still is the fact that much of Catullan poetry appears to be enabled by the very experiences that it seems to disparage or disavow. That is, Catullus's poetry foregrounds, as an integral part of its poetic fiction, the often unpleasant conditions of its production. And this is particularly evident with respect to what I have earlier called the "work of Roman imperialism." The major underlying condition that enables poem 12 is the status of nearer and farther Spain as Roman provinces. Although Rome's primary interest in Spain lay in its rich natural resources – in particular precious metals – Judith Lynn Sebesta has pointed out how the acquisition of Punic Spain and Sicily provided Rome with additional supplies of linen.[17] The divulgence of the napkins' Saetabian origin, then, functions not merely as luxury name-dropping but in fact provides their very presence with a political rationale. Not only does the napkins' availability testify to the breadth of Rome's empire but, more narrowly, their movement from Spain to Rome highlights the degree to which the political, material and emotional – and indeed the literary – are mutually imbricated. The political structures that make available the cherished napkins have also created the spatial distance between Catullus and his friends, who are ostensibly in Spain serving a provincial governor.

Regardless of their narrowly historical veracity (i.e., did the author ever receive a gift of napkins? did he have friends stationed in Spain?), the poems work hard collectively to author credible personalities that move through a broadly "real" landscape.[18] Poem 12 offers an intimate treatment of the ways in which Roman involvement in the provinces has become embedded in the social, even the emotional, fabric of Roman daily life. In marked contrast to both the irresponsible young lovers of comedy and the legendary soldiers and statesmen of epic, Catullus and his friends manage to marry sentiment and citizenship. The depth of that bond between close friends and cohorts finds its best representation and truest expression in costly Spanish linen. But the asyndetic nature of the final lines confuses the relationship between friend and napkin: "Fabullus and Veranius sent them to me as a gift. I have to love them." Literally, the next line reads "both little Veranius and darling Fabullus" (*et Veraniolum meum et Fabullum*). The names are, in grammatical terms, direct objects, but the syntax is slippery. For this reason, the preferred variant reads *et Veraniolum* as *ut Veraniolum*, in order to "fix" the line as "just as I love both Veranius and Fabullus."[19] In the former variant, however, the line invites speculation. Is the relationship between the two lines causal – "I love the napkins *because* I love my friends" – or parallel – "*just as* I love my friends?" Or are the two names merely an afterthought? While the poem's significance does not rest on this single line, its lack of syntactical clarity turns attention to the napkins' ability to elicit emotion. The napkins are the subject of the poem and are mentioned, in this instance, before the two friends. Catullus may have loved his friend first, but, as with all gifts, the napkins produce a range and a complexity of feelings that require narrative explication and ultimately suggest a causal relation between object and emotion.

I would also observe how – through a curious trick of the poem – the systems of provincial government and political advancement seem to make possible not only an occasion for poetry but also those profound sentiments that ostensibly set Catullus apart from the "big pricks" of empire. "Big plunder" does not simply create big pricks; big plunder is symptomatic of larger systems of representation that allow linen napkins to mean everything but clean fingertips at the dinner table. Hence the juxtaposition of the napkins' cost with their sentimental value remains a false dichotomy inasmuch as both cost and sentiment represent an abstraction of the napkins' materiality as napkins. At the same time, this abstraction of materiality produces heartfelt emotions or, more accurately, a seemingly novel expression of sentiment. In this way the emotional life of the poet appears grounded in – not set against – the material gains of empire that he seems to question and critique. But the deep-feeling poet is not alone in his reaction to such objects; his feelings of longing and loss are not the exclusive products of Roman imperial expansion. I have already noted how napkins figure as objects of theft in poems 12 and 25, and the great lengths to which the speaker of poem 10 goes to hide his failure to bring home some litter-bearers. While the poet and the thief seem to occupy dichotomous positions *vis-à-vis* their sense of value, both are equally affected by material objects; both appear driven by desire.

Thus far I have been reading a selection of the polymetrics with an eye towards denaturalizing the familiar distinction between monetary and sentimental value. In surveying a variety of poems, I have suggested that financial and emotional investment can productively be viewed as two aspects of the same phenomenon: an abstraction of materiality not wholly inconsistent with the notion of commodity fetishism. In this light, the poems reveal their engagement in the construction of a "broadly real landscape" in part marked by the presence of deeply meaningful material objects. The presence of such things as souvenir napkins highlights the affective potential of materiality. In the case of a poet, we also see how the mechanics of literary production and even fictionalized narratives arise from a specific historical and material context. Catullus presents a model for poetic inspiration that differs dramatically from the romantic image of the solitary and stationary poet; for Catullus, poetry is found and made along the roads of empire and through physical contact with irresistible foreign products. The acquisition of territories and the concomitant regulation of circuits of commerce are figured as providing the "raw materials" for a variety of actions, experiences and sentiments. Thus what distinguishes the work of Catullus is its overt recognition of that material world and its use of it to represent favorably the bonds of male friendship and an occasion for poetic expression. The urbane individual need not fear being unmade by contact with foreign luxury items, as occurs in the ancient historian Sallust's description of Sulla's army. Quite the contrary, Catullan poetry emphasizes the way that these new things underlie this new form of poetry. The poetry further reveals the capacity of such objects to body forth new feelings and, hence, to create a new kind of sentimental subject.

Until this point, the emotions unearthed by contact with foreign things have been largely positive. Although Catullus expresses anger at the theft of his precious souvenirs, the souvenirs themselves enable him to fall into nostalgic reverie and thereby give shape to an emotionally complex and three-dimensional model of Roman subjectivity. Still, I do not mean to gloss over the more negative aspects of empire that Catullus treats. A number of poems announce in visceral terms a distaste for the experience of service to a provincial governor. Curiously, while the poems discussed thus far open up the psychic opportunities afforded by the practices of Roman expansion, their counterparts disclose the negative attributes of Roman politics through the language of physical and sexual violation, and in this way ground the sentimentality of subjectivity in a three-dimensional body. Thus I will now turn briefly to those poems that critique Roman expansion.

The bodies of men

A number of poems from the collection appear to offer an implicit critique not just of the "biggest pricks" in Roman provincial government, but also of the system responsible for them. For instance, poem 28 begins with a dismal portrait of our friends Fabullus and Veranius; they are a "bankrupt band" (*cohors inanis*), having endured cold and hunger under the leadership of Piso Caesoninus. Lines 9 and 10, however, expand the scope of the poem to address Catullus's own experiences with Memmius in Bithynia: "O Memmius, you fucked me good and slow and I took that timber all the way down my throat" (*O Memmi, bene me ac diu supinum … tota ista trabe lentus irrumasti*). Through this comparison, the experiences of staff members in provinces as different as Spain and Bithynia emerge as identical – the staff are always screwed because the governor is always an *irrumator*. Likewise, poem 29 flattens the Roman world and represents the provinces as uniform sites of past and potential exploitation by cataloguing a whole series of provinces looted by Caesar:

> Was it on this account that you were in Britain?
> So that tired penis of yours
> could eat up twenty to thirty million HS?
> First he squandered his inheritance, secondly the Pontic prize,
> thirdly Spain, and now they're afraid in Britain.

As in poem 28, the imagery is sexual and violent. Mamurra (Caesar's cohort) is described as Caesar's exhausted penis, and Caesar is called Cinaedus Romulus (homosexually passive founder of Rome).

The figuring of politics as sex or sex as politics has a familiar ring, for Catullus is certainly not the first author to employ such metaphors. Yet the preponderance of Catullan scholarship reveals a tendency to separate the two. More specifically, critics have often addressed portions of the collection according to theme. Thus, even contemporary critics interested in pushing the boundaries of Catullan criticism have opted to treat, for instance, the "Lesbia poems" (love poems directed at a woman called "Lesbia," in reference to the Greek poet Sappho) separately from the campaign poems.[20] Yet even cursory inspection shows that Catullus regularly moves back and forth between using sex and politics as the tenor of his metaphors. While a full examination of the Lesbia poems remains beyond the parameters of this essay, I would like to return to the subject of sex and move it alongside the relations between subjectivity and empire addressed thus far.

One thing that unifies the various sex acts that serve as metaphors for unethical plundering is their unpleasant, if not graphically violent nature. Poem 28 portrays life in the provinces as analogous to homosexual rape; poem 29 represents the plundering colonial as an insatiable penis. A metaphor such as that found in poem 28 – of being slowly gagged by a timber – draws attention to the permeability of the victim's body. The use of *helluor* ("to gluttonize") and *lancino* ("to rend") represents booty as ingestible. Such terms necessarily assume, if they do not actively construct, a body – a Roman self – that is physically three-dimensional – one as capable of being penetrated as it is of engulfing.

In earlier Roman literature, bodies that appear thus marked and penetrated are most often the bodies of slaves and criminals.[21] Slaves and criminals were tortured as a form of punishment, and the evidence given by slaves was admissible in the law courts only if it was extracted through torture (Crook 1967: 275). Somewhat similarly, a sexually penetrated body marked its owner as a woman, a pathic or a slave. In appropriating the body of the victim in poems such as 28, Catullus refigures the citizen's male body, which, according to Wiseman, enjoyed at least a theoretical inviolability (1985: 8). Metaphorically, the compromised bodies of the speaker and his friends testify to the disempowerment experienced by young men on account of the erosion of late-Republican socio-political systems such as patronage:

> Aspiring young men are sent out on foreign service with the advice to cultivate useful friendships. But the patronage system is rigged against anyone born outside the tight circle of this nobility; there is no guarantee that those at the top will play fair with those beneath them.
>
> (Skinner 1979: 140)

The most striking aspect of Catullus's use of sexual violence as a metaphor for the degenerative employment of political power emerges powerfully once it is placed alongside the sentimental subjects discussed in the previous section.

As I noted above, readers and critics alike have been at something of a loss with regard to how to read the emotionally confessional voice constructed through such poems as 12. Much of this, no doubt, has to do with the fragmented nature of literary evidence. But part of the problem, as I hinted at the outset, involves the nature of the query. Thus I have been reading Catullus more as cultural evidence than as literary landmark. As a result, I have interpreted Catullus's more sentimental tones less as a literary experiment than as marking a shift in the representation of the Roman masculine subject. On the one hand, the sentimentalizing of value works to accommodate the changes in the visual landscape and personal habits of Roman citizens effected by Rome's expansion. On the other hand, the sentimentalization of material objects produces, quite simply, sentimental subjects, men who desire and care about persons and places and express those feelings through poetry, gift giving and theft. Catullus vests those subjects with compromised bodies. While Roman literature and daily life abounded with tortured and violated bodies, those bodies most often belonged to persons whose stature and sex set them well apart from men of Catullus's ilk. Thus I suggest that the appropriation of such bodies here provides the physical counterpart – a mirror of three-dimensionality – to the emotional depth given expression through Spanish linen. Therefore the marked, penetrated and penetrating bodies of those directly involved in the work of imperialism complement, rather than contradict, the model of Roman identity that I have been teasing out of poems such as 12. Ironically, that the bodies of Catullus and his friends should suffer such misuse only testifies to the sincerity of his claims, if we can associate their sexual violation with the torture of slaves. In the world of the polymetrics, one develops or acquires a sense of emotional depth through contact with the material fruits of empire just as one comes to know the body through the failure of socio-political structures. As a result, what ultimately emerges from these poems constitutes a new way of imagining the Roman masculine subject: as physically permeable and consequently possessed of a deep interiority. And both of these qualities are realized specifically through the social, political and economic climate of Catullus's Rome.

My reading of Roman identity as it emerges from Catullus's poetry rebuts those cultural theorists who see antiquity as a simpler time populated by "flatter" individuals. It also seems to depend upon an implicit belief in the possibility of something tendentiously analogous to commodity fetishism in Catullus's Rome. I would not, however, argue that the Late Republic ought to be regarded as a proto-capitalist society. As I noted earlier, the ancient economy was fundamentally agricultural, while supporting urban centers of consumption – not manufacture or commerce. It is also evident that Roman culture, as seen through the eyes and words of Roman writers, endured a prolonged anxiety about the effects of material objects upon its very being. From the very beginnings of territorial and economic expansion and of the literary record, exotic or luxury items were viewed as threats to *Romanitas*. The poetry of Catullus in a sense addresses this anxiety without constituting that poetics of mourning or nostalgia so familiar to readers of work on post-coloniality and tourism. Rather than compensating for lost authenticity, the imperial "commodity" appears to be materially and metaphorically implicated in a new rhetoric of Roman masculinity. To the degree that we can speak of something akin to commodification or commodity fetishism in antiquity, its relationship to subjectivity is reciprocally formulative. A critical move towards identifying various proto-capitalistic phenomena in antiquity runs the risk of setting up a relentlessly Western teleology at odds with more recent work that treats non-Eurocentric histories of capitalism and alternate and multiple modernities. This is not my intent. At the same time, terms such as "commodity" and "commodity fetishism" – if they can be freed from a specific teleology of Western economic development – speak most pointedly to the relationship between economics and subjectivity and, as a result, enable substantial critical work. Thus in the remaining portion of this essay, I will employ such items, albeit gingerly. As W.V. Harris has recently suggested, the employment of economic terminology deriving from the study of more modern societies (he speaks, in this instance, of the term "capitalism") can result in a different categorization (and, likewise, a critical reconsideration) when applied to the Roman economy (1993: 24). Thus broader definitions of terms such as "commodity" and "capitalism" suggest alternate histories of economic development in the West as well as reconsiderations of such hallmarks of modern capitalistic economies as "rational" accounting and the "commercialization" of the economy. Further, employment of terms such as "commodity" and "commodity fetishism" underscores, like nothing else, the complicated interplay between the realms of economics and subjectivity.[22]

Concluding thoughts

How, finally, are we to reconcile Catullus's rhetoric of sentimental materialism with the anxious indeterminacy of the material gift found in the legal discourse?

To begin with, the "big pricks of empire" and the thieves who pay no respect to private ownership reflect the kind of thinking inherent in the prohibition of gifts between spouses and as payment for legal advocacy. Underlying their behavior is a recognition of the gift's ability to function merely as a bearer of economic value. The poet, on the other hand, claims no interest in such a base form of value. In this way, his feelings mirror the logic that allows gifts between spouses and close family members: gifts essentially concern bonds that remain, for want of a better term, "priceless." While poem 12's speaker appears only to recognize this sentimental form of value, the poem itself upholds the cultural illogic already seen in Roman legal treatment of the gift. The linen napkins are priceless but worth a payback of three hundred lines of invective poetry or trade for a *talentum*. In this way, poem 12 does not provide the kind of comfortable logic offered by a "purely economic" explanation of, for example, the traditional prohibition of gifts between spouses. Instead, its own schizophrenia mirrors both the paradoxical nature of Roman legislation on gifts and the vexed attitude that Romans held towards material wealth. Thus the example of Catullus clarifies the validity of Bourdieu's claim that "economism is ethnocentrism." Like gifts in the legal sphere, Catullus's gift betrays its own over- and underdetermination. It is not enough, however, merely to recognize that Roman law and Catullan poetry depict similar limitations on economic logic. Not only does Catullan poetry appear to mirror prevailing attitudes towards the gift, but it actually seems to put those attitudes – in particular, the gift's ability to embody the fluid shift between various forms of value – to use.

As already noted, a variety of cultural pressures rendered the gift a highly charged yet indeterminate category of objects. To a certain extent, much of the legislation regulating gifts appears highly rhetorical. Take, for instance, the coexistence of dichotomous rules governing spousal gifts. The fact that the *lex Cincia* actually permitted gifts between spouses seems, in this context, negligible – unless we assume that the object of the law was something other than gifts themselves. The Romans themselves, one suspects, recognized the impossibility of stabilizing occasions for, limits on, and definitions of the gift. The gift could always be a suspect object. And laws such as the *lex Cincia*, along with the writings of various jurists, appear to use that indeterminacy in order to fix other objects or relations. Thus the *lex Cincia* establishes a group of intimate familial relations ideally endowed with a certain inviolability. Gifts, in this instance, embody close family bonds. In forbidding payment for legal advocacy, the *lex Cincia* reaffirms the existence of both the patron's generosity and his lack of interest in acquisition *per se*. Thus, gifts here either cannot embody personal ties without the taint of material gain, or the ties between patron and client are so categorically different from those between family members that they render the exchange of gifts impossible.

Poem 12 and the collection that contains it clearly take advantage of the gift's indeterminacy. The gift of linen napkins straddles the line between the gifts addressed in the above legal contexts: like the gift between spouses it embodies a close personal tie; like the gifts forbidden between patrons and clients, the napkins are exchanged between men and constitute recognizable economic value. The nature of this gift is, moreover, given substantial material specificity when Catullus identifies it as a set of souvenir napkins. The souvenir (like the gift), for which Catullus employs the obviously Greek term *mneumosyne*, represents another category of objects demanding substantial narrativization. In this case, its primary signal, through the term of its identification and its "biography" as an imperial product, is foreign. But the specific marking of this souvenir as a gift both permits an elaboration on its material specificity and opens the possibility of a "universal" sentimentality. The marking of the napkins as a gift allows poem 12 to slip between the realms of politics and friendship, of cost and sentiment. The linen napkins embody the amicable feelings of friends and cohorts. They thus signal a highly emotional bond between men while at the same time contributing to a shift in our sense of Roman masculinity. The glut of description – personal, material and otherwise – that accompanies the napkins further contributes to our sense that they function, at least for the speaker, as a kind of fetish. Concomitantly, it is exactly the sentimental fetishizing of the napkins that enables them and other such items to work towards the recuperation not merely of the objects brought by Roman expansion but also of the larger political and economic systems that make those objects available.

At this point I run the risk of hailing Catullus and Catullan poetic intention as responsible for initiating a shift in Roman individuation. I would like, then, finally, to shift emphasis away from Catullus as a poetic producer to Catullus as a symptomatic vehicle through which Republican society could voice its negotiation of newfound wealth, foreign luxury items, and their like. As seen through the examination of legal discourse, Roman society already had, in the notion of gift, an available indeterminate category of object able to accommodate new meanings and forms of value. Thus, for example, the melodramatic discourse of the *Digest*, to my mind, above all represents the highly emotional form of individualized subjectivity characteristic of later antiquity – the era of Hellenistic novels, Christianity, etc. What we see emerging in Catullus, on the other hand, is a more slippery and, I suggest, incipient form of subjectivity. Curiously sentimental and paired with a body more akin to that of a slave than a citizen, the Catullan subject appears at once novel (in terms of prior modes of representation) and, at the same time, very much a product of the material, political and other such conditions of the late Republic. That such subjectivity should be effected through the politics of empire, the medium of its products, and be transmitted through the medium of poetry is provocative, to say the least.

In the broadest sense there lies an analogic relationship between fetishism and poetry through the common grounds of abstraction and representation. I write here conscious of Gayatri Spivak's (1985) arguments against such "culturalization" of economics. Yet in the specific context of (1) the "non-economy" of Republican Rome; and (2) the relentlessly discursive nature of the gift within that context, I would argue that such a move is not only necessary but productive. To argue against the culturalization of economics is to assume the autonomous existence of an economy, against which we have already seen argued. To look, on the other hand, at the abstraction of value within the nexus of Roman economics/culture/representation is to glimpse alternate ways of negotiating the press of economic shifts. In this light, the gift not only provides a conveniently logical object for a poetics of sentimental masculinity, but the fact that it is given voice through the medium of poetry becomes forcefully logical as well. Ultimately, this move rebuts strictly teleological arguments about economic history and development. Still, I make no claim to press Bourdieu's "universally respected forms of respect for the universal." For, while providing equally valid indications of a cultural and economic imperialism, the dining couches of Catullus's Rome lie at a far remove from supermarket take-out sushi, the prevalence of KFC in Sumatra, and the interconnectedness of global cultures and economies that such phenomena signal today. At the same time, my look back at the complex cultural and individual negotiations of value, sentiment, culture and politics in ancient Rome suggests that the relative plurality of globalization(s), universalisms and capitalisms is not merely horizontal and synchronic but also vertical, with deeper and more complicated histories. Thus in advancing a treatment of Roman antiquity that places it both inside and outside the discourse of economic criticism and theory, I contribute to the production of non-linear, multiple and alternate histories of capitalism which can lead, ultimately, to non-ethnocentric economic thinking.

Notes

Portions of this essay, in various forms, were delivered at the Annual Meeting of the American Philological Association, December 1996, New York and at Culture and Economics, An International Conference sponsored by the Society for Critical Exchange, July 1998, Exeter, UK. I owe many thanks to the interlocutors in attendance. Special thanks to Mark Osteen for his insightful suggestions, and to Andrew Riggsby and Cannon Schmitt, as always, for their probing questions and helpful suggestions.

Wherever possible, I cite the Oxford Classical Text editions of Latin sources such as the *Carmina* of Catullus or the *Ab Urbe Condita* of Livy. The *Digest*, along with *Institutes* and the *Codex Iustianius*, were compiled under the Emperor Justinian in the sixth century CE. The standard edition of the *Digest* is the *Digesta*, edited by Th. Mommsen and P. Krueger. Some juristic writings on the *lex Cincia* are contained in the *Fragmentum Vaticanum* (298 ff), also post-classical.

1   According to Jerome, the Roman poet Catullus was born in 87 BCE and died in 57/58 BCE. There is evidence to suggest that the dates are slightly off; hence, his dates are usually given as c. 87–54 BCE. The collected works are derived, for the most part, from two 14th-century manuscripts, G (no. 14137, National Library in Paris) and O (no. 30, Canonici Latin mss in the Bodleian Library). The poems or carmina are generally referred to by number, although some distinction is often made between the shorter polymetrics (the first 60), the longer poems (61–68b), and a second group of shorter poems all written in elegiac couplets (69–116). For obvious reasons, the literature on Catullus and his works is vast. Two recent works by Michaela Janan (1994) and William Fitzgerald (1995) offer fresh approaches and contain substantial bibliographies.

2   On the specifics of neoteric style and vocabulary, see D.O. Ross. Some of Ross's interpretations of specific poems have been contested, but his work on diction and word association remains valuable.

3 The word *amicitia* ranges in meaning from personal friendship to something closer to party affiliation.

4 Academic historians and cultural critics working in latter eras are used to thinking in terms of decades or even years. Those of us ensconced in the world of antiquity often think of events separated by decades as, in some vague sense, simultaneous. Thus we speak of fifth-century BCE Athens or the Roman Republic (c. 510–27 BCE) as constituting discrete eras.

5 The terms *dona* and *munera* both refer to gifts. *Munus* (singular) is somewhat broader, encompassing notions of "office" or "duty," as well as "charge" or "tax." On the *lex Cincia* in general, see Berger 1953; Gardner 1986: 74–7; Watson 1968: 229–32; Treggiari 1991: 365–6.

6 Thus, for instance, the *lex Claudia* of c. 218 BCE forbade senators and their sons from owning vessels of any but the smallest capacity, presumably to exclude them from maritime commerce. Livy offers an account of the law's passing in Book XXI, 63.3–4. Further, it is something of a rhetorical convention to feign a lack of interest in money, finery and other such things associated with the acquisition of wealth, as seen in the writings of figures as disparate as Cato the Elder (*de Agricultura*), Catullus (poem 12) and Cicero (the Verrines).

7 Laws by custom are practices accepted as the rule despite the absence of recorded law. To be sure, Roman jurists drew a distinction between laws according to custom and "mere social observances" (Crook 1967: 28). For a brief discussion of law according to custom, see Crook 1967: 27–30. Regarding the prohibition of spousal gifts, the date is speculative. It has been suggested that the ban dates to the *lex Iulia et Papia* of Augustus (9 CE), but ancient authorities agree that the rule was not dependent upon legislation. Most likely, the ban came into practice during the late Republic. See, for example, Watson 1968: 229–30; Treggiari 1991: 370. Extensive commentary on the ban, including discussions of exemplary cases, is found in book 24 of the *Digest* of Justinian. Susan Treggiari offers a redaction of many key points (1991: 366–74).

8 *Hoc autem receptum est, ne mutuo amore invicem spoliarentur donationibus non temperantes, sed profusa erga se facilitate.* It should be noted that there were exceptions and/or loopholes to this rule. Detailed examination of the subject extends well beyond the parameters of this paper. For further discussion see Treggiari 1991: 365; Corbett 1930: 202.

9 On marital love and affection see Treggiari 1991: 229–61; Williams 1958.

10 Crook is hardly the only scholar to advance an economic interpretation of the ban on spousal gifts. David Johnston, in his *Roman Law in Context* (1999), states "The purpose of this was clearly not to discourage birthday or anniversary presents but to prevent large capital settlements being made from one side of the family to the other" (1999: 34).

11 *[N]e concordia pretio conciliari videretur.*

12 "The 'consumption city' is one that derives its maintenance on the basis of legal claim, such as taxes or rent, without having to deliver return values" (Hopkins 1983: xiii, quoting M.I. Finley).

13 The various divisions that marked Roman society are complex and do not map easily onto more contemporary conceptions of class. For a thorough consideration of this problem, see Finley (1985: 35–61), who addresses the problems inherent in adopting the term "class" to describe various segments of the Roman population, and argues for the adoption of the term "status": "an admirably vague word with a considerable psychological element" (1985: 51).

14 Caesar means Julius Caesar. Mamurra, also called *mentula* (prick), has been identified as an engineering overseer for Caesar and a member of the class of knights. Pliny the Elder and Cicero both mentioned Mamurra's ill-gotten wealth. The identity of Furius is not known.

15 For an overview of indemnities amassed from conquests, booty, taxation, mining profits, etc. see Jones 1974, especially 114–16.

16 *Similiter etiamin Italiae regione Aliana inter Padum Ticinumque amnes, ubi a Saetabi tertio in Europa lino palma, secundam enim vicina Alianis capessunt Retovina et in Aemilia via Faventina.* The town was also known for its production of linen hunting nets. See Blazquez 1978: 325. The fame of Spanish linen dates back several centuries at least to the time of Hannibal (Livy 21.15).

17 The cultivation of flax in Italy dates to prehistoric times, but the linen produced in Egypt and Spain was of a finer weave. See Sebesta 1994: 65–76.

18 Although the landscape of the Catullan collection is broadly real, it is, at the same time, highly literary. Catullus often substitutes allusive phrases or epithets for simple placenames or chooses to identify those places with literary associations (for example, the birthplace or home of a Greek author). The doubled significance of the cities and regions he mentions, I would suggest, contributes to the enabling representation of Roman imperialism. Not only does movement through the provinces make souvenir napkins available, but it also lies at the heart of his poetic production. This poetic discourse becomes a kind of "thing" embedded in the work of Roman expansion and government.

19 The version I present, "*et ... et*" is derived from an assumed source manuscript V dating from ca. 1280 from which three surviving fourteenth-century manuscripts O, G and R are thought to derive (directly or indirectly). Manuscripts rendering the line "*ut ... et*" date back to the fifteenth century. Most modern editors prefer this reading because it resolves the meaning of the line. Most recently, D.F.S. Thomson has argued for "*ut ... et*" on the basis that "*et* has most certainly crept in from the preceding line" (1997: 241), which can hardly be taken as conclusive. See Thomson 1997 for an overview of the history of the text as well as further bibliography.

20 I do not mean to imply that there has been no satisfactory work on Catullus. In fact, Marilyn Skinner has written amply and persuasively on the specific problems of Catullan sexuality (1981) and the implications of Catullus's political poems (1979).

21 Slaves are threatened with beatings, torture and crucifixion with great regularity in Roman comedy. On the level and nature of public violence in Catullus's Rome see Wiseman 1985: 5–14. The most notable exception to the correspondence between marked bodies and non-citizens is the scarred body of the Roman soldier. To bear the scars of battle was, of course, a mark of nobility and courage – but even in this case the scars ought to mark the front and not the back of a man's body.

22 On the problem of commodity fetishism as a category, see Amariglio and Callari 1993.

References

Amariglio, Jack and Antonio Callari. "Marxian value theory and the problem of the subject: the role of commodity fetishism." In Emily Apter and William Pietz (eds) *Fetishism as Cultural Discourse*. Ithaca: Cornell University Press, 1993, pp. 186–216.

Apter, Emily and William Pietz (eds). *Fetishism as Cultural Discourse*. Ithaca: Cornell University Press, 1993.

Berger, Adolf. "Encyclopedic dictionary of Roman law." *Transactions of the American Philosophical Society* (NS) 43.2 (1953).

Blazquez, J.M. *Economia de la Hispania Romana*. Bilbao: Ediciones Najera, 1978.

Bourdieu, Pierre. "Marginalia – some additional notes on the gift." Trans. Richard Nice. In Alan D. Schrift (ed.) *The Logic of the Gift: Toward an Ethic of Generosity*. New York: Routledge, 1997a, pp. 231–41.

—— "Selections from *The Logic of Practice*." Trans. Richard Nice. In Alan D. Schrift (ed.) *The Logic of the Gift: Toward an Ethic of Generosity*. New York: Routledge, 1997b, pp. 190–230.

Corbett, P.E. *The Roman Law of Marriage.* Oxford: Oxford University Press, 1930.

Crawford, Michael. *The Roman Republic.* Second edition. Cambridge, MA: Harvard University Press, 1992.

Crook, J.A. *Law and Life of Rome, 90 B.C.–A.D. 212.* Ithaca: Cornell University Press, 1967.

Evans, John K. *War, Women, and Children in Ancient Rome.* London and New York: Routledge, 1991.

Finley, M.I. *The Ancient Economy.* Second edition. Berkeley: University of California Press, 1985.

Fitzgerald, William. *Catullan Provocations: Lyric Poetry and the Drama of Position.* Berkeley: University of California Press, 1995.

Gardner, Jane F. *Women in Roman Law and Society.* Bloomington: Indiana University Press, 1986.

Garnsey, Peter, Keith Hopkins and C.R. Whittaker (eds). *Trade in the Ancient Economy.* Berkeley: University of California Press, 1983.

Hallett, Judith P. and Marilyn B. Skinner (eds). *Roman Sexualities.* Princeton: Princeton University Press, 1997.

Harris, W.V. (ed.). *The Inscribed Economy: Production and Distribution in the Roman Empire in the Light of Instrumentum Domesticum. The Proceedings of a Conference Held at the American Academy in Rome on 10-11 January, 1992.* Ann Arbor: University of Michigan Press, 1993.

Hopkins, Keith. "Introduction." In Peter Garnsey, Keith Hopkins and C.R. Whittaker (eds) *Trade in the Ancient Economy.* Berkeley: University of California Press, 1983, pp. ix–xxv.

Janan, Michaela. *"When the Lamp is Shattered": Desire and Narrative in Catullus.* Carbondale and Edwardsville: Southern Illinois University Press, 1994.

Johnston, David. *Roman Law in Context.* Cambridge: Cambridge University Press, 1999.

Jones, A.H.M. *The Roman Economy: Studies in Ancient Economic and Administrative History.* Ed. P.A. Brunt. Oxford: Blackwell, 1974.

Lyne, R.O.A.M. *The Latin Love Poets: From Catullus to Horace.* Oxford: Clarendon Press; New York: Oxford University Press, 1980.

Parker, Holt N. "The teratogenic grid." In Judith P. Hallett and Marilyn B. Skinner (eds) *Roman Sexualities.* Princeton: Princeton University Press, 1997, pp. 47–65.

Ross, David O. Jr. *Style and Tradition in Catullus.* Cambridge, MA: Harvard University Press, 1969.

Rudd, Niall. "Romantic love in classical times?" *Ramus* 10 (1981): 140–58.

Sebesta, Judith Lynn. "Tunica ralla, tunica spissa." In Judith Lynn Sebesta and Larissa Bonfante (eds) *The World of Roman Costume.* Madison: University of Wisconsin Press, 1994, pp. 65–76.

Sebesta, Judith Lynn and Larissa Bonfante (eds). *The World of Roman Costume.* Madison: University of Wisconsin Press, 1994.

Schrift, Alan D. (ed.). *The Logic of the Gift: Toward an Ethic of Generosity.* New York: Routledge, 1997.

Skinner, Marilyn. "Parasites and strange bedfellows: a study in Catullus' political imagery." *Ramus* 8 (1979): 137–52.

—— *Catullus' Passer: The Arrangement of the Book of Polymetric Poems.* New York: Arno, 1981.

—— "Ego mulier: the construction of male sexuality in Catullus." *Helios* 20.2 (1993): 107–30.

Spivak, Gayatri Chakravorty. "Scattered speculations on the question of value." *Diacritics* (Winter 1985): 73–93.

Thomas, J.A.C. *Textbook of Roman Law.* New York: North-Holland, 1976.

Thomson, D.F.S. *Catullus*. Toronto: University of Toronto Press, 1997.

Treggiari, Susan. *Roman Marriage: Iusti Coniuges from the Time of Cicero to the Time of Ulpian*. Oxford: Oxford University Press, 1991.

Watson, Alan. *The Law of Property in the Later Roman Republic*. Oxford: Clarendon Press, 1968.

Williams, Gordon. "Some aspects of Roman marriage ceremonies and ideals." *Journal of Roman Studies* 48 (1958): 16–19.

Wiseman, T.P. *Catullus and His World*. Cambridge: Cambridge University Press, 1985.

8 Gabriele D'Annunzio

The art of squandering and the economy of sacrifice

Nicoletta Pireddu

From his early poems to the decadent phase of *Il piacere*, from his lyrical novel *Il fuoco* to the autobiographical works of his last years, the Italian writer Gabriele D'Annunzio (1863–1938) consistently investigated and pushed to the edge a leading idea: that art resists the utilitarian and materialist orientation of modern Western society by functioning as a gift. In D'Annunzio's ongoing meditation on aesthetic activity in terms of gift giving, the gift acquires the status of both a material and an ideational entity. It operates as a tangible ceremonial object that eschews the mercantile logic of the commodity by replacing value with worth. But, more abstractly, it is also the principle of a collective ritual founded upon unconditional expenditure. In other words, the gift becomes the catalyst, if not the metaphor, for a state of exaltation and creativity promoting emotional bonds among individuals, in a disinterested, hence noble, social space.

As significant for Italian decadence as Oscar Wilde is for Great Britain and Joris-Karl Huysmans for France, D'Annunzio cultivated a mythographic imagination in art and life alike, and was an unrepentant worshipper of pleasure and of political notoriety. Therefore, he has always been portrayed as a provocative public figure who influenced art and social mores with his flamboyant writing as well as with sensational, although debatable, military actions. The controversies he stirred among critics were as lively as the influence he exerted upon a variety of late nineteenth- and twentieth-century Italian and foreign authors. James Joyce, to be sure, begins to use the term "epiphany" almost simultaneously with his discovery of D'Annunzio's texts.[1] Joyce may also owe to the Italian author a portion of his blend of naturalism and symbolism, as well as some of the sensitivity to the musical aspect of words so prevalent in his works. With admiration and irony, Henry James highlights the simultaneously hedonistic and colonial adventure of "Signor D'Annunzio," who, "organized for real discovery," really "sailed the sea and brought back the booty" (1904: 419). Yet this paradoxical coexistence of aesthetic disinterestedness and imperialist thirst for appropriation does not seem to have diminished, as evidenced by, for example, Ramón del Valle-Inclán's admiration for D'Annunzio. This Spanish writer of the Generation of '98 movement passionately transposes in his texts those "pangs and pities of the flesh" (1904: 398) which, for James, have "the firmest hand" (1904: 398) in all of D'Annunzio's works. With no less enthusiasm the Haitian novelist Fernand Hibbert (1923) extols *Il fuoco* as "a wonder of lyricism," the crazy and tiring accomplishment of a writer who, better than anyone else, has succeeded in communicating to the soul the shiver of voluptuousness.[2]

D'Annunzio's aesthetic conception of life as the apotheosis of a languid and heroic beauty continues to arouse interest both in Italy and abroad.[3] Beyond reviving D'Annunzio's cult of personality, however, a study of his texts reveals a surprising richness that newly substantiates his truly European stature. More than any other Italian writer of his epoch, D'Annunzio participates in and interrogates a wider cultural discourse that, at the end of the nineteenth century, begins to ascribe an ethical and aesthetic value to the ritual significance of exchange. At a time when progress, profit and utility seemed to triumph as the principles of the Western bourgeois world and were further sanctioned by the instrumental mimesis of realism, anthropologists and artists alike increasingly depicted archaic and primitive ceremonies as the sacred and elitist locus of the symbolic, and hence as a source of reenchantment.[4]

How does D'Annunzio incorporate and transform anthropological discourse in his texts? Unquestionably, his intuitions about the role of ceremonial exchange as the foundation of an allegedly innocent cultural otherness and about its implications for aesthetic activity surpass those of other intellectuals of his time. In D'Annunzio's thought we already find the basic premises about symbolic economies that run from Émile Durkheim through Marcel Mauss and Georges Bataille. Indeed, not only does D'Annunzio articulate the aesthetic object as gift and as the symbolic focus of a unifying experience; he also represents the disposition to unconditional squandering, without any prospect of remuneration, as the aesthetic principle *par excellence*.[5] And he ultimately goes even further, raising questions that still dominate the current critical debate in the humanities and social sciences. Can art really break the circle of contractual, rational exchange? Can the divine worth of its expenditure really mark a point of incommensurability that erases the order of restitution? Is the ethics of natural reciprocity a viable alternative to utilitarian drives? Far from occasional, these issues traverse the entire corpus of D'Annunzio's writings.

As we will see, the pivotal stages of D'Annunzio's poetics also represent significant points of a conceptual trajectory leading from the gift, as the alternative or supplement to the circle of material and moral payoffs, toward a more radical measure. Ultimately at stake is the possibility of a form of expenditure that does not simply remain at the margins of contractual exchange. D'Annunzio envisions this asymmetrical gesture in terms of absolute dissolution, de-materialization, death, and attempts to stage this gesture as sacrifice – the sacrifice of the author and of the work of art alike. This extreme, total act aims to turn the economy of the gift into an economy of pure nothingness, and to bring art from a supplementary present and presence to a sublime, ineffable absence. Yet, ultimately, this is also the *aporia* of D'Annunzio's sacred, ecstatic squandering. Pushed to the limits of representation, aesthetic activity still survives as a trace. It embodies the residues of matter and memory, of the subject and of its intentionality, recapturing loss within the circuit of possession.

The gift of art, the art of giving

As I have shown elsewhere (Pireddu 1997, 2002), the notion of aesthetic activity as a gift, as a destructive form of expenditure without any prior calculation of return, has not received enough attention in studies of D'Annunzio. In fact, however, it not only characterizes D'Annunzio's decadent works, but also represents a fundamental premise of his entire literary production.

D'Annunzio adheres to decadence as to an aesthetics and ethics of ephemerality, to a cult of beauty conceived as a sequence of intoxicating and transitory sensations consumed and enjoyed as such. Not accidentally, the task of Andrea Sperelli, the protagonist of the novel *Il piacere* (1889), is to treat aesthetic activity as wasteful, disinterested dissipation. To make one's own life a work of art – the objective Andrea tries to attain – implies putting oneself in the service of squandering and forgetfulness, refusing the obsession with self-preservation and utility in favor of an idea of representation as a will to chance, as a process of creation governed by transience and loss. Andrea feels the need "to give himself freely and out of gratefulness"[6] to the superior ideal of art, rightly understanding that "the divine worth of the *gift*"[7] – his artistic talent – is not his exclusive property. Indeed, a line of poetry is for him "independent of any constraint and any control: it no longer belongs to its maker; it belongs to all and yet to nobody."[8] No less than his readers, the artist is a temporary beneficiary, and not the master of the gift of art, and as such he is expected to circulate the fruit of his creative spirit by treating it as perishable property – as Lewis Hyde would say[9] – instead of exploiting its essence as personal wealth.

For Andrea Sperelli, then, the poetic word establishes contact with a revitalizing, non-instrumental form of exchange. His contempt for the democracy of taste and for its utilitarian bias makes him refuse "any benefit which is not of love"[10] and conceive of the work of art as a unique specimen to be offered to a unique recipient, since, as he states, "the real reader is not the one who buys me but the one who loves me."[11] The work of art provides a less commonplace model for social interaction based upon a non-conceptual, emotional impulse to bestow and to receive. Here the correspondence between the purposelessness of aesthetic activity and the propensity to give for its own sake emerges with surprising clarity. Aesthetic disinterestedness, and its subjective universality *à la* Kant, are, we could say, equivalent principles to those underlying the impulse to give, according to Marcel Mauss's seminal *Essai sur le don*. The practice of gift exchange is set in motion and regulated by a set of obligations which, like the lawfulness without law of the Kantian beautiful (1997: 228), are not imposed from above as a categorical imperative but rather harmoniously integrated in the texture of the community, or, better, coterminous with the birth of the community itself. It is precisely through the circulation of the ceremonial object that individuals are connected to one another, according to Mauss:

> Everything is tied together: things have personality, and personalities are in some manner the permanent possession of the clan. ... If things are given

and returned it is precisely because one gives and returns "respects" and "courtesies." But in addition, in giving them, a man gives himself, and he does so because he owes himself – himself and his possessions – to others.

(1967: 44–5)

Mauss's vision of gift exchange as a "much less prosaic" (1967: 70) social practice (hence, we might extrapolate, more poetical and more beautiful) remains the paramount source to substantiate the correspondence between aesthetics and the principle of ceremonial expenditure. But D'Annunzio's *Il piacere* already contains all the essential points of the formal conjunction of art and gift, of symbolization and fetishization. Nor does the ultimate failure of its protagonist, who is still too anchored to material and rational speculation to be able to let go, expel the paradigm of symbolic economy from D'Annunzio's aesthetic and social vision. Thirty years after *Il piacere*, its author provides us with a practical example endorsing the circulation and consumption of the aesthetic object and the unifying sensations it generates within the community. I am referring to the *Carta del Carnaro* (the Carnaro Charter), the constitution to which D'Annunzio contributed during his occupation of the Dalmatian city of Fiume in 1919–20, at the apex of his epic ardor for Italy's redemption of territories lost in the peace negotiations that closed World War I. Here, a D'Annunzio who seems to have forsaken the languor of decadent beauty and aesthetic disinterestedness to plunge into heroic conquests nonetheless still desires to extinguish the appeal of materialism and of scarcity-induced production by molding popular consciousness through art.

The gist of the document, mainly prepared by D'Annunzio's collaborator Alceste De Ambris, is to sanction D'Annunzio's project to unite all the oppressed people of the earth in order to fight imperialist and financial forces. Yet D'Annunzio's allegedly idiosyncratic additions reinstate the primacy of the aesthetic as a collective, ritual experience separate from purposeful actions. In the slightest trace of decoration, in the institutionalization of music, and in the civic ceremonies that should be integral parts of that ideal counter-society, D'Annunzio locates a mysterious force that can restore the spirit of freedom and solidarity of a pre-capitalist, non-technological world. Hence the working class must learn how to endow its existence with spiritual and aesthetic meaning. The task of the College of Aediles, for instance, is not simply to preside over the "decoro" (both "decorum" and "embellishment") of civic life, but, more specifically, to convince workers that "to adorn with some sign of popular art the humblest dwelling is a pious act, and that there is a religious feeling of human mystery and of deep nature in the simplest sign which is transmitted, through carving or painting, generation after generation."[12] Similarly, music guarantees the greatness of a people precisely for its ritual, noble and creative faculty:

If every rebirth of a noble people is a lyrical effort, if every unanimous and creative feeling is a lyrical power, if every new order is a lyrical order in the

> vigorous and impetuous sense of the word, Music considered a ritual language exalts the act of life, the work of life.[13]

Echoing Durkheim's aestheticizing interpretation of archaic religious ceremonies as generators of collective effervescence (Durkheim 1991: 363–417), D'Annunzio here implies that joyful dissipation of imaginative energy beyond utilitarian constraints and practical activities is a universal and permanent source of reciprocity in mankind as a whole, and hence the only stable guarantee of social harmony and redemption.

However, in the so-called Overman phase of D'Annunzio's work, of which *Le vergini delle rocce* (1991a [1895]) is the central text, the aristocratic ability for sacred squandering was not so much a matter of a potentially universal greatness of soul as of belonging to a noble household, in line with Nietzsche's scorn for any institutionalized community. The blatant influence of the German philosopher on D'Annunzio has received considerable attention.[14] What seems still to be neglected, however, is that the Italian author promptly grasps the *anthropological* underpinnings of Nietzsche's thought, and in particular the inseparable link between the instinct for rank, from which the master's prestige derives, the nobility of taste, and the disposition to bestow. Aristocracy in *Le vergini delle rocce* may well be more specifically related to ancestral lineage, contrary to the less defined status of the Nietzschean master, but it is important to notice that D'Annunzio endorses the interpretation of art as the essence of the will to power, associating it with the practice of what Nietzsche defines as a "large-scale economy" (Nietzsche 1968: 451), and hence with that active nihilism distinguishing the noble individual and the artistic creator from the passive nihilism of laymen, who are mere recipients of art and unable to transcend a morality of utility.

Indeed, the protagonist of the novel, Claudio Cantelmo, aspiring to defend and perpetuate the ideal of beauty and virtue, wants to generate a kind of Overman – the king of Rome – belonging to a racial *élite* distinguished by a sense of reciprocity founded upon the ability to bestow, rather than upon the rational balances of utilitarian transactions. Just as the Nietzschean noble soul gives as it takes, prince Luzio, the father of the three women from whom Cantelmo will choose his spouse, appears to Cantelmo as "an exemplary model of a superior humankind, manifesting in each of his actions his different essence, the feeling of his absolute separation from the multitude, from common duties, from common virtues."[15] Not accidentally, the tangible sign of Luzio's aristocracy is his hands, beautiful and pure because they practice a "liberality only comparable to the ancient, which loved to reward profusely for small services."[16] By adopting unconditional giving as the prerequisite for the "sovranità interiore" (inner sovereignty, the Nietzschean autocracy of consciousness),[17] the protagonist of *Le vergini delle rocce* can thus conceive of the world and of the poetic word as "a magnificent gift bestowed by the few upon the many, by the free upon the slaves: by those who think and feel upon those who have to work."[18]

Nevertheless, if we look more carefully at the way in which D'Annunzio interprets the noble propensity for aesthetic rather than for utilitarian production, we can see that, whether it be a ruse or simple naiveté, D'Annunzio questions the transvaluation of all values, exposing how the gift of art is inevitably reabsorbed within the circuit of value-production. The honor of the Nietzschean master is not simply an instance of *noblesse oblige*: rather, it results from the force of super-abundance, beyond order and control. The greatness of the Nietzschean genius lies in prodigality: in his works and deeds "he expends himself … he uses himself up" (Nietzsche 1990: 109). What suspends his instinct of self-preservation, allowing him to discharge his excess energy, is neither heroism nor indifference to his own interests. In fact, he overflows only under the irresistible pressure of his own vital force, "with inevitability, fatefully, involuntarily" (1990: 109). However, despite the totally physiological and automatic nature of his deed, this superior, "explosive being" is bestowed a "higher morality" (1990: 109) in return. In other words, human gratitude calls the genius's gesture "sacrifice," although this is only the result of a misunderstanding (1990: 109). In uncannily analogous terms, D'Annunzio, as we can see in one of his letters to his French lover Angèle Lager, underscores this equally inevitable reward that repays the genius's self-consummation, but ultimately shows how the apparent resignation with which the superior being accepts this symbolic gain is not immune to a strategic component. As if making a virtue of necessity, D'Annunzio explains that he has to be "so heroically patient,"[19] since the suffering he has to undergo for the sake of his work – a martyrdom "far more atrocious than Saint Sebastian's" – is precisely "the terrible condemnation and damnation of the genius. … It is the eternal misunderstanding."[20]

Is it possible to avoid this misunderstanding? That is, is it possible to conceive of an absolutely pure act of giving that can challenge every rational standard? Is it possible to think of an exchange without feedback or profit? D'Annunzio's "ascensional" reading of the German philosopher – his transfiguration of Nietzsche's sarcasm into a heroic and sensual state (Schnapp 1986: 255) – suggests a negative answer. The allegedly automatic, magical, disinterested impulse that propels aesthetic activity as extravagant expenditure cannot remain outside the grip of consciousness, hence it cannot but slide into grandiosity and reward. Whereas for Nietzsche the relation between will and action in the economy of the genius's drives escapes intelligibility, D'Annunzio skillfully manages and reinvests the emotional squandering involved in aesthetic activity. Thanks to his heroic patience, he can deliberately push his labor of art to the extreme level of exhaustion required of him to be worthy of the master's symbolic prestige. We could say that the *pathos* of distance that separates the master's prodigality from servile consciousness here becomes agonistic. As D'Annunzio reiterates in many other personal meditations, he is haunted by "the anxiety of not having given enough"[21] because only a beautiful soul "feels no joy except by giving itself lavishly."[22] Only by giving more than is asked and more than is promised can the artist break with the circle of finite commerce. Indeed, referring to the herd's ethos of scarcity and material utility that has trodden over the ideals of culture and beauty, D'Annunzio despises money in *Il Libro Segreto* (1995a) since it debases passion and poisons heroism:

> Real passion does not know utility, it does not know any kind of benefit, any
> kind of advantage. it lives, like art, for itself alone. art for art's sake, prowess
> for prowess's sake, courage for courage's sake, love for love's sake, intoxica-
> tion for intoxication's sake, pleasure for pleasure's sake.[23]

How, then, can D'Annunzio's soul be truly beautiful? Through what gesture can
it attain such an absolute, self-referring disinterestedness? Is there an unaccountable experience that can consummate this passionate expenditure alien to any
stable order of equivalences? These fundamental aesthetic and ethical questions
emerge systematically in D'Annunzio's more confessional writings, such as *Le
faville del maglio* (1995b [1911–14]), *Notturno* (1991b [1921]), and *Libro segreto*
(1995a [1935]) which – like Baudelaire's *Fusées* – are fragmentary autobiographical memories and meditations on art and life.

Sublime sacrifices: beyond the gift?

In the last stage of his literary career – the so-called nocturnal phase –
D'Annunzio understands, more subtly, that if the alleged truly disinterested pleasure, that of poetic creation, wants to break with the exchange of values and really
be noble, it cannot respond to the mere "bisogno del superfluo" (the need for the
superfluous). It cannot simply consist of the *enjoyment* of art for its own sake, the
expenditure of fleeting sensations: rather, it must go as far as the *destruction* of art
by art. Aesthetic ephemerality must be pushed to its extreme, to absolute loss and
self-dispossession. It must entail "the gift of one's own self, the dedication of one's
whole being,"[24] the sacrifice of the artist, and simultaneously the dissolution of a
transmissible aesthetic experience. For this kind of project, the subversion of
grammatical laws and sentence construction is not enough. More radically, what
D'Annunzio now aspires to is the disintegration of the work of art, "an art of the
word … created upon the total abolition of literary conventions,"[25] which ultimately should coincide with the abolition of literature altogether. The sacrificial
mechanism subtracts the artist and the disinterested pleasure of his aesthetic
expenditure from the circle of collective consumption. It turns the writer and his
production into the embodiment of an absolute – the origin of value, literally *abso-
lutus*, detached, beyond all measure, comparable to nothing.

We can hence recuperate the pattern of radical self-negation through
suffering and detachment from the world underlying D'Annunzio's nocturnal
writings. If we reexamine it under this new light, we can see it as something
different from an acknowledgment of failure, an exhaustion of poetic creativity,
an expression of political disillusionment, or an itinerary of renunciation on the
road of Schopenhauer's *noluntas* – which are the most frequent explanations
given by critics. Rather, the sacrificial and ascetic paradigm, and the rarefaction
of the word on the page, lead to the apotheosis of the aesthete's magnificent
inimitable life, founded upon an economy of death – death of the author and
annihilation of the work – through which D'Annunzio explores the possibility of
a form of expenditure that cannot be appropriated or assimilated by anyone else.

Jacques Derrida, positing the link between gift and writing, claims that neither death nor an immortal life can give. Only a life can give, but a life in which this economy of death manifests itself and lets itself overflow (1991: 132). For his part, D'Annunzio wants to test precisely this borderline, this impossible experience. He now abandons the communitarian aspect of donation, in which his work would be engaged in a process of hetero-affection, hence of circulation, and by representing the consumption of the artist and of his work, he conceives of the production and expenditure of pleasure as non-exchangeable productivity. Literally staging what, in Derrida's term, would be "la mort de l'instance donatrice" (Derrida 1990: 132), the death of the act of giving through the death of the giving agent, D'Annunzio aims at a creative process no longer lacerated by the distinction between gift and debt, and hence a creative process conceived as an autoaffective emotional expenditure.[26]

Rearticulated in aesthetic terms, this shift entails the passage from the principle of the beautiful as a gift propelled by and consolidating a *sensus communis* to the singularity of the sublime. D'Annunzio's art now wants to designate an experience of the limit consisting in an emotional expenditure that frames a hierarchical space without being recuperated within its boundaries. This liminal state does not simply abolish pleasure *tout court*. Rather, it becomes the locus of pleasures that cannot be represented and hence cannot be shared. Significantly, this attempt to verbalize a non-discursive condition while keeping it non-communicable and non-communifying goes hand in hand with D'Annunzio's paradoxical representation of himself as the sacred individual, made *sacer* through sacrifice, and hence excluded, unable to be assimilated by the community.

Limits, heroic exclusion, consumption, and self-effacement are extremely frequent in D'Annunzio's "nocturnal" meditations. Sacrifice and abolition hinder exchange as hetero-affection, so as to accord to the artist absolute ownership and power over emotional and creative experiences that are to remain unique:

> I lived, and I have always liked to live on the border of risk and on the border of the secret. On both of them, the common sense of time is entirely abolished. On both of them, just as at the top, the only kind of time that reigns is the very fluidity of interior life.[27]

Or, again,

> I do not tell anybody what I expect; I do not tell anybody what I suffer; I conceal my real life and I conceal my real art for the supreme heroism and for the supreme book. And I am sure that I will attain both summits. ... And I feel on a par with the most extraordinary event, beyond history, and beyond any other known limit.[28]

"All is sealed in myself, very deep, secret"; "And even the word of the mystic was mine, only mine, only of myself."[29]

Indeed, in *Le faville del maglio* D'Annunzio's reticence regarding the circulation of poetic matter emerges from the *topoi* of absence and nothingness through the frequent use of negative adverbs and prepositions such as "non" ("not") and "senza" ("without"). In the imperishable casket that he builds with imaginary wood splinters, D'Annunzio would like to enclose "the book I have not written,"[30] agreeing with Keats that "Dolci sono le melodie udite ma quelle non udite sono ancora più dolci" ["Heard melodies are sweet, but those unheard [a]re sweeter" ("Ode on a Grecian Urn")] (D'Annunzio 1995b: 14–15). The aim of D'Annunzio's continual distillation of the word will thus be a trilogy of "*novels of flesh without flesh*,"[31] the only possible product of a form of art that must be revealed by "a kind of substance without substance, of divested matter, of naked abundance."[32] Similarly, the word written in the darkness loses its letters and its meaning not simply to become music but to be absorbed by the empty formalism of a "Musica muta" [mute music] – that is, "music without music in itself."[33] These images stress D'Annunzio's yearning to "esprimere l'inesprimibile" (1995a: 217), to express the inexpressible, that is, the attempt to deprive representation of its referential value, of "segni materiali" [material signs] (1995a: 128), to protect the poetic word from the risk of intellectual investment so as to avoid reducing its elusive presence to a manageable present.

This gesture cannot be separated from D'Annunzio's action on the level of literary form. Both the fragmentation of his writing and the emptying out of the poetic word try to enact an aesthetic experience as the errant, wasteful, non-acquisitive display of poetic language outside the instrumentality of speech, to thwart the assumed goal of transparency and immediacy of meaning, which he equates to a servile act. As D'Annunzio himself states in *Libro segreto*, "I do not consider the word as a means of exchange. I feel I can no longer use what Ugo Foscolo calls 'linguaggio itinerario'" (that is, mercantile language, a kind of commonplace, practical, communal language).[34] The need to snatch language from the grasp of accumulative power leads D'Annunzio toward a form of unaccountable expression, one that is nominated in its own impossibility: "The most arcane forms of communication of the soul with things cannot be grasped, as of today, but in pauses; which are the words of silence,"[35] namely, words that cannot circulate, that cannot be exchanged or transmitted.

Not accidentally, D'Annunzio invokes the worshipper of nothingness *par excellence*, Stéphane Mallarmé, by borrowing images of absence like the "Liocorno" (D'Annunzio 1995b: 33) (the unicorn, "la licorne" in Mallarmé's poems), the "aurora non nata" (1995b 30) (a dawn not born), or – the most peculiar and insistent one – the Amazon. We may remember that at the end of the sonnet "Mes bouquins refermés," Mallarmé opposes the real breast of his lover to the "sein brûlé d'une antique amazone" (1985: 82) – that is, not so much a visual object of desire as a purely verbal desirability, since this object is unattainable. Yet, precisely for its formal nature, this burnt breast, far from exhausting desire, stimulates an even more sensuous reverie, one that, significantly, is more attractive than the one aroused by its bodily equivalent. In *Libro segreto* D'Annunzio rehearses "up to the catastrophe the amazon's fate,"[36] associating the creatures'

mutilation with their being "in vain more desirable."[37] However, a crucial difference between the two writers highlights how D'Annunzio revises the context
created by the French poet precisely in favor of an auto-affective operation. As it
makes the mechanism of desire inseparable from sacrifice, Mallarmé's sonnet
also underscores how their common origin lies in violence. Precisely because the
"sein brûlé" is the opposite of an erotically desirable object, the Amazon
denounces the founding sacrificial gesture at the roots of masculine culture by
exerting against herself a kind of violence that is the negative counterpart of
masculine erotic desire (Gans 1981: 285–303). For his part, D'Annunzio rather
appropriates the Amazon's sacrifice as a device that generates sophisticated and
private pleasures. Significantly, from impersonation of the last Amazon's deadly
lot, the description shifts to the author's ultimate acquisition of that rare object
of desire. Severed from the woman's body and purified of all traces of cruelty,
the left breast has now become D'Annunzio's exclusive property – the reservoir
of precious aesthetic stimuli: "Now it is I who own this cup of perfection. It is I
who guard it in the casket of the jewelers Boehmer and Bassenge, in the golden
and enameled small wooden chest."[38]

This greed for appropriation through consumption triumphs in D'Annunzio's
fullest profession of decadent faith: in his representation of his own trespass as
the most rigorous adherence to an aesthetics and ethics of transience, hence as
the extreme act of giving. D'Annunzio announces his inevitable death, staged by
his body through a progressive dematerialization, "according to the ascetic
canon,"[39] to the point of absolute spiritualization: "So much soul is growing
inside my flesh that I seem to have almost no flesh left."[40] And, more importantly, he underscores the agonistic value of self-annihilation by asserting that no
other ascetic "could ever disembody himself" as he could.[41] On the one hand,
the reference to contemplation seems to deprive the dramatization of death of
all pathological content, and thus to decree the triumph of a kind of empty
formalism. On the other hand, however, the outcome of D'Annunzio's
encounter with death is precisely – evoking the title of another autobiographical
meditation – the splendor of sensuality made more precious by pain. As we read
in *Notturno*, his "thirst for life is similar to the need to die. … Death indeed is
present as life, inebriating, promising, transfiguring."[42] Death supplies
D'Annunzio with a surplus of *jouissance* allowing him to attain self-aggrandizement
through spoliation: "I do not have sovereignty over myself, nor can I measure my
moments, nor can I follow the continual dissipation of my substance. My life, in
turn, dissolves and re-seals itself … and suddenly I feel that within myself there
lives another one, greater than me."[43]

Indeed, the "Third place, on this side of life, and beyond death"[44] that
D'Annunzio looks for and ultimately identifies as the site of the ascetic is also the
place where "VOLONTÀ" (will) and "VOLUTTÀ" (voluptuousness) (1995b:
75) coexist, turning his will to death into a "miraculous transfusion of life."[45]
This supplementary spatial dimension – which, significantly, is also the title of a
work that D'Annunzio envisioned but never carried out – should be a liminal
space able to erase the distinction between, in Bataille's well-known terms, a

restricted and a general economy: respectively, an economy of production, accumulation, and circulation, and a non-utilitarian, sumptuous expenditure without reserve based upon the positive property of loss (Bataille 1967: 57–80). D'Annunzio here wants not only to break the circle of binary oppositions. He also reveals how the apparent contrast between restricted and general economy disguises the sameness of those two modes of exchange. Indeed, this "third place," which in D'Annunzio's mind is at once an aesthetic unity and a geographical domain, inaugurates an economy of negativity that D'Annunzio invokes as the radical "other" of *any* collective form of exchange. This hypothetical transaction is supposed to be alien to both the extended and the elitist economic circle, to both a material and a symbolic deal, and takes on the character of a free productivity contracting a debt with itself and returning the gift to itself.

This auto-affective breach of all forms of circular economy acquires further significance insofar as it seems to condense Derrida's observations about artistic genius in his discussion of the economic underpinnings of the Kantian sublime. For Derrida, the Kantian poet "is the voice of God who gives him voice, who gives himself and by giving gives to himself, gives himself what he gives ..., plays freely with himself, only breaks the finite circle or contractual exchange in order to strike an infinite accord with himself" (1981: 11). D'Annunzio's individual economy of pleasure as absence and of absence as pleasure owes a great deal to Kant's and Schopenhauer's notion of the sublime, and absorbs its paradoxical nature. To grasp the sacrificial strategy of D'Annunzio's aesthetics and ethics we should remember that Kant's sublime is of course a "negative pleasure" (Kant 1987: §23, 98) – that is, one produced by privation and as such resisting "the interest of the senses" (1987: §29, 127) – but also "an emotion" (1987: §23, 98), hence an empirical and interested condition. It is precisely the sacrificial nature of the sublime that links these two extremes. The "momentary inhibition" of the imagination (1987: §23, 98) that opposes Kant's experience of the sublime to the "charms" (1987: §23, 98) and to the feeling of life furthered by the beautiful in fact rewards the mind with a subsequent, stronger gush of vital forces. "*[I]n return for*" (1987: §29, 131; emphasis added) the immolation of its freedom, the imagination can partake of the "unfathomable depth" (1987: §29, 131) of the moral law to which it has succumbed. Hence, one can attain a "pure and unconditioned intellectual liking" (1987: §29, 131) only by constraining the imagination to a ruthless expropriation and renunciation of itself. Ultimately, however, the refund for such a loss is a surplus of "supersensible power" (1987: §29, 131) – "an expansion and a might that surpasses the one it sacrifices" (1987: §29, 129).[46]

Therefore, there is still a commerce underlying the Janus-like nature of the sublime experience, although, as Derrida also observes, it is an immaculate one (1981: 9). From the aesthetic side – the side of sensibility – such liking is negative, that is, "opposed to this interest" (Kant 1987: §29, 131). Yet, considered from the side of the intellect, it is "positive and connected with an interest" (1987: §29, 131). The *counter-interest* of the Kantian sublime, then, is a veritable counter-prestation at the roots of the sacrilege of productive imagination. The Kantian sacrificial economy of the faculties requires the destruction or consumption of the given, so as to obtain in return the counter-gift of the unpresentable, as Lyotard has shown. And the revenue yielded by the experience of spoliation is precisely a liking of a higher order, one that transcends those vulgar mental states in which the agitation produced by affects renders the mind unable to engage in free deliberation. As it touches the limit of representation, the sublime imagination feels its powerlessness, but such feeling still belongs to the order of representation and sensibility. The imagination presents itself as touching the limit; it renders sensible the vanishing of the sensible. Therefore, the emotion provided by the sublime sacrifice is not simply "*apatheia*" (Kant 1987: §29, 132) but, more subtly, the pathos of apathy – the joy of being offered.

Even more interestingly, in response to the many readings of D'Annunzio's nocturnal phase as a *via negativa* towards Schopenhauer's *noluntas*, we should remember that Schopenhauer's own itinerary of spiritual liberation from the *principium individuationis* reproduces the very collusion of spoliation and enrichment underlying the Kantian sublime. It is "a secret joy" (1958: §68, 396) that accompanies Schopenhauer's *askesis* through suffering "to the most disinterested love, and the most generous self-sacrifice for others" (1958: §68, 378). His denigration of pleasure as satisfaction of a need, hence as the mere cessation of pain, does not prevent his purely intellectual *via negativa* from providing a higher form of pleasure, one accessible only to an *élite* of spirits, to those few consumers with extremely refined taste. The loss is compensated by a greater gain: the "vastness of the world, which previously disturbed our peace of mind, now rests within us; our dependence on it is now annulled by its dependence on us" (1958: §39, 205).

In the light of what we have observed so far, D'Annunzio does not simply repudiate Schopenhauer's doctrine because of its pessimism and passivity. Rather, he endorses the aristocratic nature of his ascetic ideal, and, above all, the supplementary interest of sense and power produced by the sacrifice of oneself. In its shift from gift to sacrifice, the nocturnal phase of D'Annunzio's poetics underscores the contractual and calculating nature of sacrifice. As we know, in Mauss's essay the gift is far from a free and voluntary individual gesture. If the three famous obligations to give, receive and return that bind donor and recipient (Mauss 1967: 10–12) are enough to dissipate the ideal of spontaneous generosity, Mauss's opening remarks on the gift-giving ritual as a transaction in fact based upon "economic self-interest" (Mauss 1967: 1) may seem at first to confirm even more decisively the utilitarian nature of the phenomenon. In fact, however, the ambivalence of the Maussian gift, being at once a gesture of superior munificence and of poisonous aggressiveness, does not fully justify such a straightforward interpretation. Gift giving is triggered neither by the individual's material speculation nor by mere self-abnegation. In the collective network of conjunctions and disjunctions that the gift creates around the principle of loss, the ostentation of disinterestedness and the symbolic return of prestige ultimately overshadow the supposedly real material interest. In other words, although calculation may well be a component of gift exchange, it does not emerge as its essence. The agonistic nature of the gift is a challenge to generosity, an incitement to disinterestedness that emphasizes the non-contractual under-pinnings of any contractual human relation (Caillé 1995: 282). Sacrifice, by contrast, emerges as an explicitly interested operation: from a more openly utili-tarian standpoint, it is not possible to conceive of a sacrificial act devoid of contractual elements.[47]

D'Annunzio allows us to see very well that it is impossible not to conceive of a proportional relation between what one intentionally renounces and what one expects to receive in return. In his treatment of sacrifice as a contract, D'Annunzio seems to agree with Schopenhauer that the "affirmation of one's own will becomes the denial of another's" (Schopenhauer 1958: §62, 342). Yet, more importantly, he also knows that the mortification of one's own will "by refusing the agreeable and looking for the disagreeable," and the "voluntarily chosen life of penance and self-chastisement" (1958: §68, 392) are not simply finalized to the *summum bonum*, to the absolutely disinterested love for others. Above all, they grant the aura of the *arbiter elegantiarum* – of an aesthetic and ethical legislator who, like Schopenhauer's saint, detains the law of "the highest joy and delight" (1958: §68, 398).[48] No less than Oscar Wilde in *De Profundis*, D'Annunzio thus conceives of a "real Symphony of Sorrow" (Wilde 1990: 55) able to kindle, rather than vanquish, that tragic sense of suffering celebrated by Nietzsche in the Dionysian ritual. Not accidentally, the apotheosis of the dismembered god in *The Birth of Tragedy* (1956) reverberates not only in the refer-ences to the mythological episode of Pan and Marsyas (D'Annunzio 1995a: 45), but also in the many passages where D'Annunzio identifies with the agonizing Christ, as in the first section of *Libro segreto*, titled "Via Crucis." Its usual defini-tion of "negative hagiography" is often taken to substantiate D'Annunzio's vocation for suicide as renunciation. Yet, in fact, D'Annunzio can be said to combine the Nietzschean Dionysus with the Crucified in order to exorcise the "necessity of expiation," typical of "servile men,"[49] through a heroic conception of sacrifice.

Here we are already beyond the victimization of the *Miles patiens*, the topos of the Italian soldier who witnesses a sacrifice, which, as Paolo Valesio has observed (1992: 18–19), D'Annunzio develops to subvert the optimism of the fascist regime. Rather, with a supreme auto-affective gesture, the artist now wants to produce and to consume the powerful emotional impact of the spectacle of extinction, by embodying simultaneously "the cadaver and he who contemplates it."[50] D'Annunzio's constant aristocratic greed for a dimension beyond utility, which makes him extol play for the feeling of boundlessness that is the true nobility and the true beauty of his life, finds in death the most excessive, destruc-tive of events. We could add: the most *sovereign* event, in Bataille's sense. Indeed, in D'Annunzio's need for annihilation as an intoxicating experience of "joy … mixed with suffering"[51] we can see intimations of Bataille's ecstatic sovereign expenditure, the exposure of the individual to nothingness, to an incommensu-rable "outside," through the unchaining of passion. However, unlike Bataille, D'Annunzio does not want to loose the knot tying passion as passivity and nihilism from active passion, *dynamis*, potency. The pathos of the suffering artist who, as a Christ-like figure, writes with blood, and is marked by stigmata, is inseparable from the power of the noble, heroic individual. Until the last stage of D'Annunzio's writings, then, the aesthetic experience as expenditure remains founded upon the very paradox of subjectivity inscribed in Western metaphysics. As Giorgio Agamben observes, the subject "thinks of nothing other than its own pure receptivity as original self-affection and, in this way, *gives* itself to itself, suffers itself, undergoes *passion*, and thus and only thus, opens out to the world" (Agamben 1986: 15–16). Significantly, this is the very essence of the Nietzschean will to power: pure passion affecting itself, a passionate self-referentiality endlessly brought back by the vicious circle of the eternal return, which D'Annunzio synthesizes enthusiastically as follows: "Every great artist is intoxicated with himself."[52]

Returns: closing the circle

This return, be it eternal or immediate – or, better, paradoxically eternal and immediate – is represented by D'Annunzio as a homecoming. He restores the household as the privileged locus for sacred transactions, which he reduces to the instantaneous circularity of his immaculate commerce of passionate expenditure and distinction. This imaginary household recalls D'Annunzio's mansion "Il Vittoriale," where an inscription at the entrance, accompanied by the symbol of the cornucopia, announces "Io ho quel che ho donato" (I have that which I have given). But, above all, the household is a mystical domestic space now incarnated in the very image of the artist. D'Annunzio resurrects the autarkic and ennobling practice of sumptuousness by reinventing himself as an archaic, enchanted *oikos* where art can emerge in all its redemptive power: "I made my whole self my home; and I love each of its parts. If I interrogate it in my own language, it answers me in my own language."[53] And this private language aims to transcend narrowly utilitarian and alienating human ends by returning to the magical, fetishized sources of culture, by innovating art not so much through "sottigliezza" [subtlety] as through "non so quale potente rudezza ingenua" [I do not know what powerful, innocent roughness] (1995a: 129). D'Annunzio appeals to our ancestral, ceremonial inheritance, convinced that, if we abandon the polished gods of Phidias and Praxiteles to go back to primitive Greek wooden idols, we do not move away but rather get closer to divinity (1995a: 129).

What, we may ask to conclude, are the implications of this spiritual and artistic testament? If the space of gift exchange destabilizes the restricted order of equivalences but still entails reciprocity, debts and counter-gifts, then D'Annunzio attempts to perform, in the domain of art, what Emmanuel Lévinas, referring to his own conception of poetic activity, has defined as a "départ sans retour" (1967: 189–92) – a voyage away from exchange, circulation, speculation, a radical movement from the self towards alterity that never returns to the same, and that exceeds symmetries and structures of subordination. At the end of the Levinasian journey, it will be the unintentional but inevitable encounter with the Other that will reveal the possibility – or, better, the inevitability – of giving, of a gratuitous ethics that empties out the subject in the discovery of duty without debt. By transforming the prestigious force of expenditure from an archaic sacred hearth to an aesthetic and ethical principle, D'Annunzio sets out on a parallel voyage, one towards pleasure without debt, which *does* conclude with a "return," at once "comeback," "revenue," and "*revenant.*" It is the comeback of the irreplaceable singularity of the subject, exhibited as intentional self-possession. It is the revenue of self-givenness as a form of restitution, of ecstatic reappropriation, with the plus-value of magnificence. It is the *revenant* of sacrifice, with its calculating logic and its contractual structure, as the threat haunting the pure gift.

The ultimate question that D'Annunzio leaves us with, then, is not simply "Is the gift possible at all?" but, rather, "Is the gift possible at all *without sacrifice*?" He thus opens up the paramount ethical issue of what form of communication and community we can conceive – be it an unavowable, inoperative, or coming community,[54] but one certainly coming after the subject, after the death of the author and the dissolution of the work of art – beyond an economy of negativity.

Notes

1 "Epifania" already appears in *Il fuoco.* For fascinating details about D'Annunzio's pervasive influence on Joyce, see Ellmann 1982: 82–8; Lobner 1989.

2 "*Le Feu* que j'ai lu il y a quelque trois ans est une merveille de lyrisme. C'est fou et fatiguant. … D'Annunzio, à mon sens, est l'écrivain qui a le mieux su communiquer aux âmes le frisson de la volupté" (Hibbert 1923: 100). I am grateful to Professor Jean Jonassaint for signaling this reference to me.

3 This interest is further substantiated by Woodhouse's (1998) and Andreoli's (2000) recent biographies.

4 In the panorama of the European *fin de siècle*, indeed, connections emerge between the purposelessness underlying the decadent cult of "art for art's sake" and the anthropologists' attention to the disinterestedness and the ritual dissipation typical of archaic or "primitive" cultures. For a study of the relationships between late nineteenth-century anti-realist aesthetics and the anthropological discourse of the same period see Pireddu 2002.

5 This bi-directional correspondence between the gift and aesthetic activity, at which Marcel Mauss already hints in various parts of his *Essai sur le don*, emerges with more evidence from Georges Bataille's assimilation of art and poetic language to forms of expression beyond the usefulness of words, and hence as instances of general economy. This relationship has received renewed attention in the works of Lewis Hyde (1983), Jacques Derrida (1991), Vincent Pecora (1997) and Jacques T. Godbout (1998), among others. For a critical summary of these treatments, see Mark Osteen's introduction to the present volume.

6 "darsi, liberamente e per riconoscenza" (D'Annunzio 1990: 138). All English translations of D'Annunzio's works are mine. With the aim of remaining as close as possible to D'Annunzio's original words and syntax, I will try to adhere to a very literal rendering of the quoted passages. In the specific case of *Il piacere*, I chose not to adopt the translation by Georgina Harding, *The Child of Pleasure* (Langford Lodge: Dedalus, 1991), which is incomplete and often inaccurate.

7 "il divino pregio del *dono*" (D'Annunzio 1990: 141).

8 "indipendente da ogni legame e da ogni dominio; non appartiene più all'artefice, ma è di tutti e di nessuno" (D'Annunzio 1990: 142).

9   Throughout D'Annunzio's novel, the role attributed to art and the artist substantiates the interpretation of the gift as "property that perishes" given by Lewis Hyde (1983: 8).

10 "ogni benefizio che non sia di amore" (D'Annunzio 1990: 57).

11 "il lettore vero non è chi mi compra ma chi mi ama" (D'Annunzio 1990: 57). For an exhaustive analysis of gift exchange in *Il piacere*, of which I can only synthesize a few points here, see Pireddu 1997, 2002.

12 "ornare con qualche segno di arte popolesca la più umile abitazione è un atto pio, e che v'è un sentimento religioso del mistero umano e della natura profonda nel più semplice segno che di generazione in generazione si trasmette inciso o dipinto" (D'Annunzio 1978: LXIII, 252).

13 "Se ogni rinascita d'una gente nobile è uno sforzo lirico, se ogni sentimento unanime e creatore è una potenza lirica, se ogni ordine nuovo è un ordine lirico nel senso vigoroso e impetuoso della parola, la Musica considerata come linguaggio rituale è l'esaltatrice dell'atto di vita, dell'opera di vita" (D'Annunzio 1978: LXIV, 253).

14 See, for instance, Tosi 1973; Michelini 1978; Piga 1979; Schnapp 1986.

15 "un esemplare di una superiore umanità, manifestante in ogni suo atto la sua essenza diversa, il sentimento della sua assoluta separazione dalla moltitudine, dai comuni doveri, dalle comuni virtù" (D'Annunzio 1991a: 157).

16 "liberalità non paragonabile se non all'antica che per piccoli servigi amava ricompensar grandemente" (D'Annunzio 1991a: 157).

17 See D'Annunzio's articles "Il Caso Wagner" and "La bestia elettiva," in *Il caso Wagner* (1996). For an English translation of "La bestia elettiva," see "The beast who wills" (1986).

18 "un dono magnifico largito dai pochi ai molti, dai liberi agli schiavi: da coloro che pensano e sentono a coloro che debbono lavorare" (D'Annunzio 1991a: 31).

19 "si héroïquement patient" (D'Annunzio 1988: 84).

20 "la terrible condamnation et damnation du génie … C'est l'éternel malentendu" (D'Annunzio 1988: 84).

21 "angoscia di non avere abbastanza donato" (D'Annunzio 1995a: 96).

22 "non ha gioia se non nel donarsi grandemente" (D'Annunzio 1991b: 195).

23 "La passione vera non conosce l'utilità, non conosce alcuna specie di benefizio, alcuna specie di vantaggio. vive, come l'arte, per sé sola. l'arte per l'arte, la prodezza per la prodezza, il coraggio per il coraggio, l'amore per l'amore, l'ebrezza per l'ebrezza, il piacere per il piacere" (D'Annunzio 1995a: 228).

24 "il dono di sé, la dedizione dell'essere intiero" (D'Annunzio 1995a: 229). For a discussion of the notion of art for art's sake as destruction of art by art itself with the aim of annihilating its own use value and intelligibility, see Agamben 1986: 47–55.

25 "un'arte della parola […] creata su l'abolizione totale della consuetudine letteraria" (D'Annunzio 1995a: 128).

26 For the notion of hetero-affection and auto-affection in relation to the act of giving and to aesthetic activity as an instance of giving, see Derrida 1981.

27 "Io vivo, a me sempre piacque di vivere, su l'orlo del rischio e su l'orlo del segreto. Su l'uno e su l'altro è intieramente abolito il comun senso del tempo. Su l'uno e l'altro come sul vertice, non vige se non quella specie di tempo che è la fluidità stessa della vita interiore" (D'Annunzio 1995b: 55).

28 "Non dico a nessuno quel che attendo; a nessuno dico quel che patisco; Celo la mia vita vera e celo la mia arte vera, per l'eroismo supremo e per il libro supremo. E sono sicuro che toccherò l'una e l'altra cima […]. E al più alto e al più straordinario evento, di là della storia e di là di ogni altro limite noto, io mi sento pari" (D'Annunzio 1995b: 93).

29 "E tutto è chiuso in me, ben profondo, segreto" (D'Annunzio 1995b: 28); "E mia, mia solamente, di me solo era anche la parola del mistico" (D'Annunzio 1995b: 57).

30 "il libro che non ho scritto" (D'Annunzio 1995b: 12).

31 *"romanzi di carne senza carne"* (D'Annunzio 1995b: 292).

32 "una specie di sostanza senza sostanza, di materia spogliata, di dovizia ignuda" (D'Annunzio 1995b: 291).

33 "musica senza avere in sé musica" (D'Annunzio 1995b: 74). And again: "amore senza figura. malinconia senza figura" (1995a: 69), "bellezza senza figura" (1995b: 85), "parole non intese, non interpretate, non raccolte" (1995b: 96), "forme senza nome" (1995b: 184).

34 "Non considero la parola come mezzo di scambio. Mi sembra di non poter più adoperare quel che Ugo Foscolo chiama 'linguaggio itinerario'" (D'Annunzio 1995a: 217).

35 "Le più arcane comunicanze dell'anima con le cose non possono essere colte, fino a oggi, se non nelle pause; che sono le parole del silenzio" (D'Annunzio 1995a: 128). The dichotomy that D'Annunzio establishes between the instrumentality of "linguaggio itinerario" and the distilled immateriality of the poetic word recalls, indeed, the separation fancied by Stéphane Mallarmé between the two states of the word, "brut ou immédiat" and "essentiel" (Mallarmé 1985: 278).

36 "sino alla catastrofe il fato amazonio" (D'Annunzio 1995a: 87).

37 "invano più desiderabili" (D'Annunzio 1995a: 85).

38 "Ora io la posseggo, questa coppa della perfezione. io la custodisco nello scrigno dei gioiellieri Boehmer e Bassenge, nel forzieretto di sorbo a lamine d'oro e a smalti" (D'Annunzio 1995a: 89).

39 "secondo il canone ascetico" (D'Annunzio 1995a: 156).

40 "Tanta anima mi cresce nella carne, che mi sembra di non avere quasi più carne" (D'Annunzio 1995b: 119).

41 "seppe scarnirsi mai come scarnire io mi seppi" (D'Annunzio 1995a: 246).

42 "sete di vivere è simile al bisogno di morire. … La morte è infatti presente come la vita, inebriante, promettitrice, trasfiguratrice" (D'Annunzio 1991b: 155).

43 "Non ho signoria di me, né so misurare i miei attimi, né seguire la dissipazione continua della mia sostanza. a vicenda la mia vita si dissolve e si riserra (…) e sento improvviso che dentro me vive un altro più grande di me" (D'Annunzio 1995a: 125).

44 "'Terzo luogo', di qua dalla vita, di là dalla morte" (D'Annunzio 1995a: 63).

45 "una miracolosa trasfusione di vita" (D'Annunzio 1995b: 220).

46 For the economic implications of the Kantian sublime, see Lyotard 1990.

47 In addition to the discussion on sacrifice as a calculating act emerging from Mauss's and Hubert's *Essai sur la nature et fonction du sacrifice* (1968), I am endorsing the standpoint of Roger Caillois in *L'Homme et le sacré* (1950) about the intentional and self-interested generosity of the sacrificial act. Any form of renunciation and asceticism is for Caillois a strategy of restriction imposed upon oneself as an anticipation of a more lavish return.

48 As early as in *Il piacere*, privation and contemplation disguise and transform voluptuousness. Andrea Sperelli interprets contemplation as that state in which the death of desire coincides with a "mai provato godimento" [a never experienced enjoyment] (D'Annunzio 1990: 131), that is, not so much with absence of pleasure, but with a formal pleasure, a pleasure emptied of pleasure. Similarly, it is this coincidence of pleasure and renunciation, of ego-loss and self-aggrandizement, that D'Annunzio later extols in *La beata riva* (2000), a treatise written by his friend Angelo Conti on Schopenhauer's aesthetics where D'Annunzio appears as a character.

49 "necessità dell'espiazione"; "uomini servili" (D'Annunzio 1995a: 98). It is significant that among his projects for future works D'Annunzio includes a life of Jesus rendered as the greatest of voluntary victims. See LaValva 1991: 235.

50 "il cadavere e colui che lo contempla" (D'Annunzio 1991b: 63).

51 "gioia … mista a patimento" (D'Annunzio 1991b: 98).

52 "è ogni grande artista 'ebro di sé'" (D'Annunzio 1995b: 292).

53 "Ho fatto di tutto me la mia casa; e l'amo in ogni parte. Se nel mio linguaggio la interrogo, ella mi risponde nel mio linguaggio" (D'Annunzio 1995a: 125). For an

extensive treatment of the household as a domestic and symbolic redemptive space, see Pecora 1997.

54 I am here referring to three contemporary works exploring the concept of community in the light of the aesthetic and ethical issues raised by disinterestedness, lack of normativity, and expenditure: Blanchot's *The Unavowable Community* (1988), Nancy's *The Inoperative Community* (1991), and Agamben's *The Coming Community* (1993b). D'Annunzio's meditation on the possibility of a community founded upon the practice of giving and the principle of unconditional loss already points at the central questions in those philosophical inquiries.

References

Agamben, Giorgio. "The eternal return and the paradox of passion." *Stanford Italian Review* 6.1–2 (1986): 9–17.

—— *Stanzas*. Trans. Ronald L. Martinez. Minneapolis and London: University of Minnesota Press, 1993a.

—— *The Coming Community*. Trans. Michael Hardt. Minneapolis and London: University of Minnesota Press, 1993b.

Andreoli, Annamaria. *Il vivere inimitabile: vita di Gabriele D'Annunzio*. Milano: Mondadori, 2000.

Bataille, Georges. *La part maudite. Précédé de la notion de dépense*. Paris: Minuit, 1967.

Blanchot, Maurice. *The Unavowable Community*. Trans. Pierre Joris. Barrytown: Station Hill Press, 1988.

Caillé, Alain. "Sacrifice, don et utilitarisme." *A quoi bon (se) sacrifier? Sacrifice, don et intérêt. La Revue du M.A.U.S.S.* 5 (1995): 248–92.

Caillois, Roger. *L'homme et le sacré*. Paris: Gallimard, 1950.

Conti, Angelo. *La beata riva. Trattato dell'oblio*. Venezia: Marsilio, 2000.

D'Annunzio, Gabriele. *Carta del Carnaro. D'Annunzio Politico. 1918–1938*. Ed. Renzo De Felice. Bari: Laterza, 1978, pp. 227–54.

—— "The beast who wills." Trans. Jeffrey Schnapp. *Stanford Italian Review* 6 (1986): 265–77.

—— *Lettere a Jouvence*. Milano: Rosellina Archinto, 1988.

—— *Il piacere*. Milano: Mondadori, 1990.

—— *Le vergini delle rocce*. Milano: Mondadori, 1991a.

—— *Notturno*. Milano: Mondadori, 1991b.

—— *Cento e cento e cento e cento pagine del libro segreto di Gabriele D'Annunzio tentato di morire*. Milano: Mondadori, 1995a.

—— *Le faville del maglio*. Milano: Mondadori, 1995b.

—— "Il caso Wagner" and "La bestia elettiva." *Il caso Wagner*. Ed. Paola Sorge. Roma: Laterza, 1996.

Derrida, Jacques. "Economimesis." Trans. Richard Klein. *Diacritics* 11 (1981): 3–25.

—— *Donner le temps*. Paris: Galilée, 1991.

Durkheim, Émile. *Les formes élémentaires de la vie religieuse: le système totemique en Australie*. Paris: Librairie Générale Française, 1991.

Ellmann, Richard. *James Joyce*. New York and London: Oxford University Press, 1982.

Gans, Eric. "La femme en X: Mallarmé anthropologue." *Romanic Review* 72 (1981): 285–303.

Godbout, Jacques T. with Alain Caillé. *The World of the Gift*. Trans. Donald Winkler. Montreal: McGill-Queen's University Press, 1998.

Hibbert, Fernand. *Le Manuscrit de mon ami*. Port-au-Prince: Imprimerie Cheraquit, 1923.

Hyde, Lewis. *The Gift: Imagination and the Erotic Life of Property*. New York: Vintage, 1983.

James, Henry. "Gabriele D'Annunzio." *Quarterly Review* 199.398 (April 1904): 383–419.

Kant, Immanuel. *Critique of Judgment*. Trans. Werner S. Pluhar. Indianapolis: Hackett, 1987.

LaValva, RosaMaria. *I sacrifici umani. D'Annunzio antropologo e rituale*. Napoli: Liguori, 1991.

Lévinas, Emmanuel. *En découvrant l'existence avec Husserl et Heidegger*. Paris: Librairie Philosophique J. Vrin, 1967.

Lobner, Corinna. *James Joyce's Italian Connection: The Poetics of the Word*. Iowa City: University of Iowa Press, 1989.

Lyotard, Jean-François. *Leçons sur l'analytique du sublime*. Paris: Galilée, 1990.

Mallarmé, Stéphane. *Œuvres*. Paris: Garnier, 1985.

Mauss, Marcel. *The Gift: Forms and Functions of Exchange in Archaic Societies*. Trans. Ian Cunnison. New York: Norton, 1967.

Mauss, Marcel and Henri Hubert. *Essai sur la nature et fonction du sacrifice. Œuvres de Marcel Mauss*. Volume I. Paris: Minuit, 1968, pp. 193–324.

Michelini, Gaia. *Nietzsche nell'Italia di D'Annunzio*. Palermo: Flaccovio, 1978.

Nancy, Jean-Luc. *The Inoperative Community*. Trans. Peter Connor, Lisa Garbus, Michael Holland and Simona Sawhney. Minneapolis and London: University of Minnesota Press, 1991.

Nietzsche, Friedrich. *The Birth of Tragedy and the Genealogy of Morals*. Trans. Francis Golffing. New York: Doubleday, 1956.

—— *The Will to Power*. Trans. Walter Kaufmann and R.J. Hollingdale. New York: Random House, 1968.

—— *Twilight of the Idols/The Anti-Christ*. Trans. R.J. Hollingdale. Harmondsworth: Penguin, 1990.

Pecora, Vincent. *Households of the Soul*. Baltimore: Johns Hopkins University Press, 1997.

Piga, Francesco. *Il mito del superuomo in Nietzsche e D'Annunzio*. Firenze: Nuovedizioni Vallecchi, 1979.

Pireddu, Nicoletta. " 'Il divino pregio del dono': Andrea Sperelli's economy of pleasures." *Annali d'italianistica* 15 (1997): 175–201.

—— *Antropologi alla corte della bellezza. Decadenza ed economia simbolica nell'Europa fin de siècle*. Verona: Edizioni Fiorini, 2002.

Schnapp, Jeffrey. "Nietzsche Italian style: Gabriele D'Annunzio." *Stanford Italian Review* 6 (1986): 247–63.

Schopenhauer, Arthur. *The World as Will and Representation*. Trans. E.F.J. Payne. Clinton, MA: Falcon's Wing, 1958.

Tosi, Guy, "D'Annunzio découvre Nietzsche." *Italianistica* 2.3 (1973): 481–513.

Valesio, Paolo. *Gabriele D'Annunzio: The Dark Flame*. New Haven and London: Yale University Press, 1992.

Wilde, Oscar. *De Profundis. The Soul of Man and Prison Writings*. Ed. and Introduction by Isobel Murray. Oxford and New York: Oxford University Press, 1990.

Woodhouse, John. *Gabriele D'Annunzio Defiant Archangel*. Oxford and New York: Oxford University Press, 1998.

9 Conrad's guilt-edged securities

"Karain: a memory" via Simmel and Benjamin

Anthony Fothergill

"*Was Du für ein Geschenk hältst, ist ein Problem das Du lösen sollst.*" With this cryptic remark, which comes without a fuller context, Wittgenstein opens up a range of problems (1998: 49). In (my) translation they multiply: "What you take for a gift is a problem you must solve," perhaps implying, "What you take to be a gift is a problem *for you* to solve," or "What you take to be a gift is (really) a problem – which you must solve." Is the "you" the person giving or receiving, and does it matter? And why is it a problem for (only?) "you" to solve? Are gifts only such insofar as they are so regarded? If I give something to someone, under what conditions do I take it to be a gift? Can I give someone a false gift? Or give someone a gift without knowing it? If nothing else, what's clear about Wittgenstein's remark is that we should look gift horses in the mouth. By examining a literary moment of similarly problematic gift giving and reading it within a framework offered by two, more philosophical, accounts of material and symbolic circulation and exchange, I hope to extend notions of gift giving into the space of aesthetic performance.

The moment of high modernity produced its own finest critical voices – not just after the event, and not just in later academic, theoretical writing. A triad of near-contemporaries, Joseph Conrad (1857–1924), Georg Simmel (1858–1918) and the somewhat younger Walter Benjamin (1892–1940), were first-hand witnesses to and profound critical commentators on that cultural-historical moment of radical innovation, destruction and transformation we call modernity. They were simultaneously the hypersensitive cultural seismographs and shapers of the fundamental cultural changes they lived through: that accelerating process of technological, economic and social revolution, which in Europe and America culminated in the international commodity capitalism of the late nineteenth and the early twentieth century.

My purpose in bringing Conrad, Simmel and Benjamin together in conversation – a writer of modernist fiction and two thoroughly idiosyncratic and individual thinkers whose writings bridge the categories of philosophy, sociology and cultural commentary – is threefold. First, I wish to bring together from across a putative disciplinary divide works that differently engage with historicized moments of gift giving. Second, in doing so I want to argue that literary works can "theorize" or offer theorizable instances of cultural/economic exchange that are as particular and sophisticated as ostensibly more abstract theoretical works. I do not intend to line up thematic coincidences revealed between them, nor to "apply" a theoretical text to a literary one, subordinately treating the latter as exemplar of the arguments and structures of the former. Rather, I would see each as shedding light on the other in a significant mutuality. Third, I want to suggest that all three writers challenge conventional notions of the gift, obliging us to investigate perhaps unexamined assumptions about the conditions of gifting.

In different ways, Georg Simmel and Walter Benjamin have offered us theoretical paradigms for understanding modernity in relation to capitalist commodity transfer. However, they have not done so in any narrow theoretical economic sense, but rather in ways that have completely transformed our social and cultural understanding of the Modern. While often taking as their starting points aspects of everyday cultural life, Simmel and Benjamin adopted as their fields of inquiry the socio-psychological implications of new technologies and new economic formations. Their work thus offers a broad diagnosis and critique of cultural practices under the conditions of high and late capitalism, and their accounts of the crisis of modernity have proven seminal in redefining the ways in which we now think about the Modern. Such works as Simmel's *Philosophie des Geldes* (1900), and his excursions into the sociology of the Modern, particularly "The metropolis and mental life" (1971), "On thankfulness and gratitude" (1984), and "On the sociology of space" (1964), are works that are only now beginning to be recognized as foundations of modern cultural theory. Benjamin, who attended Simmel's university lectures in Berlin before World War I, acknowledges his debt to Simmel in such essays as "On some motifs in Baudelaire" and "Leskov: the storyteller" (Benjamin 1973), both of which shed light on the complex economic and cultural relationships represented in art works of "high modernism."

This latter term, of course, is a label that has been the subject of endless debate and contested definition, which I cannot rehearse here. For my present purposes I will briefly make two observations. Though modernism is a historical category of artistic development, roughly corresponding to cultural movements from the 1880s to the 1930s, it does not denote a simple or direct artistic reflection of the broader socio-economic category, modernity. Indeed, and this is my second point, the aesthetic self-preoccupation of much modernist culture has tended to assert an autonomous existence separate from the broader economic and social life. It often stands in self-proclaimed isolation from and in hostile relation to tendencies in the broader culture we would identify with modernity. But this self-proclaimed autonomy is too often taken (for good or ill) at face value by supporters and critics alike. Too often it is assumed that such modernist works keep an aesthetic distance from the everyday, bearing no relation to the economics of lived, working reality. I would argue to the contrary. Taking Conrad's story, "Karain: a memory" (1898),[1] as my specific example, I shall demonstrate in this essay that Simmel's and Benjamin's theories make visible the economic drama rendered in literary works of modernity, a drama that remains invisible to classical economic theory. Seeing the economic drama in a specific moment of gift giving, enacted in and by the story, enables us more fully to understand the complexities, both cultural and social, of the drama of the gift.

Underpinning their critique of modernity are Simmel's and Benjamin's notions of an alteration in sensibility that accompanies technological and economic transformation. Particularly in their construing of "experience" in pre-capitalist and late capitalist societies, Simmel and Benjamin seek to describe the cultures and psychologies of exchange at a moment of radical transition into modernity. Their psychologizing of the socio-economic – that is, the attempt to register in the psychological details of individual phenomena the fullness of their social reality – was not particularly fashionable at the times of their writing. Both thinkers were institutionally marginalized and only now, posthumously, enjoy a centrality as cultural critics that they were denied in their own lifetimes. Joseph Conrad, himself an outsider – a Polish emigré to Britain who turned down a literary knighthood there – would have somberly appreciated this irony and the value and advantages of that exclusion. Both Simmel and Benjamin challenge the boundaries of accepted areas of academic debate, moving outside and, theoretically, beyond the more tightly defined orthodoxies of established disciplines. Benjamin was intrigued that Simmel wrote on the sociology of the Alps, on fashion, on flirtation, and on the experience of the everyday in the city. Both writers defied a classical Marxist analysis of economics and the then-seedling forms of positivist sociology.[2] Their very marginality and their embrace of the unsystematic, the fragmentary and the impressionistic led them to non-mainstream sociological fields for their critiques of the Modern. For Simmel, it might be the psychology of jewelry, or the socio-psychology of the secret; for Benjamin, the social resonances of old photographs and keepsakes, or the cultural politics of strolling (see Simmel 1993; Benjamin 1979). These excursions into the marginal and the "trivial" teach us to attend to the everyday accidental that literature – in particular, the short stories and novels of Conrad – can bring to life. Indeed, when we come to read the textures of Conrad's work, we should pay attention not so much to the abstract grand theme, but, as he urged, to "the secondary notions," seeming incidentals where the real meaning of the story lies obscured from casual view (1986: 157–8).

Simmel and Benjamin structure their economic theories diachronically, on the notion of change from a pre-capitalistic to a capitalistic polity. Simmel describes the development from a traditional subsistence economy (using gift exchange and bartering) to a proto- and then an established money economy, which evolved into later capitalistic forms. Among other things, this development involves a change in money use, from a society where money circulates as a sign functioning in its substantial form, directly representing its actual material value – say, its weight in gold or salt – to one where the money sign takes on an increasingly symbolic function (as, for example, with paper money). Paradoxically, though, this shift to the more symbolic, abstract function of money as the medium of exchange between persons has the effect of reducing the non-economic interpersonal aspects of object exchange that pertained in

simpler societies where gift exchange and barter prevailed. In these latter societies, the social relations between individuals and groups – those
non-quantifiable aspects of exchange such as mutual dependency, long-term
trust, gratitude, etc. – become crucial factors of social bonding. For Simmel,
these symbolically expressed subjective social relations are by no means of
secondary importance to material, objective ones in questions of material
exchange. As Simmel puts it, "ultimately it is not the objects [of gift or
exchange] but rather the people who carry on the processes [by which objects
stand in relation to one another]; and the relations between objects are really
relations between people" (1990: 176). These relations between people become
increasingly anonymous and objectified under the conditions of the market, and
money use enacts and symbolizes that distancing.

Although Benjamin does not address in direct theoretical terms questions of
material economic circulation, I would suggest that he engages with an analogous
argument concerning the "economy" of narrative circulation and exchange. In
his essay "The storyteller," based notionally on the Russian short-story writer
Leskov, Benjamin places the activity of storytelling within a broad social historical
context, and theorizes a shift from orally-based narrative transmission in "traditional communities" to increasingly anonymous forms of communication under
the conditions of modernity and consumer capitalism. Resembling Simmel's
socio-psychological account of monetary exchange in its increasing historical
disenchantment, Benjamin's historical story about storytelling sees it as originating in the transmission of narrated experience – that is, wisdom – within closed
communities from teller to avid listeners who, in their turn, can become tellers of
the story to future listeners. "Experience which is passed from mouth to mouth is
the source from which all storytellers have drawn" and crucial to the process is the
faculty of memory: "It has seldom been realized that the listener's naive relationship to the storyteller is controlled by his interest in retaining what he is told … to
assure himself of the possibility of reproducing the story" (Benjamin 1973: 84,
97). But economic and social change – the breakdown of smaller rural, maritime
or artisanal urban "knowable communities" (see Williams 1973) and the rise of
mass-urban, now even global, communities – led to the decline of this oral form of
cultural transmission. The transmission of knowledge (and wisdom) through
storytelling and communal memory, which "passes a happening on from generation to generation" (Benjamin 1973: 98), cedes its cultural centrality to
modern-day globalized information sending (for Benjamin, newspapers; for us,
electronic media).

Simmel's and Benjamin's diachronic accounts show that, just as forms of
material circulation and exchange, so forms of symbolic cultural exchange are
determined by but also radically affect historically (and geographically) different
kinds of social relation. The beginnings of modernity therefore signal a fundamental modification in forms of and ideas about *experience* and *memory* – at both
the individual and community level. To simplify their argument somewhat, for
the individual in mass society events in one's life (*Ereignisse*) may be emotionally
absorbed as particular episodes or experiences (*Erlebnisse*) but modern conditions

militate against their being inwardly assimilated, combined and modified into a body of personal experience (*Erfahrungen*) which, traditionally, could be passed down to others through stories. Referring to the mass of information and knowledge we receive through newspapers, for example, Benjamin comments that "man has become increasingly unable to assimilate the data of the world around him by way of experience. … [T]he replacement of the older form of narration by information, of information by sensation, reflects the increasing atrophy of experience (*Erfahrung*)" (1973: 160–1). These notions correlate to different modes of memory. Experiential memory (*Erinnerung*) is the vital form of remembering, the inward recalling, through which experience and self-understanding can be achieved. This is to be distinguished from other faculties of memory (*Gedächtnis*), which, as "file-recording recollections," are more calculable. There is a further socio-economic homology, frequently evoked among sociologists and cultural critics, in the concepts of *Gemeinschaft* and *Gesellschaft* ("community" and "society"), often seen as analogous models for this historical-cultural shift and the ensuing experiential changes Benjamin describes.[3] The kinds of continuity that memory and story telling used to vouchsafe at both a personal and communal level are what the radical tendencies of modernity now undermine.

For Simmel and Benjamin, the importance of acts of exchange (of gifts, of stories) lies as much in their very *performance* as in their material value or contents. Like gift giving, storytelling in a "traditional" social community was the gifting of experience – the passing on, through narration, of memory and experience – without expectation of a direct return. Narration may thus be thought of as symbolic gift exchange.

To summarize thus far: Simmel and Benjamin share a historical model of economic and social development that is registered in terms of changing psychological and inter-personal relations. Their interest in marginal fields – fashion, style, literature, cultural ephemera – leads them to find precisely in "superstructural" forms material for their broad cultural critique. We may, in a sense, put Simmel and Benjamin back to back. For Simmel, questions of economic value are aligned (though not identified) with discussions of aesthetic value and effects on and of sensibility. For Benjamin, the aesthetic exchange that occurs in storytelling, the gifting of a narrative to a community of listeners or readers, always has a social and economic context. I hope to show that these socio-economic theories shed particular light on Conrad's tale. Caution is necessary in making alignments or perceiving homologies between such theories and psychological, cultural and socio-economic formations; we need to attend very carefully to the way they are articulated by cultural historians such as Simmel and Benjamin. But they themselves, to arrive at their subtle and broad-ranging critiques, drew on and followed in the path of their literary contemporaries and forerunners such as Conrad, to whose work I now turn.

To my knowledge, neither Simmel nor Benjamin was familiar with Conrad's work, though they could have been, as his writings had been appearing in Germany since 1897 and in translation since 1908. But my purpose in placing them together is not to urge a case for influence in either direction, which might anyway tend to be reductive at the expense of one of the parties. Rather, it is to argue that as witnesses to the globalization of modernity they all share a constellation of cultural perspectives and insights that defines their specific historical moment. Literature, above all, has articulated the tensions that Simmel and Benjamin diagnose. In turning to Conrad's short story, "Karain: a memory," I will concentrate on a crucial and particular moment of gift giving in the narrative, around which notions of community and memory revolve. An analysis of it will show, I hope, that cultural theory and literary imagination can inform one another. I draw from Benjamin the notion of the particular interdependency of experience, memory and narration. From Simmel, I draw on the account of historical economic changes, which begin with personal-experiential forms, lively in pre-capitalistic economies, and move to the more objectified, indeed reified, forms of anonymous commodity exchange that characterize high capitalism. The common denominator shared by the three writers is their recognition that the gift can be read both literally and symbolically, so that it is seen to belong not simply to the realm of material exchange but even, and more importantly, to the realm of psychology, imagination and aesthetics. Here, the performance of narration – the passing on not of an object but of a story – creates a certain sort of imaginative exchange economy.

At the heart of my argument will be the assumption that gift giving, be it in material or narrative form, involves exchange, a cycle of reciprocation. But recent work on the notion of gift exchange has tended to be more straitened than the complex theorizing of it evident in the thinking of Simmel and Benjamin. Derrida's powerful argument in *Given Time* (1992), for instance, is centered on the Heideggerian view that a "true" gift cannot be reciprocated. For Derrida, a true gift cannot entail a return, for by (his) definition, it must break the cycle of exchange, disrupt an economy of circulation. With this argument, Derrida offers a critique of Mauss's seminal essay, *The Gift*. Marginally, or at first sight, Derrida might be thought to be correct. We all know about false gifts, the so-called "free gifts" given away by banks and supermarkets. We know, too, if only from *Godfather* movies, about gifts we can't refuse, gifts whose reciprocation is deferred but inevitable and usually accepted with a grimace. In this latter case, as Derrida, following Nietzsche, reminds us, the Germanic etymology of "gift" (from *geben/Gabe*), is cognate with the German word *Gift* (meaning "poison"). This antithetical meaning shadows the seemingly positive associations of the word: even the gifted child may carry a poisonous burden.[4] Contra Derrida, and drawing support from Conrad's story, I would argue that the structure of reciprocity need not be denied *once we recognize its varied forms.* For such exchange need not be an economic-material one. That is, it need not be, indeed cannot be, quantifiable. Conrad's story, read by way of Simmel and Benjamin, offers instances of the sophistication of "primitive" forms of gifting. Furthermore, I want to argue that the nature of gift giving represented in the tale is heavily predicated on notions of the symbolic, performative importance of the act. That is, the performance of the gifting, and *not* the gift as abstracted object, is the crucial factor. If that is the case, the participation of the *recipient* in the performance of gifting can also be a form of reciprocity. If gifts are not objects as such but the predicates of certain believed-in kinds of action, it is not stretching the argument too far to say that the listener is giving a gift by his or her listening to the teller. I would argue that we need to allow for the coexistence of differing economies of belief in exchange. A multiple or multifaceted economy (which is what Simmel and Benjamin propose) allows for relations that are not solely defined in capitalistic terms (labor/profit as a measure of quantifiable value, etc.) but that leave space for other forms of personal and cultural exchange. This kind of economy, which includes narrative as exchanged gift, can be verified by other cultures and other histories, and is represented in "Karain: a memory."

The story appeared in the collection *Tales of Unrest* (1898). It is set in the Eastern (Malay) Archipelago, where the narrator, an unnamed English sailor, and fellow sailors Hollis and Jackson, operate an illicit gun-running business, supplying weapons to native insurgents fighting small tribal wars against colonialist Spain and Holland. Over the years the gun-runners have traded with Karain and established a closer friendship with him. This axis – trader/friend – is centrally important. Karain is the warrior ruler of a small collection of villages in an isolated corner of the Archipelago. His appearance is heroically magisterial, and metaphors of the stage, theatricality and performance abound in descriptions of him. Furthermore, he regales the Englishmen aboard ship with stories, mainly about his own travels and his people's turbulent history. In constant attendance on him is an old man, his sword-bearer and spiritual protector, a sort of shaman. The climax of the story finds Karain back on the Englishmen's schooner; the old man is dead and a frightened Karain comes to the "unbelieving" white men to tell them his guilty story of friendship and betrayal and to seek spiritual asylum or a protective charm against the ghost of Karain's best friend, Matara. Years earlier Karain had deliberately shot Matara dead as a result of a complicated love quadrangle, and Karain has since borne with him a massive sense of guilt, manifested in Matara's haunting specter. No longer protected by his shamanic old attendant, the desperate Karain asks to be taken by the Englishmen back to their country, in effect abandoning his people. "With you I will go … to your land of unbelief, where the dead do not speak, where every man is wise, and alone – and at peace," he pleads. Hollis offers an ironic snort at this "Capital description" of the English. Karain continues, "Take me with you. … Or else give me some of your strength – of your unbelief. … A charm!" (Conrad 2000: 35).

At this moment, in a highly ritualized act of gift giving, Hollis takes from a keepsake box a coin, a Jubilee sixpence bearing the image of Queen Victoria. "A charm for our friend," he says to his fellow Englishmen. "The thing itself is of great power – money, you know – and [Karain's] imagination is struck" (2000: 39). He then explains to Karain: "'This is the image of the great Queen, and the most powerful thing the white men know.' … 'The Invincible, the Pious,' [Karain] muttered. 'She is more powerful than Suleiman the Wise, who commanded the genii, as you know,' said Hollis, gravely. 'I shall give this to you'" (2000: 39).

But lest we think that Hollis (or Conrad) is sentimental about Queen Victoria, he says to his fellows: "She commands a spirit too – the spirit of her nation; a masterful, conscientious, unscrupulous, unconquerable devil. ... Don't look thunderstruck, you fellows. Help me make him believe – everything's in that." Then he adds, "Hang it all, he's a good fellow. I'll give him something that I will really miss" (2000: 40). He returns to the keepsake box full of tokens from his beloved and takes a ribbon from it, cuts some delicate leather from a white glove, sews the coin up in the leather and with the ribbon as neckband, places it ceremoniously about Karain' s neck. It acts, for Karain, as a mystical token bearing magical power far beyond its face-value (sixpence), a protective charm against Karain's memories and ghosts. It seems to do the trick. Karain seems awakened from a nightmare, his ghosts banished. He leaves, his identity, dignity and authority re-established by this symbolic transfer. He passes out of the white men's lives – except for the profound memory of the man and his stories, his memories, which he has given to and leaves with the Englishmen.

Three main issues arise with this incident of gift giving: the gift itself, gift giving as performance, and forms of memory and storytelling. All of these are kinds of actual or metaphorical exchange, the passing on or the passing over. First, however, we need to consider the larger historical and cultural context of the exchange in the story. It would be easy to read the cross-cultural gift giving at the heart of the tale as conducted by a patronizing Westerner, bemusedly indulgent towards a native who believes in the magic of a coin and coinage. The rather skeptical attitude of the anonymous narrator of the tale tends to encourage this reading. Many critics, including most recently Christopher GoGwilt (1995) and Daphna Erdinast-Vulcan (1991: 31–2), have so argued. They thus tend to attribute to Conrad the belief that traditional economies and their underlying belief systems (superstitious, religious, tribalistic, etc.) have rightly and inevitably given way to the demystified, rational economy of monetary exchange. They see the story as mapping the evolution of social and economic systems toward the period of high capitalism in which Conrad was writing. Such a reading takes Conrad as condoning the superior attitude evinced by the unnamed narrator.[5] I will argue, however, that this perhaps cynical view of cross-cultural gift giving and its attendant form of cultural superiority is not that of Conrad, nor of his complex text.

We need to pause here and return briefly to Simmel. Although by and large a historical, developmental account of economic change, Simmel's *The Philosophy of Money* (1990) is, in an important sense, also a *socio-psychological* history of money. His discussion of gift giving in the work, as well as in his essay "On thankfulness and gratitude," offers space for thinking of gifting as bearing a symbolic value that exists "outside of [material] exchange" (Simmel 1964: 389).[6] Indeed, the very shift he describes, the development of money from a materially-valued entity (e.g., lengths of copper wire) into its symbolic forms (e.g., paper money) for exchange, opens up the possibility that the symbolic is invested wherever "confidence" and "shared belief" play an increasingly crucial part in determining value. Primitive magical belief has not simply given way to the rationality of the money market. "Magical belief" is nowhere more evident, of course, than in stock exchange transactions. Recent fevered share-buying in US internet companies demonstrates real belief in virtual profits made from virtual realities. Or as Alan Greenspan of the US Federal Reserve puts it, recent share-trading has shown "irrational exuberance."[7] Shared belief, indeed.

For Simmel, gift giving nevertheless disrupts "pure" or concrete models of exchange (i.e., those in which something is materially offered in exchange). Gift giving is part of a social interaction not reducible to objectified (for Simmel "reified") economic exchange. There is an economy of circulation and exchange in gift giving, but it functions at a symbolic level. "[Although] it cannot be expressed in terms of definite concepts and measures, every act of giving is an interaction between giver and receiver" (Simmel 1964: 389).[8] This questioning of "definite concepts and measures" is precisely to the point. A symbolic as opposed to a "purely" concrete understanding of the exchange liberates other notions of gift giving. It complicates, in an interesting way, Derrida's relatively purist attempt to give an account of the gift that is by definition neither returned nor returnable. Simmel's model permits a return, but not necessarily one in kind. The underlying emphasis Simmel places on social interaction as a crucial form of (non-monetary/goods) exchange can re-introduce us to the role of the performance in gift giving and what is at stake in it. A reductively economistic account of exchange (itself historically specific and determined) that takes the capitalist Western model as a general theory is blind to more varied cultural practices. In these, other religious, ritualistic and social-psychological formations provide a personal and social adhesive over and beyond the relatively anonymous relation of producer and consumer, profit-maker, buyer and seller through which capitalism defines exchange. Simmel's theory provides for what I may call a mixed economy of beliefs, one rationalized and "objective" (exemplified in capitalist structures, and in labor theories of value); the other more dependent on intra-subjectivities, as he calls it, which modulate and extend our notions of the economies of interest we all inhabit.

In this Simmel is not without predecessors. Earlier German Romantic economic theorists, to whom Simmel, incidentally, does not tend to refer, have an equally complex understanding of the social relations of economic exchange. Foremost among these is probably Adam Müller, whose lectures in 1808–9, *Vom Geiste der Gemeinschaft* (*The Spirit of the Community*), offer a critique of Adam Smith. Müller's *Theory of Money* (1931 [1816]), differentiating between price and value, discusses the complicated relation of material object (say, a silver coin) and representational value. Paper money, he argues, becomes like the word, a discourse, a symbolic medium of social exchange. But so silver or gold or salt has always been. Legal tender is whatever you tend to believe in. "Man stands in an equally present relation to other people and to things ... but he cannot act as if either of these relations existed in isolation from one another." Müller further argues against a material theory of objects and their value by pointing out (and Simmel later takes this up) that even in the case of the seemingly material fact of metal coinage, it is through the minting of the coinage and its institutional control that the metal carries credit. So whether in the form of metal coin, or paper money or credit – what Müller calls literally "Wordmoney" (Wortgeld) – monetary exchange partakes of the symbolic and functions as a communicative social act. "When solid metal [i.e., gold] is meant to become actual money, then it must be coined, the word must be stamped on it" (Müller 1931: 268–9; my translation).[9] We are reminded of this quasi-linguistic activity when we recall the authorizing words on English paper money, "I Promise to Pay the Bearer on Demand the Sum of One Pound."

What I have just called in Simmel a mixed economy can, in fact, be traced in "Karain: a memory" in two ways. The story represents a "dualistic economy" not only at a level of material exchange, complicating even a conventional notion of uniform monetary economy. It also represents the spiritual exchange – of love and wisdom – inherent in the performance of gifting and narration. Karain and the English gun-runners occupy two positions, two economies, simultaneously. The gun-runners start as traders with, but become friends to, Karain. He buys guns from them to fight his local wars against the colonial presence, but he also tells them stories. The tale's dual positioning of English traders and native prince produces and results from two economies of exchange. The gift of the sixpence embodies a complex mix of both kinds of circulation.

Let us first take the strictly material economy of gun-running. A question immediately arises: how, in this so-called "primitive economy," does Karain actually engage in trade with the English? The story answers: with a case full of (Singapore) dollars. Moreover, the whites, though they regard as futile Karain's desire to obtain old guns to fight off the irresistible domination of European colonizers, being his friends (and more or less honorable English types, of course), broker an honest commercial deal: "All we could do for him was to see to it that the powder was good for the money and the rifles serviceable, if old" (Conrad 2000: 16). Why, then, given his long familiarity with (European and Indian) modes of monetary circulation, can Karain at the same time so mystify an English sixpence and believe it can magically protect him? I am asking, in effect, how the material and the magical can co-exist in competing economies. For surely we in the West, as rational "unbelievers," would deny any spectral aspect of the market. But this denial is barely tenable. Remember Mr. Greenspan: Western belief and "confidence" in the market daily reinforce such "speculations." Another more fruitful way to approach the question is to re-examine our assumptions about economic and social models based on progress, especially as we apply those models to other non-Western cultures. This is what Simmel's and Benjamin's arguments enable us to do.

Julius Boeke's and G.J. Resink's studies on Indonesia have identified ways in which Western economic theories – on production and consumption and the labor theory of value, for example – have been universalized and de-historicized, and how they have been misleadingly applied to the cultures and economic formations of the Archipelago. Western economic theories were inadequate to the socio-economic and historical complexities of the Eastern Archipelago in the 1890s when Conrad was living in and writing about the area, as they are to this day. For they project onto a much more intricate historical and geographic space the relatively simple patterns that their diachronic story of "progress" tells them. The comfortable story of a clash between a simple native and a sophisticated colonizing culture does not work. There are fault lines in it, and they point to a much more complicated socio-economic and cultural formation.[10]

In its small details Conrad's story lets us see the traces of two economic systems existing side-by-side within the Archipelago: it is a "dualistic economy" rather than a simple confrontation between a "primitive" native economy and the Westerners' monetary economy. As Resink (1968) has argued, when Korzeniowski (as Joseph Conrad was then properly called) sailed in this area in the late 1880s, his close observation of the prevailing political, legal and economic conditions gave him material for his subsequent writing. While the story's representation of gift giving *seems* to smack of what Westerners might call false magic, other exchanges of coin in the story point to a different economy of belief, a rudimentary money economy. This doubleness is epigrammatically summed up in the narrator's description of Karain: "Our friend paid us like a banker, but treated us like a prince" (Conrad 2000: 17). When Karain buys guns from the English, the narrator is anxious that the powder and rifles "are good for the money." When the last shipment of guns is delivered, the gun-runners are paid with "a case of dollars." In this and other works set in Malay, Conrad accurately registers the wide range of currencies in circulation – chief among them, the Singapore dollar. However, and this is the crucial point, money was generally used only for transactions with Europeans, Indians or Chinese, and therefore tended to be geographically restricted in its circulation to those villages along the shores of Indonesia's islands, particularly Java. In Conrad's years there and for decades afterwards, there was an international, ephemeral, peripheral and heterogeneous shipping and trade economy of "white and brown." But beyond that, just a few miles inland and in more isolated coastal areas, one found the more homogeneous traditional micro-economies of the Indonesian petty fiefdoms.

In his major study of the economic system and economic history of Indonesia, Boeke (1953) describes this as the simultaneous co-existence of a traditional pre-capitalistic and a tropical-colonial, or dualistic economy. We are not talking here about lag or slow economic development but about the dualistic economy to which I have referred, an economy our Western categories and historiography cannot easily entertain. What distinguishes such an economy and its social structure is that, of the two prevailing systems, one (the more "advanced") is imported from abroad and partially overlays but does not oust or assimilate the indigenous system. Reading the dualistic economy and its attendant cultural, ethical and social formations back into the story, we can see that Karain, who is described as both "banker" and "prince," has indeed to play both roles. As Simmel and Boeke emphasize, in traditional social systems far more weight is laid on exchange/gifting as fulfilling other social functions and activities beyond simple market exchange. Such exchange depends on ceremony or ritual performance as a form of social bonding and identification.

This brings me, finally, to the idea of performance. For Simmel (as for Derrida), a gift is not a thing. That is, the gift status of an object is not a quality inherent in it but rather the function of a particular relationship between giver and recipient. Further, this relationship can be defined as a social performance, i.e., the act of giving. A gift is thus constituted by the performance, the enactment, of an inter-subjective relation. Following and adapting J.L. Austin (1962) and John Searle (1971) on performative/illocutionary utterances, I suggest we see gifting as such an utterance. I would say that only in my *performance* of giving a ring or a silver dollar, and doing so under certain conditions, does the object become a gift. As Austin and Searle suggest, among other things it has to be mine to give (I can't have stolen it). In most cases the act of donation must be consciously intended to be received: if something falls off the back of a truck into my outstretched hands it has not been given to me as a gift. In a quasi-ritualistic way, I have to *present* the present to the recipient who must, generally speaking, also want it. There is thus an element of non-material exchange always present.

If its performance is crucial to gifting, then the performance of storytelling can also be seen as a gift: the symbolic passing on of narrated experience and memory. Viewing the performance of (Karain's) story telling as a gift, as Benjamin and Simmel allow us to do, we find that Conrad has prepared the way with constant allusions to Karain as an actor occupying a stage: "he presented himself essentially as an actor," and the gun-runners' ship, where he recounts his memories so dramatically, is "the stage where, dressed splendidly for his part, he strutted, incomparably dignified" (Conrad 2000: 7). In the story, Karain's narrative is a performed gift, shared among equals. As the narrator says:

> There are those who say that a native will not speak to a white man. Error. No man will speak to his master; but to a wanderer and a friend, to him who does not come to teach or to rule, to him who asks for nothing and accepts all things, words are spoken by the camp-fires, in the shared solitude of the sea, in riverside villages, in resting-places surrounded by forests – words are spoken that take no account of race or colour. One heart speaks – another listens; and the earth, the sea, the sky, the passing wind and the stirring leaf, hear also the futile tale of the burden of life.
>
> (Conrad 2000: 21–2)

We might recall here Derrida's notion of the non-reciprocity of the gift, in the sense that storytelling is, as it were, a pointless, unconditional act, one that expects nothing in return. But the situation is more complex. There is a sort of exchange apparent here, a double gift. On the one hand we have the artistic gift: the giving of a narrative, and the shared skill to make it enthralling. On the other we have the gift of the listener, the audience's giving of its attention, its interest, its time. Therein lies the non-material economy of reciprocity, uncoerced and equal. In his Preface to *The Nigger of the "Narcissus"* (1897) Conrad speaks of the complementarity of artist and audience:

> [The] artist appeals to that part of our being which is not dependent on wisdom; to that in us which is a gift and not an acquisition – and therefore, more permanently enduring. He speaks to our capacity for delight and wonder, to the sense of mystery surrounding our lives: to our sense of pity, and beauty, and pain: to the latent feeling of fellowship with all creation – and to the subtle, but invincible, conviction of solidarity that knits together the loneliness of innumerable hearts to the solidarity in dreams, in joy, in sorrow, in aspirations, in allusions, in hope, in fear, which binds men to each other, which binds together all humanity – the dead to the living and the living to the unborn.
>
> (Conrad 1923: viii–ix)

This is not sentimentality. Conrad is describing an economy of mutual interest in which the gift is the giving and receiving of the artistic – more specifically, of narratives, storytelling. The unusual feature of this economy of exchange – and for him, as for Benjamin, it clearly *is* exchange – is twofold. First, there is no coercion or obligation in the reciprocal exchange. The listener is always free to walk away from the performance. Second, with the gifting of the story, nothing is lost. Nor can there be anything lost. There is no transfer of property in story-telling, although there may be gain. I have already stressed the ways in which Conrad's descriptions of Karain's and Hollis's gifting emphasize performance, theatricality. It is a theater in which all perform freely. Karain has passed over to the whites his memories. The narrator remembers these memories, and performs them for us, his, Conrad's, audience. Hollis performs a reciprocal gifting whose value lies not in its material but its personal, emotional measure.

The mode of the aesthetic can more easily accommodate notions of performance than can the mode of the marketplace, although the latter is as determined by it as the former. Confidence and the willing suspension of disbe-lief, as Coleridge describes our participation in the economy of the aesthetic, are not alien concepts to either mode of exchange, although they are not equally acknowledged. Benjamin's account of storytelling as performance presupposes a reciprocity of giving: from storyteller to listener, from listener to storyteller. What is transferred is wisdom. As I have indicated, Benjamin distinguishes in his essay on Leskov between two types of experience: *Erfahrung* and *Erlebnis*, the accumu-lated body of experience of "the lived through" and the isolated experiences which have simply "happened to one" at particular times. For Benjamin, the traditional storyteller (Karain in this case) conveys his *Erfahrung* by telling of his experience of love, guilt and betrayal. Hollis can also empathize with this experi-ence, acknowledging that "every one of us, you'll admit, has been haunted by some woman. … And … as to friends … dropped by the way" (Conrad 2000: 38). This gift of the story provides the cement for the form of social/filial bonding that Conrad endorses in his Preface to *The Nigger of the "Narcissus"*.

The friendship which Karain's presence and storytelling has founded – which in Conrad's rendering does not lack a homoerotic energy – is the premise, the quid pro quo ante, for Hollis's gift. But just as Karain has done, Hollis and the others also need to perform the gifting. The suspension of disbelief that most artistic performances famously require is demanded also by Hollis when he ceremonially passes over the coin in its pouch. "Make them believe" is the constant injunction of all theater.

But what of the gift itself? If we look more closely at *what* is offered to Karain, another complication arises in the economy of belief. For the coin, a gilt Jubilee sixpence, is in fact a counterfeit.[11] It is a silver sixpence which has been gilded over. Jubilee silver sixpenny pieces bore a close resemblance in size and weight to the more valuable gold half-sovereign, and it was not unusual for the former to be gilded to convey the higher value. Guilt-edged securities, one might call them, particularly when given to someone, like Karain, to exorcise his guilt. So we are in fact dealing with a counterfeit coin. Is it therefore a false gift? I think not. A counterfeit, like a forgery, is only a counterfeit within a specific economy of exchange, and gifts exist independently of the market. If the act of giving and not the object itself is what constitutes the gift, then provided that the act is authentic, the gift is true. There is no reason to believe that a false or counterfeit coin is, as a gift, less authentic than a genuine gold or silver coin.

Simmel's argument in *Philosophie des Geldes* (1989) describes the historical transformation (or development, as he sees it) of money from a substance that carries value (the materiality of coinage) to an increasingly symbolic form. It is an account of the symbolization of transfer. Here we come, albeit by the back door, to a justification for the giving of a counterfeit coin. Its value lies not in its exchangeability in the marketplace, as it would within a strict material economy, where it would carry but one symbolic evaluation. Rather, the "false" coin, particularly in its carefully sewn leather pouch with ribbon, belongs for Karain but also for Hollis to a differing economy of belief, not one of the market, but one of trust and personal confidence, of friendship and love between persons. Here Conrad's tale confounds easy post-colonial assumptions about cross-cultural distinctions and superiorities. Once we have acknowledged, with Simmel, the shift from a material or substantial to the symbolic form of exchange that money embodies, then *what* that symbolic symbolizes is determined by the contexts in which it is mobilized, by the exchanges enacted. For Karain, the coin apparently offers magical protection. But the gift is hardly less magical for Hollis – he has kept the coin, the leather glove and ribbon stored lovingly in his keepsake box full of "the amulets of white men! Charms and talismans! … Gifts of heaven – things of earth" (Conrad 2000: 38–9). For Jackson and Hollis, giving to Karain such invaluable trinkets is recompense for the friendship won through the storytelling and for the wisdom of the story that Karain has offered them.

Conrad provides a coda to his tale. It is a moment in the narrative in which memories, gift giving, and storytelling fall together to challenge the material realities of the present. Years after their last encounter with Karain, a chance meeting on a busy London street brings the anonymous narrator and Jackson together again. Jackson stands peering into a gun shop window and that triggers his thoughts about Karain. Both reminisce about him, but it is Jackson, clearly more affected than the narrator by his experience of Karain and his story, who really meditates on Hollis's gift of the charm, on whether it worked, and on "whether [the haunting by the specter of Matara] really happened to [Karain]" (Conrad 2000: 43). Clearly, for Jackson, who is meditative and troubled, the effect of Karain's storytelling, the experience and memories evoked in it, and the drama of the gift, have been not merely episodes (*Erlebnisse*) in his life. They have been absorbed by Jackson into his own experience (*Erfahrung*). They have changed, if ever so slightly, his way of thinking about the world. The "reality" and value of his immediate material surroundings are challenged by the alternative "realities" of the more immaterial world of Karain's stories. The narrator, forever confident of superior Western values, scoffs at Karain's superstitious naïveté and his simple Eastern ways. By implication he also scoffs at Jackson's ponderings about reality. "My dear chap ... you have been too long away from home. What a question to ask! Only look at all this" (2000: 43). As if demonstrating the superior realities of "home," London, advanced Western culture and commerce, he cheerily waves at the crowds in the street, in all their poverty, pomp and circumstance.

There follows a description of the London scene as phantasmagoric as any Karain may have given of his specters. Effectively undercutting the narrator's complacent sense of the material real, Conrad offers an almost expressionistic picture of the metropolis as an urban jungle:

> Our ears were filled by a headlong shuffle and beat of rapid footsteps and an underlying rumour – a rumour vast, faint, pulsating, as of panting breaths, of beating hearts, of gasping voices. Innumerable eyes stared straight in front, feet moving hurriedly, blank faces flowed, arms swung ... and a line of yellow boards with blue letters on them approached us slowly, tossing on high behind one another like some queer wreckage adrift upon a river of hats. ... [A] ragged old man with a face of despair yelled horribly in the mud the name of a paper; while far off, amongst the tossing heads of horses, the dull flash of harnesses, the jumble of lustrous panels and roofs of carriages, we could see a policeman, helmeted and dark, stretching out a rigid arm at the crossing of the streets.
>
> (2000: 43–4)

This vision of the City of London, epitome and embodiment of the superior values of the West and its capitalist achievements, Jackson sees rather as an image of the primitive, an untethered and indifferent beast in the jungle: "It is there, it pants; it runs, it rolls; it is strong and alive; it would smash you if you did not look out." Remembering Karain, he is more impressed by the alternative realities and spiritual values he represented: "I'll be hanged if it [London] is yet as real to me as ... the other thing ... say, Karain's story" (2000: 44). Against the beast of the capital, the friendship forged and the memories shared with Karain and the gifts mutually given transact a cross-cultural economy of experience that is, finally, more abiding and otherwise valued.

The complex ironies of Conrad's story now finally confront us. We have seen, through Simmel's and Benjamin's arguments on the non-material exchanges involved in gift giving and its particular version enacted in storytelling, that these forms of exchange defy the rules and calculus of monetary exchange. The immaterial values the former enjoy are not commensurate with the rationalized and abstract money economy of the market. But in "Karain: a memory" these ostensibly separate worlds of material economy and gift are bound together in an inseparable and dizzying way. Clear distinctions are dissolved. The figures in his tale, primarily connected through the economics of trade, are suddenly united in the experience of the gift. The gift is, paradoxically, a piece of money: precisely that which normally represents materiality, material value. But not here. It is a coin that possesses virtually no material value, even though as a gift it carries life-redeeming worth. It is given in recompense for the gift of Karain's stories about his memories; and the virtual realities of these gifts, and the performance of these gift exchanges have been powerful enough to be believed in and to affect the material world. So much so that at the story's conclusion the English gift givers (or at least Jackson) have become the gift receivers – of experience and memory sufficient to effect a sort of transvaluation of values. The gift of Conrad's story to the reader leaves the latter perhaps to ponder Wittgenstein's remark on the gift as a problem to be solved and to conclude that the economy of the gift and gift giving dramatize human relations held in solution.

Notes

1 This story was first published in *Blackwood's Magazine* (1898) and later appeared in a collection of short stories, *Tales of Unrest* (1898).
2 It is therefore ironic, as Zygmunt Baumann has recently pointed out, that Simmel and Benjamin are now regarded as founding fathers, or critical confounders, of ideas on modernity. See his *Modernity and Ambivalence* (1991).
3 The terms are ones which Ferdinand Tönnies elaborated, romanticized one might say, in his *Gemeinschaft und Gesellschaft* (1887). Simmel was constantly being compared to Tönnies in his broad-ranging critique of modern social forms.
4 In German, the only positive cognate of *Gift*, nowadays, is *Mitgift* ("dowry"). Though playing with such linguistic oppositions, Sigmund Freud's influential essay, "The Antithetical Meanings of Primal Words" (1910), does not directly address the word but is nonetheless of theoretical interest. Behind my current argument is this cultural and psychological, as well as the etymological, linkage. In "Conrad's 'nightmarish meanings'" (Fothergill 1992: 11–24), I have dealt with a similar transgression involving "tradition" – a carrying over (to the next generation) – and "betrayal" – a carrying over (to the foe).
5 In her more recent work on Conrad, Erdinast-Vulcan (1999) has modified this position, partly by drawing briefly on Simmel in the context of "Karain: a memory," stressing his usefulness in arguments about cultural relativity. However, she does not pursue the importance, elaborated in his *Philosophy of Money*, of the immaterial, interpersonal functions of exchange, particularly found, I argue, in the performance of gifting.

6 Simmel continues:

> Giving is by no means only a simple effect that one individual has upon another: it is precisely what is required of all sociological functions, namely interaction. … The manner of [a recipient's] acceptance, gratefully or ungratefully, having expected the gift or being surprised by it … all this keenly acts back upon the giver, although it can of course not be expressed in definite concepts and measures.
>
> (1964: 389)

7 As reported on the 6pm News, BBC, Radio 4, 21 July 1998.

8 Simmel adds that "'benefit' is not limited to a person's giving things to another: we also thank the artist or poet who does not even know us" (1964: 389). So for Simmel, and in answer to one of the Wittgensteinian "problems" with which I started, we can give a gift without knowing it.

9 For alerting me to the relevance of this earlier German theoretician I am indebted to Richard Gray and his unpublished paper on Müller, delivered at the Conference on Culture and Economics, University of Exeter, July 1998, where an early version of my essay was also presented.

10 See Boeke 1953 and Resink 1968, particularly the latter's chapters, "Europocentric historiography" and "The Eastern Archipelago under Joseph Conrad's Western eyes."

11 For more commentary on this, see my edition of *Tales of Unrest* (Conrad 2000: 164).

References

Austin, J.L. *How To Do Things With Words*. Cambridge, MA: Harvard University Press, 1962.

—— *Philosophical Papers*. Oxford: Oxford University Press, 1970.

Baumann, Zygmunt. *Modernity and Ambivalence*. London: Polity, 1991.

Benjamin, Walter. *Illuminations*. Ed. and introduction by Hannah Arendt. London: Fontana, 1973.

—— "A small history of photography." *One-Way Street and Other Writings*. London: New Left Books, 1979 [1931].

Boeke, J.H. *Economics and Economic Policy of Dual Societies*. New York: International Secretariat, Institute of Pacific Relations, 1953.

Conrad, Joseph. *The Nigger of the "Narcissus."* Preface. London: Dent, 1923.

—— *Collected Letters*. Vol. 2. Ed. Frederick R. Karl and Laúrence Davies. Cambridge: Cambridge University Press, 1986.

—— "Karain: a memory." In Anthony Fothergill (ed.) *Tales of Unrest*. London: Everyman, 2000.

Derrida, Jacques. *Given Time: I. Counterfeit Money*. Trans. Peggy Kamuf. Chicago: University of Chicago Press, 1992.

Erdinast-Vulcan, Daphna. *Conrad and the Modern Temper*. Oxford: Oxford University Press, 1991.

—— *The Strange Short Fiction of Joseph Conrad*. Oxford: Clarendon, 1999.

Fothergill, Anthony. "Conrad's 'nightmarish meanings': betraying the tradition in *Nostromo* and *Under Western Eyes*." *L'Epoque Conradienne* 18 (1992): 11–24.

Freud, Sigmund. "Über den Gegensinn der Urworte" ["The Antithetical Meanings of Primal Words"]. *Gesammelte Werke*. Vol. 8. Frankfurt: S. Fischer, 1977 [1910].

GoGwilt, Christopher. *The Invention of the West: Joseph Conrad and the Double-Mapping of Europe and Empire*. Stanford: Stanford University Press, 1995.

Müller, Adam. *Vom Geiste der Gemeinschaft*. Leipzig: Kröner Verlag, 1931.

Resink, G.J. *Indonesia's History between the Myths*. The Hague: W. van Hoeve, 1968.

Searle, John (ed.). *The Philosophy of Language*. Oxford: Oxford University Press, 1971.

Simmel, Georg. "On the sociology of space." In K.H. Wolff (ed.) *The Sociology of Georg Simmel*. Second edition. New York and London: Free Press, 1964.

—— "The metropolis and mental life." In Donald N. Levine (ed.) *On Individuality and Social Forms*. Chicago: University of Chicago Press, 1971.

—— "On thankfulness and gratitude." *On Women, Sexuality and Love*. New Haven and London: Yale University Press, 1984.

—— *Philosophie des Geldes. Gesamtausgabe*. Volume 6. Frankfurt: Suhrkamp, 1989 [1900].

—— *The Philosophy of Money*. Trans. Tom Bottomore and David Frisby. London: Routledge, 1990.

—— "Psychologie des Schmuckes." *Aufsätze und Abhandlungen, Band II, 1901–1908, Gesamtausgabe*. Volume 8. Frankfurt: Suhrkamp, 1993 [1908].

Tönnies, Ferdinand. *Gemeinschaft und Gesellschaft*. Leipzig: Fues, 1887.

Williams, Raymond. *The Country and the City*. London: Chatto and Windus, 1973.

Wittgenstein, Ludwig. *Culture and Value*. Second revised edition. Oxford: Blackwell, 1998.

10 Formed by homages

H.D., Robert Duncan, and the poetics of the gift

Stephen Collis

Originality is now rare, if not extinct. That is why we overestimate it. But in this, our present-day literary Alexandria, even the most "original" among us may take a sort of perverse delight in finding a new writer daring to discard his personality to follow, remotely or unconsciously perhaps, the tradition of an earlier generation.

H.D., "The farmer's bride" (1916a)

from 1944 on, she already was turning back and did all her life – formed by homages. It's from her that I really learned to or became a disciple or claimed to be of the same school, and that was literature. You find out; you give the line of your heritage, and the line of her heritage was analogous to the line of the Moravian Church.

Robert Duncan, "A lecture on H.D." (1994/5)

There have been a number of attempts to explain authors' works – in terms of their creative "origin" and textual "meaning," as well as in terms of their authors' production and distribution strategies – in light of the anthropological category of gift exchange. Adelaide Morris, in an essay on the American poet H.D., "A relay of power and of peace: H.D. and the spirit of the gift" (1990), notes that it is "the spirit of the gift that gives H.D.'s life and work its distinctive structure," and she goes on to apply the gift theories of Marcel Mauss and Lewis Hyde to three aspects of H.D.'s career: her relationships with money, her name, and her child (Morris 1990: 52–3).[1] More recently, in *Sacramental Commodities* (1995), Charles Rzepka has examined Thomas De Quincey's attempts to figure the literary exchange between author and reader as a form of gift economics – an attempt, according to Rzepka, to "exorcise" the material relations involved in the production and distribution of the literary commodity (1995: 8). Interestingly, these discussions of two widely divergent writers both hinge upon questions of influence and the literary communities and traditions to which those influences link their authors: Morris notes that H.D.'s "gift" has its source in a series of influential literary "masters" and familial ancestors, while Rzepka argues that the supposed gift relationship between author and reader involves "Oedipal rivalry" and a "crisis" of "indebtedness." These are the aspects of the supposed literary gift economy – the relationships between authors of different generations and between authors and their readers – that I wish to explore in this paper by considering the relationship between H.D. and fellow American poet Robert Duncan. Thirty-three years H.D.'s junior, Duncan carefully positioned himself as a member of the elder poet's "school" and openly recognized her central influence on his work. In "The H.D. Book" (1966–1985), his monumental study of his literary inheritance, he tells us that it is from H.D. that he learned that "[t]he poem is a gift in exchange" (1969a: 28), and his critical work on her poetry might be read as an attempt to return the gift his "master" gave him.[2] "The H.D. Book" itself might also be seen as colored by its status as part of a gift (rather than a commodity) exchange, as it is a text that has never been published whole, appearing instead in fragmentary installments, its circuitous discourse dispersed amongst a host of mostly forgotten little magazines and short-lived literary journals. Like material to be consumed at potlatch rather than hoarded as a packaged commodity, Duncan's criticism is returned to the avant-garde world of little-magazine poetry from which his work springs.

H.D. and Duncan both write of their influences as "initiations," H.D. calling those figures who have most affected her life and work (Sigmund Freud and Ezra Pound among them) "initiators" to whom she would return "the debt I owe" in "some literary form": her "homages," *Tribute to Freud* (1974 [1956]) and *End to Torment* (1979).[3] While it is the case that some of H.D.'s literary homages contain a degree of the "anxiety" Harold Bloom has attributed to the influence relationship – perhaps none more so than *End to Torment*, her Pound homage – she is nevertheless at pains to negotiate an enabling, empowering and positive relationship between herself and her "initiator." Duncan appears to see even less that is problematic in the influence relationship, at times in his career gleefully tabulating lists of poets he would "emulate, imitate, reconstrue, approximate, duplicate" (1960b: 406). He even suggests that the "initiate" reader must show "obedience" in coming "under the orders of meanings and inner structures he must follow" (1968e: 108). Apparently, in this paradigm other poets are the source of gifts for the struggling poet, who owes a debt of gratitude shown in his or her "obedience" to the tradition from which he or she has learned.

Such a notion of influence seems a far cry from Harold Bloom's well-known anxiety theory, in which "priority" (or originality) is the "property" most coveted by poets who compete with their powerful predecessors for this scarce commodity (1973: 64). Obviously, in such an Oedipal struggle, the successor poet is decidedly disadvantaged simply by being "belated," and he will be at pains to repress any evidence of his father-poet's influence in order to "usurp" his priority. However true this may be, much of twentieth-century American poetry appears to be surprisingly free of Bloomian anxiety. H.D., in the passage I have quoted above as an epigraph, decries "originality," and Duncan does the same when he willingly accepts the title of "derivative" poet. Comments such as H.D.'s and Duncan's come out of a vision of poetic abundance, whereas Bloom's version of influence is tied to a vision of scarcity and depletion. When influence processes, typically read in the agonistic terms of psycho-social development, become a matter of gift economics, with its three obligations to give, receive, and return (Mauss 1967: 37–41), a different picture of literary history is revealed.[4] Pound's comments on the "tribe" of poets and Eliot's description of the literary tradition may make more sense when read from this position, and certainly the fragmentary complex of exchanges between poets such as H.D. and Duncan, which includes letters, manuscripts, books and dedications, suggests a particular sort of personal economy. Nevertheless, one still has to wonder how applicable an anthropological description of the gift is to the aesthetic situation of poetics and the psycho-social situation of influence, let alone to the modern marketing strategies of literary laborers.

Lewis Hyde is one writer who has no problem in treating the literary market-place through the anthropology of gift exchange, applying Mauss's theories to the production and distribution of art. Hyde argues that "works of art exist simultaneously in two 'economies,' a market economy and a gift economy," and that "where there is no gift there is no art" (1983: xi). As I will demonstrate below, on first glance, it does appear that poets like H.D. and Duncan are attempting to position themselves in some sort of alternative economic space. This is exactly what David Bergman argues in applying Hyde's ideas to the poets' attempts to "avoid the commercialization of art" (1988: 14). However, Charles Rzepka has criticized Hyde for maintaining that division between gift and market "economies" and rightly points out Hyde's tendency to "mystify the real origins of the literary work of art in labor" (Rzepka 1995: 53). Rzepka argues that figuring the literary exchange between author and reader as a gift exchange obfuscates the means by which the author exerts his or her Foucaultian "author function" (1995: 9).[5] Furthermore, even if we do assume that an author's work has been exchanged as a gift, the result is that the reader as receiver of that gift is placed in a "subordinate, debtor position," unable to make a return gift (as he or she must, according to the logic of gift exchange) because "the apparent bestower of the immaterial gift-text has assumed the sublimated, ahistorical form of an 'author' or 'transcendental anonymity'" (1995: 55–7). In light of Rzepka's comments, we need to question whether the logic of gift exchange applies at all to the literary marketplace. If gift exchange can be seen as merely a *metaphor* of the influence relationship and those particular influence situations where Bloom's "anxiety" model falls particularly flat, are we making too great a leap to extend its provenance into the realm of material relations? In *Stone Age Economics* (1972), Marshall Sahlins accuses Mauss of making just this sort of logical error when discussing the Maori concept of *hau*, that "principle of fertility" so crucial to the dynamics of gift exchange (1972: 168). Arguing that Mauss misread or misinterpreted his source, Sahlins suggests that "the Maori was trying to explain a religious concept [*hau*] by an economic principle [gift exchange], which Mauss promptly understood the other way around" (1972: 157). What I am asking is whether or not we similarly mix our metaphors when we extend poets' explanations of the "source" of their work as a "gift" to the economics of that work's fate as a commodity. The rest of this paper will explore exactly this question.

Before considering the specifics of the exchanges between H.D. and Duncan, something more needs to be said about "The H.D. Book" as a gift passed between the poets. "The H.D. Book" has a unique textual history, one that, as with H.D.'s texts, may bear the stamp of the book's status as a gift. Intended to be a brief, personal study of H.D.'s work, it grew into an extensive "essay in essential autobiography," stretching to some 485 pages and appearing in sporadic installments, a chapter at a time, between 1966 and 1985.[6] The dozen small press journals and little magazines in which its seventeen chapters appeared have for the most part long since ceased publication, and only the assiduous collector or university rare book archive now possesses its scattered remains. In an analogy David Bergman has made, like Isis retrieving the various pieces of Osiris' body, one has to track down, as an act of love, the lost and hidden pieces of the book's broken body (Bergman 1988: 14). This is also where the shadow of potlatch enters the equation, for "The H.D. Book" seems to be a literary product that has been entirely consumed and destroyed in its extravagant distribution amongst the poetic "tribe." Mauss notes this destructive aspect of the potlatch, and opens the door for its unsettling of the very concept of the gift that he has used it to exemplify – a paradox of which Jacques Derrida has made much in *Given Time* (1992). As the gift by definition implies "dissemination without return," in order for it to be a part of a circle of reciprocity (as Mauss and others claim it is), it must, Derrida argues, annul itself *as* gift, break the circle it implies by being destroyed in its very dissemination.[7] The gift, for Derrida, is a "figure of the impossible" and a paradox (1992: 7) – something that "The H.D. Book" may portray quite nicely in being an unpublished "publication." Nevertheless, following its paradoxical nature, to break the circle of gift exchange the gift must first establish such a circle.

Hyde notes that, as "two people do not make much of a circle … most of the stories of gift exchange have a minimum of three people," the point being that gift exchange is not typically a simple back-and-forth "bartering" between two individuals (1983: 16). In the story I will tell here, Norman Holmes Pearson, H.D.'s friend, archivist, and unofficial literary agent, joins H.D. and Duncan to form such a "circle" in the last years of H.D.'s life. Pearson acts as go-between for the poets, passing on Duncan's request to correspond to H.D., and then passing back H.D.'s positive response; but more than this, the poets themselves increasingly view him as a servant of the gift, seeking its increase as it moves through their various exchanges. It is Pearson who encourages H.D. to give the younger poet her ear, and Pearson again who encourages Duncan to write reviews, notices, and eventually a full-length study of H.D.'s work, all the while feeding his interest with manuscript drafts of unpublished works and the occasional "buck" for postage.[8]

Pearson's efforts on H.D.'s behalf, as the letters between them demonstrate, ranged widely. He acted as her "literary cavalier servante," finding publishers for her work, handling the whole economic side of her literary affairs, collecting the archive of her unpublished manuscripts at Yale where he was a professor, and even making editorial suggestions for works in progress. All the while Pearson saw himself as simultaneously serving literature itself, and the particular traditions to which H.D.'s work belonged, writing to her in August of 1943 of his efforts to collect her manuscripts, that "I simply want there to be in America the materials for those who some day will want to write about a fellow American" (Hollenberg 1997: 27). Like Duncan, Pearson protests that he is interested in more than simply promoting the careers of individuals. When Duncan writes to him of his fears that "The H.D. Book" will never be completed and that it has become "monstrous," with too little of H.D. and too much of "R.D." in it, Pearson, despite having "commissioned" Duncan to write "a book about H.D.," writes:

> As to the manuscript you have been writing … I welcome it already as a success. You have done all the things I wanted and hoped you would do, which was to fashion and formulate something from your own loins and heart. It could not be other than that on your terms and mine if indeed it was to be "some account of how H.D.'s work is a source and a goal for the literary consciousness of my generation." You show precisely this in its dynamics. You are a poet …[9]

Pearson offers his benediction – a gift, it would seem, returned to Duncan for the gift Duncan has given to H.D. He even echoes Freud's healing words to H.D. – that "you are a poet" – as she records them in the poem "The master" (1983) and in *Tribute to Freud* (1974), conferring his "permission" on the poet's straining psyche.[10] Both H.D. and Duncan deeply appreciated Pearson's mediation, and considered him a vital part of their artistic circle. For H.D., Pearson was an "initiate," able to understand the true scope of her work. She wrote to him, in a letter accompanying the typescript of her "memoir" *The Gift* (1998) (another homage, this time to her Moravian ancestors) "that you might understand a few things in it, as hardly anyone can or will," and Pearson responded appropriately by noting that "*The Gift* was a gift which I shall cherish and am cherishing" (Hollenberg 1997: 26–7). Duncan, in turn, addresses Pearson as "not only [a] guide, but companion of the way," and Pearson responds by noting how Duncan "helped to bring her [H.D.] a sense of belonging in the world of younger poets."[11]

Perhaps the most important exchange between H.D. and Duncan occurs in an exchange of inspirations. On 10 August 1960 Duncan included his poem "Risk" with a letter to H.D.[12] The older poet responded on 6 September, writing that "I just wasn't going to write any poetry & then your letter came & the poem, & Aug. 17, it started me off. Does one *have* to write? It seems so, from your *Risk*. Mine is a *Risk* too" (Bertholf 1992: 30). On 17 August 1960 H.D. began her last long poetry sequence, eventually published as *Hermetic Definition* (1972), and she includes with her letter the lines from her poem which, in some way, Duncan's poem apparently inspired – the injunction to "write, write or die":

> ... She draws the veil aside,
>
> unbinds my eyes,
> commands,
> write, write or die.
>   (H.D. 1972: 7)[13]

An inspiration of some sort is received, and it is returned when Duncan receives, on 2 March 1961, a copy of H.D.'s unpublished "Pound book" (later published as *End to Torment* ([ETT]), sent to him by Pearson. Within days Duncan reports to Pearson that, after reading the "Pound" manuscript he "began 'a little day book' as the center piece of my H.D. study."[14] This is the largest and most "inspired" section of "The H.D. Book," and it seems to have come about rather spontaneously, in response to a gift received. Duncan once again makes his indebtedness clear when he eventually titles his "day book" section "Nights and Days," echoing the last line of H.D.'s *Hermetic Definition*, "Night brings the Day."

Duncan's ultimate gift to H.D. was, of course, to be his "study."[15] In April 1960, Pearson, feeling that H.D. "needs the dignity of a book about her," and that Duncan "talks better about her than anyone I've ever heard," commissioned the younger poet to write a "critical study" of H.D.'s work for her 75th birthday (in 1961).[16] With the promise of $1,000 out of Pearson's own pocket "to keep him going while he finished it," Duncan almost immediately set to work on his study. Reflecting back upon this time years later, Duncan wrote that he "had warned him [Pearson] that I saw H.D. as the matrix of my finding my work in Poetry itself," and thus that any study he wrote would be as much about himself – and about the poetry he "served" – as it would be about H.D.[17] Pearson encouraged him nonetheless and sent two installments of $500 each while Duncan worked on his untitled "H.D. Book" from May of 1960 until H.D.'s death in September of 1961. Like H.D.'s own "tributes" to her "initiators" Freud and Pound, Duncan's study was meant as a homage to his "master," a poet from whom he learned his own craft – another gift received.

We may, however, describe the interactions between these individuals in terms other than those chosen by the participants themselves. Thus, while all three conceive of their activities in terms of homage, tribute and "service" (with Pearson as H.D.'s "literary cavalier servante" and poetry, so Duncan writes in a letter to H.D., "a womb of souls which we as poets attend" (Bertholf [1992: 22]), and while H.D. and Duncan repeatedly write of their "battle" against "squalor and commercialism" (H.D.) and "the dominant motives of profit and industry" (Duncan), aspects of the material production of literary commodities are never far from their activities and discussions.[18] As one would assume of a literary agent, Pearson relieves H.D. of some of the more "crass," material tasks associated with authorship, such as arranging for the publication of her later works and running her literary estate, as well as preserving her legacy and assisting in canonizing her poetic achievement.[19] His relationship with Duncan is even more straightforwardly colored by economics: Duncan requests an honorarium for reading at Yale, and Pearson complies; Duncan sends

H.D. copies of books as a "gift" for which Pearson (aware of Duncan's precarious finances) makes a return "gift" of $25.[20]

The most obvious material circumstance here is of course Pearson's patronage of Duncan's writing of "The H.D. Book." As a "commission" (a word used by both Pearson and Duncan), it would clearly lie within the bounds of market exchange: a cash payment for goods and/or services rendered. However, Duncan's "failure" to deliver on this commission, and Pearson's acceptance of this failure, casts the whole concept of a "commission" into doubt. The commissioning of "The H.D. Book" might, then, be more correctly characterized as an act of patronage: Pearson is willing and able financially to support Duncan's literary activities, whatever the final product. This would be, nevertheless, an act of patronage with particular motivations, to which I will turn in a moment. For now, it is important to see that the commissioning of "The H.D. Book" involved more than gift economics. As Lee Anne Fennell shows in her essay in the present collection, monetary gifts are generally earmarked to imply obligation and even to specify the form of that obligation. Thus when a patron donates his support he generally expects to gain at least added prestige, and the recipient of the patron's support is expected to produce publicly recognized (i.e., published) work that will contribute to that prestige. These obligations and expectations hover in the background of the correspondence between Duncan and Pearson. Duncan would appear to be asserting his financial independence from Pearson when he writes, in January 1961, that he may not require the second installment of $500: "There is enough then for me to go on working on my own on the HD Book as far as the economy goes." The writing of critical prose was at the time a great struggle for Duncan, and it seems he was despairing of finishing the task from very early on in the project. Refusing the second payment from Pearson was a necessary step in dealing with his anxiety over the commission's obligations, as he writes on 13 March: "Releasing myself from your gift that was also a commission was part of the magic necessary for the work." Nevertheless, the second installment is paid in June 1961, and Duncan appears still to be working actively on the text. By the autumn of 1962, a year after H.D.'s death, there is little talk of "The H.D. Book" in the letters Duncan and Pearson are continuing to exchange, with drafts of poems having replaced drafts of the H.D. study as accompanying material in their correspondence.[21]

Clearly, even Duncan was aware that Pearson's patronage was both a "gift" *and* a "commission," that it both "served" H.D. and her tradition by paying homage *and* that it obligated Duncan to contribute to that tradition. The "gift" of poetry, seen by poets such as H.D. and Duncan as coming from some external source, also brings such paradoxical pressures: as Duncan writes in "The truth and life of myth," "the event of the poem gives the poet *both a permission and a challenge*" (1985c: 48; emphasis added). David Bergman argues that Duncan's difficulties in writing "The H.D. Book," as well as the difficulties he created for readers in finding the text, relate to its special status as a "gift" that necessarily avoids commodification (Bergman 1988: 12). However, if the text truly is a gift, it necessarily struggles under the doubled pressures of being both a boon and a demand. I would also suggest that these difficulties are more clearly the result of Duncan's anxiety over financial obligations and, at the same time, his growing realization that "The H.D. Book" was functioning more to prompt and trans- form his own poetry than to produce the kind of criticism he or Pearson originally envisioned. Furthermore, returning to the motivations for Pearson's commission in the first place, it might be argued that Pearson was seeking a deferred return on his "investment": the acquisition of what Pierre Bourdieu has referred to as cultural capital, which can, over time, be converted into monetary capital (Bourdieu 1993: 54). In their troubled relationship with the market and their desire to position their publishing activities within a gift economy, both H.D. and Duncan may also be seeking another sort of capital in their cultural activities. According to Bourdieu, symbolic capital takes the form of peer recog- nition and status; in the homologous competition over a scarce "commodity" Bourdieu finds a correspondence between the various "fields" (the small-scale field of artistic production and the large-scale field of market production – the typical division between "high" and "low" modernisms; 1993: 37–44).

Peer recognition is indeed one motive for H.D.'s and Duncan's homages. However, the fact that both H.D. and Duncan underwent self-imposed absences from the literary scene, the former in the 1930s and the latter in the 1970s (a period at the height of his career when Duncan published no major collection), does trouble the idea that they were struggling for some identifiable form of capital.[22] This problem is also seen in the publication histories of the works they conceived as homages. H.D.'s *The Gift*, written in the early 1940s, was not published until 1982, and did not appear in unabridged form until 1998.[23] While H.D. did appear to consider publishing the work from the beginning, she was definitely not in a hurry to do so, writing to Pearson as early as 1943 that a copy of the manuscript had been sent to Houghton Mifflin "but as Chapter 4 and Chapter 7 were badly cut about by censor [sic], and the point of the whole story lost, I asked them to hold it with a book of poems they have, till later. I do not think they are any too keen, anyhow" (Hollenberg 1997: 26). *End to Torment* follows a similar pattern, but even more than *The Gift*, there seems to have been little intention of publishing the manuscript, as H.D. wrote to both Pound and Pearson at the time.[24]

As I have noted above, "The H.D. Book" follows a similarly troubled path into print. While H.D.'s death ended any notion of a "birthday gift," Duncan continued to work, sporadically, on the text of "The H.D. Book" well into 1964. The text came close to publication on several occasions – with Scribner's in the mid-1960s, and again with Black Sparrow in the early 1970s. Both times Duncan seems simply to have been unable, or unwilling, to complete the task – to draw to a close a text that had long ago become an open-ended process, the prose counterpart to his open-ended serial poems "The Structure of Rime" and "Passages."[25] What we begin to see here is a conflict between personal gift and public homage and revaluation. In one sense "The H.D. Book" has only H.D. as its intended reader, as Duncan writes to Pearson shortly after her death:

Now that H.D. is gone, the book seems to me more than ever (perhaps because now the person of H.D. as well as the form of the book belongs to the spirit world of the human) to be hers, to have her as its reader. A confidence.[26]

Like H.D.'s own homages, it seems to have been meant only for the limited circle of the "gift community" – the "lending" of unpublished manuscripts being the most common exchange between the two poets. But "The H.D. Book" is more than this too, for it both constructs a tradition and enacts Duncan's own self-positioning within that tradition. It is an important re-evaluation of a body of literature, a poetic history, and also an act of self-definition. And it is the very "figure of the impossible" itself, simultaneously disavowing and ensuring its status as gift in its very means of distribution. All of these factors seem to have determined the book's liminal existence as an "open secret," published but not its entirety and not readily available; known but not read; rumored but not certain; for the few but also for anyone who desires to remember its parts.

Returning to the question of patronage raised above, I would suggest that it is a useful concept when considering the reluctant publishing activities of H.D. and Duncan, as well as of modernism in general, as Lawrence Rainey has shown in *Institutions of Modernism* (1998). Rainey argues that "Modernism marks neither a straightforward resistance nor an outright capitulation to commodification but a momentary equivocation that incorporates elements of both in a brief, necessarily unstable synthesis" (1998: 3). This "unstable synthesis" in modernist publishing practices involved a "revived patronage," "disguised" as something more palatable to a market economy: capital investment (1998: 73–4). The strategy chosen by the agents participating in the production of literary modernism was "to accept ... the status of art as a commodity, but simultaneously to transform it into a special kind of commodity, a rarity capable of sustaining investment value" (1998: 39). The institutions through which this system of investment-patronage would be played out were the little magazine and the limited or deluxe edition, a form of "niche-marketing" that allowed modernism to be produced in a liminal space simultaneously removed from and connected to the market economy.

Both H.D. and Duncan employed just these publication strategies, particularly in the years in which they are typically seen as having "withdrawn" from the public sphere of publication, and particularly in regard to those works that reveal the trace of gift exchange in their methods of dissemination. Thus, as Rainey notes, H.D. published only small-press, limited editions (in runs of one or a few hundred copies) of her works in the 1930s, specifically addressing them to an audience of "friends" (Rainey 1998: 154), while Duncan published only cheap chapbooks in the 1970s, either privately printed or with small presses such as Black Sparrow. Rainey, however, criticizes H.D.'s continued use of this strategy in the 1930s, by which point he sees it as "outmoded," the system of investor-patrons having collapsed with the Great Depression (1998: 105, 154). Certainly Rainey is correct in noting the disappearance of a market for expensive deluxe editions; however, poets continued to publish in limited, small-press editions (often very cheaply produced chapbooks) and little magazines long after the supposed end of modernism. These products continued to increase in value over time, providing substantial returns on invested symbolic and, eventually, economic capital – the difference being that the "investors" in poetry were now more often than not poets themselves.[27] Rainey's criticism of H.D.'s activities in part misses the point: that there is a more decided shift from capital investment to investment in symbolic capital at this period, that the deferment of the return on the literary investment is further extended, and thus, that the initial investments are also diminished (we might recall here Pearson's desire to squirrel H.D.'s unpublished manuscripts away "for those who some day will want to write about a fellow American"). With less money circulating in the production of avant-garde literature after the Depression, it was perhaps more appealing for poets to describe their activities as part of an economics of gift giving – to step, in other words, more firmly away from a destabilized market economy that had made the narrow market for literary modernism one of its first victims.[28]

Whatever can be made of the shifting dynamics of post-Depression literary markets, it seems likely that after this point poets such as H.D. and Duncan were even more dependent than ever upon mutual aid and support, often in the form of a limited kind of patronage such as Pearson's "commissioning" of "The H.D. Book." At the same time, this situation was in part necessitated by their choice to acquire cultural capital in the restricted field of avant-garde publishing rather than to move toward the more openly commodified productions of the popular, market economy. In this regard, discussion of the literary product as a "gift" meant that its exchange-value contained more "symbolic" than material meaning, and thus registered a particular type of capital.

Such rhetoric would indeed appear to be an attempt, as Rzepka (1995) reads in De Quincey, to disguise material relations behind a smokescreen of gift exchange – as long as we are discussing the production of a literary commodity. However, it is also necessary to consider the "symbolic production of the work" of art, as Bourdieu notes (1993: 37), and this requires us to consider the complex influence-relations inscribed in any text, especially the openly intertextual modernist texts of poets such as H.D. and Duncan. In this light, as I have tried to suggest, the rhetoric of gift exchange may be appropriately descriptive. In Bloom's model, intertextual relations are commodified as "originality" becomes a "property" exchanged in the creation of new poems out of old. Both H.D. and Duncan, on the other hand, seek access in their writings to a particular tradition which they see as inherently "heretical" and opposed to a culture of militaristic aggression and capitalist exploitation: thus, they decry both "originality" and "property." The "anxiety" these authors experience is not over the crushing "priority" controlled by their devouring poetic parents, but an anxiety over the loss of continuity with a poetic past jeopardized by the social and intellectual costs of commodification. Their anxiety is also economic, in that it is related to their discomfort with the reality that their literary labors inevitably produce literary commodities – a situation they tend to disguise behind the rhetoric of gift giving. However, what I question here is the mixing of metaphors: applying the economic description of market commodification to intertextual relations (as in Bloom), or viewing intertextual gift exchange as also applying to a commodified market exchange (as in Hyde [1983] and Bergman [1988]). The majority of the comments H.D. and Duncan themselves make on gift giving relate not to the material conditions of the published commodity but to the tradition to which they attach their own literary efforts: most of their letters discuss this topic, and the books they exchange deal largely with aspects of it. The very notion of a poetic or cultural "inheritance," of having anything to *be* influenced *by*, is described by Duncan as a gift: "The shaping of every spiritual and psychic imagination has its ground in these things that I did not originate but that came to me as an inheritance of what I was, a gift of life meanings" (1985c: 2). H.D.'s work is a part of this "inheritance" for Duncan, and it comes to him, in their interactions, as the living embodiment of the tradition to which he would attach his own work.

To clarify the description of influence as a gift exchange I will briefly consider some of the gestures toward their chosen tradition that H.D. and Duncan deploy. If it is H.D.'s "heresy," as both Eileen Gregory and Cassandra Laity have argued, to attempt to reconcile "male modernism" with its rejected feminine Other, Duncan takes up this same task, attempting to recognize, in Laity's words, the "gift of [the male modernist's] former Romantic personae" (1996: 153). H.D. reveals a feminized occult current rippling just beneath the surface of modernism and reads it backwards, through late Victorian aestheticism and the romantics and an underground "occult" tradition, to an "Alexandrian" source, a gesture not unlike Pound's speculation upon a persisting "light from Eleusis."[29] Enacting a critical "return of the repressed," Duncan in turn (re)places H.D., and thus the occult tradition, in the modernist canon; in so doing he recognizes the gift of the most crucial influence he has received.

It is the recovery of a feminine and occult "heart tradition" that occupies H.D.'s thought and work. This tradition is made manifest in her explorations of the re-emergence of a feminine principle of erotic connection and community opposed to a phallogocentric culture of divisive and fragmented commerce and war. As Jane Augustine has recently written in her introduction to the complete text of *The Gift*, that text

> embodies H.D.'s belief in an eternal creative feminine spirit continually manifesting itself as the living bearer of peace to the world. Incarnate in her, it is a spiritual gift bestowed through her reinvocation of the female Holy Spirit celebrated by her maternal Moravian Christian ancestors.
>
> (H.D. 1998: 1)[30]

H.D.'s Moravian tradition forms a "hidden" or "invisible church," a heretical "heart religion" which for her, in its worship of the Holy Spirit as female (the archaic notion of *Sophia* as the *Anima Mundi*), links back to "a special Spirit that some of the Crusaders had worshipped" (1998: 155), and beyond this, to a

Greek mystery tradition she links with ancient Alexandria. This heart tradition is her "gift," as she characterizes it in the text of that name – what has been bestowed upon her by her heritage – and her task in *The Gift* is to recover what she has been given so that the gift may be passed along. Once recovered, her gift is one she feels "might have changed the course of history" had it not been lost (1998: 160). Writing in London in the midst of the blitz, H.D. retrieves what her war-torn world lacks, the gift of peace and communion shared by the Moravian's *Unitas Fratrum*.[31]

In "The H.D. Book," Duncan, like H.D. in *The Gift*, grounds service to the tradition in the personal roots of his own life – in, as H.D. writes, "one's own private inheritance" (H.D. 1998: 50). He retells the story of his first contact with H.D.'s poetry, and the wellspring of his calling as a poet, in his high-school teacher's reading of H.D.'s poem "Heat" (later re-titled "Garden"). This poem "came as an offering," and Duncan characterizes the experience as "Falling in love, a conversion or an obsession" (1966: 11). Duncan again conjoins gift and tradition in the second chapter of "The H.D. Book":

> Love showed me the way and bid me to follow. ... I was to undertake the work in poetry to find out – what I least knew myself – what I felt at heart. But in the beginning the work was a gift to my teacher ... who wished for just that gift for love's sake. I was to undertake the work in order that Eros be kept over me a Master.
>
> (1967a: 32–3)

Duncan quotes H.D.'s lines from *Trilogy* (1973):

> never was my mind stirred
> to such rapture,
>
> my heart moved
> to such pleasure,
>
> as now, to discover
> over Love, a new Master
>
> (H.D. 1973: 10)

Duncan then pointedly places himself in this same Eros-tradition, finding "a new Master over Poetry in the work of H.D." (1967a: 34). In *Trilogy*, the "Master" is at this point Kaspar, the "Mage, ... bringing myrrh," who returns in the poem's third sequence, "The flowering of the rod." But the Master is a symbolic essence of some sort for H.D., and she works over the various images of her spiritual "masters" in a chain of associations (where Kaspar is also Hermes, Ares, Ra, Osiris and *Amen*) in the course of her retelling, seeking the archetypal source beyond them.

Duncan's retellings in "The H.D. Book" are structured by similar patterns of association, following links ever backward into the "hidden" story of modernism and H.D.'s work. The primary "texts" Duncan works on are the "story" of modernism itself and H.D.'s "War Trilogy" (although many other texts are considered). In unfolding the on-again-off-again interactions of his modernist "parents," Duncan connects H.D., Pound and William Carlos Williams as Imagists during World War I, and then again as the authors of epic "open" poems during the time of World War II (associating H.D.'s *Trilogy* with Pound's *Pisan Cantos* and Williams's *Paterson*). Duncan sees these poets as initiated members of a community opposed to the economic and martial forces of the contemporary world. "They alone of their generation," he writes, "saw literature as a text of the soul in its search for fulfillment in life and took the imagination as a primary instinctual authority" (1968e: 113).

In acknowledging H.D., Duncan acknowledges the tradition in which he places her, and in which she has placed herself – the modernist tradition and, behind that, the occult traditions as a vessel of an ancient, transformative wisdom – thereby resituating a poet who had become divorced from the ground to which she originally belonged. Placing H.D. beside Pound, Williams, and Eliot changes the picture of modernism that was already well formed by the 1950s. It assaults the canon formed by the New Critics, sanitized by the omission of women and by the removal of the modernists' own occult interests. Pearson refers to Duncan's "missionary work" on H.D.'s behalf, and Duncan notes his desire to keep her work "in circulation," which led him to copy personally out-of-print books that he would then mail to interested readers. This was canon-busting at the grass-roots level.[32] Nevertheless, there are aspects of Duncan's counter-tradition that necessitate its occlusion and the struggle to remember its scattered remains. As another "figure of the impossible," such a tradition, like the gift, is unavoidably paradoxical, erasing itself in order to remain itself: to be an occult tradition of secret knowledge it must disperse, scatter and disseminate its productions. Thus the roadblocks to gaining access to their work (small-press runs, limited distribution) set up by poets like Duncan and H.D. mirror the occluding practices of the tradition in which they seek participation. The gift, demanding return, disguises itself so that it can appear to be unencumbered gift, without such demands; the occult tradition, demanding return, hides itself from its seekers so that it remains occult.

One could also argue that H.D.'s and Duncan's efforts to position themselves within a particular tradition are no different from their efforts to claim the status of "gifts" for the fruits of their literary labors: in either case the goal may be the production of symbolic capital. However, it is questionable as to how much cachet these particular acts of positioning would have conferred. H.D. was, at the time Duncan chose to declare her his "master," "unfashionable," and the occult tradition H.D. and Duncan placed so much stock in has, until recently, rarely been met with anything but critical embarrassment.[33] Whether self-deluded or not, these two poets felt that they were serving a tradition, rather than their own careers, and thus experienced little or no anxiety regarding their "indebtedness." In contrast, in discussing the "crisis of indebtedness" experienced by a reader unable to return an author's gift, Charles Rzepka replicates the structure of Bloomian anxiety. But Duncan escapes this master/pupil, parent/child dichotomy, in which "the child is forever obliged, and thus forever subordinated, to his parents" (Rzepka 1995: 55), by noting that H.D., too, is "formed by homages" – that she too is a pupil and servant. The source of the "gift," for these poets at least, is, as I have argued, "The Tradition"/"Poetry" capitalized – rather than any given practitioner. In this way there are, in a sense, no "authors," only readers who record their gleanings, for authority is deferred back along the tradition until it disappears in some unspecifiable Alexandria or Eleusis – a more fundamentally "*transcendental* anonymity" than any author could ever aspire to be. Gift-debts are thus experienced as returned when the tradition is preserved by a poet "daring" to be unoriginal: as Derrida notes of Mauss's frequent use of the motif of "returning," one must "come back" in order to "give back" (Derrida 1992: 66).

Notes

1 Morris's essay originally appeared in *Contemporary Literature* 27 (Winter 1986): 493–524. Here I use the reprint of the essay from *Signets: Reading H.D* (1990). See also Mauss (1967) and Hyde (1983).

2 A full bibliography of the sources of the various chapters is available in the References.

3 H.D. lists her "initiators" in two unpublished manuscripts in the Collection of American Literature, Beinecke Rare Book and Manuscript Library, Yale University – *Compassionate Friendship* and *The Sword Went Out to Sea*; letter from H.D. to Havelock Ellis, January 1933, quoted in Guest 1984: 214.

4 Diehl makes a similar observation in attempting to delineate an influence paradigm appropriate to the "relations between and among women." She suggests that "*the true subject of literary influence could be understood as the capacity to give and receive gifts*" (Feit Diehl 1993: 45; italics in original). Such a notion would obviously be quite different from the masculinist struggles of Bloom's "anxiety" theory; however, Diehl's treatment of influence, based on psychologist Melanie Klein's theories of pre-Oedipal development and object-relations, is still colored by anxiety and envy. For other non-Bloomian versions of influence in the context of women's writing see Gilbert and Gubar 1987; Kolodny 1987.

5 For a definition and discussion of the author-function, see Foucault 1977.

6 This is the subtitle of Duncan's later essay "The truth and life of myth," originally published in 1968 and bearing obvious signs of "The H.D. Book"'s influence. See 1985c: 1–59. In a letter dated 16 September 1959 H.D. refers to the autobiographical urge, asking Duncan "Have you written your story?" (Bertholf 1992: 19). The first chapter of "The H.D. Book" shows some attempt to do so, and "The truth and life of myth" even more.

7 See Derrida 1992: 14, 24, 30, 48; Mauss 1967: 35. Derrida's interest is, for the most part, in the gift's semantic paradoxes as a troubled signifier.

8 Letter, Pearson to Duncan, 7 December 1959. Pearson Papers, Collection of American Literature, Beinecke Rare Book and Manuscript Library, Yale University. Duncan and H.D. corresponded most intensely from July of 1959 until August of 1961, shortly before H.D.'s death, exchanging thirty-five extant letters collected by Robert Bertholf in *A Great Admiration* (1992). Duncan and Pearson also began a correspondence during this period that lasted until Pearson's death in the mid-1970s. The extensive (over a thousand letters) correspondence between H.D. and Pearson ran from 1937 until 1961, and a large selection of it has recently been compiled by Donna Krolik Hollenberg in *Between History and Poetry* (1997).

9 Letter, Pearson to Duncan, 31 August 1962. Pearson Papers, Yale.

10 "The master" (H.D. 1983: 451–61); *Tribute to Freud* (H.D. 1974: 173).

11 Letter, Duncan to Pearson, 27 May 1960; and Pearson to Duncan, 1 October 1961, Pearson Papers, Yale.

12 Duncan's poem "Risk" appears in 1964: 56–9.

13 Part One of *Hermetic Definition*, "Red rose and a beggar," is dated 17 August–24 September 1960 (1972: 3).

14 Letter, Pearson to Duncan, 2 March 1961, Duncan Collection, The Poetry/Rare Books Collection, SUNY Buffalo; "Here is H.D.'s Pound for you to see" (Duncan to Pearson, 13 March 1961, Pearson Papers, Yale). The first day-book entry is dated 10 March. Given time for the mail to arrive, the movement from reading "H.D.'s Pound" to beginning the day-book must have been very swift – almost instantaneous. *End to Torment*'s (1979) journal entries begin 7 March 1958; the coincidence of dates may also have been an inspiration.

15 In letters to Pearson, Duncan refers to "The H.D. Book" as a "gift" on several occasions, writing on 3 April 1961, that "it must be a gift," and again, on 14 December 1961, that it is "a kind of child and gift" (Pearson Papers, Yale).

16 Letter, Pearson to Bryher, 23 April 1960, Pearson Papers, Yale. It is fairly typical that Pearson would write of financial matters to Bryher, H.D.'s lifelong companion and financial supporter and another important agent in the would-be gift circle. It should also be noted that in the late 1950s and early 1960s, H.D. was virtually forgotten artistically. If she was remembered at all, it was as an Imagist poet of the 'teens; her later work was for the most part critically ignored.

17 Author's note on "The H.D. Book" from *Ironwood* 22 (1983): 65.

18 H.D 1916b; Duncan 1969c: 49.

19 Of course Bryher, whose enormous fortune allowed both women to live comfortably without having to worry about making profits from their literary endeavors, was another buffer between H.D. and economic reality.

20 Letters, Pearson to Duncan, 8 August and 7 December 1959, Pearson Papers, Yale.

21 Letters, Pearson Papers, Yale.

22 One critique of Bourdieu's model is that it is reductive. However, the problem is not that artistic or potentially gift-giving communities are "reduced" to "mere" economics – they *are* economies, though they are, as Bourdieu notes, "upside down" economies – the problem is rather that purely economic logic, in particular, the logic of competition over scarce goods, is applied to a field that may be operating under a different logic – the *illogic* of abundance. John Guillory, in commenting on Bourdieu's thought, also notes this problem: "the persistence of the charges of economism or reductionism point to what is genuinely problematic in Bourdieu's theory[:] … the adequacy of a socio-logic to express the illogic of social existence" (Guillory 1993: 327).

23 *The Gift* was originally published by New Directions in an edition abridged by Griselda Ohannessian. The University Press of Florida Complete Text edition used here restores almost a third of the text's total length cut from the New Directions edition.

24 H.D. writes to Pound that she has no intention of publishing her "Pound" piece on 2 January, 10 November and 18 November 1958, and to Pearson on 21 September 1958 (H.D. Papers, Yale).

25 "The Structure of Rime" serial begins in *The Opening of the Field* (1960a), and continues to appear throughout Duncan's remaining publications. "Passages" first appears in *Bending the Bow* (1968a), and continues through Duncan's final two collections in the 1980s.

26 14 December 1961 (Pearson Papers, Yale).

27 To cite a single example, Duncan's book *Letters*, published by Jonathan Williams's Jargon Books (a poet-run small press) in 1958 and originally selling for around $10, now typically costs hundreds or even thousands of dollars.

28 See also Delany 1999. The efforts of Duncan and H.D. to describe poetry as a gift may be likened to Delany's description of Pound's attempts "to establish a modernist myth of economic innocence" (1999: 343). Delany discounts the modernist notion that their works were "anti-commodities," calling them instead "super-commodities" (1999: 345), in that "Exclusiveness does not conflict with commodification; it may even be the highest form of it" (1999: 338).

29 See Pound's *Selected Prose*: "a light from Eleusis persisted throughout the middle ages and set beauty in the song of Provence and Italy" (1973: 53). Tryphonopoulos describes the occult as follows: "An ancient body of literature, formulating a profound and coherent system, is thought to pass on occult [i.e., "hidden"] or esoteric knowledge whose source is divine" (1973: 25).

30 Friedman makes similar statements regarding H.D.'s feminine conception of divinity (1981: 179–83).

31 According to H.D.'s family tradition, members of the Moravian church held a feast and exchange of name giving with a local tribe of Native Americans shortly after their arrival in the environs of Bethlehem, Pennsylvania. It was, for H.D., symbolic of the best that gift exchange can create: peace and understanding.

32 Letter, Pearson to Duncan, 2 March 1974, Duncan Collection, Buffalo; Duncan to Pearson, 15 August 1959, Pearson Papers, Yale. Pearson was not completely comfortable with Duncan's "circulation" of manuscripts, even though he was their main source. Many people note having received such manuscripts from Duncan over the years.

33 Duncan writes to Pearson on 16 September 1960, that "Part of the story I'd like to tell" is how "H.D. was unfashionable" (Pearson Papers, Yale). It was part of his "heretical imperative," his desire always to seek the return of the repressed, that prompted Duncan always to turn toward what was being ignored. Recent studies of modernism in light of the occult include those of Surette and Materer.

References

Bergman, David. "The economics of influence: gift giving in H.D. and R.D." *H.D. Newsletter* 2.1 (Spring 1988): 11–16.

Bertholf, Robert (ed.). *A Great Admiration: H.D./Robert Duncan Correspondence, 1950–1961*. Venice, CA: Lapis, 1992.

Bloom, Harold. *The Anxiety of Influence: A Theory of Poetry*. Oxford: Oxford University Press, 1973.

Bourdieu, Pierre. *The Field of Cultural Production: Essays on Art and Literature*. New York: Columbia University Press, 1993.

Delany, Paul. "Who paid for modernism?" In Martha Woodmansee and Mark Osteen (eds) *The New Economic Criticism: Studies At the Intersection of Literature and Economics*. New York: Routledge, 1999, pp. 335–51.

Diehl, Joanne Feit *Elizabeth Bishop and Marianne Moore: The Psychodynamics of Creativity*. Princeton: Princeton University Press, 1993.

Derrida, Jacques. *Given Time: I. Counterfeit Money*. Trans. Peggy Kamuf. Chicago: University of Chicago Press, 1992.

Duncan, Robert. *The Opening of the Field*. New York: Grove, 1960a.

—— "Pages from a note book." In Donald Allen (ed.) *The New American Poetry*. New York: Grove, 1960b, pp. 400–7.

—— *Roots and Branches*. New York: Scribner, 1964.

—— "The H.D. Book" (Part 1, Chapter 1), *Coyote's Journal* 5–6 (1966): 8–31.

—— "The H.D. Book" (Part 1, Chapter 2), *Coyote's Journal* 8 (1967a): 27–35.

—— "The H.D. Book" (Part 1, Chapter 6, part i), *Caterpillar* 1 (October 1967b): 6–29.

—— *Bending the Bow*. New York: New Directions, 1968a.

—— "The H.D. Book" (Part 1, Chapters 3 and 4), *TriQuarterly* 12 (1968b): 67–98.

—— "The H.D. Book" (Part 1, Chapter 5), *Stony Brook* 1/2 (1968c): 4–19.

—— "The H.D. Book" (Part 1, Chapter 6, part ii), *Caterpillar* 2 (1968d): 6–29.

—— "The H.D. Book" (Part 2, Chapter 1), *Sumac* 1.1 (1968e): 101–46.

—— "The H.D. Book" (Part 2, Chapter 2), *Caterpillar* 6 (1969a): 16–38.

—— "The H.D. Book" (Part 2, Chapter 3), *IO* 6 (1969b): 117–40.

—— "The H.D. Book" (Part 2, Chapter 4), *Caterpillar* 7 (1969c): 27–69.

—— "The H.D. Book" (Part 2, Chapters 7 and 8), *Credences* 1.2 (1975): 53–94.

—— "The H.D. Book" (Part 2, Chapter 9), *Chicago Review* 30.3 (1979): 37–88.

—— "The H.D. Book" (Part 2, Chapter 11), *Montemora* 8 (1981): 79–113.

—— "The H.D. Book" (Part 2, Chapter 10), *Ironwood* 22 (1983): 47–64.

—— "The H.D. Book" (Part 2, Chapter 6), *The Southern Review* 21 (1985a): 26–48.

—— "The H.D. Book" (Part 2, Chapter 5), *Sagetrieb* 4.2/3 (1985b): 39–85.

—— "The truth and life of myth." *Fictive Certainties*. New York: New Directions, 1985c, pp. 1–59.

—— "A lecture on HD." *Talisman* 13 (Fall 1994/Winter 1995): 41–61.

Foucault, Michel. "What is an author?" *Language, Counter-memory, Practice: Selected Essays and Interviews*. Ed. Donald F. Bouchard. Trans. Donald F. Bouchard and Sherry Simon. Ithaca, NY: Cornell University Press, 1977, pp. 113–38.

Friedman, Susan Stanford. *Psyche Reborn: The Emergence of H.D.* Bloomington: Indiana University Press, 1981.

Gilbert, Sandra and Susan Gubar. *No Man's Land: The Place of the Woman Writer in the Twentieth Century. Vol. 1: The War of the Words*. New Haven: Yale University Press, 1987.

Gregory, Eileen. *H.D. and Hellenism: Classic Lines*. Cambridge: Cambridge University Press, 1997.

Guest, Barbara. *Herself Defined: The Poet H.D. and her World*. New York: Doubleday, 1984.

Guillory, John. *Cultural Capital: The Problem of Literary Canon Formation*. Chicago: University of Chicago Press, 1993.

H.D. "The farmer's bride." *The Egoist* 3.9 (1916a).

—— "Marianne Moore." *The Egoist* 3.8 (1916b).

—— *Hermetic Definition*. New York: New Directions, 1972.

—— *Trilogy*. New York: New Directions, 1973.

—— *Tribute to Freud*. Boston: Godine, 1974 [1956].

—— *End to Torment: A Memoir of Ezra Pound*. New York: New Directions, 1979.

—— *Collected Poems 1912–1944*. Ed. Louis L. Martz. New York: New Directions, 1983.

—— *The Gift. The Complete Text*. Ed. Jane Augustine. Gainesville: University Press of Florida, 1998.

Hollenberg, Donna Krolik. *Between History and Poetry: The Letters of H.D. and Norman Holmes Pearson*. Iowa City: University of Iowa Press, 1997.

Hyde, Lewis. *The Gift: Imagination and the Erotic Life of Property*. New York: Random House, 1983.

Kolodny, Annette. "The influence of anxiety: prolegomena to a study of the production of poetry by women." In Marie Haris and Kathleen Aguero (eds) *A Gift of Tongues: Critical Challenges in Contemporary American Poetry*. Athens: University of Georgia Press, 1987, pp. 112–41.

Laity, Cassandra. *H.D. and the Victorian Fin de Siècle: Gender, Modernism, Decadence*. Cambridge: Cambridge University Press, 1996.

Mauss, Marcel. *The Gift: Forms and Functions of Exchange in Archaic Societies.* Trans. Ian Cunnison. New York: Norton, 1967.

Morris, Adelaide. "A relay of power and of peace: H.D. and the spirit of the gift." In Susan Stanford Friedman and Rachel Blau Du Plessis (eds) *Signets: Reading H.D.* Madison: University of Wisconsin Press, 1990, pp. 52–82.

Pound, Ezra. *Selected Prose, 1909–65.* Ed. William Cookson. New York: New Directions, 1973.

Rainey, Lawrence. *Institutions of Modernism: Literary Elites and Popular Culture.* New Haven: Yale University Press, 1998.

Rzepka, Charles J. *Sacramental Commodities: Gift, Text, and the Sublime in De Quincey.* Amherst: University of Massachusetts Press, 1995.

Sahlins, Marshall. *Stone Age Economics.* Chicago: Aldine Atherton, 1972.

Part IV

Posing new questions

11 Gift or commodity?

Mark Osteen

One of the primary challenges for gift theory has been to distinguish gift exchanges from market exchanges, and thereby to discriminate between gifts and commodities. Usually the distinction is presented historically: with the rise of bourgeois individualism and industrial (and then post-industrial) economies, the realms of gift and commodity have become ever more estranged. This is the position of, among others, Lewis Hyde, who further argues that market exchanges also alienate those who practice them; in contrast, he writes, gift exchange constitutes an "erotic commerce" that expresses and creates social bonds (1983: 155).[1] This Jekyll-and-Hyde dichotomy subtends a number of other dualities in social theory: the domestic vs. the public spheres; female vs. male domains; "society" vs. "economy" (Carrier 1995: 192); Georges Bataille's general vs. restricted economies; the *oikos* vs. the *agora* (the home vs. the market-place); alienable vs. inalienable objects. As Arjun Appadurai notes (1986: 11), the tendency to view the two realms as "fundamentally opposed" remains a marked feature of anthropological discourse.[2]

These descriptions are not, of course, neutral; rather, in both Left and Right theory, in Mauss as well as in Marx, the commodity is treated as the sign of a fall from grace, a demonic phenomenon emerging horns intact from capitalism's drive toward total commodification. In Marxist discourse, commodification is always linked to alienation and fetishism – the reverse modalities of a utopian or prelapsarian economy of barter, gift, and pure use-value that was allegedly, as Jonathan Parry and Maurice Bloch describe it, "non-exploitative, innocent and even transparent" (1989: 9). But whereas Mauss describes systems of "total prestation" that blend barter, commerce and gift exchange, thereby mixing altruism and self-interest, analyses of contemporary society invariably emphasize the gulf between gift and commodity circulation. Yet this tendency may stem not from the diagnosis of a universal social reality, but rather from the fact that "*our* ideology of the gift has been constructed in antithesis to market exchange" (Parry and Bloch 1989: 9; emphasis in original): we lament the condition that our own discourse has helped to generate.

My aim in this paper is to examine several theoretical treatments of the gift/commodity distinction, to question and complicate their polarization, and finally to outline and critique the major limitations in most of these accounts. To my mind, there are three: first, an inability or refusal to acknowledge that objects exchanged may be fully understood only in the context of objects withheld from exchange; second, a stubborn adherence to the ethos of individualism and its attenuated notion of human subjectivity; and third, an elision of the spiritual or sacred dimension – the immaterial but indispensable aura – of the gift. I hope to suggest that making sense of the gift vs. commodity distinction does not merely involve, as Appadurai suggests, taking account of the "calculative dimension" of gifts (1986: 13), but requires that we question our very conceptions of identity and sociality.

Before focusing on the gift, I wish briefly to challenge the reflexive notion that commodification and commodities are inevitably impure or disabling. In fact, commodification can, in some instances, be enabling and productive. For example, in *Time and Commodity Culture*, John Frow suggests that the sale of Australian aboriginal art permits money to flow toward the impoverished artisans while also keeping a version of their culture alive, albeit in kitschified form (1997: 136–8). Jonathan Parry cites the case of gifts – *dana* – given to Brahmin priests in Banaras, India, which are generally regarded as dirty, loaded with the sins of the donors, and hence unwelcome and morally opprobrious. In contrast, the chicanery of merchants – and the commodities involved in these transactions – can be treated neutrally (see Parry 1989).[3] We might also point to a curious relationship between aesthetic objects and their market value. In the case of, say, literary manuscripts, commodity-value encourages preservation, which often, in turn, enhances the manuscripts' aesthetic value by encouraging continued scholarly access, if not attention. In short, commodification is not necessarily at odds with "culture." Moreover, as Arjun Appadurai (1986) and Igor Kopytoff (1986) have shown, commodity status is not permanent for most objects; rather, the term may accurately name only one phase of an object's "career" (Appadurai 1986: 16). A commodity is not a thing but a process or, better, a system of relations. I want to show a little later how the status of objects may change, and discuss the ways that commodities may be decommodified. But for now it seems clear enough that total non-commodification and complete commodification are extreme conditions that seldom exist in reality (see Kopytoff 1986: 75, 87).

Yet social theorists at both ends of the political spectrum continue to use these polarities as explanatory tools, and some even act as though these ideals have real-world instances. For example, in the perfectly decommoditized world described by Kopytoff, every single item would be "singular, unique and unexchangeable" for money (1986: 69). There would be no sale, but only a wide range of gift exchanges, none of which would be competitive or even self-interested (whether there would therefore be a self, in the sense we know it, is a separate question). In his Maussian study of the gift/commodity distinction, James Carrier delineates a similar "ideology" of the perfect gift. Ideally, Carrier claims, the perfect present is timeless, and its material expression irrelevant: hence, we have "the gift that keeps on giving," and "it's the thought that counts" (1995: 149). Second, the perfect gift is free, unconstrained, and unconstraining: no return is expected (1995: 157). Finally, the parties involved are as free and unconstrained as their presents, so that perfect gift givers are just like *Homo economicus*, only nicer (Carrier 1995: 158–9). Russell Belk's (1996) description of the perfect gift, while overlapping with Carrier's to some degree, ultimately paints a very different picture. For him, the perfect gift involves sacrifice and altruism (the giver must give of him- or herself), so that, far from being unconstrained, its aim is to imbricate the donor in social relations. Second, the gift must not be an object needed for mere sustenance and must be appropriate for the recipient (food gifts should be fancy fruit or candy, not bags of potatoes): in contrast to Carrier's outline, the material qualities matter immensely. Finally, the perfect gift must surprise and delight the recipient (presumably because of its appropriateness and luxuriousness; see Belk 1996: 61–8). As I'll suggest, Carrier's vision presupposes an autonomous self, whereas Belk's adheres to the principles of spontaneity and superfluity that I outline in the introduction to this volume.

Although James Laidlaw's contribution to the present volume describes an instance that approaches Carrier's description of the perfect, unconstraining gift, it still seems more an abstract ideal than a concrete social practice, at least in Western societies. Nevertheless, few theorists have been content to leave the perfect gift undisturbed. Moreover, both Belk and Carrier admit that a discrepancy exists between the level of articulated cultural values and the level of everyday behavior, so that although we imagine that we give freely, in fact we understand that giving and receiving incur obligations, and we may also exaggerate the sacrifice and pleasure involved (Carrier 1996: 157; Belk 1996: 69).[4] Less sympathetic theorists – especially neoclassical economists – readily re-explain the gift in their own terms. David Cheal lists three ways that such theorists reappropriate gift exchanges into the discourse of the marketplace: by capitalist transformation (in which gifts are viewed as vestigial holdovers from an earlier era); by emotional sequestration (gift exchanges are said to occur only within the realm of the family or household, and thus do not challenge the separation of spheres); and by economic rationalization (wherein gift giving is simply reanalyzed as self-interest; Cheal 1988: 4–8).

As Margaret Radin observes, the chronic use of "market rhetoric" renders invisible anything outside of the market. Thus the only explanation neoclassical economists can muster for why some things are withheld from market exchange is market failure (1996: 7, 22). Further, neoclassicals such as Gary Becker and legal theorists such as Richard Posner employ market rhetoric to paint a caricatured picture of human relations in which every person engages in constant cost-benefit analyses of such matters as bearing children and perpetrating rape. For these theorists even babies and body parts are fungible items, and in their schemata, all values are commensurable, objectively measurable, and alienable (see Radin 1996: 6–8, 92–4).[5] Obviously there is no place in such theories for gifts, which are represented as commodities in sheep's clothing; gift exchange, likewise, is just an alias for self-interest. But this conceptual scheme is powerful because it can translate virtually any human interaction into its own terms; indeed, as Radin points out, it is impossible to refute its arguments while staying within its frame. One must ask, however, whether market rhetoric provides a complete or even accurate picture of social life, and whether the obsessive recurrence to it creates a self-fulfilling prophecy in which formerly sacred or non-fungible things – babies, kidneys – become commodities precisely *because* they are habitually treated as such by economistic ideologies.

Although theorists such as Cheal, Carrier and Jacques T. Godbout also recognize that the perfect gift is largely a mystification, they retain a belief in the possibility of extravagance and altruism; for them, even though gifts create obligations, they are not to be extorted, expected or perhaps even fully explained. Cheal, for example, argues that the special nature of gift exchanges derives from their condition as "redundant transactions." They are redundant because they do not conform to conventions, always going beyond the merely expected; they are balanced exchanges that bring no net advantage to their recipients; the objects received are those that the recipients could have provided themselves; and they are ritualized and multiple (Cheal 1988: 12–13). But Cheal's theory presents some serious difficulties. First, if gifts are redundant and exceed convention, then they must be designed to produce not balance but imbalance. That is, "going beyond" expectations will prompt the recipient to do the same, and then again, thereby perpetuating a permanent, spiraling imbalance in which each tries to outdo the other (this phenomenon, I should add, is by no means a bad thing; Godbout describes this alternating disequilibrium as the essence of the gift economy; Godbout 1998: 33, 93). Perhaps more importantly, Cheal's description, like Carrier's, presumes that gifts are given by those same maximizers of utility so ubiquitous in neoclassical economics. For in order for there to be extravagance, there must first be at least an implicit calculation of the merely adequate. Although Cheal (like Marshall Sahlins) suggests that the closer to perfect balance a transaction lies, the less likely it is to be friendly, nonetheless his definition of "redundancy" provides little resistance to "economic rationalizations" that propose that givers give in order to get more back.

Is there really a free gift, then? And if so, do we even want to make one? Perhaps we should distinguish between the first and subsequent gifts, as does Georg Simmel, who argues that only the original gift is truly "free," because in making a return we are always "obliged ethically" and operate under a "coercion" (1950: 392). But what prompts the first gift? Is it also made with some expectation of reward? According to Jacques Derrida, the instant an action is even conceived of as a donation it becomes freighted with expectation, if only of that warm feeling we get when a loved one opens our Christmas package. Thus, as Rodolphe Gasché argues, there is no such thing as an originary gift; if the principle of reciprocity obtains, every gift is already a response, "a counter-prestation" (1997: 111): every gift always repays or responds to some imagined or remembered emotional or material obligation. If even the recognition or remembrance of the gift as such obliterates it, then, as Derrida claims, the gift must be defined as whatever escapes the measure of discourse and memory; it is therefore unnameable and perhaps even unthinkable (1992: 16). Yet we cannot dispense with our belief in it. Hence, Derrida argues, the gift is paradoxical: "there is no gift without bond, without bind, without obligation or ligature," but there is also no gift that does not try to "untie itself from obligation, from debt, contract, exchange" (1992: 27). The only way out of this bind for Derrida is to reclaim for the gift economy "chance … the involuntary, even unconsciousness or disorder" (1992: 123). As I suggest in the introduction to this collection, Derrida's paradox is founded upon a set of misrepresentations. In any case, how can one make an involuntary gift? A gift without volition is an accident, not a present. The deeper problem for Derrida is that the same intention that makes the gift possible also makes it impossible.[6] If we restrict ourselves to the rational and the material, to the presumption of reason and choice, to the identification of reason with calculation, there seems to be no way out: like Derrida we are hemmed in by the very dichotomy between generosity and calculation that we aim to deconstruct (see the introduction to this volume for further discussion of these ethical dilemmas). For him, our only hope is to make intention and chance somehow, "miraculously, graciously" agree (1992: 123).

Anthropologists provide a sounder solution: we seek a means of keeping while giving. According to Annette Weiner, the essential problem in gift economies is precisely how to "*keep-while-giving*" (1992: 5), because what motivates reciprocity is in fact its reverse: "the desire to keep something back from the pressures of give and take" (1992: 43). In her enlightening discussion of gift exchange in Melanesia, Weiner adapts C.A. Gregory's concept of inalienable possessions – objects that speak to and for an individual's or group's social identity (Weiner 1992: 43). The notion of inalienability is the key term in Gregory's distinction between the two economies: commodity exchanges involve *alienable* objects exchanged between reciprocally *independent* transactors that thereby establish *quantitative* relationships between the objects transacted; in contrast, gift exchanges involve *inalienable* objects exchanged by reciprocally *dependent* people that establish *qualitative* relationships between the transactors (Gregory 1983: 104; emphasis added).[7] Whereas commodities are alienable possessions, gifts are inalienable possessions; or, to use Carrier's terms, gifts are possessions while commodities are merely property (1995: 28). Commodity transactions are thus determined not by whether money is involved, but by the relative alienation of the transactors from the objects and from each other. According to Gregory, inalienable possessions are the perfect converse of Marx's fetishized commodities, so that "things and people assume the social form of objects in a commodity economy while they assume the social form of persons in a gift economy" (Gregory 1982: 41). In a gift economy, objects are personified; in a market economy, persons are objectified.[8]

What makes a possession inalienable? According to Weiner, the quality is its "exclusive and cumulative identity with a particular series of owners through time" (1992: 33). There are two forms of inalienability. In the first, a possession may be given from one person to another, but will retain the "aura" or imprint of the original owner. Although the object moves from hand to hand, it is never really given away. (One notes in passing how the idea of inalienability violates the ideal of the "perfect gift," which is alleged to be "free and unconstraining" – alienable, not inalienable.) These possessions generate value because they are simultaneously kept when (and *because*) they are given. In the second form of inalienability, certain objects essential to the identity of a family, clan, tribe or community are withheld entirely from exchange; they never pass from the original owners, or do so only under extreme duress. In this case, the distinction between gifts and commodities may be reconceived as the distinction between objects that are freely circulated and those whose circulation is restricted (Frow 1997: 127), because these second types of inalienable possessions may be circulated *only* within the family or community whose essence depends upon them.

Inalienability of the second kind is essential to grasp because it moors the floating, fluctuating values of both gift objects and commodities. As Godelier argues,

> there are two opposing forces which must always be combined: exchanging and keeping, exchanging for keeping, keeping for transmitting. In every society, alongside those things which circulate ... there must be fixed points ... which anchor the social relations and the collective and individual identities: it is these which allow the practice of exchange and which set its limits.
>
> (1999: 161)

An inalienable possession acts "as a stabilizing force against change because its presence authenticates cosmological origins, kinship and political histories" (Weiner 1992: 9; cf. Godelier 1999: 33). These origins may be either authentic or inauthentic, because such possessions may allow their owners to fabricate histories of association with the object in order to manufacture prestige. In our society, heirlooms constitute such inalienable possessions. Thus the quilts sewn by one's grandmother are never used to warm her descendants' chilled feet, but hang on the walls as art works or symbols of memory, kinship and continuity. Although the quilts have commodity value, which probably accrues as they age, to consider them as such would be in poor taste, or even a kind of obscenity: to sell one would be to sell grandma herself. But because such objects must outlast their owners, "transferability is essential to their preservation" (Weiner 1992: 37); they are therefore at once symbols of stability and symbols of change. In so-called "primitive" cultures, such inalienable possessions form the very ground of value because they remain associated with the ancestors (real or imaginary) who founded the society through exchanges with the gods. Paradoxically, then, the very things that are "uncoupled from the exchange sphere" are "the very instrument of these exchanges" (Godelier 1999: 29): circulation may proceed only if some things remain uncirculated or restricted. Likewise, alienability exists only if certain objects are *in*alienable. Thus inalienable possessions prove, writes Weiner, that the basis of exchange is not reciprocity, but the "principle of difference" (1992: 40) – not balance but power and prestige.

Hence we arrive at the first premise I sketched at the outset: that the distinction between gifts and commodities may be understood only by acknowledging that certain objects are neither, and never pass, at least symbolically, from their original owners. In this vein Godelier concludes that:

there can be no human society without two domains: the domain of exchanges ... from gift to potlatch, from sacrifice to sale, purchase or trade; and the domain in which individuals and groups carefully keep for themselves, then transmit to their descendants or fellow-believers, things, narratives, names, forms of thinking.[9]

(1999: 200)

Such *sacra*, Appadurai observes, cannot be "permitted to occupy the commodity state ... for very long" (1986: 23) without losing their power. And they cannot be given as gifts outside of the group without threatening the very social identities that underpin their inalienability.

Nevertheless, by itself this concept doesn't solve the problem of distinguishing gifts from commodities within the realm of exchange. The difficulty lies in what Nicholas Thomas (1991) calls the entanglement of gift and commodity economies. As Godelier suggests, "gift objects and valuables are caught ... between two principles: between the inalienability of sacred objects and the alienability of commercial objects" (1999: 94). I will return to the first of these terms below. But it seems obvious that commodities can be – temporarily or permanently – rendered inalienable. Through what Carrier calls the "work of appropriation" (1995: 110) and Koptyoff terms "singularization" (1986: 73), previously alienable objects become imbued with personhood – whether or not they are actually given as gifts.[10] Thus people who give gifts employ a variety of strategies – packaging, removing the price tag, and so on – designed to camouflage the commodity status of the objects given. In every household, Carrier further shows, members appropriate the commodities that reside within it (1995: 116). Indeed, the act of shopping itself may appropriate or singularize objects to the degree that the purchaser labors to buy them (1995: 121–2). A favorite chair, for example, although ultimately purchased at the department store down the street, may have required a good deal of planning, saving and comparison; it becomes further appropriated when it comes to bear both the physical and emotional imprint of its habitual occupants. Conversely, an inalienable possession may become alienable once again: when the springs poke through, the old chair is unceremoniously deposited on the curb for pickup by the Salvation Army.

Let me adduce two literary examples to illustrate further the changing biography of objects. The first is from Louise Erdrich's story, "The red convertible," from *Love Medicine* (1984). In it two Native American brothers, Henry and Lyman Lamartine, purchase a red Oldsmobile convertible, partly with the money that Lyman gains from an insurance settlement – a market exchange. When the brothers first spot the car sporting its For Sale sign, it doesn't just sit, but seems rather to "repose"; here it seems to epitomize Marxian commodity fetishism (Erdrich 1984: 144). The brothers use it for adventures, including a trip to Alaska, after which it comes to symbolize freedom and their fraternal bond: now it is no longer just property, but a joint possession. When Henry is drafted to serve in Vietnam, he gives the car to Lyman (Erdrich 1984: 147), who nonetheless still refers to it as Henry's. It has now become a gift – an inalienable possession – bearing the personhood of both brothers: for Lyman, it symbolizes Henry; for Henry, it represents his attachment to his brother. After a traumatized and distant Henry returns from the war, Lyman attempts to draw him out by beating the car with a hammer to induce his brother to fix it; his gesture is a way of offering the car back to his brother. Henry fixes the car and thereby seems to heal himself. In the story's final scene, the brothers go drinking in the car, and Henry attempts to give the keys back to Lyman, who at first refuses – probably sensing that in relinquishing the car Henry is also giving up on life – but finally accepts. Henry then abruptly commits suicide by jumping into the river. To complete the cycle of reciprocity, Lyman runs the convertible into the river. This object, then, is given back and forth, but only between the brothers. At first a gleaming commodity, the car becomes "singularized" and appropriated into the brothers' individual and fraternal identities – a sign of the kinship relations described by Weiner. The car exemplifies the condition that Radin calls "market-inalienability": it may be exchanged as a gift, but has been permanently removed from the realm of the fungible (Radin 1996: 19–21). The convertible, then, is just that: a commodity that has, in being passed back and forth, been converted into a person. Its demise is the final sign of its inalienability: when one of the brothers dies, it must die as well.

My second example comes from Don DeLillo's novel *Underworld* (1997). One strand of this epic of Cold War America traces the biography of the baseball hit into the bleachers by Bobby Thomson on 3 October 1951 to beat the Dodgers and win the National League pennant for the New York Giants. The next day the ball passes from the hands of Cotter Martin, an African-American teenager who sneaks into the game and snatches it from the grasping hands of a white businessman; to those of his father, who pilfers it and then sells it for $32.45 to a white advertising executive named Charles Wainwright. Wainwright eventually bestows it upon his uncaring son, Chuckie; later it becomes the property of Judson Rauch, videotaped as he is murdered while driving his Dodge; then it is sold to mordant sage and memorabilist Marvin Lundy, who astutely recognizes how the ball betokens baseball's "deep eros of memory," and remarks on an unseen force within it that invites each owner to "surrender … to longing" (1997: 171). Lundy eventually sells it to former Dodgers fan Nick Shay, now a fiftyish waste analyst haunted by his father's disappearance and a killing he committed as an adolescent. Through the years the ball's market value appreciates a thousandfold – Nick buys it for $34,500 – but its deeper value accrues through its association with those "origins, kinship and political histories" that Weiner delineates (1992: 81). That is, although the ball is sporadically treated as a commodity, for each owner it also functions as an inalienable possession speaking the language of desire: the yearning for father/son atonement, for vital community, for political innocence, and, in Nick Shay's mind, for the "mystery of loss" itself (DeLillo 1997: 97). The Thomson baseball is one of those ambiguous objects which, as they become more singular and worthy of being collected, become at the same time economically more valuable, and hence acquire a commodity price that conflicts with their inalienability.

Emitting a "radiant amaze" (DeLillo 1997: 176), it exudes a paradoxical aura in which its inalienability expresses nothing so much as each of its owners' profound alienation from mainstream culture.

The car and the ball bear out Frow's conclusion that inalienability may apply to different objects at different times, and that the relationship between gift and commodity is always a "hybrid" condition (Frow 1997: 124). Both of these fictional objects instance what Radin dubs "incomplete commodification": a condition in which commodification (or alienability) and non-commodification (inalienability) characterize an object at different times – though probably never at the same time for the same person. Some gifts, too, seem to cross the line into commodity relations. Such is the case with those "instrumental gifts" recorded by Yan (1996), in which parties give gifts with the recognized intention of currying favor with high-ranking officials. These gifts occupy a gray area very near to bribes; yet personalized social relations are often established or solidified by such gifts, thus personalizing further commodity exchanges between the same parties (Yan 1996: 218–19).

But is there really no such thing as the perfect commodity? What about money? After all, its peculiar role is to act as a supercommodity, a universal equivalent by means of which all other values are made commensurable and abstract. For this reason Simmel suggests that a gift of money is never an "adequate mediator of personal relationships," because money "distances and estranges the gift from the giver much more definitely" than any other kind (1990: 376, 333). Likewise, for many of Cheal's Canadian informants, money was perceived as an "inferior gift," because giving cash requires little time or thought and therefore depersonalizes what should be personal (Cheal 1988: 131). Money gifts also seem to violate Belk's requirement of sacrifice (although they exemplify Carrier's "free and unconstrained" ideal gift). As Viviana A. Zelizer notes, money gifts seem deaf to the call to display "intimate knowledge of the recipient and the relationship," and remind us of the many impersonal situations in which cash is exchanged (1994: 90–1).

Can money ever be singularized or appropriately be given as a gift? The answer is yes, as Zelizer demonstrates in detail (Anthony Fothergill also provides a compelling literary example in Chapter 9 of the present volume). People convert money into a proper gift by various strategies of personalization that generate what Lee Anne Fennell, in her contribution to this volume, calls "illiquidity": by giftwrapping; by using special kinds of cash (crisp new bills, shiny new coins, large denominations); by earmarking ("this is to go toward your new stove"); or by inventing new currencies (not counterfeits, but false bills such as gift certificates, which were devised for precisely this purpose; see Zelizer 1994: 107–8). Fennell, Fothergill and Zelizer show that, by itself, monetization does not deplete the social meaning of gifts, because people designate an array of different forms of money to "discriminate among a surprising range of meaningful social relations" (Zelizer 1994: 114, 115).[11]

Let us take another brief excursion into literature to see dramatized some of the complex ways that money informs gift relationships. The text is Zora Neale

Hurston's 1933 story "The gilded six-bits," which traces the healing of Joe and Missie May's marriage through a symbolic coin. When Joe returns home from work on Saturdays, he habitually tosses silver dollars against the door; he and his wife then engage in erotic games in which she digs through his pockets for the gifts he has brought her. These simple tokens – chewing gum, soap, handker-chiefs – represent the authenticity of their love. Both become fascinated with a city man named Otis Slemmons, whose urbanity and wealth are symbolized by his gold stick-pin and watch-charm. Arriving home from work early one evening, Joe catches Slemmons and Missie May in the middle of a sexual liaison; after kicking Slemmons out, Joe appropriates his gold watch-charm. Rather than discarding it, however, the wounded husband hangs onto the gold piece for months, placing it between himself and his wife at meals. His meaning is painfully obvious: this golden charm represents his anger, the debt that his wife owes him that he will not let her repay. Slemmons is still here in the form of his gold token, which has also become linked with Joe's damaged pride. The gold piece has become inalienable, but its inalienability is a sign not of a gift but of a grudge, an emblem of the rift in their relationship.

One day Joe leaves the gold charm under the pillow, where Missie May finds it. Upon examination, she discovers that it is not a solid gold charm but a gold-painted half dollar (the stick-pin is, likewise, nothing more than a gilded quarter). Slemmons's inauthenticity (and perhaps the exploitative and inauthentic capi-talist world he represents) is thus epitomized by the fake gold piece, a counterfeit coin that pretends to be more valuable than it really is. Now revealed as a sham, the gold token simultaneously stands for Slemmons's inauthenticity and Joe's failure to let go of his anger; likewise, his refusal to spend the money concretely represents his refusal to "spend" sexually with his remorseful wife. But Joe finally begins to loosen his grip on the coin, and eventually the relationship is healed when he and his wife have sexual relations again, and Missie May bears a son. At the end of the story Joe takes the gilded half dollar and spends it for exactly fifty cents' worth of candy kisses for his wife. The story concludes as it began, with Joe tossing money against the door to signal to Missie May that gifts are to be found in his pockets – right next to his now restored manhood.

The significance of the story for our purposes is threefold. First, it dramatizes how inalienability, in which objects are associated with persons, may signify not trust but an absence of trust, hostility rather than kinship. Second, the fact that the inalienable possession is a gilded coin implies that money too can become singularized, removed from the commodity realm and imbued with all of the signifiers of personhood – here Slemmons's dishonesty and Joe's probity. Third, and perhaps most importantly, the story emphasizes that the money must be spent before the relationship can be fully healed; that is, the money's alienability must be restored so that it can be expended on gifts. Alienability here is a requirement, rather than an impediment, for a functioning gift relationship. Joe gives up his jealousy of Slemmons (represented by the gilded watch charm), in effect spending Slemmons to recapture his wife. The nature of gift here is anti-thetical to hoarding; as Hyde notes, the gift must move, must be passed along

(1983: 9, 21). Yet its circulation also depends upon the market economy that enables Joe to earn money at the fertilizer (!) plant and spend it in the store in Orlando. In short, as Frow notes, the notion of inalienability cuts across the gift/commodity distinction (1997: 130). Far from being entirely separate, the two realms are mutually dependent: even money, at first blush the most fully commoditized of all objects, may, at least temporarily, become an inalienable possession.

This example reinforces Appadurai's conclusion that commodity status is but one "phase in the life of some things," and that those things are the rope in a "perennial and universal tug-of-war between the tendency of all economies to expand the jurisdiction of commodities and of all cultures to restrict it" (1986: 17). The real distinction, then, is not between different types of objects but between different orders of social relations. This tentative conclusion brings us to a question that I have so far kept at bay. I have suggested that objects are inalienable when associated with persons. Well, then, what is a person? The competing versions of the gift economy and its relationship to the market economy seem to be founded on different definitions of personhood, itself a concept that has changed philosophically and legally throughout history and that bears different meanings in different societies. A person is a living exemplar of his or her society: different societies produce different kinds of persons and different conceptions of personhood, and these persons and conceptions in turn produce those different societies. According to Marilyn Strathern, our society is founded upon "Western proprietism," in which the unitary self has the power "freely to alienate its possessions or to acquire possessions which become a separable component of its identity" (1988: 159); in contrast, in gift-based societies "persons simply do not have alienable items, that is, property at their disposal; they can only dispose of items by enchaining themselves in relations with others" (Strathern 1988: 161). Similarly, as we saw, all of the exchanges depicted in "The gilded six-bits" reinforce or establish such erotic or social bonds. Frow thus concludes that a person is "neither a real core of selfhood nor a transcendental principle that inherently resists being alienated in the market, because it is always the product of the social relations formed by the distinction between alienable and inalienable possessions"; hence, the person is at once "the opposite of the commodity form and its condition of existence" (Frow 1997: 152).

But this statement begs the question of whether our definition of personhood is adequate – whether it limits or enriches human existence. This question, and its implicit answer, lies behind virtually all serious studies of the gift, including that of Mauss, who believed that we should emulate the "primitive" societies about which he wrote, where gift exchanges constituted a total social fact, and where persons and things were positively identified. So what, if anything, is wrong with our Western definition of personhood? Radin describes the commodified personhood assumed by neoclassical economics (and to a lesser degree, by liberal political theory) as a "thin" theory of self, because nothing in it "is intrinsic to personhood but the bare undifferentiated free will"; everything else is alienable (1996: 62). Its association with market rhetoric, she argues, fosters an "inferior conception of human flourishing" because it fails to account for significant ways in which human beings interact with other humans and with objects – kinships and friendships being only the most obvious. A thicker theory of the self would recognize that "much of the person's material and social context [lies] inside the self, inseparable from the person" (Radin 1996: 62). Although this theory lends itself to the establishment of fixed hierarchies, it at least recognizes the degree to which individuals both make and are made by their social relations. Still, even in our society no person is entirely commodified: just as the same object may be at different times a gift or a commodity, so an individual's "personhood" is constantly redefined through shifting social and kinship relations.

We have thus arrived at the second assumption to which I pointed at the beginning of this essay: that many proponents of the "free gift" are just as wedded to the idea of the autonomous individual self as are the neoclassical economists they seek to refute. As Parry notes, both rely on the same faith in freedom and rational choice, the same belief that "those who make free and unconstrained contracts in the market also make free and unconstrained gifts outside it" (1986: 466). As a result, the "ideology of the pure gift may thus itself promote and entrench the ideological elaboration of a domain in which self-interest rules supreme" (1986: 469). We have met the enemy and he is us: the perfect altruist is nothing more than the obverse face of *Homo economicus*. With these ideas in mind, I offer a tentative, second conclusion: we will achieve no deeper understanding of gift exchanges and their relationships to economic and social behavior until we discard or at least modify the notion of persons as free, unconstrained transactors, which always leads to the Derridean double-bind that I outlined earlier. For gifts are not only made by subjects but also make subjects; and all transactions are imbricated in the complex skein of made and withheld exchanges through which our fluctuating, convertible social identities are fashioned.

The definition of personhood in gift-based societies is, according to Godelier, far more expansive than our own. Indeed, for societies such as that of the Baruya of Papua New Guinea, there are no things as we conceive of them, only persons, sometimes in the guise of human beings, sometimes in the guise of objects (Godelier 1999: 105). For them the precious items that circulate in gift exchanges are "substitutes twice over: substitutes for sacred objects and substitutes for human beings" (Godelier 1999: 72). This statement leads to my third thesis. When Mauss wrote about Maori gift exchanges, one of his key concepts was that of the *hau*, or spirit of the gift (Mauss 1990: 8–9). I do not wish to add my interpretation of that phenomenon to those of Hyde, Sahlins, and many others.[12] I wish instead to highlight an underlying presence to which this concept points, one elided by almost all contemporary writers on the gift: its association with the sacred.[13] Most writers on the gift are aware of the three obligations that Mauss delineated – to give, to receive and to reciprocate. But there is a fourth obligation that has been ignored: the obligation to give to the gods (see Mauss 1990: 14). This obligation is just as essential as the other three, because without a connection to persons beyond the human, inalienable objects could not exist. Why? Because what creates inalienability is objects' inextricable connection to a group identity, and this identity ineluctably derives from the tales devised and handed down regarding origins – that is, from myth and religion. Inalienable objects always retain some vestige of the sacred, which Godelier therefore defines as a *"certain type of relationship that humans entertain with the origin of things"* (Godelier 1999: 171; emphasis in original). Inalienable objects create wealth and status by permitting clans and communities to batten upon a stable past, thereby enabling them to recall the original gifts that issue from those sacred beings who are the source of all power. In concealing the human origins of social relations, sacred narratives give back a society's laws and mores in idealized, authoritative form (Godelier 1999: 173–4). Inalienability, then, is a function of narrative, which endows possessions with temporal continuity and which generates both prestige, through affiliation with gods, and humility, by reminding us of our inferiority to them. Inalienable possessions cannot exist as such without the stories that accompany them: in the case of heirlooms, the objects embody family or communal continuity; in the case of gifts, the story grows longer as the object is passed along, but always retains at least a vestige, a memento, of its original owner – its author, as it were. But finally, all gifts are but shadows of the original gift from the gods – the gift of our very existence. Thus, to secularize the spirit of the gift (as many social theorists do reflexively) or represent it merely as a series of objects or reciprocal exchanges is merely to recapitulate the history of commodification and desacralization, in which commodification profanes humans and their labor, and which results in the "mystical," fetishistic reconceptualizing of objects and persons that Karl Marx so powerfully analyzed.

What makes an object sacred? An object may be considered sacred if it is unique; if it is inextricably connected with some spiritual practice or moral quality; or if it is a direct gift or relic of divinity. Perhaps examining the relationship between humanity and divinity will help to explain the dilemma of the gift's "impossibility." Certainly in Christian doctrine, as St. James writes, "Every good gift and every perfect gift is from above, and cometh down from the Father of lights" (James 1:17). Yes, such a gift involves obligations, but both we and God know that these obligations can never be fully repaid, no matter how grateful we are or how many sacrifices we perform or prayers we utter. According to many Christian denominations, these gifts are not objects at all, but charisma, those "gifts of the spirit" cited by Paul in I Corinthians 13 and celebrated (some would say fetishized) in Pentecostal churches. For them language – or rather *glossolalia*, the gift of tongues, the language that is not language – constitutes the greatest gift. Therefore only the most extravagant spiritual practices – worship that "goes beyond" the norm – can begin to repay God's grace.

I would like now to make one final foray into a literary text that provides an exemplary instance of the movement from a market to a gift economy and that also dramatizes one possible pathway for a logic of resacralization. The text is Don DeLillo's 1982 novel *The Names*. Its protagonist, James Axton, a "risk analyst" working in Athens for a multinational insurance corporation, prides himself on avoiding commitments: he refuses to visit the Acropolis, for example, because of the "obligations attached to such a visit" (1982: 3). Axton strives to be the perfect maximizer of utility, and carefully maintains his freedom from accountability. Like his fellow Americans, he is in Greece to "do business" (1982: 6), which largely involves exploiting the native economies and manipulating their political systems for profit. Axton's "business" is shielding the investments of insurance companies by assessing the political stability of countries where they insure executives. His job is a glorified form of actuarial accounting whereby he protects "the parent" company by selling portions of policies to syndicates, thereby spreading the risk (1982: 48). As the term "parent" indicates, in Axton's business familial relations have been replaced by economic ones. He and his associates also objectify the people they study, pinning them to the wall with Orientalist stock phrases. This "subdue and codify" (1982: 80) mentality is also displayed in their refusal to learn the languages of the countries they study: they "do business" only in English. Like persons and investments, for Axton's crowd words are just tools to be written down and manipulated for gain.

Axton's isolation ends when he becomes obsessed with a cult that matches its prospective victims' initials with those of a place and then hammers these human letters to death. At first Axton and his friend, archaeologist Owen Brademas, believe that the cultists seek to restore the sacred by reversing the history of linguistic and economic representation – that is, by returning to a simpler relationship between persons and objects – in which bodies become words and money and acquire enhanced value through violent death. The cultists seem to be practicing the kind of excess described by Bataille (1988), in which rituals rid the social body of the "accursed share" – the abject, or waste – and thereby resacralize the world through holy expenditure. If so, their murders would function as a kind of anti-sacrifice, a gift to the God that doesn't exist: since for the cultists God is dead, only meaningless violence can truly affirm the void. Ultimately, however, Axton and Brademas discern that the cult's murders are merely a form of "austere calculation," another kind of accounting (DeLillo 1982: 171) in which they give nothing but instead mechanically follow "the premise" they have established (1982: 302). They take no risks. Far from conse- crating their victims through violence, they only turn them into blank counters – literal currency – and then obliterate them. Rather than reaffirming the sacred connection between persons and things, they turn persons into alienable objects. Axton's own sense of self is similarly obliterated when he learns that the CIA, unbeknownst to him, has been using his information; curiously, the Names cult has been re-enacting his own violent calculations. Stunned by an attempt on his life by unknown terrorists, Axton finally visits the Acropolis, which he discovers to be not a relic but "an open cry" (1982: 330). What we bring to the temple, he declares, "our offering" to the gods, "is language" (1982: 331) – not literal but oral. Axton thus moves from alienation to attachment, from accounting to gift, from writing to conversation, from alienation to a recognition of the inalien- ability of humans and our works.

The final catalyst for his conversion, however, is an excerpt that he reads from his son Tap's novel, based on Brademas's childhood memory of tongue-speaking in a Pentecostal church. Written in exhilaratingly mangled prose, the excerpt finds the protagonist Orville in the "middle of a crowd, tongue tied!" (DeLillo 1982: 335): though he is unable to speak, he strives to bond with the other worshipers "tied" together by tongues. Glossolalia – that immaterial "gift of the spirit" – has people "realing" (i.e., both "reeling" and becoming real) in a "daise" (at once swooning and blooming like a daisy; 1982: 335), in what Hyde might call the "transcendent commerce" of "recreation, conversion or renaissance" that is gift exchange (Hyde 1983: 93). Freeing speakers from the boundaries of selfhood, the gift of tongues comes as a graceful provision, an endlessly circulating stream that issues from the Holy Spirit and returns not as object but as oblation. Pouring from heaven like rain, this liquid, lingual speech counteracts the rockbound doubt and rational calculation of the hammer and accountant. The act of tongue-speaking epitomizes the uncertainty and risk identified by Bourdieu (1997: 191) and Godbout (1998: 7, 97) as the essence of the gift, since one cannot plan or will it to occur.[14] Moreover, this act both creates and embraces a communal or situated self defined by group connections – the antithesis of the cost-calculating reasoners who populate so many economists' accounts of the world. God and humans are united in a cycle of gift and countergift that is possible only because there is no calculation, thought or memory. Language is resacralized, and humans become sacred instruments – gifts within a larger commerce. Here glossolalia seems to satisfy Derrida's paradoxical requirement of a gift without presence, at once binding and unbinding, in which the parties receive and reciprocate without intention. Axton (and perhaps DeLillo) suggests that glossolalia enables humans to be "tongue tied" within a web of obligating but unhobbling gift exchanges. *The Names* thus portrays gifts as issuing from a primal urge to engender and embody the sacred, as a ligature that binds individuals into a larger whole.

Yet the novel offers no way out of the paradox of its own creation: it praises the gift of speech in the chiseled prose of a book. We might speculate that novels require a form of gift exchange in which the reader is asked to contribute or respond to the author's present; but such homologies are fraught with problems, as I point out in my introduction to this volume. Further, the novel does not really destroy the duality between gifts and commodities; it restores it. For Orville fails to receive, let alone reciprocate, the gift of tongues. Lamenting his strange "laps of ability" (DeLillo 1982: 338), he flees from the church into the "nightmare of real things, the fallen wonder of the world" (1982: 339). Most of us, I would reckon, are in Orville's predicament, resigned to unreciprocated gifts and incomplete returns, deaf to divine grace and alienated in most of our transactions. This is likewise the condition of materialist gift theory: without some recourse to a transcendental signifier, sacred source or communal force, it can offer only a withered vision of human relationships to Other(s), one fettered rather than freed by paradoxes. Still, perhaps ordinary, "fallen" gift exchanges retain a trace, a remnant, a penumbra, of the unfallen condition of that pure present, of that direct communion with the Other within and without.

What makes possessions inalienable, I conclude, must be neither time nor the drive for power but an immaterial aura of connection to other humans and to something greater than any individual human. This proposition is the missing link between the three assumptions outlined at the beginning of the paper. Thus inalienable things are withheld from exchange in the same way that a secret is withheld: they are given only in privileged circumstances, and given only to Others who are part of ourselves – brothers, mothers, gods. In being withheld they are more truly given, and more firmly establish the filial, familial and communal connections that engender a fuller sense of personhood. Unless it recovers some respect for these immaterial qualities – the spirituality and sociality – of subjects and objects, the discourse of the gift will leave us no richer; rather, we will remain the neoclassicals' poor, forked beings crying alone in the storm, frantically calculating self-interest and exchanging commodities that do nothing more than confirm our alienation.

Notes

1   For more detailed historical narratives regarding these phenomena, see Carrier 1995: 39–105; Parry 1986; Godbout with Caillé 1998: 129–67.

2   Pecora offers an extended argument tracing the permutations of Aristotle's *oikos* in gift theory. For other treatments of this dichotomy see Sahlins 1972; Carrier 1995: 154. The distinction has recently been challenged by Parry and by Yunxiang Yan's research on Chinese gift practices.

3   Parry speculates that the source of Western moral associations may lie in the separation between urban and rural communities established in the middle ages, whereby the city (the realm of commodities and the market) came to be viewed as sinful and corrupt (1989: 83–4).

4   Mauss, of course, emphasizes the mutual obligations – to give, to receive, and to reciprocate – built into gift exchanges (1990: 37–41). It is perhaps telling that both Carrier and Belk find their example of the perfect gift not in actual social life but in O. Henry's sentimental story, "The gift of the Magi."

5   Radin lists four indicia of complete commodification: objectification, fungibility, commensurability of value, and money equivalence (1996: 118).

6   This is similar to what Godbout and Caillé dub the "Dale Carnegie paradox": the gift is only valuable if it is spontaneous; but if we try to cultivate spontaneity we are guilty of calculation and hence obviate the purity of the intention. See Godbout with Caillé 1998: 82, 97.

7   Frow treats Gregory and other theorists in his excellent discussion of the notion of inalienability and the distinction between gift and commodity exchanges (Frow 1997: 102–30). For further critiques of Gregory, see Cheal 1988: 10–12; and Laidlaw's essay in the present volume. For his part, Cheal may be confusing the legal definition of gifts, in which the donor has the right to dispose of an object, with the cultural understanding of gifts, which retain the familial or social "marks" of the relationship between the transactors.

8   Cheal thus misses the point when he writes that in modern Western societies, gifts' "alienability is a precondition of their being gifts" (1988: 10). He means that presents must be intentionally "alienated" by being passed from one person to another. But as Schwartz and other theorists show, gifts not only retain the personhood of the giver, inasmuch as the giver singularizes the present or puts his or her "signature" on it, but

also reflect the donor's vision of the recipient (see Schwartz 1996: 70). In that sense they are doubly inalienable. Parry and Bloch elide another important distinction when they claim that capitalist commodity fetishism is the same as Gregory's inalienability (Parry and Bloch 1989: 11–12; Pecora makes the same error [1997: 229–30]). But for Marx the commodity is a fetish because it conceals the social relations involved in its production; hence, in the absence of a capitalist economy producing surplus value, true Marxian commodity fetishism cannot exist. Contemporary use of the term is looser, but its "fetishistic" association between persons and things remains different from that in gift objects. The source of commodity fetishism lies in desire: one perceives in purchased goods certain qualities that one lacks and wishes to obtain. In contrast, in gift economies objects are *already* imbued with the personhood of those who have previously owned them. The immaterial qualities of such objects are not the imaginary social properties ascribed to them by advertisements, but the imprimatur of preceding possessors, including their prestige, history, kinship relationships, and so on. In the first case, the qualities are invented; in the second case, they are inscribed.

9 See also Frow 1997: 127; Parry 1989: 88.

10 Appadurai 1986: 16. For a more complete taxonomy of "decommoditization" see Appadurai 1986: 6–16.

11 Zelizer's conclusion seems to hold for non-Western societies too: the essays in Parry and Bloch's collection suggest that "the meanings with which money is invested are quite as much a product of the cultural matrix into which it is invested as of the economic functions it performs." What money means, then, "is not only situationally defined but also constantly renegotiated" (Parry and Bloch 1989: 21, 23). Yan also shows that money plays an important role in Chinese gift-giving practices (1996: 215–16).

12 See Sahlins 1972: 157–67; Hyde 1983: 36–7. For more discussion of this issue, see the introduction to the present volume.

13 Recently gift theorists have begun to re-examine this association. Godelier's (1999) study, for example, is essentially an attempt to explicate this fourth obligation through an analysis of Mauss. My discussion here is strongly indebted to Godelier's work. See also Laidlaw's contribution to this volume.

14 For a further discussion of these attributes, see the introduction to this volume. For a more detailed analysis of the economic and religious aspects of DeLillo's novel, see Osteen 2000: 118–41.

References

Appadurai, Arjun. "Introduction: commodities and the politics of value." In Arjun Appadurai (ed.) *The Social Life of Things: Commodities in Cultural Perspective.* Cambridge: Cambridge University Press, 1986, pp. 3–63.

Bataille, Georges. *The Accursed Share: An Essay on General Economy.* Trans. Robert Hurley. New York: Zone, 1988.

Belk, Russell W. "The perfect gift." In Cele Otnes and Richard F. Beltramini (eds) *Gift-Giving: A Research Anthology.* Bowling Green, OH: Bowling Green State University Popular Press, 1996, pp. 59–84.

Bourdieu, Pierre. "Selections from *The Logic of Practice.*" Trans. Richard Nice. In Alan D. Schrift (ed.) *The Logic of the Gift: Toward an Ethic of Generosity.* New York: Routledge, 1997, pp. 190–230.

Carrier, James G. *Gifts and Commodities: Exchange and Western Capitalism since 1700.* London and New York: Routledge, 1995.

Cheal, David. *The Gift Economy.* New York and London: Routledge, 1988.

DeLillo, Don. *The Names*. New York: Knopf, 1982.

—— *Underworld*. New York: Scribner, 1997.

Derrida, Jacques. *Given Time: I. Counterfeit Money*. Trans. Peggy Kamuf. Chicago: University of Chicago Press, 1992.

Erdrich, Louise. *Love Medicine*. New York: Holt, Rinehart and Winston, 1984.

Frow, John. *Time and Commodity Culture*. Oxford: Clarendon Press, 1997.

Gasché, Rodolphe. "Heliocentric exchange." Trans. Morris Parslow. In Alan D. Schrift (ed.) *The Logic of the Gift: Toward an Ethic of Generosity*. New York: Routledge, 1997, pp. 100–17.

Godbout, Jacques T. with Alain Caillé. *The World of the Gift*. Trans. Donald Winkler. Montreal: McGill-Queen's University Press, 1998.

Godelier, Maurice. *The Enigma of the Gift*. Trans. Nora Scott. Chicago: University of Chicago Press, 1999.

Gregory, C.A. *Gifts and Commodities*. London and New York: Academic, 1982.

—— "Kula gift exchange and capitalist commodity exchange: a comparison." In Jerry W. Leach and Edmund Leach (eds) *The Kula: New Perspectives on Massim Exchange*. Cambridge: Cambridge University Press, 1983, pp. 103–17.

Hurston, Zora Neale. "The gilded six-bits." In Ann Charters (ed.) *The Story and Its Writer: An Introduction to Short Fiction*. Fourth edition. Boston: Bedford/St. Martin's, 1995, pp. 620–8.

Hyde, Lewis. *The Gift: Imagination and the Erotic Life of Property*. New York: Random, 1983.

Kopytoff, Igor. "The cultural biography of things: commoditization as process." In Arjun Appadurai (ed.) *The Social Life of Things: Commodities in Cultural Perspective*. Cambridge: Cambridge University Press, 1986, pp. 64–91.

Mauss, Marcel. *The Gift: The Form and Reason for Exchange in Archaic Societies*. Trans. W.D. Halls. Foreword by Mary Douglas. London: Routledge, 1990 [1925].

Osteen, Mark. *American Magic and Dread: Don DeLillo's Dialogue with Culture*. Philadelphia: University of Pennsylvania Press, 2000.

Parry, Jonathan. "*The gift*, the Indian gift, and the 'Indian gift.'" *Man* (NS) 21 (1986): 453–73.

—— "On the Moral Perils of Exchange." In Jonathan Parry and Maurice Bloch (eds) *Money and the Morality of Exchange*. Cambridge: Cambridge University Press, 1989, pp. 64–93.

Parry, Jonathan, and Maurice Bloch. "Introduction: Money and the Morality of Exchange." In Jonathan Parry and Maurice Bloch (eds) *Money and the Morality of Exchange*. Cambridge: Cambridge University Press, 1989, pp. 1–32.

Pecora, Vincent P. *Households of the Soul*. Baltimore: Johns Hopkins University Press, 1997.

Radin, Margaret Jane. *Contested Commodities*. Cambridge, MA: Harvard University Press, 1996.

Sahlins, Marshall. *Stone Age Economics*. Chicago: Aldine, 1972.

Schwartz, Barry. "The social psychology of the gift." In Aafke E. Komter (ed.) *The Gift: An Interdisciplinary Perspective*. Amsterdam: Amsterdam University Press, 1996, pp. 69–80.

Simmel, Georg. "Faithfulness and gratitude." In *The Sociology of Georg Simmel*. Ed. and Trans. Kurt H. Wolff. New York: Free Press, 1950.

—— *The Philosophy of Money*. Ed. David Frisby. Trans. Tom Bottomore and David Frisby. Second edition. New York: Routledge, 1990 [1907].

Strathern, Marilyn. *The Gender of the Gift: Problems with Women and Problems with Society in Melanesia*. Berkeley: University of California Press, 1988.

Thomas, Nicholas. *Entangled Objects: Exchange, Material Culture, and Colonialism in the Pacific.* Cambridge: Harvard University Press, 1991.

Weiner, Annette B. *Inalienable Possessions: The Paradox of Keeping-While-Giving.* Berkeley: University of California Press, 1992.

Yan, Yunxiang. *The Flow of Gifts: Reciprocity and Social Networks in a Chinese Village.* Stanford, CA: Stanford University Press, 1996.

Zelizer, Viviana A. *The Social Meaning of Money.* New York: Basic Books, 1994.

12 The ghost of the gift

The unlikelihood of economics

Antonio Callari

You hear remarks such as "Philosophy leads to nothing," "you can't do anything with philosophy." … There is no denying the soundness of these two phrases, particularly common amongst scientists and teachers of science. … It is absolutely correct and proper to say that "You can't do anything with philosophy." It is only wrong to suppose that this is the last word on philosophy. For the rejoinder imposes itself: granted that we cannot do anything with philosophy, might not philosophy, if we concern ourselves with it, do something with us?

Martin Heidegger, *An Introduction to Metaphysics* (1987: 11–12)

The most ordinary and even the seemingly most routine exchanges of everyday life, like the "little gifts" that "bind friendship," presuppose an improvisation, and therefore a constant uncertainty, which, as we say, make all their charm, and hence all their social efficacy. … The simple possibility that things may proceed otherwise than as laid down by the "mechanical laws" of the "cycle of reciprocity" is sufficient to change the whole experience of practice and, by the same token, its logic.

Pierre Bourdieu, *The Logic of Practice* (1990: 99)

Enter the ghost …[1]

Derrida has summoned the figure of the ghost to evoke an image of epistemological tremor – the tremor-inducing effect of Marx on European capitalism[2] being the most notable instance. It is an effect of the ghost that the one to whom it appears finds her own identity shaken, as a result of what Derrida calls a *visor effect*: "This Thing meanwhile looks at us and sees us not see it even when it is there. … We call this the *visor effect*: we do not see who looks at us" (1994: 6–7). Since the ghost is not so much chosen by as it is the chooser of the one to whom it appears, this last one is not in control of her own identity, because she cannot see the seeing "eyes" of the ghost and cannot thus "fix the other" that calls upon her. Unable thus to "close the space" of her own being, the seer of the ghost cannot be her own confident subject, and her identity, which had perhaps hitherto been thought secure, is now thereby threatened. The ghostly apparition produces a threatening mix of being-as-subject (seeing) and being-as-object (seen), and so these states of existence remain suspended above the more definite geography in which they normally have their bearings fixed – in a gap, as it were, between identities.

That the figure of such a gap[3] would be useful for Derridean deconstructions and disseminations is easily intuited. More important for us is that Derrida uses the figure to theorize the philosophical conditions of the ethical and the political; in fact, Derrida's deconstructions and disseminations may be but modes of philosophical exploration that, grounded neither in any fixed geography nor any economy of meaning (that is, any discipline), invite the possibility and need for ethical and political suturings.[4] For our case, in the gap between subject and object, the ghost remains irreducibly (because of the visor effect) and yet compellingly other, and can, therefore, metaphorically represent that "totally-other" other towards which Derrida directs the concept of responsibility as he tries to reconstruct radically the space of ethics and politics: "If I ... speak at length about ghosts, ... it is in the name of justice. ... No justice ... seems possible or thinkable without the principle of some *responsibility* ... before the ghosts of those who are not yet born or who are already dead" (1994: xix; emphasis in original).

In this paper I would like to discuss the relationship of the gift to "economics" in these ghostly terms. The gift *can* destabilize economics, question its subjectivity/objectivity, and threaten its confidence because its conception is unstable. Derrida (in *Given Time* [1992]) represents this instability as a paradox, or aporia, at the basis of which are two contradictory states of the gift: at one pole is generosity, giving without any expectation of a return; at the other pole is reciprocity, the return of the gift, or even the expectation of a return. The aporia consists of the fact that the condition of the gift's possibility is simultaneously the condition of its impossibility: to be a gift, the thing must be intended as gift, but the very act of consciousness whereby the one who gives is acknowledged (or acknowledges himself) produces a type of symbolic return, no less real for being cultural or immaterial. The gift, then, is unstable because it cannot but be suspended between these two poles – in the gap, as it were.[5] The instability of the gift makes it impossible for economics to set its gaze upon the thing and fix the terms of its relationship to it. The instability, that is, produces the functional equivalent of the *visor effect*, and the gift thus wears well a ghostly garb, haunting economics.

The instability of the gift has been well noted: "*The Gift*, by Marcel Mauss, ... is the 'master narrative' of economic anthropology, and anthropology's gift to neoclassical economics. ... But the idea of a gift also represents economic anthropology's postmodern moment, for it seems to elude every fixed understanding we erect" (Gudeman 2001: 459). And "In economic anthropology, all roads to the gift lead back to Marcel Mauss. ... [T]he primary attraction of *The Gift* is, self-reflexively, its radical undecidability" (Mirowski 2001: 438–9). But whereas Gudeman and Mirowski seem moved to overcome the gift's instability (we shall see how), I wish to welcome it: because it can shake longstanding conceptions of "the social" which, as a result of their structuralist and functionalist forms, cannot think the ethical or the political; because it can beckon us to replace these conceptions with more open-ended ones, wherein the ethical and the political modes can become thinkable; and finally, because it can make these modes not only thinkable but compelling ways of condensing the otherwise frightfully rich indeterminacy of being that the (ghost of the) gift evokes out of the gap between reciprocity and generosity.

Social science has indeed found the gift slippery and has been unable to make it the center of community, or to structure its concept of society around it. Mirowski (1994, 2001) explains why the efforts of economic anthropologists, Marshall Sahlins in particular, to make the gift an alternative to exchange as the foundation of society exhausted themselves: to the extent that the very concept of the "*social*" *implies reciprocity*, any attempt to understand society through the gift must abide by the logic of reciprocity, with the consequence that the gift concept slips inevitably back towards one of its two poles and becomes theorized as exchange: economics absorbs anthropology.[6] I think, however, that the inability of the gift to substitute for exchange in structuralist and functionalist conceptions of society, rather than speaking to a limitation of the gift itself, speaks to the limitations of these conceptions, highlighting in particular their inability to accept undecidability in the social, to understand that society is always more *and* less than its structures and that these structures are themselves performances. In this regard, the gift's instabilities, ambivalences and aporias can break up the social science economies of structure and function and offer the conditions for a sociality with ethical and political dimensions – even if only as the measures of the gift's need to suture its own excesses and deficits in relation to exchange. We can echo Heidegger (see epigraph) here, in trying to turn social science's verdict on the gift back upon it: even if we grant that the gift cannot replace exchange as a center of society, it would still be wrong to suppose that this is the last word on the gift, for the function of the gift may lie not within science but in relation to it. If social science can't carry out its self-given task of structuring the social around the gift, might not the gift do something for social scientists? In the face of the confidence with which economics has disciplined the ethical and the political (e.g., in the name of efficiency), the destabilizing tremor of the gift would be of no small consequence: at stake in this tremor, uncontrollable to the extent that Derridean undecidability marks it, may indeed be nothing less than the recovery of the space of ethics (responsibility) and politics (capacity) – a recovery unavailable, perhaps, in any other way.

Enter the ghost ... of the gift, then, to beckon us, even (or especially) as economists, to resist, diffuse and ultimately reject the prerogative of economics to "discipline" our knowledge of ... pangs of hunger, aches of anomie, cries for justice, or pleas for dignity, and to *respond* instead to their injunctions, ethically and politically, out of the well of a poetic sociality.[7] From each according to his abilities, to each according to his needs ... perhaps ... *perhaps*! Perhaps this is the gift.

Exit the ghost ...

By economics I refer to its disciplinary conception as a science of exchange. The idea of exchange as a structure has required economics to discipline concepts, such as the gift, that would otherwise open gaps on the surface of the structure (society, economy) and thus suggest an independent, performative or suturing role for the ethical and the political. I use the metaphor of the ghost to allude to the effect of this disciplinary need, since the response of economics to the challenge of the gift (which threatens to be the totally-other other of exchange) recalls rituals of exorcism: exit the ghost of the gift, so that the structure of exchange may keep whole the disciplinary confidence of economics. In the next section, we will see the ghost re-enter: everyone knows, after all, that exorcisms are never final and that, rather than annulling the ghost, they merely displace it to another location, whence it can, and normally does, reappear (one hears echoes of Freud, Lacan). In this section, however, I first sketch the nature of the exorcism; I try to explain not only the need economics feels to exorcise the gift, a relatively easy point to make, but also the form this exorcism has taken, in order to expose (and would that I could make tremble) the epistemological grounds on which the rite has been performed.

It might at first appear that the exorcism could be attributed to selfishness, and to the self-interested, calculating rationality that is its theoretical principle. Indeed, the concept of the gift was first introduced by Malinowski, and then conjured by Mauss, as a critique of the type of self-interested behavior that economics, from Adam Smith to Herbert Spencer to Alfred Marshall, had normalized in modern, commercial society.[8] Indeed, the more recent theoretical maneuver of economics, enacted notably by Nobel laureate Gary Becker, has been to absorb the gift into the orbit of self-interest by reducing it to the expression of an altruism that can itself be calibrated and expressed in the dosage proper to the giver's underlying utilitarianism – an example, *par excellence*, of disciplinary imperialism.[9] This reduction of the gift to an underlying utilitarianism indeed strikes one as a denial of a more pristine and popular principle of generosity.[10] Thus appearing as a triumph of selfishness, the economic absorption of the gift could be read as another *mise-en-scène* of that conversion of Adam Smith from a moral philosopher concerned with sympathy to a political economist smitten by self-interest, which is the mystery stock of traditional histories of economics. And to be sure, this appearance of a victory of selfishness over generosity would not be false: orthodox economics does celebrate the principle of self-interest, and selfishness is but the fleshy form of this principle; with public spaces and social sympathies increasingly channeled into market patterns, and as we find ourselves carried down the tracks of a sociality engineered in selfishness, we indeed seem to confront the fading of poetic sociality.

There are, however, two reasons why matters cannot rest with a simple opposition between selfishness and generosity.[11] The first is, as Mirowski (2001) shows, that a simply moral opposition to selfishness has not been an effective tool for critics of economics.[12] As we have seen (see notes 9–11), economists have found effective ways of resisting the more radical moral critiques, absorbing generosity and altruism into the utilitarian terrain. The absorption effectively resists the impulses to the extent that it provides orthodox economics with a perfectly plausible defense against charges of ethical indifference: indeed, as we have seen, a form of generosity is even "analytically" authorized in economists' construction and, in the face of this authorization, the charge of ethical lapse loses its sticking power. In order to keep the gift from being swallowed by economics, it is thus not sufficient to oppose generosity to self-interest; the conditions for a recovery of the gift (and of poetic – ethical and political – sociality) are more likely to be found, instead, in an exposure and critique of the paradigmatic operation by which economics does the otherwise unthinkable: reshaping generosity in the image of self-interest.

The second reason matters cannot rest with a simple opposition between self-ishness and generosity is that we would, in that case, find ourselves unable to account for the rich anthropological legacy of the gift. As is well known, the legacy of the gift is not exhausted by the mode of generosity, nor by the opposi-tion between generosity and selfishness, but encompasses a variety of more "total" social modes (aggression, ceremony, etc.) through which social agents (groups and institutions as well as individuals) symbolically and materially perform their relationships. In this respect, of course, Mauss's text, with its Durkheimian inspiration and attention to the "poison" meaning of the gift, remains seminal. In economics, however, the discussion has been conducted as if it were simply a matter of accommodating generosity, and the "total" dimension of the gift has remained invisible. Now, the absence of this otherwise well-known dimension in the economic reconfiguration of the gift would be perplexing indeed, except that one cannot help suspecting that the invisibility might itself be paradigmatic, a necessary condition of the gift's absorption into utilitarianism. The richer anthropological legacy of the gift produces a spilling of the self beyond the utilitarian parameters. Moreover, the contrast between economists' impoverished opposition between selfishness and generosity and anthropologists' richer understanding of the gift suggests, in the end, a contrast between different constructions of sociality – between different ways of constructing the "self" and "society," and indeed different configurations of "interest" and "generosity." If we are not to be complicit in occluding the richer understanding of sociality that the gift can give, then, our gaze must extend beyond the simple opposition between self-interest and generosity. For this reason too we must discover, precisely in order to look beyond them, the epistemic conditions for the invisi-bility in economics of the gift's richer legacy.

What, then, might underlie the ability of economics to restrict and absorb the gift? I would like to suggest that this underlying condition is the image of the economy as a *world of goods*, and of the world of goods as a *homogeneous field*. This image explains simultaneously the intellectual poverty with which economists have defined, and the ease with which they have absorbed, the gift; in fact it reveals that this poverty of definition and ease of absorption are but two sides of the same epistemic coin. I begin with a brief discussion of the function of self-interest in a structuralist concept of society and of the need of this concept to neutralize (exorcise, by absorption) the gift. I then show that self-interest can play the structuralist function given to it only if it is itself conceived as a behavioral trait defined over a homogeneous space of goods. It will thus become clear that it is this premise of goods homogeneity, rather than any originary ethical lapse on the part of economists, that permits the centrality of self-interest which requires the gift's exorcism. And it will also become clear that, while serving as a condition for the exorcism/absorption of the gift, the homogeneity premise requires as its own condition precisely the invisibility of the anthropological legacy of the gift. After all this, then: QED, the economic absorption of the gift and the poverty of economics relative to anthropology are indeed but two sides (the first an effect, and the second a condition) of the disciplined epistemology of economics: it knows the good, and what it knows are the goods.

Albert Hirschman (1977) traced the Enlightenment transformation of the conceptual center of society as a political problem of social order: from "passions" that, ultimately untamable, could at most be politically managed (a pre-eighteenth-century view), to calculable "interests" that could be folded directly into a mechanism of social gravity (a post-eighteenth-century view). This Enlightenment transformation goes some way towards explaining why the generosity of the gift rubs economics the wrong way: the problem of society as an order or structure requires in principle that every action be connected with every other action in a *measured* (that is, analytically calculable) way; the gift, were it not collapsed into reciprocity, would threaten this calculability condition. Adam Smith's metaphorical construction of the economy as a system of gravity was inscribed within an emerging conception of society as a mechanism, the parts of which were connected to each other through the type of precise fittings (every turn of a wheel producing a measured turn of another) with which clock-makers were beginning to make time: every act of giving requiring a precise balance of taking.[13] Born by analogy with celestial mechanics, economics had to transform giving and taking into buying and selling – a giving-and-taking, in other words, with no room for the give-and-take that, Bourdieu would say, makes the charm of life.

But the idea of a social *structure*, though it explains the function of the concept of interest, does not explain what in the nature of interest allows it to perform that function. The ability of interest to perform its required function must be explained independently, and it is here that one can appreciate the importance of the epistemological construction of the economy (and society) as a homogeneous field of goods: *the order of things is a condition of, a substitute for, the order of persons*. In order for interest to function as a trustworthy calibrator of individuals' behavior, composable into a mechanism of social order such as a market system, there must first be a field over and through which interest can be calculated in a stable and consistent manner across space (individuals) and time (society). The episte-mological condition by which interest could be presented as the central code of the social was, thus, the construction (unacknowledged, as epistemic conditions often are) of a field over which interests could be connectively measured. The economists' homogeneous field of goods is just such a field.[14] This presumption of a homogeneous field of goods underlies *all* constructions of the economy and of the market as a mechanism and can therefore be thought of as *the* epistemo-logical condition of economics. The presumption explains the theoretical –

universalizing and disciplining – humanism peculiar to bourgeois rationality, wherein emancipation consists of the ability to navigate over the world of goods freely, unimpeded by, for example, traditions and social obligations – untouched, that is, by the poetry in intercourse with nature or community.[15] Significantly, it also explains the special place that value theory has traditionally had in economics, with the value field providing both measure and borders – that is, homogeneity – to the goods field.

Now, not only is the gift unnecessary in such a construction, but it may actually be incompatible with it: when gifting does take place, to the extent that it introduces any difficulty of calibration, it becomes a theoretical bother. (Indeed, this seems to be the key point of economic anthropology: that gifting is inscribed in systems of reciprocities that are uncertain in form – appearing either as generosity or hostility, or an undecidable combination thereof – and in calibration: the timing, quality, and quantity of the return.) More than a bother, in fact, from the perspective of the exchange system, the introduction of an uncalculable reciprocity appears as a throwback to the "passions" and the problem of their political management. Thus, the only way in which the gift could be included in the economists' cast of characters was for it to be shorn, by baptism and/or exorcism, of its extra-utilitarian dimensions. From this the absorption and definitional poverty of the gift in economics soon follow.

Some might think that Becker-type economists exhibit ingenuity in reducing the world of human affections (and therefore of the gift) to utilitarian principles, but it is not difficult to see that this ingenuity consists of nothing more than a mechanical (if gutsy) expansion of the logic of goods homogeneity; given the inclination, the operation is easily performed whenever and wherever "the goods" are invoked. Not much depth of thought is necessary to realize that the economists' concept of altruism is merely the obverse of self-interest and does not challenge either the parameters of the social or the nature of the self that economics has traditionally constructed: whereas self-interest is about getting the goods for oneself, altruism is about the goods of another, but the construction remains entirely about the goods. If economics can so easily fit altruism into self-referential utility functions, that is because selfishness and generosity are, for it, but two sides of the same coin, two alternative but not contrasting, let alone problematically conjoined or incompatible, ways in which the calculus over the world of goods can be conducted. The other to whom the goods are given can function as much as a utilitarian machine as can the giver and is therefore but a functional equivalent of the giver.[16] In fact, once one gives prominence to the world of goods and to the homogeneity of the economic space thus constructed, altruism can as easily yield to economic calculus as can selfishness. As I have already suggested, this construction even authorizes generosity.[17] But authority also implies discipline, and it will be clear, in fact, that the nature of this altruism remains limited by the utilitarian character of the body that manifests it – limited, that is, to a matter of a "preference" to see another consume goods – and cannot become a more general, more open, alterity. In other words, the only quality of the gift that economics can absorb is that of a calculable generosity, and, clearly, the condition for this absorption (so that the absorption does not contaminate the utilitarian construction) is the invisibility of the other qualities given in the anthropological legacy of the gift.

These are the ways, then, that the exorcism – an impoverishment of the gift and its absorption into economics – was enabled, even compelled, by the imperialistic sweep of the epistemology of goods homogeneity. But these ways sharply contrast with the wealth of anthropological imagination and the depth of philosophical inquiry that the gift has historically drawn out and beckons us to recall – invoking Derrida and even a Derridean Mauss. Derrida's work on the gift, moving the ethical (and political) in the direction of radical alterity, has in mind an other that would be irreducible even to a complexly constructed self, let alone to that utility function deployed over a homogeneous field of goods through which the order of persons is regulated by the order of things. In this Derridean context, the appeal of Mauss's *Gift* might come from its suggestion that the order of persons cannot be reduced to the order of things – this, more than any mystical fusion of goods and people, must be the intent of Mauss's lament that Malinowski's original venture into the gift suffered from the Western differentiation between persons and things.[18] In contrast to the economists' absorption of the gift into exchange, the Derridean perspective, by pointing toward a "totally-other other," can link the gift to an irreducible ethical and political sphere. By refusing to reduce it to reciprocity, Derrida claims an irreducible heterogeneity for the gift; he therefore suggests how we might replace the social homogeneity (centricity, essentialism, modernism) produced in the economistic equation of things and persons with a social *heterogeneity* embedded in a culture of ethical and political performativity.

Given the cultural dominance of economics, however, the path to such a replacement will need to be carved against the grain. To clear such a path, therefore, we must break the force of the image of goods homogeneity that so powerfully contains the gift in the circle of reciprocity, structure and homogeneity. A recovery of the gift that falls short of such a rupture will also fail to deliver the theoretical means to restore the gift to a site of intellectual knowledge. It is with this shortfall in mind that I posited, in the first section of the paper, a difference between the thread we would be unraveling and the approaches of two other critics of neoclassicism, the economist Philip Mirowski and the anthropologist Stephen Gudeman. While Mirowski and Gudeman do indeed rescue the gift from the invisibility given to it by economics, their rescue fails to question the very disciplinarity of economics and underlying epistemology of goods homogeneity that has tipped the scales toward the reciprocity pole of the gift. As an economist, Mirowski denaturalizes the traditional, essentialist, economic conception of the *value field*, instead highlighting its social construction: he argues that goods do not *have* value; rather, the value field is constructed (through social measuring practices and through analytico-mathematical representations) and symbolically attached to goods. While Mirowski's value field, like the traditional value field, leaves no room for the gift, the gift still remains visible outside the value system, and indeed remains capable of upsetting that system.[19] Gudeman's concern is, naturally, anthropological, and for him, given the concept of community as a system of reciprocal relations, the gift, embodying both the potential for and uncertainty of reciprocity, functions in relation to strangers as an offer of community: the gift is what invites community, but community itself only comes after the gift, or after the gift has been resolved into reciprocity. But while both Mirowski and Gudeman thus rescue the gift from the oblivion of neoclassicism – the one by de-essentializing the economists' value and the other by questioning the origin of community – the space they open for the gift remains at the margins of the social. The rescue they perform therefore does not undermine the concept of society as a system of reciprocities that is originally responsible for the exorcism of the gift, and one wonders if the gift so rescued has any enhanced capacity to resist the call of the exorcist, authorized as that is by economic disciplinarity, and thus all the more clearly audible for the impoverished, uniform code of bourgeois "virtue."

The thread we have been unraveling suggests that the deliverance of the gift must take place in a deconstructive relation to the very idea of the social: that is, the discussion must move beyond the question of whether the gift is inside or outside of society. If the gift offers possibilities for intellectual enrichment and for a recovery of ethical and political performativity, those possibilities will not be charted on the inside or outside of society – or even at the very border between inside and outside the circle (value, or community), since the existence of borders is what authorizes the very idea of the inside. Those possibilities will come instead out of the gift's eroding effects on the very notion of borders.[20] As I will argue next, in a way that arches back to the "visor effect" of the ghost, the possibilities of the gift are inscribed in its ability to distance theorists *of* the gift from the concept of the social and thus allow us to to gaze upon it – to suspend the social, as it were, in a gap above any geography of borders – and to evoke the suturings of the ethical and the political. This approach, to be sure, will expand the focus beyond the gift *qua* object of analysis (within society; within or without, but nonetheless in a specified relation to, borders) to encompass it *qua* perspective, *qua* Other from which to keep perspective on the notion of the social (or economy or disciplinarity). This expansiveness will reveal what the gift gives to us, and especially to economists: the freedom to transcend the narrow borders within which economic disciplinarity would keep us, and thus to retain the grounds for ethics and politics. From the site of *perspective* (and hence of the *other*), the ghost of the gift would return.

Re-enter the ghost!

Contrary to what is sometimes asserted, Derrida does not argue that the gift is impossible. He says that the gift is *the impossible*, which is much stronger and quite different.

> If the figure of the circle [i.e., return, reciprocity, calculation] is essential to economics, the gift must remain *aneconomic*. Not that it remains foreign to the

circle, but it must *keep* a relation of foreignness to the circle, a relation without relation of familiar foreignness. It is in this sense that the gift is the impossible. Not impossible, but the impossible. The very figure of the impossible.

(Derrida 1992: 7; emphasis in original)

For Derrida the gift exists as a Heideggerian *Dasein*, as event. In fact, only because "there is gift" can there be a philosophical (and intellectual) problem wrapped in it: the word gift

> would not name what one thinks it names, to wit, the unity of a meaning that would be that of the gift. Unless the gift were the impossible but not the unnameable or the unthinkable, and unless in this gap between the impossible and the thinkable a dimension opens up where *there is* gift – and even where *there is* period, for example time, where it *gives* being and time (*es gibt das Sein* or *es gibt die Zeit*, to say it in a way that anticipates excessively what would be precisely a certain *essential excess* [emphasis added] of the gift, indeed an excess of the gift over the essence itself).
>
> (1992: 10)

The gift's aporia speaks not to *its* impossibility, then, but to *the impossible*, and yet *given*, combination of the possibility and impossibility of the gift. So, lying neither on this side nor on the other of the (im)possible but in the gap between the impossible and the thinkable, the gift cannot be mapped on a geography of borders. Thus we find Derrida, representing the gift, using a term that moves it beyond the calculable, as a state of *excess* – a state that, he makes sure to note, marked the gift's first appearance in anthropology: "The madness that insinuates itself even into Mauss's text is a certain excess of the gift" (Derrida 1992: 45). Throughout *Given Time* Derrida expresses the excess of the gift over the circle (that is, the economy of goods or the economy of identity, knowledge, time, consciousness, or even an economy of the unconscious) in a way that does not deny the circle but tries instead to *keep* the "relation without relation of familiar foreignness" (Derrida 1992: 7) to it. He does this by combining *desire* and *responsibility*. Unable to be satisfied and disciplined, desire has no economy and is itself *excess* over economy. But the gift is nonetheless excess *over economy* and must thus keep its relation to the circle of reciprocity, to the idea of a "return." Thus, if *Given Time* works throughout on the moment of the gift's separation from economy, it ends (in a long, absorbing deconstruction of Baudelaire's "Counterfeit money") by reinscribing the gift within a form of reciprocity, *responsibility*: what responsibility do people have to use well (that is, to "return") the gifts that nature has given them? Moreover, in a way that captures the excess of the gift over *itself*, Derrida anticipates the reinscription of the gift in the circle of responsibility in the very opening pages of *Given Time*, where the very figure of desire itself is the desire to give (back).

Desire, the desire to give back (response/ibility), excess – a gap perhaps, but not borders between the impossible and the thinkable. ... Now *re-enter the gift* in *relation to* economy, society, community, neither inside its border (as social science would have it, whether as a form of exchange or as the center of society), nor outside its border (the fact that disturbs the regime of value, or the origin, and thus still out, of society), but in a "relation without relation of familiar foreignness" to it, as it were: *the gift, then, is neither in economy, nor out of it, but in excess over it.* In a way, Gudeman's and Mirowski's recuperations could not help but pass through a geography of borders, for in the face of the invisibility of the gift within economics, its specter cannot but emerge from the outside. Yet, even if it must seize the moment of the outside, the gift cannot remain there, lest its position confirm the border and thus reaffirm the inside that has historically so efficiently absorbed it and would no doubt re-absorb it. A continued presence of disciplinary borders reproduces a dichotomy between the economic and the (political and ethical as) non-economic and privileges the economic. In this context, Mirowski argues that the temptation "to creat[e] a space within economics for ethics … is a tender trap" (2001: 450; see note 12) and concludes that critical economists must instead formulate an alternative theory of value. But as valuable as such a formulation might be, basing an opposition to orthodox economics on it accepts the givenness of disciplinarity and permits an all-too-easy evacuation of the ethical.[21] The gift, its aporia and the state of excess that condenses its two sides, would be useful precisely insofar as it would allow us to go beyond the traditional dichotomy of ethics and economy, or of the economic and the non-economic, and to think differently of the relationship between them, such that the ethical (or the non-economic) can overflow the economy while still responding to it (that is, be precisely in excess over economy) – as the gift, in Derrida, overflows knowledge and yet enjoins one to take responsibility for knowledge: to respond to it, to give a return of a kind.

Re-enter the ghost, then, haunting disciplinarity, conjuring the unlikelihood of economics. By threatening disciplinary consequences, the ghost will speak to unsettle the certainty of borders, produce the visor effect on what is on the inside and shake its confidence, bringing into question its sub- and objectivity. But whence does the ghost return and to whom does it speak? While rescuing the gift from the oblivion of economics, Mirowski also rescues it from the natural essentialism that characterizes romantic anthropological accounts of the gift as the foundation of the social. That the gift will not return from nature, that it is not inscribed in an essence and that it is not a matter of returning to an origin, are points that Derrida also makes in *Given Time.* Our given is that the relation between gift and economy lies within one horizon, variously characterizable as imaginary, discursive, cultural, ideological, analytical. The gift and exchange mutually define each other: "Gifts are an attempt to transcend the system of value; but that system transcendence already presupposes some form of monetary structure. Without money (or some similar imposition of equivalence classes), there is no 'outside' to which to escape" (Mirowski 2001: 453–4). Unanchored in an origin outside of and yet not bound within economy, the gift can return only as something that invites playing with the inside and outside, in the form of a gaze which, itself unseen behind the visor, unsettles economists' confident borders. Mirowski, although he problematizes the border between gift and economy by making the inside the condition of the outside, stops short of playing with it. While he correctly concludes that, since the gift acquires meaning only in relation to exchange, it is not possible to ground exchange on the gift, he also concludes something that does not necessarily follow, namely that the critique of orthodox economics (and of the selfishness it celebrates) cannot draw on the gift, or draw inspiration from the gift. For him, the critique must move within, and he thus embraces the disciplinarity of economics, privileging the task of developing an alternative theory of value. Correctly explaining the undecidability of the gift as the result of its simultaneously being inside and outside economy, Mirowski simply accepts the *fact* of the gift and does the considerable intellectual work necessary to make room for this fact, but he does not seize the opportunity the gift gives to stand back and gaze upon the very idea of economy. It is possible, however, accepting Derrida's strategy, to develop such a gaze, taking the undecidability of *the thing* as an opportunity not only to read the gift in relation to economy, to make the inside a condition of the outside, but also to read economy in relation to the gift, to make the gift the standard by which to gaze upon economy, to make the outside a condition of the inside, and to feel this conditionality as a moment of dispersal of the borders. While accepting Mirowski's insight that the gift is constructed in relation to value, one can also argue that value's own identity is constructed in relation to the gift. In this mutuality of reference there can be play: instead of making the gift more decidable, seeing it from the solidity of the circle of value, we can see the economists' very circle of value (regimes of calculations, suturings of the social space, homogenizations of social identities, needs and desires) as itself undecidable, an impossible and yet thinkable attempt to close off the undecidabilities of the gift.

To be clear, this is not only a matter of the instability (uncertainty, undecidability) of the value regime, which is a question within economics. It is more a matter of opening up a gap where would lie the borders that constitute the very idea of a circle of value, a gap that would contain the simultaneous inevitability and impossibility of this idea. It is not a matter, in other words, of coming up with a theory of value or exchange that can highlight how economies are socially constructed, and thus realizing that the value regimes that encode them are contingent and fluid, capable even of accepting the gift; nor is it a matter of resurrecting the anthropologists' task of making the gift the center of sociality, for that too would keep the gift on the inside and eliminate its intellectual excess. It is instead a matter, first of all, of how to retain a perspective on the economists' circle of value, neither accepting nor being bound by a limiting disciplinarity. Only by keeping perspective, or gaze, can we keep "relation without relation of familiar foreignness" with the circle, thereby permitting us to envisage the excess over it. A remarkable example: "From each according to his abilities, to each according to his needs."[22] Perhaps! Economists cannot make disciplinary sense of such poetic sociality that, like Marx's, would break the homogeneous reciprocity that undergirds their economy. Their confident refusal of poetic sociality rests on the solidity of their circle of value. Yet suggestions of poetic sociality retain their ethical and political power, remaining compelled by, it would seem, a desire – desire itself, the desire to give – by a *hau* inscribed in a circle much larger than the economist's circle, a *hau* we need not explain, but only accept poetically, as what is *given*. This gift summons itself as the specter that gazes upon the economists' circle of value, producing the visor effect, haunting the economists' circle and yet keeping the "relation of a relation of familiar foreignness" with it. We gain our perspective by gazing with it.

In this respect, the most significant condition of value theory is perhaps its historical heterogeneity, which is as good as if the history of economics had been punctuated by periodic appearances of the specter of the gift to break one circle with another, in an incessant process to keep the circle in the gap between the impossible and the thinkable, between economy and generosity, between the objectivity and the subjectivity of economy. Beyond the analytics of this or that value theory – which, of course, economists have the professional responsibility to dissect – what will loom large in any outer glance at the discipline, and what does loom large in everyday consciousness, is analytical heterogeneity, that which is arguably irreducible. To the traditional classical and neoclassical theories of value, we may now add other, so-called overdeterminist approaches, for which Mirowski indeed provides more stringent mathematical conditions. This simple fact of the heterogeneity of value tends to be neglected in most histories, which give the impression that the history of economics can only be reconstructed as a search for one common value principle and consequently domesticate the heterogeneity around a presumed common *logos*. Mirowski's reconstruction, though making room for the gift, follows this pattern. And yet, there is perhaps more truth, or at least as much truth, in the outsider's historiographical gaze upon economics as a fragmented discipline characterized by the absence, rather than the presence, of a common value principle. This absence of a common value principle seems to me characteristic of the discipline and certainly of its historiographical condition. *Given* this history, one could argue that only hope, not any sense of realism, motivates anyone who, like Mirowski, believes that any single theory of value settles any ethico-ideological matters. The undecidability of the gift, *per contra*, signifies the undecidability of value, an undecidability that expresses itself within economics as a heterogeneity of value. The absence of a common value principle: it is in the presence of this absence that the ethical and the political can return to give force to poetic sociality.

Notes

I wish to thank Jack Amariglio, Stephen Gudeman, Colin Danby, Yahya Mete Madra, Philip Mirowski, David Ruccio, Richard Wolff and Eiman Zein-Elabdin for comments they made on various versions of this paper. I benefited from their comments even when I did not follow their leads.

1 "Enter the ghost, exit the ghost, re-enter the ghost." Derrida quotes from *Hamlet* in *Specters of Marx* (1994: xx). I have used the three clauses of this stage direction as titles for this paper's three parts.

2 "A specter is haunting Europe" are the opening words of the *Communist Manifesto*.

3 Homi Bhabha uses an analogous construction to treat Franz Fanon's production of a postcolonial presence through tropes of invisibility (the "evil eye," and the "secret art of Invisible-Ness") that destabilize, in depth and time, Western identities of slave and master: "The gaze of the evil eye alienates both the narratorial I of the slave and the surveillant eye of the master. It unsettles any simplistic polarities or binarisms in identifying the exercise of power – Self/Other." The analogy extends to the gap, as Bhabha refers to a "strategy of duplicity or doubling (not resemblance …), which Lacan ["Alienation," in *The Four Fundamental Concepts of Psychoanalysis*] has elaborated as 'the process of gap' within which the relation of subject to Other is produced" (Bhabha 1994: 53–5).

4 Derrida is more concerned with the ethical than with the political. However, insofar as both can be defined by their suturing abilities, the Derridean gap can, *mutatis mutandis*, introduce the political as well as the ethical. Bhabha's concern (see note 3) is more political.

5 Of course, the gap is eventually closed somehow: one pole or the other, at one time or another, the one (giver) or the other (recipient), or a particular mix of one and other, will always put its face on the thing. Now, insofar as there is a gift event, one might say at least that which of the two poles will prevail must remain unknown beforehand – were it known beforehand, one would speak directly of exchange or of generosity, with nothing left of the charm Bourdieu speaks of in my epigraph. But the instability of the gift is not simply a matter of not knowing beforehand how the contradiction between generosity and reciprocity might play itself out; in whatever way the contradiction or ambivalence plays itself out, the name of the gift must continue to echo the possibility that things "might (have) proceed(ed) otherwise": Bourdieu's charm must be after-effect as well as pre-condition of the gift.

6 Mirowski writes: "As [Mary] Douglas insists [in her introduction to Mauss's *Gift*], to give with no discernible interest as to consequences is to deny the very existence of social ties" (2001: 447).

7 In the third section, we will see that Derrida resolves the fundamental aporia of the gift, the source of its instability and undecidability, exactly into the concept of responsibility.

8 Whereas Malinowski introduced the concept of the gift in a more positivist way, Mauss's Durkheimian approach absorbed the gift's more symbolic and ceremonial functions. As Mirowski reports, Mauss accused Malinowski of basing his account of the gift on the false opposition (in Western positivism) between persons and things. Mauss's account of the gift, then, is itself written within a gap that refuses the fixed separation of subjects and objects upon which Western knowledge is based.

9 In the 1970s economists began increasingly to attend to norms of social behavior that seemed at odds with the principle of self-interest. To the extent that such behavior existed – or, even more significantly, seemed to produce efficient social outcomes – the economists' theory of social organization, dependent as it was on a model of self-interest, seemed threatened. The responses of market-centered economists to such ideas as Titmuss's gift relationships and Kenneth Boulding's grants economy are reviewed extensively by Mirowski (1994, 2001) and Fontaine and, in passing, by Harcourt (1983). In response to this intervention, economics sought to reabsorb the gift. However, I would characterize this concern with the gift as merely a disturbance of, rather than a rupture with, the disciplinarity of economics, because it quickly subsided, to be resuscitated only more recently by feminist economics. The question of the gift has traditionally been formulated in relation to some concept of society, but, to the extent that society has been understood as a "structure" (as opposed to, say, a "performance"), the concern with the gift has been unproductive. On the one hand, the simple recognition of the "fact" of the gift did nothing to change the concept of society itself and thus left the gift out there as a kind of dangling modifier. On the other hand, as Mirowski explains (2001), when the gift was offered as an

alternative to exchange as a structural principle, it inevitably seemed to slip back into a form of exchange. The sterility of simply insisting on the "fact" of the gift and the impossibility of the gift to substitute for exchange are why it makes sense to use other ways, such as our ghostly analogy, to discuss its relationship to exchange economics.

10 A variation on this subsumption to utilitarianism considers gift giving (e.g., blood donation) as a practice undertaken in the absence of certain requisite market conditions – for example, symmetric information. This approach is based on the neoclassical logic of the market's efficiency in organizing the circulation of goods in society (this is a self-evident logic, once efficiency is defined as a maximization of utility and utility functions, or preferences, are given to individuals, who are thus the only ones capable of determining what transactions will yield them the most utility). This approach, however, still aims to reject the gift (and along with it, all forms of sociality other than market processes), since it produces the social conditions that would allow such interaction to become exchange. An example of this social engineering is the creation, in the USA, of markets for the trading of state-issued pollution permits.

11 In fact, the ways of exorcism can be all absorbing. Fontaine outlines how some economists (e.g., a certain Culyer) have used exactly the concept of generosity to absorb into economics not only the idea of the gift but also the practice of gift giving. Distinguishing between altruism as a mode of interpersonal relations and generosity as a behavioral trait (i.e., actually giving), Culyer argues that although preferences were what they were and could not be themselves changed through social policies, actual behavior could be changed by giving people incentives, that is, by changing the cost-benefit calculations behind their generosity. In this sense, economists could argue that their absorbing the gift into the calculus of self-interest is actually motivated by a desire to induce more giving. It is a short step from there to arguing that the very organization of giving should be left to the market, thereby analytically devaluing institutional (including state) modes of gift giving or redistribution. Thus economists have spoken of the presence of a "charity market." This analytical operation was complemented by rhetorical references to Aristotelian-inspired reflections on the virtue-enhancing powers of private giving. However, this Aristotelian garb violates the logic of economics (hence I say that references to it are merely rhetorical) because, as I will try to show, the logic of economic analysis is based on a metaphysical representation of value as a property of goods, not of social relations among people. Thus, whereas the rhetoric of virtues must refer to relations between people, economic logic treats the world of goods as a system in itself.

12 Mirowski describes the "attempt to define liberal or left politics as creating a space *within economics* [emphasis added] for ethics or communal goals or generosity or compassion" as "a tender trap" (2001: 450). Morever, he continues, "as soon as these ideas about generosity are mooted in public, they are neutralized by the rhetoric and reality" of politics. "For to 'give' communally one must 'give' reasons to get support, and then the protagonists become desperately embroiled in the calculations of cost and benefit, the apparent antithesis of the gift."

13 Merchant provides the classic statement of this thesis. In "Economics as a patriarchal discourse" (Callari 1996) I use Merchant's basic insight to discuss the birth of economics as inevitably patriarchal.

14 Mirowski (1991) identifies the mathematical conditions for a theory of value, and the most significant of these conditions, for our purposes, is the construction of a "commodity space." Implicit in Mirowski's treatment is the idea that a "commodity space," or "homogeneous field of goods" is the product of a particular episteme, a discursive construction. Among economic anthropologists, Karl Polanyi (1968) best understood this point, but his insight has not been sufficiently explored and developed. On this last point, see my "Towards an anthropology of economics" (Callari n.d.)

15 The bourgeois form of property is different from other forms of property because of the greater degree to which ownership over goods and resources is absolute, not bound by tradition, or by such legal forms as use-rights.

16 Two different scenarios are possible here. In one scenario, the recipient's enjoyment of the goods can remain an element in the giver's utility function. This is the simple case. The more complex scenario envisages the recipient's expression of a separate utility calculation. This last scenario provides ample opportunities for economists to display their mechanical skills, to describe the possible interactions between giver and recipient and calculate the efficiency outcomes. Mirowski (2001) presents a number of interesting examples.

17 We have seen (in footnote 11) how, working within the logic of this construction, some economists distinguished between altruism (a desire to see others consume) and generosity (actual willingness to give).These economists must have been in full form, for the distinction enabled them to analyze how these altruistic, but still inherently selfish, persons would strategize in order to have others give the goods – this being a case of what, in economics, is known as the free-rider problem. The predictable upshot of this discussion was that the best way to organize "charity" was to leave it as a private matter, a charity market yielding a more efficient outpouring of generosity than, say, social redistribution programs. All of this is outlined in Fontaine 1999. This calculative dexterity exemplifies the ability of economics to produce analytically sound ethical nonsense.

18 Derrida himself laments that social scientists, including Mauss, have failed to explore the philosophical horizons the gift makes visible: "This problematic of the difference … between 'the gift exists' and 'there is gift' is never, as we know, deployed or even approached by Mauss, no more than it seems to be, to my knowledge, by the anthropologists who come after him or refer to him" (1992: 26). Nonetheless, while it is true that Mauss does not directly cross the philosophical bridge between the gift's existence and *Dasein*, his refusal to structure his work around the distinction between persons and things is an act of philosophical courage.

19 In "Postmodernism and the social theory of value" (1991), Mirowski has outlined such a value theory. In contrast to other value theories, Mirowski gives us a value world which, instead of expressing the single presumed essence (labor or utility calculation) of economizing behavior, is but a monetary condensation of multiple, possibly conflicting, behaviors, tendencies and forces. Whereas other theories could not accept the gift because it compromised their need to map value unequivocally against an essence such as distribution of labor or of utilitarian preferences, Mirowski's value regime need not express any given essence and can acknowledge the gift and its disturbing effects.

   Into this framework Mirowski fits the gift as an element that, though it derives its significance from and contrasts with the value regime, yet threatens its structure by removing commodities from the monetary flow. In "Refusing the gift" (2001), Mirowski outlines a value regime, or "value invariance" standard [one or more theoretically specifiable set(s) of money prices, the observance of which would structurally link into one system the multiple and separate acts of exchange] which combines systemic (top-down, monetary control) forces and particularistic (bottom-up, self-interest) forces and reflects a mix of intended and unintended effects. It is, moreover, unstable, its theoretical specificity notwithstanding – Mirowski writes that "the tensions between the bottom-up and top-down forces are what allow it to be cast in the language of self-organized criticality – because it is always 'compromised,' 'challenged,' or 'circumvented' from top (monetary forces) and bottom (innovations, theft, bargaining, gifts)" (2001: 452).

20 This is different from positing the gift as the origin of society, which is what Gudeman (2001) does. Positing the gift as origin does not question the constitution of society as bordered, as a system of reciprocity; indeed, it confirms that conception, since it is

the very absence of unequivocal reciprocity that defines the gift as outside of or prior to society. The representation of the gift as eroding the bordered character of the social instead conveys a refusal to think of the inside or the outside, and hence of any origin, of the social and a consequent refusal to place the gift either outside or inside of the social. For a related critique of Gudeman's concept of the social, see Mark Osteen's introduction to this volume.

21 Mirowski's proposed turn away from the ethical and towards the analytical as a strategy for the left implies a dubious confidence in disciplinarity. To eschew the ethical and rely exclusively on the analytical, one would need some reassurance that the analytical is quite powerful in itself and rhetorically effective. Mirowski is right to note that the resort to "ethical" arguments has been a "trap," but he has not noted the equally remarkable failure of any analytical opposition to the cultural hegemony of orthodox economics, a failure that has little connection to the abstract theoretical disputes that have punctuated the heterodox theories of value. Clearly, neither an "ethical" nor an "analytical" opposition has succeeded. One suspects, rather, that the root of the failure lies in the very belief in the separability of the ethical and the analytical. One must therefore erase this separability. This cannot be done by bringing ethics into economics (as Mirowski rightly argues), nor can it be done by making the economic ethical – in short, by retaining the distinction between the two, the inside and the outside, and then trying to merge one into the other: the merger is epistemically outlawed. However, it can be done if, with the gift, the separation between the two is itself eroded.

22 Interestingly, the sentence in which this principle appears is marked by the traces of a material "excess," which we might place in a relation of *différence* with the "excess" of the gift. Marx writes: "In a higher phase of communist society … after labor has become not only a means of life but life's prime *want*, after … the springs of cooperative wealth flow more *abundantly* – only then can the narrow horizon of bourgeois right be crossed in its entirety and society inscribe on its banners: from each according to his ability, to each according to his needs" (Marx 1938: 10; emphasis added). Of course, the notion of an overflowing of material wealth is no longer tenable in itself, and the condition of socialism or communism would be more in the overflowing, the excess, of the ethical and political over the circle of economic necessity. In this sense, recovering the gift in excess over economy would constitute a prelude to a gift theory of Marxism.

References

Bhabha, Homi K. *The Location of Culture*. London and New York: Routledge, 1994.

Bourdieu, Pierre. *The Logic of Practice*. Trans. Richard Nice. Stanford: Stanford University Press, 1990.

Callari, Antonio. "Some developments in Marxian theory since Schumpeter." In W.O. Thweatt (ed.) *Classical Political Economy*. Boston: Kluwer Academic, 1988, pp. 227–58.

—— "Economics as a patriarchal discourse." In Laurence S. Moss (ed.) *Joseph A. Schumpeter, Historian of Economics: Perspectives on the History of Economic Thought*. London and New York: Routledge, 1996, pp. 260–76.

—— "Towards an anthropology of economics." Unpublished manuscript, n.d.

Derrida, Jacques. *Given Time: I. Counterfeit Money*. Trans. Peggy Kamuf. Chicago: University of Chicago Press, 1992.

—— *Specters of Marx*. Trans. Peggy Kamuf. New York and London: Routledge, 1994.

—— *The Gift of Death*. Trans. David Wills. Chicago: University of Chicago Press, 1995.

Fontaine, Philippe. "Ethics and the market: Richard Titmuss and the economists on the gift relationship." Presented at the 26th annual meeting of the History of Economics Society. Greensboro: University of North Carolina, 1999.

Gudeman, Stephen. "Postmodern gifts." In Stephen Cullenberg, Jack Amariglio and David F. Ruccio (eds) *Postmodernism, Economics, and Knowledge*. London and New York: Routledge, 2001, pp. 459–74.

Harcourt, G.C. "A man for all systems: talking with Kenneth Boulding." *Journal of Post-Keynesian Economics* 6.1 (Fall 1983): 143–54.

Heidegger, Martin. *An Introduction to Metaphysics*. New Haven and London: Yale University Press, 1987.

Hirschman, Albert O. *The Passions and the Interests. Political Arguments for Capitalism Before Its Triumph*. Princeton: Princeton University Press, 1977.

—— *Rival Views of Market Society*. Cambridge: Harvard University Press, 1992 [1986].

Marx, Karl. *Critique of the Gotha Programme*. New York: International Publishers, 1938.

Merchant, Carolyn. *The Death of Nature: Women, Ecology, and the Scientific Revolution*. New York: Harper & Row, 1980.

Mirowski, Philip. "Postmodernism and the social theory of value." *Journal of Post-Keynesian Economics*. 13.4 (1991): 565–82.

—— "Tit for tat: concepts of exchange, higgling, and barter in two episodes in the history of economic anthropology." In Neil De Marchi and Mary S. Morgan (eds) *Higgling: Transactors and Their Markets in the History of Economics*. Durham and London: Duke University Press, 1994, pp. 313–42.

—— "Refusing the gift." In Stephen Cullenberg, Jack Amariglio and David F. Ruccio (eds) *Postmodernism, Economics, and Knowledge*. London and New York: Routledge, 2001, pp. 431–58.

Polanyi, Karl. "Aristotle discovers the economy." In G. Dalton (ed.) *Primitive, Archaic, and Modern Economies*. Boston: Beacon Press, 1968, pp. 78–115.

13 Give the ghost a chance!
A comrade's shadowy addendum

Jack Amariglio

Antonio Callari's luminous essay casts a long and deep shadow. I prefer to think of these comments as living in that shadow. There is much to be said for the shade, or perhaps living both in and as a shade. For the shade, in the sense of Antonio's ghost, is both of and "other" than what it may shadow. While my comments are therefore an open acknowledgment of my trailing Antonio's paper, in both originality and luminescence, still I think that I can contribute something both of and other than what he has put forth. After all, since we have known each other and worked and written together (even lived together, for a spell) for close to thirty years, I think it befits such comrades to think of each other as both of and other. Whether, as he suggests is appropriate to shades and specters, these comments can produce the "visor-effect" and the keenness of sight he describes will be up to others (perhaps also living in/as shadows) to discern. There is no question, though, that in this particular instance, the epiphenomenon (my shadowy commentary) can do little to surpass the phenomenon (his vital analysis), nor is it intended to do so. Being of, secondarily, and other is all I can hope for at this juncture.

Being of and other is, in an important sense, the key analytic framework underlying the arguments Antonio Callari makes here about the relationship between the idea of the gift and the idea of exchange. Indeed, being of and other is also the relationship he describes as existing between academic economics proper (the discipline of economics, as a set of professional discourses about the terrain of "goods") and the discourses that have emerged over the past century about the gift. I would like to continue along the lines Antonio has laid out, probing some things a bit more to see whether I can show that gift and exchange are, indeed, constructed as both of and other than each other. Indeed, such a simultaneous desire for belonging, for identity, and for alterity characterizes many of the past debates on this matter. I will also take up the idea of chance (as in "give the ghost a chance") since much of importance in current distinctions between the gift and exchange rests upon the attribution of "indeterminacy" and "chance" to one concept of sociality as opposed to the other. Along these same lines, I will take up, if briefly, the issue so imperatively and poetically put by Antonio, that of the appropriate conception of sociality (gift or exchange) that necessarily implies the intervention – indeed, the very existence – of ethics and politics. For, as Antonio argues, the gift's gift to contemporary discourses, and perhaps its greatest threat – currently practiced as a haunting – to economists' notions of the social via "the economy" as a world of goods, is to make explicit the "responsibility" and the necessity of ethics that such gifting interactions imply in their undecidability.

My own point of departure (being of and other than Antonio's essay) is the question of the "impossibility of the gift." Antonio does Jacques Derrida justice in recovering what has been overlooked by some cultural and economic critics, which is that Derrida's gift is not only "impossible" but, moreover, marks the realm of "the impossible." It is this latter marking that Antonio explores, challenging the more one-sided reading of Derrida that some, such as Philip Mirowski, have proposed. Callari is right to challenge in particular Mirowski's reading, largely since Mirowski has also insightfully summarized and scrutinized the anthropological and economic literatures to demonstrate the "impossibility" of the gift so long as it remains within the same regime of value that characterizes exchange (that is, the regime within which value is a measuring device for the relationship between "equivalence classes"). Callari rightly questions Mirowski's glum but exaggerated conclusion that, like all anthropologists before him, Derrida cannot sustain the difference between exchange and gift, as the latter dissolves into the former. I will leave for now the question of which reading of Derrida is more satisfying and take up the question that intrigues me more.[1] And that is the question of the impossibility of exchange.

For there is no doubt that, for Mirowski and a host of others who conclude that reciprocity involves some notion, in the last instance, of equivalence (the master code underlying exchange) exchange remains largely unchallenged as to its own "possibility." To put this differently, it seems that exchange – understood as a site or activity in which notions of value are brought to bear and perhaps even actualized – is identical to itself, with no "shadow" or "ghost" to which it partly owes its own existence, of which it is both of and other. It is "present" and therefore "possible" precisely because it is thought to be a master code that, paradoxically, sublates any sublation. Exchange cannot be "reduced" to the gift, in this view. The gift is not exchange's shadow. The gift is only "of" exchange, and can rarely be truly "other."

Now, Antonio Callari argues that, to the contrary, the gift is what haunts economists' figure of exchange. Indeed, in some ways, exchange is a pale figure compared to the robustness of the gift, since the latter connotes forms of social practice that exchange is thought either to subordinate or transcend, such as ethics and politics. There is just as much benefit in thinking about exchange as simply "impossible" (but thinkable) since, as it is discursively constructed by most practicing economists, it occupies the perhaps ridiculous space of "self-reproduction" and therefore self-determination. This move – the claim that the realm of exchange, or for that matter any act of exchange, contains within itself most if not all of its conditions of existence – makes the figure of exchange exactly impossible. To borrow liberally here from Antonio (though I'm not sure he would authorize this reading), the impossibility of exchange ironically involves a veritable exorcism of the gift – that is, a denial of the possibility of the gift in terms of the gift's supposed absorption within the realm of exchange. Yet, once again, Antonio is prescient in seeing that exchange cannot, without altering itself and becoming other, truly "absorb" the undecidable gift, since to do so would be to import elements – in my view, these elements are crucial for any act of exchange – that represent the "excess" of the gift.

Callari argues, implicitly if not explicitly, that the gift can be characterized as the *excess* over exchange. With this idea I would mostly concur. To be clear, this is not to say that the gift only exists as an excrescence of exchange. Indeed, the point may be that exchange could be seen as a subsumed figure occupying one corner of the social space cleared by the gift, and is always overrun by any attempts to preserve its corner borders as a private space. But if so, then the notion of exchange as a regime of value that can dissipate the specter of the gift is absurd, and thus impossible.

For some cultural critics, and perhaps Antonio agrees with them here, the gift is both a figure of excess and expenditure, overflowing the bounds of "controlled" (because ultimately calculable) exchange, as well as *the* master code of excess itself. Perhaps, in this last guise, gift discourse promises to become one with economics, but also to abolish it at the same moment. It is in this sense that David Ruccio and I (Amariglio and Ruccio 1998) argued that for many cultural critics the concept of the gift is the key term for an "anti-economics." That is, the gift is often viewed, or at least desired,[2] to be that which is "outside" economics, but which, more menacingly, possesses the capacity to infiltrate and ultimately replace economics. Antonio Callari, however, embraces a different position, one that seeks to keep in play the tension between being of and other than economics. Nevertheless, I think more needs to be said about the economy as a "world of goods" and exchange as a site of value before we draw any conclusions about "insides" and "outsides" of economic discourse, at least as far as the economic status of the gift is concerned.[3]

Here I am in complete agreement with Callari that the discourse of economic value, as a crucial condition for its own possibility, renders a world in which things exist as objects that can be alienated and that are prone to a type of reduction in which some "common element" or substance can make them more or less quantifiable and calculable by all potential trading partners. It is this point – or at least a similar one that Antonio and I made a decade ago in our essay "Marxian value theory" – that I think has significant consequences for the claim that, in its self-reproducing guise, "the economy" or exchange has no need for the excess that anthropology's gift brings. It continues to fascinate me that any conception of the economy as self-reproducing could be so naturalized it requires great effort to demonstrate, in contrast, its ideological/discursive constituents and determinations.

For it should be by no means obvious that "things" exist as "others"; that these things should therefore enter the realm of what can be alienated from self or community or other entities or good(s); that these things should be looked on primarily as means to satisfy sensual needs; that these things should be seen to possess something in common (even if that common thing is that they satisfy needs or that they are the results of a labor process); and that these things can and should be numbered and calculated. The world in which these are all encountered – as Antonio calls it, the world of goods[4] – is of course a world that must constantly be produced and reproduced precisely because there is nothing more "natural" about this set of practices than any other way of thinking about and experiencing selves and things.[5] To put this another way, the production and reproduction of such a world of goods require all sorts of cultural, ideological, political, moral and other practices in order for the "events" (such as exchange) that constitute its supposed manifestations to occur.

The tendency to see nearly every act in which things change hands as involving value (if not exchange) is clearly grounded in this reduction of things to "goods." This holds even if one argues that some goods are regulated by a "law of value" (the realm of "equal exchange") while others are outside that realm and have a more casual or at least indeterminate "economic value" – the latter being an argument sometimes made for the uncertainties attendant upon gift giving (just what is required in return, if a return is required at all?). As Antonio states, the *a priori* discursive construction of a world of goods is sufficient to lay the trap for any who wish to claim that the gift resists economic value considerations. This is why, for example, even those who are interested in distinguishing the gift from exchange find it difficult to fend off the claim that, at bottom, a question of value binds them together. Discussions of "symbolic exchange" or symbolic value do little to alter the terms of the argument since in the end, as Mirowski notes, some notion of equivalence classes – something implicitly calculable – will likely creep in (2001: 442–6).

But there is also a sense that exchange describes better than gifts a transaction involving goods since exchange, it is often thought, is less symbolic, less constitutive of subjectivity, and more regulated by considerations of equality and/or realized preferences.[6] For many economists, as well as for gift theorists, exchange is seen as more transparent, more able to represent already given value considerations, including the meeting of trading partners' needs, and already constituted subjectivities. This view is mistaken. For there is nothing at all "certain" about any act of exchange, and nothing in it less symbolic or less "about" power, responsibility, meaning, and so forth.[7] Likewise, there is something fundamentally "constituted" and "constituting" about identities and subjectivities in every act of exchange. Leaving aside the question of the multiplicity within selves who enter into trades, the fact remains that exchange is a very overloaded activity, and trading partners not only may be of several different minds about the transaction, but are often uncertain as to what exactly such transactions "mean" in terms of their own and others' wealth and property, the effects on their wellbeing, who or what subject positions they occupy, what exactly is being traded, and so forth.[8]

Even though the special province of the gift seems to be to cast doubt on the issue of time and return (hence its vaunted indeterminacy), there are countless occasions in which what we normally consider exchanges involve exactly this lack of clarity and this question of time's passage. Exchange is also a damnably difficult action to pin down, since it is never clear which part of the activity (is it the talk involved? the physical exchanging of things? the moments before and after a purchase?) is considered its essence and defining moment. For example, I swear I couldn't tell when it was that I actually bought my first house, which I did, presumably, just recently.

Exchange, then, is privy, just as is the gift, to a whole host of perturbations and undecidables. Why not view every event of exchange as uncertain, as requiring many different determinations for its constitution? Why not view the suturing then done in the ideological realm, such that exchange economy is considered the crowning if not founding act (as in some readings of Adam Smith) of sociality, as itself indicating how something complexly overdetermined can become naturalized into "self-determination"? Why not posit the fundamental uncertainty and indeterminacy of every act of exchange, including those that seem to involve such a high degree of routine and habit that the fragility (in the sense of needing to stand on "others'" legs) of their social practice has been obliterated from economic discourse?[9] Why not, in this sense, make clear that the gift is at least one of the necessary concepts that calls attention – even if only as a spectral gaze – to just those limb supports?

Antonio Callari does a great service in pointing out that there is nothing necessary in conceiving of a world of goods and thinking that value is ubiquitous.[10] In this sense, he joins all those who seek in the concept of the gift a way of "othering" an economy of exchange by suggesting that value discourse captures nothing omnipresent or quintessentially natural. It still seems shocking, for some, to suggest that living and thinking in the "thingified" world of commodities is not only historical (and perhaps transient), but also redolent of all things cultural, ethical and political. That is, living in the world of goods does not mean the death of the gift, a death attended by no consequent traces of exchange's ghost. To the contrary, living in such a thingified world can bring out of the shadow the many elements of the gift – power, aggression, community, responsibility, care, indeterminacy – that may inhere as well in every act of exchange.

The weight of elements that rush in when we begin to investigate the possibility of exchange is overwhelming. An analysis of the overdetermination of exchange provides insight into the tentative and improvisational nature of transactions that involve degrees of calculation.[11] Antonio and I argued previously that for transacting members of any community to view exchange as involving relations of more or less equivalence, these members must be "socially constituted" by the practices and processes that promote identities of proprietorship, relations of social equality, and economic rationality (the ability to see things as things and as likewise calculable). Now, I dare say that he and I both think that we left out or underappreciated many other complex identities that help to produce an exchange economy (including the idea that there is no reason for people to possess *any* particular type of identity, or to hold *any* particular notion of exchange in order for them to engage in the activity). But one thing I do believe we wanted to suggest through our analysis was the "openness" (and now I would add, the impossibility or undecidability) of the process of exchange: by which I think we meant the inability of any act of exchange, and any discourse about the same, successfully to suture *itself* – at least in a "permanent" act of closure. Indeed, when we tried to specify the many non-economic determinants of any act of "equal exchange," we had in mind something opposite from presenting an exhaustive list of these determinants (here again, we could easily read our own endeavors as different in intent from "rescuing" value theory). Certainly we didn't regard our list as an attempt to close the circle on exchange by accounting for all of its moments.

In contrast, I think we were attempting to show what earlier I called the fragility and utter impossibility of exchange ever being identical to itself. That is, we were seeking to produce an analysis that could lead economists and others toward conjunctural analyses of exchange and away from any grand *economic* theory of value. It is Antonio's additional contribution in his paper for this volume, as I read it, to summarize these gestures toward the uncertainty of conjuncture in the figure of the gift. The study of the aleatory nature of exchange and economy, in fact, marks much of Antonio's recent work, as is evidenced by his introduction with David Ruccio to a book dedicated to the work of Louis Althusser (Callari and Ruccio 1996). Althusser's aleatory materialism has spurred Callari, I think, to conceive of uncertainty and indeterminacy (in the sense of a conjuncture) as constituting a critical moment to theorize about and intervene in ethics and politics.

This leads me to a central part of his essay: the gift as the space or figure that impels ethical and political considerations, even for a regime of economic value. There is much to be said on this topic. First, it is clear to me that, coincidentally, Antonio has seen what the neo-Austrian economist G.L.S. Shackle understood in his lifetime of criticizing mainstream neoclassical and Keynesian economic models. That is: when economic behavior is reduced to a matter of preference, and when this preference is viewed as an object of predictable regularity and can therefore be modeled with a degree of certainty, then "choice" involves no choice – no freedom – at all. Instead choice becomes a misnomer for mechanism, and the realm of preference is emptied of all aspects that require ethical consideration (which, for Shackle, would require true freedom for its operation) or political practice, which would likely involve freely choosing between different states of existence. In Shackle's libertarian world, individual freedom is the highest virtue, and any model of an exchange economy that renders transactions knowable or at least predictable (and, in this sense, contrary to the indeterminacy of conjuncture) contributes to shackling, by ignoring, acts of "pure" choice.[12]

Now, of course, Antonio Callari is no advocate of the illusion of "pure choice" that Shackle promises in his pursuit of individual freedom in exchange economies (codified, more importantly, in the discourses about the same). But where Antonio is in potential agreement (potential, of course, because "the gift" is not Shackle's worry) is in his emphasizing that the exorcism of the gift – a figure of social complication, because undecidable – performed purportedly by value theorists conspires to prevent the full force of the uncertainty of economy and its consequent flooding (hence, *over*determination) with morality, politics and choice. The ghost of the gift is, in many ways, about chance. It is about realizing the implications of chance to provide precisely the opportunity – or even the necessity – both to suture and to reopen (even temporarily) so-called "economic" practices by and through ethics and politics.

Here I might differ slightly from Antonio, since he seems both to accept and to deny the possibility of locating ethics and politics on the terrain of economic value. Or, rather, for Antonio, the undecidability of the gift is what makes such a "raising" possible, and perhaps he is right if he means here the idea that, once again, the self-determination and determinacy of "economy" may be always already overrun by the figure of the gift. I want to stay just a bit longer, though, on the field of value, preferring like Arjun Appadurai to argue that "politics (in the broad sense of relations, assumptions, and contests pertaining to power) is what links value and exchange in the social life of commodities" (1986: 57). That is, perhaps there is some worth not only in seeking an anti- or non-economics through the gift, but also, as Antonio notes, in spending some time thinking through the implications of the sociopolitical construction of this world of goods.

On this note, I think we cede too much if we permit other economists to continue to think that when they discuss preference and choice they are writing about a world that is anything but ethical and political. Much is lost in allowing preference to stand as an icon for individual economic self-realization in exchange rather than seeing it as always already a question of power (over nature, over things, over needs, over one's and others' bodies) and moral choice (between different possible outcomes that affect nature, things, needs, bodies, etc.). So while we may conceive the gift as the summation of all these concerns, nevertheless value theory – even the most individualistic – is open to a decon-struction in which uncertainty and the practices it inspires (politics and ethics certainly, and perhaps aesthetics as well) may be found to dwell in the gaps, tautologies and absences that attend any discourse.

Another aspect to the critique of treating economics as a world of goods, or circle of value, bears directly on the question of the exorcism of the gift's ghost. This is the issue, mentioned in passing by Antonio, of constructing the circle of value from a world populated mostly by separate and separable individuals. Stephen Gudeman (2001) has been most adept in showing that reconstructing the field instead from the initial premise of *community* (and the extension of its boundaries) can provide the impetus to enshrine reciprocity, if not the gift, as a leading concept, even an entry point, into all theories of transactions (that is, events when things change hands). Antonio Callari too notes that conceiving of social space as, first, a space occupied by relatively autonomous selves and bodies is not only the hallmark of most economic thought during the past 200 years, but also a corollary (though, in my mind, not a necessary one) to representing the economy as a world of goods. There is no question that for many critics of economics, this presupposition is the most offensive one, and in place of it the gift is touted as representing an alternative starting point, that of irreducible community. This alternative starting point may impel us to imagine every act in which things change hands as stemming from and solidifying or dissolving (and often both) social ties. Again, this starting point further implies the necessity to view economic activity as "embedded" within community practices. What then remains is to discuss the norms and interests that pertain to the reproduction or destruction of community.

This view that the field of value begins with an individualistic conceit, and that, therefore, demonstrations of the "impossibility" of the gift retain such a conceit, has recently concerned feminist economics. As Antonio notes, the debate over selfishness versus generosity retains the supposition that these decisions are taken by individuals who "act" in the world for themselves or for others. But this means that in some important way these selves are never simultaneously "of" and "other than" such others, and thus, critics argue, we can continue to deny the possibility that sociality is itself, in the first instance, a matter of caring and responsibility. Hence, some contemporary feminist economists view the debate over the gift as really being about the role of such notions as caring, affection and responsibility, all of which point historically mostly to the activities of and ties forged by women.

Various tensions mark these discussions. One involves the question of whether to retain a discourse of value, in which case one part of the feminist contribution is to suggest that generosity, caring and affection cannot be reducible to self-interest and need to be accounted for (even in economic statistics involving the money value of gross domestic product). This is the crucial contribution that such writers as Nancy Folbre and Heidi Hartmann (1998) make in distancing themselves from both neoclassical and Marxian value theories since, according to Folbre and Hartmann, both of these approaches subsume the affective realm and acts of sharing and caring to other, masculinist master codes. In a way, the problem over the economic value of caring and generosity has led some, such as Irene van Staveren (2001), to specify different economic value spheres (for van Staveren, these are the spheres of freedom, justice and care, which imply, respectively, exchange, rules and the gift). But, of course, van Staveren and others note that any particular transaction can and often does involve all three value considerations (thus, making the value – if measured in money terms – quite difficult to specify, let alone predict). The difficulties experienced in seeking to be both of and other than the regime of exchange give rise to a different desire for gift theory. That desire is based upon the view that economic discourse is so inextricably bound up with value discourse that it is impossible – starting with nearly any existing value theory – to reground notions of economy on responsibility and caring. Perhaps, then, in this view, a truly feminist economics can refashion the gift as a way to give voice to these foundational ideas.

Yet, there is also a sense in which traditional gift theory, from Mauss and Malinowski to Sahlins and the French poststructuralists, retains a masculinist edge as well.[13] This can be seen in the view that the gift is not just about "generosity," as Antonio notes, but about all kinds of constraining and aggressive political and social acts that construct community (such as the potlatch). In fact, to look for the "glue" that holds society together in these acts of prestation and status is to focus largely on the activities of men.[14] Feminist economists prefer instead to concentrate on the activities in which care and responsibility are socially binding, thus implying that the concentration on power and status and impressed obligation behind much gift theory only differs from traditional economic value theory in choosing masculinist "community" over masculinist "individuals."[15]

I am not one for foundations of any type, so I have no desire to posit here any particular first or last cause of sociality, individual, community, or otherwise. I am more interested in leaving in play the tensions Antonio identifies between multiple, supposedly "originary" causes of the social as enacted in the gift. But, perhaps more importantly for these comments, the preceding options suggest quite different notions of ethics and politics, which in the end is what Antonio seems to be most concerned with. After concluding with some brief remarks on this issue I will step back into the shadow.

The undecidability of the gift, for Antonio, is the occasion to interject the ethical and political dimensions that academic economics has long since exorcised.[16] Yet he leaves open (a deliberate gap?) the precise ethical questions and political arrangements that different conceptions of the gift might imply – that is, unless we take seriously his repeated reference to Marx's dictum (from each according to his/her abilities, to each according to his/her needs) as an ethical position. He hints that this dictum may now overflow its original interpretation as a hoped-for "economic" arrangement, and that it is implied in the concept of the gift. I don't know if this is Antonio's position, so I won't debate the point one way or another.

But I think it is at least worth asking if this famous dictum isn't positioned precisely in the gap Antonio finds between the gift and economic discourse. This is because the dictum can be read simultaneously as presuming the existence of a world of goods, a world in which value is still the main means of making homogeneous what is heterogeneous, and as precisely the material to deconstruct this idea. We cannot decide, in my view, whether it constitutes a continuation of value discourse (and "economics") or the founding moment of something outside of economics and value altogether. Or, indeed, whether it is content to live in the gap between this "inside" and "outside." Perhaps this is what Antonio wants to support: a mechanism through which things change hands that also precipitates the kinds of ethical and political discussions he wishes to promote, brought about by the gap that the gift opens up. What partialities (on whose "side" is it on?) Antonio sees in this dictum is left unstated, but there is no question in my mind that he prefers the social justice he reads in this dictum to many other alternatives.

On most days and circumstances, I share this preference. I think Antonio understands well the power, violence and aggression, as well as the affections of caring, responsibility and love that this particular gift implies (as do all schemes for social justice, as do all schemes for sociality in general, including the neoclassical economists' world of free and unfettered markets).[17] How the gift can illuminate the partialities inherent in all such schemes is a matter of great import, but one for which a different light will have to shine (if Antonio is up to the task), or a different shade will have to come forth (I know I will not).

The ghost of the gift. If given a chance, this wraith can, in Antonio Callari's view, lead us once to again take up such famous dicta. "Perhaps ..." . While many may say to such a specter, along with the mad Dane, "Whither wilt thou lead me? Speak, I'll go no further," still others, like Antonio and myself, maintain the mad hope that "perchance t'will walk again."

Notes

1 Though not directly concerned with Derrida on the gift, Gibson-Graham (1995) discusses the specters of the economic and non-economic that haunt the pages of Derrida's *Specters of Marx*.

2 Much of this desire speaks to a sense of profound loss. Paul Rabinow reminds us that "Mauss wrote *The Gift* to demonstrate how unique and late in world history the category of the 'economic' really was and how much social and moral solidarity had been lost through its triumph" (1996: 129).

3 I think, but am not sure, that Antonio eschews the views of those like Chris Gregory and David Cheal, who posit a dual system of transactions. For Gregory, "commodity exchange establishes objective quantitative relationships between the objects transacted, while gift exchange establishes personal qualitative relationships between the subjects transacting" (1982: 41). Cheal, differing in some important ways from Gregory (whom Cheal criticizes), describes what he calls a "moral economy," which he regards as the proper realm for the operation of the gift, living alongside "political economies" in the modern world. For more on these theories, see Chapter 11 of the present volume.

4 There is a wonderful irony in Antonio's use of the term "world of goods." *The World of Goods* (1979) is the title of an important cross-disciplinary book by the great cultural anthropologist Mary Douglas and the economist Baron Isherwood. The irony mainly consists of the fact that this book seeks to de-economize and de-materialize the terrain of goods. Douglas, the anthropologist of "meaning" *par excellence*, and Isherwood argue that we should put aside, at least temporarily, the fact that goods meet material desires and needs (including needs for status) in favor of an approach that emphasizes instead the idea that goods make "visible and stable the categories of culture" (1979: 65) because they are primarily markers to be interpreted for the cultural meanings they exemplify. It is not clear, though, that this transvaluation of the world of goods touches Antonio's concern about the homogeneity of this terrain *vis-à-vis* the imposition of a value mechanism. In fact, Douglas and Isherwood miss a chance to re-situate economics by failing to engage directly the issue of the value calculation within the context of their prior concern to see goods as markers of culture. That is, they do not extensively explore the interconnection among calculation, value and meaning.

5 Robert Garnett reminds us that, for Marx, the classical economists made the same "error" that persists today among many modern economists. To wit, "value, exchange-value, and abstract equal human labor do not appear to them peculiar or socially contrived but natural – qualities or expressions of Man which 'possess the fixed qualities of natural forms'" (1995: 50).

6 A related point is that, for some, gifts represent or even produce "identity" to a greater degree than does exchange. Komter summarizes this point:

> Gifts reveal something about the identity of the giver. ... But a gift also imposes an identity on the recipient, in the sense that the ideas which the other person's needs and desires evoke in our imagination – ideas about his or her typical characteristics and peculiarities – are exposed to a certain extent in our gift.
>
> (1996a: 6)

Advertising, marketing strategies, focus groups, and many other devices of contemporary market culture suggest the possibility that a subject's "presence" and identity may, likewise, be just as much at stake and in question in the realm of exchange.

7 Writing about the gift, Pierre Bourdieu claims that "the major characteristic of the experience of the gift is, without doubt, its ambiguity" (1997: 231). Exactly! But I would say "exactly!" to the same description of the experience of exchange. Bourdieu goes on to explain the "dual nature" of the gift, caught between a renunciation of self-interest, on the one hand, and a sometimes dim awareness of the "logic of exchange." Similar dilemmas beset the act of exchange as well.

8 In her brilliant unpublished paper on forms of cooperation and gift giving between firms, Judith Mehta (n.d.) elucidates Jean-François Lyotard's critique of Maussian notions of the gift. What is mostly at stake in this critique is Lyotard's view that the forms of transactions Mauss describes can be reduced to "giving-with-return," which presupposes fixed identities in those engaged in these trades. Mehta approves of Lyotard's reconstruction of the gift as "giving-without-return" since it highlights the indeterminate nature of the subjectivities involved in such actions, and therefore sees the gift as pertaining to the "presence" of becoming subjects rather than the "presents" exchanged by already existing subjects. While I admit to being much enamored of this distinction, I think it understates the indeterminacy of the act of exchange and the constitutive power of exchange on subjectivity.

9 Amariglio and Ruccio (1998) argue that the contrast between planning (seen to be more orderly) and markets (seen to be more quixotic) has also been greatly exaggerated. In this light, we stressed the habit and convention that marks much exchange activity. I do not wish this argument to be read as an endorsement of the greater certainty of other acts of exchange compared to that of the gift. My point would simply be that the contrasts between gift and exchange have been largely overdrawn where the issues of certainty, stability and determinacy are concerned. Furthermore, I think many people are "habitually anxious" in approaching numerous acts of exchange. Perhaps these same and others are "anxiously habitual" in regard to most transactions as well.

10 Ruccio, Graham and Amariglio (1996) have written about the ubiquity of value discourse, and not just in reference to economic value. Our point has been that value (in our article we treat mostly economic and aesthetic notions of value) is itself a historical event as well as a discursive construct. Value names no transcendent fact. As such, there is nothing "necessary" about its appearance or operation in the social space.

11 John B. Davis makes a similar point:

> There are good reasons to believe that market participants do not share in a single higher logic in their respective interactions with one another, and that we accordingly ought to attend more carefully to different and changing forms of behavior in market activity. But if this is the case, then modeling discursive interaction as market exchange in terms of a formal symmetry of behaviors explicable in terms of a single mathematics is entirely misguided. Rather, we should seek to explain the changing and often incompatible means by which very different discursive agents negotiate exchanges with one another without supposing that a determinate formal apparatus lies behind the concrete phenomena.
>
> (1999: 163)

12 For an example of Shackle's argument, readers can consult his *Decision, Order and Time* (1961).

13 Schrift (1997: 2) makes the point that the renewed interest in the past two decades in gift theory has derived in part from critical feminist investigations of the relation between gender and the gift.

14 I am a fan of Georges Bataille. But there is no question in my mind that Bataille's work on expenditure and excess in the concepts of the gift and general economy displays an extreme form of masculinism. In his early article on "the notion of expenditure," Bataille revels in the acts of libido and pure destruction that he most closely associates with men. Thus, economies of desire, pleasure and loss employ, often in Bataille's writings, the figure of the "youthful man, capable of wasting and destroying without reason" (1985: 117). Bataille moves from such a description to the more "general" phenomenon of spectacular destruction and loss. In this light he describes potlatch as "a kind of deliriously formed ritual poker" (1985: 122). It is largely in reaction to this kind of orgiastic masculinism and to the Lévi-Straussian notion that social structure is founded on the "exchange of women" that Luce Irigaray states emphatically that "the economy of exchange – of desire – is man's business" (1997: 179).

15 Komter (1996b) explores the active role women may take in gifting to acquire social and political power. Komter states that in modern western societies, where women are more likely to engage in gift giving than men, it is "improbable" that women are more altruistic than men; rather, power considerations are often chief motivators. Komter also notes that "women seem to be no exception when painful, hurting or offending gifts are given" (1996b: 130).

16 Compare Antonio's views to those of one of the most famous living economists, Kenneth Arrow: "The market is one system; the polity is another. Use of the market and its language leads to results which offend our intuitions; so does the use of political language" (1997: 765).

17 For a recent defense of the market as a site for virtues that partly encompass care, responsibility, and perhaps even love, see McCloskey 1996. For an opposing perspective that argues that market culture has more often embodied conflict, violence, and destruction, see Reddy 1984.

References

Amariglio, Jack and Antonio Callari. "Marxian value theory and the problem of the subject: the role of commodity fetishism." In Emily Apter and William Pietz (eds) *Fetishism as Cultural Discourse*. Ithaca: Cornell University Press, 1993, pp. 186–216.

Amariglio, Jack and David Ruccio. "Postmodernism, Marxism, and the critique of modern economic thought." In David L. Prychtiko (ed.) *Why Economists Disagree: An Introduction to the Alternative Schools of Thought*. Albany: State University of New York Press, 1998, pp. 237–73.

—— "Literary/cultural 'economies,' economic discourse, and the question of Marxism." In Martha Woodmansee and Mark Osteen (eds) *The New Economic Criticism: Studies at the Intersection of Literature and Economics*. London: Routledge, 1999, pp. 381–400.

Appadurai, Arjun. "Introduction: commodities and the politics of value." In Arjun Appadurai (ed.) *The Social Life of Things: Commodities in Cultural Perspective*. Cambridge: Cambridge University Press, 1986, pp. 3–63.

Arrow, Kenneth. "Innumerable goods." *Journal of Economic Literature* 35 (June 1997): 757–65.

Bataille, Georges. "The notion of expenditure." In *Visions of Excess, Selected Writings, 1927–1939*. Ed. and trans. Allan Stoekl. Minneapolis: University of Minnesota Press, 1985, pp. 116–29.

Bourdieu, Pierre. "Marginalia – some additional notes on the gift." In Alan D. Schrift (ed.) *The Logic of the Gift: Toward an Ethic of Generosity*. London and New York: Routledge, 1997, pp. 231–42.

Callari, Antonio and David F. Ruccio. "Introduction: postmodern materialism and the future of Marxist theory." In Antonio Callari and David F. Ruccio (eds) *Postmodern Materialism and the Future of Marxist Theory: Essays in the Althusserian Tradition*. Hanover: Wesleyan University Press, 1996, pp. 1–48.

Cheal, David. *The Gift Economy*. London: Routledge, 1988.

Davis, John B. "Postmodernism and identity conditions for discourses." In Robert F. Garnett Jr. (ed.) *What Do Economists Know? New Economics of Knowledge*. London: Routledge, 1999, pp. 155–68.

Derrida, Jacques. *Given Time: I. Counterfeit Money*. Trans. Peggy Kamuf. Chicago: University of Chicago Press, 1992.

Douglas, Mary, and Baron Isherwood. *The World of Goods: Towards an Anthropology of Consumption*. London: Allen Lane, 1979.

Folbre, Nancy, and Heidi Hartmann. "The rhetoric of self-interest: ideology of gender in economic theory." In Arjo Klamer, D.N. McCloskey and Robert M. Solow (eds) *The Consequences of Economic Rhetoric*. Cambridge: Cambridge University Press, 1988, pp. 184–203.

Garnett, Robert F. Jr. "Marx's value theory: modern or postmodern?" *Rethinking Marxism* 8.4 (1995): 40–60.

Gibson-Graham, J.K. "Haunting capitalism … in the spirit of Marx and Derrida." *Rethinking Marxism* 8.4 (1995): 18–39.

Gregory, Chris A. *Gifts and Commodities*. New York: Academic Press, 1982.

Gudeman, Stephen. "Postmodern gifts." In Stephen Cullenberg, Jack Amariglio and David Ruccio (eds) *Postmodernism, Economics, and Knowledge*. London: Routledge, 2001, pp. 459–74.

Irigaray, Luce. "Women on the market." In Alan D. Schrift (ed.) *The Logic of the Gift: Toward an Ethic of Generosity*. London and New York: Routledge, 1997, pp. 174–89.

Komter, Aafke E. "Introduction." In Aafke E. Komter (ed.) *The Gift: An Interdisciplinary Perspective*. Amsterdam: University of Amsterdam Press, 1996a, pp. 1–12.

—— "Women, gifts and power." In Aafke E. Komter (ed.) *The Gift: An Interdisciplinary Perspective*. Amsterdam: Amsterdam University Press, 1996b, pp. 119–31.

Lyotard, Jean-François. *Libidinal Economy*. Trans. Iain Hamilton Grant. Bloomington: Indiana University Press, 1993.

McCloskey, Deirdre. *The Vices of Economists. The Virtues of the Bourgeoisie*. Amsterdam: Amsterdam University Press, 1996.

Mehta, Judith. "Cooperation within and between firms: reflections on the giving of gifts." Unpublished paper, n.d.

Mirowski, Philip. "Refusing the gift." In Stephen Cullenberg, Jack Amariglio and David Ruccio (eds) *Postmodernism, Economics, and Knowledge*. London: Routledge, 2001, pp. 431–58.

Rabinow, Paul. *Essays on the Anthropology of Reason*. Princeton: Princeton University Press, 1996.

Reddy, William M. *The Rise of Market Culture: The Textile Trade and French Society, 1750–1900*. Cambridge: Cambridge University Press, 1984.

Ruccio, David, Julie Graham and Jack Amariglio. "'The good, the bad, and the different': reflections on economic and aesthetic value." In Arjo Klamer (ed.) *The Value of Culture:*

On the Relationship between Economics and Arts. Amsterdam: Amsterdam University Press, 1996, pp. 56–73.

Schrift, Alan D. "Introduction: why gift?" In Alan D. Schrift (ed.) *The Logic of the Gift: Toward an Ethic of Generosity*. London and New York: Routledge, 1997, pp. 1–22.

Shackle, G.L.S. *Decision, Order and Time in Human Affairs*. Cambridge: Cambridge University Press, 1961.

van Staveren, Irene. *Caring for Economics: An Aristotelian Perspective*. London: Routledge, 2001.

14 The pleasures and pains of the gift

Andrew Cowell

In this essay, rather than talking about the practice or the theory of the gift, I would like to discuss the concept of the gift as it appears in critical theory more generally, especially in France, where ideas originally expounded by Marcel Mauss have had perhaps their greatest resonance. As many anthropologists have recognized since the appearance of Mauss's essay in 1925, his own text can easily be viewed not as a work on the practice or theory of the gift, but as an example of how to use certain varied practices of exchange from both ancient and near-contemporary eras to think about Western capitalism and communism and their (to Mauss, regrettable) emphasis on pure economics. Mauss thus inaugurates, from this perspective, the use of the concept of the gift, as drawn from ethnographic sources, as a way of thinking about and critiquing the West.

A complete examination of the gift as a broader concept in critical theory is beyond the scope of a single paper. Here I would like to focus more narrowly on the connections that have been made between the concept of the gift and the body – both in pain and in pleasure. I will begin with a brief look at a series of medieval depictions of what seem to be truly gift exchanges. Interestingly, at a certain point, the Latin charters recording these ceremonies begin to speak of the "smiling donor" for the first time, rather than just the simple donor.

After thinking about the implications of this smile, I will jump to the twentieth century and the main body of the paper. Reading texts of Mauss (1967), Georges Bataille (1985a, b), Hélène Cixous (1981, 1989), Jean Baudrillard (1972, 1973) and Jacques Derrida (1992), I will argue that the texts in question are part of a larger, multi-century tendency of "the gift" to become simultaneously more productive as a theoretical concept and less bounded by the conditions of social practice. In the works of these critical theorists, I have chosen to trace a single thread – the developing connection between the gift and desire, especially sexual, which moves towards the figures of both infinity and impossibility. The treatment of the concept of the gift finally culminates in its becoming nothing more than a gift from theory to itself, and raises important questions about the relations between critical theory and social anthropology. In conclusion, I return to the medieval moment of the smile to locate, in the dynamic of pain and pleasure, the missing ground of the practice of the gift that modern theory has sought to elide.

In the beginning, there was a social practice of the gift. Medieval documents are full of descriptions of ceremonies of donation, primarily to religious houses, and many of these do seem to involve true gifts, rather than disguised sales or bartering. Reading these descriptions, one is struck by incidents of violence which surrounded the giving of the gift and which must have made gift giving and gift receiving an occasionally painful experience. In one instance, a certain Roger of Montgomery was donating to a monastery a marsh that he possessed. According to the medieval charter, after inspecting the property, he suddenly "threw his son, Robert of Bellême, dressed in a miniver cloak, into the water, in witness and memory that the domain of the abbot and monks extended up to there" (Tabuteau 1988: 151). The reason for this memorable and (for the son) unexpected event was of course precisely to make the gift ceremony, and the land boundaries in question, all the more memorable to the son. Gift giving was a serious matter, and not to be entrusted merely to Latin charters, but to the minds and words of the living.

There are many other medieval examples of the beating of witnesses at donation ceremonies for the same reasons – to make sure that the exact details of the gifts were remembered by those giving, receiving and participating. On one occasion, we read that after a gift "they there whipped many little boys and [then] refreshed [them] well in the record and memory of this deed" (Tabuteau 1988: 149). These acts of violence against the bodies of the witnesses to the gift of course testify to the orality of medieval culture, and to the fact that without such witnesses and their memories, there was really no gift at all. The gift was less an act of exchange between two individuals than a public ceremony intended to secure public order by establishing the controlling existence of these witnesses, whose existence guaranteed the sanctity of the bonds between giver and receiver, but also helped ensure the obedience of both parties to these bonds. (Indeed, in the Middle Ages, the parties often waited until the king should happen to be present before transacting especially important gifts.) In many charters, the description of the actual transfer of property occupied far less room than the many clauses designed to assure the gift's permanence. In effect, the ceremony was inscribed into a series of constraints and social pressures to ensure continued respect for what had taken place.

At the same time, the giver and receiver, to the extent that they also literally acted out, in bodily gesture and language, the process of the gift ceremony, also enacted a series of rituals (often quite similar to the rituals of homage and investiture familiar to feudalism) that formed the basis of peaceful coexistence and social order. Thus the gift ceremony promised the avoidance of the implicit alternative of violence and social disruption. In fact, many assurance clauses make this alternative quite explicit for those who would later seek to challenge the proceedings.

In another aspect of the ceremonies, various symbolic objects were often physically attached to the medieval manuscripts that recorded donations, serving through their presence to authenticate and re-animate the ceremony that the manuscripts recorded. Interestingly, the most common such object was a knife (see Clanchy 1993: 36–41). The knife, whatever its multiple meanings may have been in the individual cases of exchange, suggests the extent to which the gift ceremony represented not just the preferred alternative to socially destructive violence, but was itself the sublimated version of the repressive violence necessary for social control (there were also cases of cutting off the hair of the giver – see Clanchy 1993: 38). Indeed, as we have just seen, the violence was not always entirely sublimated. Upon reading the descriptions of the experiences of the witnesses, one thinks of Foucault's analysis in the first part of *Discipline and Punish* (1979) of how, in the early modern era, state authority was inscribed onto the subject in the form of tortures and executions. Marshall Sahlins has noted that the gift effectively replaces the state in many contexts (1972: 171–2), and one can see in these sometimes physically violent gift ceremonies and in their sublimated symbolic objects a force of social authority that would indeed eventually be replaced by the violent authority of the state itself in the later Middle Ages and Renaissance.

Thus whereas the gift has often been romanticized by writers such as Mauss and Ferdinand Tönnies as a force, missing in modern capitalist society, that encourages social cohesion and community, the exact nature of the cohesion itself is often neglected. In reading Georges Duby's (1984) recounting of the life of the famous medieval knight William Marshall, for example, one finds not only many examples of gifts of both goods and services, but also an impression of the tension, rivalry, competition and coercion that were expressed in the gifts. In this book, based on the earliest of medieval biographies, we find William on his deathbed, pressed to give away his wealth, making sure to forget nothing, in order to regulate his standing with God (1984: 23–4). But more importantly, his secular relations are marked by the same pressures. When he marries and accedes to a position of wealth and authority, he is also immediately drawn into a tightly woven web of social rivalries and jealousies. He finds himself with a network of bachelor knights in his household, to be armed and supported while he is also continually preoccupied with giving away his daughters in marriage, along with the accompanying dowries, in order to maintain political alliances (1984: 161–6). Upon taking over the regency of England, he furiously distributes both material wealth and honors in an effort to maintain order and authority and prevent revolt (1984: 181–2). The forces of authority, and the potential for violence, judicial combats and open warfare are present at every turn in the transactions of loyalty and property that dominate William's existence.

Yet William Marshall, like the subjects of the exchanges mentioned above, did adhere to the system of the gift. That is, the gift was one crucial model and form of social order, one of the vital rituals through which social order was continually rehearsed and enacted. Because of the centrality of this ritual, it was a deadly serious event, and neither the ritual forms of donation nor the memories of the witnesses were to be trifled with. But during the eleventh, and especially, twelfth and thirteenth centuries, the practice of donation began to be less common, or at least more problematic in terms of the perception of "pure" gift. Gifts were increasingly replaced by sales, for example. William Marshall's donation of his service and body itself to the Knights Templar is an example of an "outdated" attitude, according to Duby (1984: 21). But as the actual giving of gifts began to play a less important role in Western society, the appearance of the ceremony was nevertheless preserved, or at least there was an attempt to do so. This was in fact a phenomenon which appeared in numerous guises in the twelfth and thirteenth centuries.[1] In the particular case of the gift, the smile (or the description thereof) began to be an important accompaniment to ceremonies of exchange, and the phrase "the smiling donor" (*hilaris dator*) began to appear commonly in accounts and charters. The idea was apparently that for the exchanges to appear as true gifts, the smile was needed to show the donor's benevolence. Such phrases had apparently been in use since late antiquity, but were rare in the tenth and eleventh centuries, though they began to appear much more commonly during the twelfth century (see LeGoff 1997; Vercauteren 1969).

Simultaneously, of course, with the use of written documents (not so much as records of the more central – and official – ritual ceremony of donation, as the legally binding proof of what became more often a sale or other non-gift exchange form), the need for such memorable exchanges, beatings of witnesses, and so forth, waned. The decline of the gift as an economic vehicle was paralleled by the gift ceremony's decline as a vehicle of orality and memory. Thus as the actual gift ceremony ceased to play an important role, high seriousness and even pain and discomfort were replaced with a smile, though the import of that smile was often problematic.

In fact, one is tempted to speculate that the nostalgia for the gift, as located in Mauss (1967) or Tönnies (1963), really began with this smile. The smile bears witness to the moment when, at least in the economic realm, the social cohesion of the community was no longer enacted in the bodies of giver, receiver or witness, but in the exchange of money and in the written recording of the event. More abstract forms of representation and of authority – letter and coin – replaced the immediacy of word and gesture. Yet the need for the appearance of the "gift" was still felt in many cases. What role did this ritual, now gradually emptied of its original functional content, play?

The alternative to the gift appears to have shifted fields, from an opposition with social violence toward a new opposition within the realm of exchange. The gift was now the alternative to the more prosaic and coldly calculated exchange or sale. But unlike the first opposition, which had a basis in social practices, this second opposition seems to have been somewhat illusory. The need of the smile to ensure that the gift ceremony was really about a gift suggests that the typical gift ceremony was already assumed to be just a disguised barter or sale. One might see the smile as an attempt to save in appearances a distinction that the gift ceremony had already functionally lost, and thus as a true nostalgia. But the question of whether these smiling donors were really donors or only disguised sellers is less important than a recognition of the fact that in both cases the form of the exchange seems designed nostalgically to resist an economy of market and sale, and thus to be a conservative, probably aristocratic gesture against the increasing growth and dominance of market, sale and profit at the perceived expense of social relations.

This bit of medieval history serves to underline a decisive moment of transformation in the relation between the gift as social practice and the gift as formal, theoretical or heuristic concept in western Europe. But, in good medieval style, it is also a perfect tropological narration of the trajectory of the gift in twentieth-century theory. In particular, as it becomes less a social phenomenon and more a theoretical construct, the gift also becomes more and more fun. Indeed, starting from the image of the smile, we can trace the gift through the emblem of pleasure, including eventually that of orgasmic pleasure, even as it disappears as a social possibility.

In *The Predicament of Culture* (1988), James Clifford stresses the importance of the "other" for the project of French ethnographers and surrealists in the 1930s, and of so-called primitive societies as sources of aesthetic and scientific resources, to be used ultimately for the "destabilization" and defamiliarization of Western concepts of moral, economic and subjective normality and identity. This movement, especially to the extent that it focused on a critique of Western, capitalist economics, was part of a broad series of such attacks, all of which sought ways of attaining privileged vantage points of criticism through an escape from the purely economic. Another emblematic discourse nearly contemporary to this one was, for example, that of the Frankfurt School. Theodor Adorno's attempt to find in the aesthetic of high modernism an alternative to the aesthetics and economics of capitalism is a famous example.[2]

One of the greatest resources which non-Western societies gave to France in the 1930s was the idea of the gift, as elaborated by Marcel Mauss, and then subsequently by Georges Bataille. In his article "The notion of expenditure", Bataille posits that Western bourgeois society is engaged in an economy of the "zero-sum (or fixed sum) game": a system of transactions in which each expenditure must produce an equivalent gain, and where "pleasure, whether art, permissible debauchery, or play" (1985b: 117) is reduced to a concession – a non-productive expenditure producing only loss. Bataille then invokes the gift – and especially the Northwest American potlatch rite (1985b: 121) – as a model for what he terms "free expenditure." The potlatch is the emblematic form of a "loss" that nevertheless provides the social solidity and unity lacking in bourgeois society. Among other such expenditures would be "perverse sexual activity (i.e., deflected from genital finality)" (1985b: 118); in other articles from the same time period, he makes clear that the sexual act can be a paramount form of sacrifice, loss, expenditure and excess paralleling that of the potlatch and gift. He mentions the orgy as one exemplary antidote to the "conjugal union" which corresponds to "juridical and administrative society" and its focus on narrow "self-interest" (1985a: 250–1).

As James Clifford has revealed (1988: 126), Bataille's celebrated book on *L'Erotisme*, dating from two decades after the article on expenditure, owes a great debt to the work of Mauss generally, and his text "La part maudite," which appeared just prior to *L'Erotisme*, is an extended meditation on Mauss's *The Gift*

(Clifford 1988: 127). In general for Bataille the gift is a social model for interrupting the circle of constraints exercised upon the social and libidinal economy in the West. The gift is itself a form of "delirium" (1985b: 122) and orgiastic effusion. It is for Bataille a figure of desire, and more specifically of the sexual desire that lies at the center of his project and that seeks to escape the economistic determinations of bourgeois capitalism.

With the work of Baudrillard, the repressive realm expands from that of Bataille. As a result, the space of the gift is even more marginal in relation to the social center, and thus it is called upon to be all the more powerful in its critical function. Baudrillard's views have shifted radically over the course of his writings, and I will concentrate here on one crucial moment in his development – his final, complete break with Marxism and his elevation of "symbolic exchange" to the paramount, founding concept of his cultural criticism. This is the period of *For A Critique of the Political Economy of the Sign* (1972), and especially of *The Mirror of Production* (1973), in the early 1970s. I will examine a key passage of the latter book, where Baudrillard specifically invokes Bataille, in order to critique not bourgeois capitalism but Marxism itself. The passage is all the more interesting because of its comments on sexual desire and pleasure and their relation to symbolic exchange.

In *For a Critique of the Political Economy of the Sign*, Baudrillard continues his earlier analyses of economic transactions in terms of the symbolic value of commodities. He privileges the sign value associated with the purchase and use of commodities, and suggests that social signification is the governing feature of economic transactions, rather than the more obvious but ultimately illusory "use-value" or market "exchange-value" which the commodities may appear to possess. In deconstructing the very categories of utility and market value, he suggests that the contemporary economy is really no different from the original economic model of symbolic exchange – the gift economy. He entitles the section of remarks on this topic "L'échange symbolique: la kula et le potlatch" (1972: 8–9), and then goes on to make the radical claim that

> It is still as always the mechanism of social prestation which one must read in our choice, our accumulation, our manipulation, and our consumption of objects. ... [T]he kula and the potlatch have disappeared, but not their principle, which we will retain as the basis of a sociological theory of objects.[3]
>
> (Baudrillard 1972: 9)

Modern capitalism is simply a disguised and perverted form of the gift economy.

In *The Mirror of Production* (1973), Baudrillard goes on to suggest that Marx, as well as the capitalist system which Marx critiques, are both complicit in the same general logic of "production" – a logic that posits human labor, human bodily "needs," and the means of production as the basis of economic value, whether this be use-value or exchange-value. As in the previous book, he argues that "symbolic exchange" is central to understanding economic values. Baudrillard suggests that it is the semiotic logic of the system of symbolic exchange values that actually produces what appear to be the originary points of the economic system – use- and exchange-value. These two, he says, are merely products of a semiotic system.

Though Baudrillard does not explicitly invoke the gift economy as the social model of symbolic exchange in *The Mirror of Production*, the connection between these two concepts established in his previous book underlies his analysis throughout. This point comes to the surface in a key passage from *The Mirror of Production* where he alludes to Bataille and to Eros. As part of the deconstruction outlined in the previous paragraph, Baudrillard has essentially underlined the false place of the body within the logic of Marxist analysis. In Marx's discussion of true, unalienated labor, values return always to the body, he suggests, and cites passages such as the following:

> Labor is, in the first instance, a process which takes place between man and nature. Man himself plays the role in this process, vis-à-vis nature, of a natural power. The forces with which his body is endowed, arms and legs, head and hands, are put to work in order to assimilate to himself the matter of nature by giving it a form useful to his existence.[4]
>
> (Baudrillard 1973: 24)

In this passage one sees the connections between the human bodily production of commodities, and the basis of this production in a utility defined according to human needs. This is Marx's ideal state of labor, where production is, or would be, both motivated by and produced by the physical human body. Baudrillard then cites a remark by Marx that "labor is not therefore the only source of the use values which it produces, and of material wealth. It is the father of these, and the earth is the mother" (quoted in Baudrillard 1973: 31).[5] Seizing on this sexual metaphor, Baudrillard argues that

> This genesis of wealth by the genital combination of labor ... mirrors quite well a "normal" schema of production and reproduction – one makes love to have children, not for pleasure. The metaphor is that of genital, reproductive sexuality, and not at all that of a corporeal expenditure for the sake of enjoyment.[6]
>
> (1973: 32)

In other words, the "'économie sacrificielle' selon Bataille, ou l'échange symbolique" ("sacrificial economy as understood by Bataille, or symbolic exchange"; 1973: 32) is incompatible with the economy of "production." Here Baudrillard, with this "or," makes explicit the particular social model of symbolic exchange underlying his analysis. But at the same time he invokes the libidinal economy of Bataille's work, and suggests that Marx's economy of production, founded on the body, denies humans the prospect of bodily pleasure. He argues that work, for Marx, is a kind of "investment" that is "opposée à toute mise en jeu symbolique, que ce soit celle du don et de la dépense" ("opposed to any symbolic engagement, whether of gift or of expenditure"; 1973: 33). "Ce que l'homme donne de son corps dans le travail n'est jamais donné" ("That which man gives of his body in labor is never given"; 1973: 33). The expenditure or "dépense" here is clearly of the sort envisioned by Bataille, and we see that for Baudrillard, symbolic exchange can be represented not only by the gift but by any form of sacrificial expenditure or loss, including of the sexual, pleasurable kind. The argument repeats that of Bataille, but attacks Marx *and* capitalism, rather than just capitalism. Whereas Marxian labor exemplifies the "domestica-tion rationelle de la sexualité" ("rational domestication of sexuality") in the form of an "Eros productif" (1973: 34), the gift would evidently be simultaneously the realm of pleasure and "jouissance." Baudrillard suggests that if only we can escape the trap of thinking in terms of production, perhaps we can also escape from "une psychanalyse devenue spécialiste des impasses de l'économie libidinale bien plus que des voies du désir" ("a psychoanalysis that has become a specialist in the blockages of the libidinal economy rather than in the paths of desire"; 1973: 38). Symbolic exchange is all about desire, about the free play of the signi-fier, about the "jouissance" that Barthes evokes in another not so different context in *The Pleasure of the Text* (1975).[7] Thus Baudrillard takes part in a move-ment towards what Lewis Hyde has termed the "erotic" life epitomized by the gift, one opposed to the "logos" of the market (Hyde 1983: xiv). Hyde locates a "lust" that consumer goods, for example, only "bait" but do not "satisfy" (1983: 10); in the realm of the gift erotic lusts may be truly satisfied. Thus Hyde speaks of "the synthetic or erotic nature of the giving of a gift" (1983: 60).

In the writings of Hélène Cixous one finds the same zero-sum or fixed-sum game at work in the social and textual universe that Bataille posits and that Baudrillard expands. In this case, however, the game has been instituted not only by capitalism and Marxism together, but by masculine society as a whole, as she assimilates the Western and the masculine: in her famous article "The laugh of the Medusa" (1989), she analyzes the "masculine economy." The model which will disrupt this masculine construct is an explicitly non-Western phenomenon – the gift. Yet where Bataille and Baudrillard see the zero-sum in terms of repro-ductive, functional sexuality, which needs to be infused with orgasmic pleasure, Cixous sees the fixed-sum specifically in the male single orgasm, exchanged against an equivalent female orgasm (if the woman is lucky).

She finds in the male libidinal and textual economy a fear of the gift, for such a gift places the receiver in a position of debt, of Lacanian "lacking" in fact, and the male recipient's immediate desire is to return the gift, to settle accounts, to equalize the situation – to continue the circle. She also sees in the masculine sense of the lack (itself a result of the Lacanian castration complex) the founda-tion of the symbolic order. The symbolic order is the order of lacking, of debt, Cixous and Lacan suggest. Thus the lack that men seek to overcome and transfer is the foundation for the symbolic "economy." The woman, however, immune to the castration complex, lacks a sense of lack itself, and hence has no sense of "debt." Thus the woman stands outside the realms of patriarchal logic due to her particular ontological status in relation to the symbolic economy of debt and lacking. Immune to debt, woman lives in the realm of the pure gift. Cixous basically proposes that the true, ideal gift lies in the woman. The false "debt-gift" of Mauss is the gift as understood in the masculine economy. "Who could ever think of the gift as a gift-that-takes?" she asks. "Who else but man, precisely the one who would like to take everything" (1989: 1099).

The true (feminine) gift is, finally, the gift of the multiple orgasm, whose virtual endlessness obviates any need for calculation and constraint. The idea of the gift parallels her idea of a feminine "ecriture" in terms of the multi-orgasmic creativity of the woman. She writes in her article "Castration or decapitation?" (1981) of a feminine textual body that would replicate the feminine libidinal economy in being "always endless, without ending," a writing which seeks continually to "give." In "The laugh of the Medusa" she likewise states that "woman couldn't care less about the fear of decapitation (or castration), adventuring, without the masculine temerity, into anonymity, which she can merge with without annihilating herself: because she's a giver" (1989: 1099). "Her libido is cosmic … her writing can only keep going" (1989: 1099). "She doesn't 'know' what she's giving, she doesn't measure it; she gives" (1989: 1102). Cixous closes by adding that "this is an 'economy' that can no longer be put in economic terms" (1989: 1102). Thus Cixous proposes an escape from repressive forces that closely parallels that of Bataille and Baudrillard. But for her, what must be escaped becomes all the larger, and the gift thus again becomes at once more marginal and potentially more productive (and disruptive).

If both Baudrillard's and especially Cixous's analyses seem to move from the social towards the textual, Jacques Derrida's treatment of the gift reflects the intensely language- and sign-based nature of all his thought. The end of the trajectory I have set out to trace can be found in Derrida's 1989 (English translation, 1992) book *Given Time: I. Counterfeit Money*. The book is, to a significant extent, a reading (and deconstruction) of Mauss's famous essay on the gift. It thus treats quite explicitly the question that occupies us here – the intersection of critical theory and social anthropology around "the gift."

Mauss's text from the 1920s is one of the seminal works of twentieth-century anthropology, and his elaboration of the gift has been a guiding theme for modern studies of economic transactions. Nevertheless, it is less obvious why Derrida the poststructuralist should be drawn to this text, despite his earlier engagements with anthropology (most notably with Lévi-Strauss in *Of Grammatology*). In reality however, given French theory's engagement with the theme, Derrida's choice is highly appropriate,[8] and marks the culmination of a century-long development.

Derrida begins by establishing a particular meaning for the word "gift": he writes that "economy implies the idea of exchange, of circulation, of return" (1992: 6). But "for there to be a gift, there must be no reciprocity, return, exchange, countergift, or debt" (1992: 12). Indeed, the receiver must "not recognize the gift as gift. … If the gift appears to him as such … this simple recognition suffices to annul the gift … because it gives back, in the place … of the thing itself, a symbolic equivalent" (1992: 13). In fact, "at the limit, the gift as gift ought not appear as gift: either to the donee or to the donor" (1992: 14). Derrida thus posits an ideal gift which would be a gift in the very truest sense of the word, as that word is understood in contemporary colloquial French and English usage – a gift is something for which no debt is owed, and no reciprocal gift need be made. Of course, "colloquial" culture, just like the gift economy, does in fact tend to assign debt to gifts, to remember a future obligation, and thus to annul the ideal sense of the gift.

Given that "economy implies the idea of exchange" as cited above, he poses the question, "is not the gift, if there is any, also that which interrupts economy? That which, in suspending economic calculation, no longer gives rise to exchange?" (1992: 7), for "it must not circulate, it must not be exchanged" (1992: 7). As stated earlier, "the gift ought not appear as gift," for this will elicit the circle of exchange. Thus "the truth of the gift ... suffices to annul the gift" (1992: 27). He continues, "if the figure of the circle is essential to economics, the gift must remain an-economic ... it is perhaps in this sense that the gift is the impossible" (1992: 7). Derrida goes on to analyze the gift within the framework of the "supplement," as he has elaborated this term – that which is both outside of a supposedly complete and sufficient system but also necessary to the completion of that system.[9] The "gift" is finally a concept that is impossible but not unthinkable, and he pursues the question of why such a concept "gives" itself to be thought.

Like the "supplement" more generally, the gift turns out to be an originary concept for the economy, at least in Derrida's reading of Mauss's work. But "finally," he writes, "the overrunning of the circle by the gift ... does not lead to a simple, ineffable exteriority that would be transcendent and without relation. It is this exteriority that sets the circle going, it is this exteriority that puts the economy in motion" (1992: 30). The supposedly an-economic nevertheless founds the economic. In deconstructing the gift's originary, an-economic status, Derrida finally denies the status of the traditional gift – as understood by anthropology – as a "gift" at all. The traditional gift is rather a part of economic circulation and exchange, as exemplified by the famous Melanesian *kula* ring. Thus he writes that "Marcel Mauss's *The Gift* speaks of everything but the gift" (Derrida 1992: 24).

He then asks, "why desire the gift and why desire to interrupt the circulation of the circle? Why wish to get out of it?" (1992: 8). The answer lies in the question itself, which Derrida himself rephrases: "There is gift, if there is any, only in what interrupts the system" (1992: 13). Between the "impossible but not the unnameable or the unthinkable ... in this gap between the impossible and the unthinkable ... there is gift" (1992: 10). "The gap between, on the one hand, thought, language, and desire and, on the other hand, knowledge, philosophy, science, and the order of presence is also a gap between gift and economy" (1992: 29). Hence there is in the gift "a certain essential excess, indeed an excess of the gift over the essence itself" (1992: 10). He thus finds in Madame de Maintenon's phrase about "giving all her time" to the King, with which he starts the discussion I have been quoting, "the infinite sigh of unsatisfied desire" (1992: 4).

The gift is finally a figure of desire, in its most pure, gratuitous, and unmotivated form (1992: 122–4). "Desire" and the "desire to give" are finally the same thing (1992: 4–5). And that desire is infinite since the desire to give is also the figure of the desire for the impossible (1992: 4–5, 7).

Derrida's analysis takes in both the conclusion of a trajectory which passes from the smile through orgasmic pleasure to "infinite desire," while at the same time deflecting that trajectory (from an essentialist standpoint) by eliciting the (infinite) dissatisfaction of the loss of the gift's essence. In Derrida's analysis, the gift is an archetypal instance of the "excess" lying outside the "circle" of exchange. As such, and as disrupter of this circle of the economy, the gift would be the emblem of social disruption itself, as indeed it is for Mauss, Bataille, Baudrillard and Cixous. It, and its practice, would represent a privileged point from which to critique and reform the "economic" that has become synonymous, in much modern theory, with the repressive mechanisms of late-capitalist Western society.[10]

Thus, for example, Derrida's analysis captures the sense of Cixous's use of the gift. She also speaks of economic circles of exchange, driven by debt, and she also develops a concept of the gift as that which would interrupt and disrupt the circle – of the masculine libidinal economy. "Break out of the circles," she writes, and "don't remain within the psychoanalytic closure," she echoes Baudrillard (Cixous 1989: 1102). Woman, without a sense of lack, has ontologically "forgotten" the debt, and thus escapes the masculine symbolic economy and achieves a status as "giver" or even as gift itself. Woman thus becomes the essential excess or outside. Baudrillard's escape from the realm of capitalism through the emancipatory alternative of the gift is also closely echoed by Derrida's critical analysis of this process (see Kellner 1994: 6).

But it is just this exteriority, this essence of the gift, that Derrida questions and deconstructs. The trajectory of the gift reaches its culminating point of desire precisely because it has become symptomatic of an endless, unfulfillable desire for what can have no reality whatsoever in social practice – the gift, and the escape from the "circle," whether it be economic, semiotic or metaphysical. The circle from which one must escape becomes bigger and bigger in each succeeding theorist, until it overwhelms the outside.

Derrida finally says that Mauss's essay is really itself a gift from Mauss to theory (1992: 57, 62), or more precisely a "simulacr[um]" of the gift (1992: 61). More generally, Derrida implies that the gift is essentially a gift (of a simulacrum, a heuristic, a theoretical construct) by theory to itself. Or as Derrida says, "the gift is the gift of the giving itself" (1992: 28). This last sentence is crucial, because it evokes not just Mauss's initial gift, but an entire series of gifts. In fact, one could read this history of theory's use of "the gift," as outlined in our trajectory, as another form of the *kula* ring of Melanesia. The trajectory is constituted by a series of givings and regivings, of the concept of the gift, each of which is marked by an increasing excess or surplus (see Mauss 1967: 40; Bataille 1985b: 122). It is as if theory sought to enact, *through* the concept of the gift, what it learned *from* the concept of the gift. The movement of the gift further and further from social praxis and closer and closer to the impossible exposes the true nature of the gift as pure theoretical construct, as finally itself a gratuitous gift on the part of theory to itself.

Thus the gift is theory's gift to itself: an ironically essentialized construct functioning as a heroic socio-cultural "Other." Yet as the disrupter of the cycle of the West, the masculine West, the capitalist West, and the logocentric West, the gift is not just a tool of theory, but also a fitting figure for critical theory itself in its disruptive potential (see Pecora 1994). "Giving" has always seemed to be about "disrupting," Derrida suggests, and this is the case with him as well. "Giving" is "theorizing" is "disrupting." Thus theory proposes itself as a gift to those features of the West it seeks to critique. Gift theory becomes finally a tool in the service of the larger "gift" of critical theory as a whole.

But as suggested above, Derrida is simply one more recipient and regiver in this trajectory. This is why I have underlined the sense in which his deconstruction of the essence of the gift – as either social practice, or point for privileged theoretical critique of (patriarchal) capitalism from the "outside" – nevertheless also completes the gift's trajectory. This is true both in the sense outlined above whereby the gift reaches the limit of desire, and also because Derrida's own deconstruction, though elaborated from an immanent rather than a transcendent point of view, is nevertheless yet another attempted disruption – another gift. The disruption here is the claim that Mauss – and all the theorists who have followed him, we might add – have been complicit with the very logic of the economy (and logocentrism and metaphysics) they have sought to escape.[11] Their binary categories and "insides" and "outsides" only replicate this deeper logic, as both Osteen and Callari suggest in their respective chapters.

Derrida himself recognizes that such deconstructions and disruptions can never be final, but only endlessly regressive, so he is not necessarily contradictory in his logic here.[12] Indeed, *Given Time* suggests that the ideal gift must always follow a trajectory that brings it back to where it began, as if nothing had ever happened. The gift must be nothing. Derrida's deconstructive culmination of the gift's trajectory does exactly this – it turns the gift into nothing at all. He thus closes the "*kula* ring" of modern theory as it has used the gift. But Derrida also says that this nothing cannot be a non-event. Something must have occurred, a trajectory must have been traced, even if the occurrence culminates in a "forgetting" that forgets even itself. And in fact, such a forgetting has occurred, and a forgetting in which Derrida himself participates. It is a historical forgetting of the archaeology of the gift itself. This forgetting is revealed most clearly in Derrida's critique of Mauss's definition of the gift.

Reading *Given Time*, one might complain that Derrida's project seems to be no more than an overwrought quibble about definitions. Indeed, the starting point of Derrida's analysis can be found in his claim that Mauss's use of the word "gift" does not correspond to this word's meaning for Derrida in modern French. In stating that Mauss's "gift" is not a "gift" in the ideal sense that Derrida defines the word, Derrida does not truly address the series of social practices that anthropologists have called "the gift" at all. These social practices may not be "gifts" as Derrida defines the word, but they are social practices of some kind, and the argument over semantics may seem puzzling. It is as if the real concern of Derrida is over the word Mauss uses to describe these social practices, whatever they may be. The essence of Derrida's reading of Mauss could be restated as "Why does he choose to use this word 'gift' to label the practices in question, when they are not 'gift'?" (see Derrida 1992: 13). More generally, why do "the anthropologists" use this term? Derrida's argument is centered around this puzzle, and around his claim that this choice of terms is symptomatic of logocentrism's need to find originary moments and stable centers, even as it tries to avoid the disseminations that threaten to overwhelm the term "gift" itself and reveal the illusion of stability and origins (1992: 44–55).

Of course, the anthropologists use the word "gift," at least in some cases, because the "natives" do. More particularly, medieval western Europeans, when engaged in the social practices which modern anthropologists have qualified as "gift giving," did indeed use the words "gift," "give," and so forth (in Latin for the most part, of course). In fact, one could reverse Derrida's implicit central question, and ask not, "why do Mauss and the anthropologists choose an 'inappropriate' term to label the practices in question, and what does this say about our misunderstanding and misrepresentation of the practices?", but rather, "how has our own usage of the terms 'give' and 'gift,' as exemplified by Derrida's ideal understanding of them, come to mean what it does?". Perhaps it is Derrida who has elaborated a strange ideal definition of the word "gift," along with his colloquial contemporaries.

At one point Derrida criticizes Mauss in the following terms: "Mauss seems to be quite unaware of what he is naming and whether one can still call one thing by the name of gift and another thing by the name of exchange" (1992: 37). This remark goes back to his distinction between gift and the circle of economic exchange – a gift must inevitably enter into that circle of exchange, Derrida has argued. The gift is after all impossible, if not unthinkable. Derrida thus criticizes Mauss for trying to assign a signifier of the impossible to a socially possible practice. But the remark also goes back, ironically, to the medieval moment of the smile.

We can recall that the opposition between gift and economic exchange in question here is exactly the opposition enacted in the later Middle Ages in the form of the *hilaris donor* and his implicit opposites, the buyer and seller. For Derrida, as for the smiling donors, the question of the gift is an economic question, rather than a question of social order and violence. This moment of the smile, in the twelfth and thirteenth centuries, is the moment when the practice of the gift ceases to play a central functional role in medieval society. But the word "give" does not cease to exist. Rather, its meaning begins to change. That change accompanies the change in the ceremony of giving, and the opposite of the word "give" ceases to be "to engage in violence, to strike a blow" (the word *doner* in Old French means literally either "to give," or "to strike a blow," and the term is often played on in the epic), but rather to buy or sell.[13]

The origin of the semantic opposition that characterizes Derrida's version of the term "give" can therefore ironically be located at the moment when the pain of the gift – as a social practice – begins to give way to the smile, and the pleasure, of the gift as a purely representational form. It occurs when the gift is largely devoid of anything more than formal social opposition (since it is usually just an empty form). It is simultaneously devoid of any forces of social cohesion, and the term and the act are thus free to wander in meaning and in the uses to which they are put. It is free to become a signifier for what is gone and no longer possible in the world of the later Middle Ages. The "gift" comes to signify not just an alternative, no longer viable form of social order, but eventually, a vanished form of social order. Hence Derrida's question is possible only within the context of a time after the practice of the gift.

If we take Derrida's idealized definition of the gift – as that whose "having been given" must be irretrievably forgotten – then modern theoretical notions of the gift are in fact "gifts" in that the theorists seem to have forgotten something fundamental. They – and Derrida as well, as we have seen – have forgotten the gift itself. More particularly, despite the emphasis on pleasure and desire which I have traced, they have forgotten the body. This is because the body, in the act of giving within a gift economy, is at least potentially a site of pain – the pain of violence when the gift fails, or the sublimated pain of social control when the gift succeeds. To "give," originally, was to exchange. The opposition of gift and exchange comes only later. To give was simply to exchange within the social order, rather than by theft, violence and conquest. To give was to be inside the social order, to enact that social order, and to feel the pressures and constraints that all social orders impose. Remember that William Marshall gave even his body itself to the Templars, and symbolically "gave" himself to the social order of the gift. We could say that in a gift culture, the thing that one gives is finally always one's body, on which and in which the gift culture is enacted.

When the gift and the gift ceremony lost their social ordering function in the face of fully monetized economies dependent on written legal documents, then the gift began to play – at least formally – a new role: the indicator of a nostalgia for the old forms of social control. This battle, however, was, perhaps, already lost by the time donors were regularly smiling. The overwhelming dominance of the letter, the coin, and the church and state bureaucratic apparatus that accompanied them left the gift as an empty institution, sufficiently marginalized that it could take on the status of a locus of social "exteriority." The end of the gift economy freed the gift to became a floating signifier of pleasure and desire and eventually of the impossible. As late as the early twentieth century, in the example of Tönnies, the gift still carried with it some of the opposition between different forms of social control, between "*Gemeinschaft*" and "*Gesellschaft*." But ultimately it has become a figure for an even more radical nostalgic desire than simply for older systems of social control. It has come to stand for a point outside the realm of social control itself, especially as these controls take economic forms.

Derrida's deflation of the gift does correctly point out some of the emptiness of the gestures of Mauss, Bataille, Cixous and Baudrillard to the extent that they would locate true social reform in a concept of the gift devoid of any basis in social practice, in one whose connection to pleasure indicates its lack of grounding in such practices. Their gift is theory without a body.[14] Of course, the body is powerfully present in these (three pre-Derridean) theorists, in a quite sexual way. But it is linked not just to pleasure, but more specifically to non-reproductively oriented sexual pleasure. Reproduction (Baudrillard's "productive Eros") is equivalent to repression, and the gift is equivalent to both freedom and non-reproduction. It is as if bodies making more bodies, or even potentially trying to make more bodies, constitutes the economic cycle itself, while masturbation becomes the true gift, the moment of an-economic freedom. The sexual pleasure of these theorists is a peculiar form of pleasure that seems to shy away from the crucial social events – birth, marriage, death – which are in fact the most universal occasions of gift giving, to the extent that such a thing exists. These are also the social events most intimately tied to reproduction, and to the body, as well as to gifts. Yet these reproductive, "economic" moments seem to be what the theoretical gift flees, in order to attain a pleasure which seems less corporeal than metaphorical.

At this point, one can return to Mauss's essay with renewed appreciation. He must be credited with having seen the true meaning of the word "gift," at least as it functioned as a vehicle of social control and organization, an alternative to violence (see 1967: 79; and Jenkins 1998). At times of potential gift giving, people come together "in a curious frame of mind with exaggerated fear and an equally exaggerated generosity," he writes. The sense of social solidarity and of its alternative, violence, is captured in these words.

This tension mirrors that of Mauss's own socio-political project. He foreshadows Baudrillard in suggesting the inadequacy of both Marxism and capitalism due to their equally economistic bases (Mauss 1967: 66–7). This critique of the two fundamental organizing principles of the Western societies of his time implies a radical critical stance. Yet he proposes the gift as a new model of social solidarity that will function as a "happy medium between the ideal and the real" (1967: 67). The relation between the gift and pleasure, sexual or otherwise, is far more ambivalent than in the writings which follow him as well.[15] Mauss, in fact, can be situated at the liminal point of the smile; for him, the gift seems sometimes to represent a nostalgia for alternative modes of social control that were at one time inherent to the Western tradition. But at other times, the gift is presented as the model for an emancipatory, non-economy-based society that would be truly revolutionary. Does the gift, for Mauss, represent a point on a line whose endpoints would be the real and the ideal, or is it a point off the line entirely, breaking fundamentally with its social context? Since this essay is not finally about Mauss's essay but about the uses to which it has been put, I will not try to answer that question, but, certainly, since his time, critical theory has used the gift in the latter sense, and, in the examples analyzed here, given up virtually all attempts to study social practice – a possibility that Mauss's own essay at least inaugurates and enables, if not impels.

As a final remark, one should note that within anthropology proper, the gift has tended to move in exactly the opposite direction, since Mauss's essay, from the way it has moved in critical and literary theory. While French theory has pushed the gift further and further outside the circle variously defined as the economic, the bourgeois or the masculine, anthropology has drawn the gift closer and closer into the economic circle, or else questioned its theoretical utility altogether. In *The Social Life of Things* (1986), Arjun Appadurai has argued that the process of exchange is less important than the objects exchanged, and Nicholas Thomas, in *Entangled Objects* (1991), likewise argues for a move away from questions of process to considerations of specific product. In *Money and the Morality of Exchange* (1989), editors Jonathan Parry and Maurice Bloch write that rather than any "unbridgeable chasm between gift and commodity exchange," the studies in the book and elsewhere stress that "one may evolve rather easily into the other." But perhaps most perspicaciously they note that "the radical opposition which so many anthropologists have discovered between the principles on which gift and commodity exchange are founded derives in part, we believe, from the fact that our ideology of the gift has been constructed in antithesis to market exchange." They continue, "We cannot therefore expect ideologies of non-market societies to reproduce this kind of opposition" (1989: 8). In deconstructing this opposition, even Derrida nevertheless deconstructs it in its own terms, so to speak, without ever asking why these particular terms and this particular binary opposition should have arisen historically in the first place. While Parry and Bloch, as anthropologists, have presumably learned the lesson they expound from critical theory, their remarks also suggest the need for this theory to continue to examine the historical anthropology that underlies its own genesis.

Notes

1 See for example Bryce Lyon's study *From Fief to Indenture* (1957), which examines the growth of such transitional practices as the "fief rente" and the "fief de soudée," which combined the forms of the traditional medieval fief with monetary payments and even contracts.

2 See for an emblematic example, Adorno 1983: 119–32 on jazz and, contrastingly, 147–72 on Arnold Schoenberg.

3 "C'est bien toujours le mécanisme de la prestation social qu'il faut lire dans notre choix, notre accumulation, notre manipulation et notre consommation d'objets … [L]a kula et le potlatch ont disparu, mais non leur principe, que nous retiendrons pour base d'une théorie sociologique des objets." Translations of Baudrillard are my own.

4 "Le travail est, de prime abord, un acte qui se passe entre l'homme et la nature. L'homme y joue lui-même vis-à-vis de la nature le rôle d'une puissance naturelle. Les forces dont son corps est doué, bras et jambes, tête et mains, il les met en mouvement afin se s'assimiler des matières en leur donnant une forme utile à sa vie."

5 "Le travail n'est donc pas l'unique source des valeurs d'usage qu'il produit, de la richesse matérielle. Il en est le père, et la terre, la mère."

6 "Cette genèse de la richesse par combinaison génitale du travail … reprend assez bien un schème productif/reproductif 'normal' – on fait l'amour pour avoir des infants, et pas pour le plaisir. Le métaphore est celle d'une sexualité génitale reproductrice, pas du tout celle d'une dépense du corps dans la jouissance!"

7   For a more detailed analysis of Baudrillard's views on this topic, see Kellner 1994. He finds in *The Mirror of Production* a search by Baudrillard for "emancipatory alternatives" in pre-modern social models (1994: 6). It should also be added than Baudrillard himself abandoned many of the views expressed in these works as his thought evolved in the 1980s.

8   It might be added that Derrida's work does engage other economic themes at various points, most notably in his meditation on usury in the article "White mythologies." Note that Bataille also discusses usury in "The notion of expenditure" (1985b).

9   For a good introduction to Derrida's development of this term see Culler 1982: 89–110.

10 This larger point has been well examined by Vincent Pecora (1994).

11 Derrida's critique thus echoes similar criticisms made by Adorno in "Cultural criticism and society" about the complicity of cultural criticism with the economy of capitalism (1992: 17–34).

12 For this reason, as well as for the ways in which Derrida deconstructs previous uses of the gift, I believe that a greater distinction needs to be made in Pecora's "The sorcerer's apprentices" (1994) between modernism and postmodernism, though of course in arguing for Derrida's participation in the fundamental trajectory of desire, I am essentially agreeing with his larger point. In Derrida, this desire occurs despite an awareness that it is unfulfillable.

13 For another critique of Derrida's failure to escape economistic modes of approach to the gift, see Boon 1999: 216–18.

14 To be fair, one must admit that Bataille, in his writings on Eros and sacrifice, does keep a sense of pain connected to the gift, and thus remains faithful to some of the gift's original social function. His very vocabulary, centering on "loss" and "expenditure," reveals this fact. But the emancipatory nature of the gift, offering a path towards "perverse sexuality," clearly is part of – indeed a founding moment of – the trajectory in question here.

15 See Mauss 1967: 71, on gifts, marriage, and sexual favors, and also his criticism of the too easy and pleasurable mode of existence promised by communism (1967: 67).

References

Adorno, Theodor. *Prisms*. Trans. Samuel and Shierry Weber. Cambridge, MA: MIT Press, 1983.

Appadurai, Arjun (ed.). *The Social Life of Things*. London: Cambridge University Press, 1986.

Barthes, Roland. *The Pleasure of the Text*. Trans. Richard Miller. New York: Hill and Wang, 1975.

Bataille, Georges. "The college of sociology." In *Visions of Excess: Selected Writings, 1927–1939*. Ed. Allan Stoekl. Trans. Allan Stoekl, with Carl R. Lovitt and Donald M. Leslie. Minneapolis: University of Minnesota Press, 1985a, pp. 246–53.

—— "The notion of expenditure." In *Visions of Excess: Selected Writings, 1927–1939*. Ed. Allan Stoekl. Trans. Allan Stoekl, with Carl R. Lovitt and Donald M. Leslie. Minneapolis: University of Minnesota Press, 1985b, pp. 116–29.

Baudrillard, Jean. *Pour une critique de l'économie politique du signe*. Paris: Gallimard, 1972.

—— *Le miroir de la production; ou l'illusion critique du matérialisme historique*. Second edition. Paris: Casterman, 1973.

Boon, James A. *Verging on Extravagance: Anthropology, History, Religion, Literature, Arts … Showbiz*. Princeton: Princeton University Press, 1999.

Cixous, Hélène. "Castration or decapitation." *Signs* 7 (1981): 41–55.

—— "The laugh of the Medusa." In David H. Richter (ed.) *The Critical Tradition. Classical Texts and Contemporary Trends*. New York: St Martin's, 1989, pp. 1090–1102.

Clanchy, M.T. *From Memory to Written Record*. Second edition. Oxford: Blackwell, 1993.

Clifford, James. *The Predicament of Culture: Twentieth-Century Ethnography, Literature and Art*. Cambridge, MA: Harvard University Press, 1988.

Culler, Jonathan. *On Deconstruction: Theory and Criticism after Structuralism*. Ithaca: Cornell University Press, 1982.

Derrida, Jacques. *Given Time: I. Counterfeit Money*. Trans. Peggy Kamuf. Chicago: University of Chicago Press, 1992.

Duby, Georges. *Guillaume le Maréchal, ou Le meilleur chevalier du monde*. Paris: Fayard, 1984.

Foucault, Michel. *Discipline and Punish: The Birth of the Prison*. Trans. Alan Sheridan. New York: Vintage, 1979.

Hyde, Lewis. *The Gift: Imagination and the Erotic Life of Property*. New York: Random House, 1983.

Jenkins, Tim. "Derrida's reading of Mauss." In Wendy James and N.J. Allen (eds) *Marcel Mauss: A Centenary Tribute*. New York: Berghahn, 1998, pp. 83–94.

Kellner, Douglas (ed.). *Baudrillard: A Critical Reader*. Oxford: Blackwell, 1994.

Le Goff, Jacques. "Laughter in the Middle Ages." In Jan Bremmer and Herman Roodenburg (eds) *A Cultural History of Humour: From Antiquity to the Present Day*. Cambridge, UK: Polity, 1997, pp. 40–53.

Lyon, Bryce D. *From Fief to Indenture: The Transition from Feudal to Non-feudal contract in Western Europe*. Cambridge, MA: Harvard University Press, 1957.

Mauss, Marcel. *The Gift: Forms and Functions of Exchange in Archaic Societies*. Trans. Ian Cunnison. New York: Norton, 1967.

Parry, J. and M. Bloch (eds). *Money and the Morality of Exchange*. Cambridge: Cambridge University Press, 1989.

Pecora, Vincent. "The sorcerer's apprentices: romance, anthropology, and literary theory." *Modern Language Quarterly* 55.4 (1994): 345–82.

Sahlins, Marshall. *Stone Age Economics*. New York: Aldine, 1972.

Tabuteau, Emily Zack. *Transfers of Property in Eleventh Century Norman Law*. Chapel Hill: University of North Carolina Press, 1988.

Thomas, Nicholas. *Entangled Objects*. Cambridge, MA: Harvard University Press, 1991.

Tönnies, Ferdinand. *Community and Society*. Trans. Charles P. Loomis. New York: Harper and Row, 1963.

Vercauteren, F. "Avec le sourire …" In *Mélanges offerts à Rita Lejeune*, Volume 1. Gembloux: Editions J. Duculot, 1969, pp. 45–56.

Index

Printed in Great Britain
by Amazon